Sales and Marketing Environment

The Marketing Series is one of the most comprehensive collections of books in marketing and sales available from the UK today.

Published by Butterworth-Heinemann on behalf of The Chartered Institute of Marketing, the series is divided into three distinct groups: *Student* (fulfilling the needs of those taking the Institute's certificate and diploma qualifications); *Professional Development* (for those on formal or self-study vocational training programmes); and *Practitioner* (presented in a more informal, motivating and highly practical manner for the busy marketer).

Formed in 1911, The Chartered Institute of Marketing is now the largest professional marketing management body in Europe with over 60,000 members worldwide. Its primary objectives are focused on the development of awareness and understanding of marketing throughout UK industry and commerce and in the raising of standards of professionalism in the education, training and practice of this key business discipline.

The CIM Student Workbook Series: Marketing

Certificate

Business Communications 1997–98
Misiura

Marketing Fundamentals 1997–98
Lancaster & Withey

Sales and Marketing Environment 1997–98
Oldroyd

Understanding Customers 1997–98
Phipps & Simmons

Advanced Certificate

Effective Management for Marketing 1997–98
Hatton & Worsam

Management Information for Marketing and Sales 1997–98
Hines

Marketing Operations 1997–98
Worsam

Promotional Practice 1997–98
Ace

Diploma

International Marketing Strategy 1997–98
Fifield & Lewis

Marketing Communications Strategy 1997–98
Yeshin

Strategic Marketing Management 1997–98
Fifield & Gilligan

The Case Study Workbook 1997–8
Fifield

Sales and Marketing Environment 1997–98

Mike Oldroyd

Published on behalf of
The Chartered Institute of Marketing

To Rebecca, and the thought that even in adversity anything is possible, including publishers' deadlines!

Butterworth-Heinemann
Linacre House, Jordan Hill, Oxford OX2 8DP
A division of Reed Educational and Professional Publishing Ltd

A member of the Reed Elsevier plc group

OXFORD   BOSTON   JOHANNESBURG
MELBOURNE   NEW DELHI   SINGAPORE

First published 1997

© Mike Oldroyd 1997

All rights reserved. No part of this publication may be reproduced in any material form (including photocopying or storing in any medium by electronic means and whether or not transiently or incidentally to some other use of this publication) without the written permission of the copyright holder except in accordance with the provisions of the Copyright, Designs and Patents Act 1988 or under the terms of a licence issued by the Copyright Licensing Agency Ltd, 90 Tottenham Court Road, London, England W1P 9HE. Applications for the copyright holder's written permission to reproduce any part of this publication should be addressed to the publishers

British Library Cataloguing in Publication Data
Oldroyd, Michael
    Sales and marketing environment 1997–98. – (CIM workbook series)
    1. Sales promotion   2. Marketing   3. Sales promotion – Problems, exercises, etc.   4. Marketing – Problems, exercises, etc.
    I. Title   II. Chartered Institute of Marketing
    658.8'2

ISBN 0 7506 3574 6

Set in 10/13pt Baskerville by Graphicraft Typesetters Ltd, Hong Kong

Contents

A quick word from the CIM Chief Examiner	vii
Preface	ix
Acknowledgements	xi
How to use your CIM workbook	xiii

1 The organization and its environments — 1
Objectives – Study guide – Study tips – The importance of the marketing environment – Business classifications – The formal and informal economy – The legal form of trading organizations – The business as a resource converter – The micro-environment of the organization – The macro-environment – Summary – Activity debrief – Examination hints and specimen questions

2 Organizations and their objectives — 20
Objectives – Study guide – Organizational objectives – Study tips – Business growth – What causes the goals to change? – Stakeholder pressures – The concept of social responsibility – The factors affecting organizational size – Internal organizational structures – Summary – Activity debrief – Examination hints and specimen questions

3 The competitive environment — 41
Objectives – Study guide – The nature of the competitive environment – Strategies available to the competitive firm – Structural analysis and market power – The role and function of intermediaries and suppliers – The growing importance of relationship marketing – Summary – Activity debrief – Examination hints and specimen questions

4 The organization and its 'publics' — 60
Objectives – Study guide – Stakeholders: analysis of an organization's many publics – The seven steps in stakeholder analysis – How should management and the marketer respond? – Pressure groups – The consumerist movement – Environmentalism – The response – Conclusions on pressure groups – Communicating with its publics: the role of sales and marketing – Public relations – Internal marketing – Summary – Activity debrief – Examination hints and specimen questions

5 The regulatory environment — 80
Objectives – Study guide – The legal background – The regulatory framework – Role and objectives of regulation – Positive impacts – Legislation and contractual relationships – Legislation, fair trading and the consumer – Legislation and competition – Monopolies and merger legislation – Other areas of legislation and the marketer – Summary – Activity debrief – Examination hints and specimen questions

6 Forecasting the macro-environment — 100
Objectives – Study guide – The importance of monitoring the environment – The key problems – The environmental set – The main sources of environmental data – What kind of information is required? The political environment – Summary – Activity debrief – Examination hints and specimen questions

7 The macro-economic environment — 126
Objectives – Study guide – A model of the economy – Deflationary and inflationary gaps – The multiplier and accelerator – The measurement and meaning of national income – The uses of national accounting data – Limitations of the data – The business cycle – Government economic objectives and priorities – Economic indicators and economic policies – Summary – Activity debrief – Examination hints and specimen question

8 The demographic and social environment   **153**
Objectives – Study guide – Trends in population – The dependency ratio – World population – Aggregate population – Population structure – Marital status and household structure – Regional distribution – Ethnic groups – Occupational structure – The workforce in employment – Some important employment trends – The changing role of women in work and society – The social and cultural environment – Social class – Reference groups – The family – Life style – A summary of segmentation bases in consumer markets – Final thoughts on culture – Summary – Activity debrief – Examination hints and specimen questions

9 The technical and natural environments   **176**
Objectives – Study guide – Definition of terms – Characteristics of technology – The role of business – What are the technical imperatives? – Fifty-year innovation cycle – Creative destruction – Microprocessors: a metatechnology with universal applications – The technological diffusion process – Technological transfer – Technological forecasting – Information sources – Technology and sales/marketing applications – Future applications of technology – The impact of technology on the natural environment – The source of the overload – Conclusions – Summary – Activity debrief – Examination hints and specimen questions

10 The global environment   **199**
Objectives – Study guide – The basis for international trade: at the macro level – The basis for trade: at the micro level – Growth in international trade – Limitations to the growth of international trade – Barriers to trade – The role of international institutions and trade blocs – The European Union (EU) and the Single European Market (SEM) – Maastricht and future uncertainty – Sources of information – The multinationals – Government policies and the global environment – Summary – Activity debrief – Examination hints and specimen questions

11 Guidance on revision and examination   **224**
Study guide – A businesslike approach – Key elements in learning – Key elements in examination success – Examinations in practice – Key point summary from the senior examiner's reports – The marketing environment: December 1996 examination paper – Model answers to the December 1996 examination questions – Alternative compulsory practice question

Glossary of terms   **254**

Index   **260**

A quick word from the Chief Examiner

I am delighted to recommend to you the new series of CIM workbooks. All of these have been written by either the senior examiner or examiners responsible for marking and setting the papers.

Preparing for the CIM exams is hard work. These workbooks are designed to make that work as interesting and illuminating as possible, as well as providing you with the knowledge you need to pass. I wish you success.

Trevor Watkins
CIM Chief Examiner,
Deputy Vice Chancellor,
South Bank University

Preface

This workbook has been written to help you understand how businesses and their environments merge and interact. Political, economic, social and technological environments affect virtually every organizational function and activity, not least those of selling and marketing.

The primary objective, however, is to provide a student-centred framework for studying the Certificate level subjects, Selling and Marketing Environment, launched in the CIM Syllabus 94 initiative. Syllabus 94 was the product of an extensive consultation process with relevant stakeholders and has, in the case of the Certificate in Selling and Certificate in Marketing, led to a fundamental syllabus revision designed to make them much more relevant to the current and future needs of sales and marketing practitioners.

The Selling and the Marketing Environment are completely new syllabi, although elements of the old law and economics remain. The treatment of these, along with the other essential components of the business environment, are now treated at the 'appreciation' level rather than in-depth. The approach taken in this workbook is to provide a blend of academic knowledge and practical activities/applications which will meet the needs not only of sales executives and marketers, but also of many other types of students. This is particularly the case for those on BTEC HNC/D equivalent level courses studying for qualifications requiring a broad appreciation of the business environment within their curricula.

The author has had considerable experience in teaching various levels of students in this area, and the methodology adopted should be ideally suited to the needs and requirements of both tutors and students in the subject. The workbook material and activities have been designed to have more general application even though the specific focus taken has been concentrated on the activities of sales and marketing departments.

It should be recognized that while there are some minor differences between the Selling and Marketing Environment syllabi, the predominant core of knowledge is identical. The differences between the two are as follows:

- While the aims and objectives are effectively the same, the Selling Environment specifically stresses the linkage to the sales role.
- Learning outcomes emphasize the role of selling as against marketing and how the activities of each are influenced by the environment.
- Organization elements account for 20 per cent indicative weighting and the micro environment 40 per cent for Selling as against 15 per cent and 30 per cent for the Marketing Environment. This is entirely appropriate given the heavier internal and micro focus of the selling function. The external orientation of the marketing environment is confirmed by a 45 per cent indicative weighting for the macro environment.
- Some texts on selling are recommended on one reading list, and marketing on the other, otherwise they are the same.

This workbook provides you with the means of making sense of the complex relationships that exist between an organization and its environment. It heightens your awareness of changes that are taking place and their implications for your day-to-day work activities. The environment is by its nature dynamic, and any text might easily become quickly dated. Every effort has been made to minimize this process of 'decay' by generalizing the concepts discussed and many of the activities related to them. The workbook is revised annually with particular emphasis on the currency of the examination questions and model answers. The emphasis throughout, however, is to reinforce the intention of the CIM that students should be given every encouragement to relate their knowledge to understanding, and that understanding to sales and marketing applications.

As Senior examiner/author of the Marketing Environment syllabus and Moderator for the Selling Environment, I have tried to design a workbook that is sufficiently comprehensive so that candidates are not confronted with the necessity to consult and purchase myriad sources in order to complete their studies. Very few texts are currently available in this area, or provide the necessary breadth and level of coverage required. Books that do exist either fall into the category of being academic with limited or no examples and activities, or provide a succession of activities and rapidly dating newspaper clippings with very little explanatory text. I hope you find that this workbook has achieved a more balanced blend that would be equally valuable to the marketer at certificate level as it would to a stage one DMS or even non-business background MBA student.

Writing this workbook for a clearly identified group of students has served to simplify the structure, which breaks down into ten similar sized study units:

- The first five units concentrate on the organization and its micro environment.
- The final five units focus on the wider macro environments.

These must not, however, be seen as separate compartments of knowledge but rather as interlocked pieces of an intricate jigsaw.

The layout of what follows is designed to be as student-friendly as possible. The text is broken up into digestible chunks by definitions and activities. Debriefs are provided to many of these at the end of each unit, but have been purposely limited to encourage maximum contribution from you! All the questions provided are either actual specimens produced for the CIM or their equivalents. You should use them to cement your understanding of the subject matter to the applications of the knowledge in question.

One topsy-turvy recommendation I hope you will consider implementing before you progress very far in this workbook is that you carefully read and digest the first five pages of Unit 11 where guidance on revision and examinations is provided. Waiting until you have completed all ten workbook units will probably be too late to obtain maximum benefit from this section with the examination just around the corner.

To conclude, this workbook is intended to be a resource; a source of information and explanation as well as a framework for study. Use it systematically and use it well and I sincerely hope you meet with the examination success you deserve.

Mike Oldroyd

Acknowledgements

Very special thanks are due to my darling wife Karen for her good humour and hard work in preparing and editing the manuscript; to Martin Murphy for the benefit of his considerable legal expertise and very useful comments in the development of Unit 5; to the team at Butterworth-Heinemann for expediting the manuscript so efficiently; and finally to my good friend Angela Hatton for her creative stimulus in helping me get to grips with effective workbook format. All their assistance was invaluable but any deficiencies that remain are entirely my own.

Regarding this 1997–98 edition, I wish to add my thanks once again to those tutors and students who provided such invaluable comments through their inspection copies and 'bite back' (see page 262) returns. I welcome this objective feedback from my own particular marketing environment in order to further refine the product. Please return your 'bite back' when you have completed the workbook to help me adapt it more effectively to meet your changing needs.

Finally, I would like to acknowledge the contribution of my own students, past and present, at the Huddersfield University Business School. For their sins they are regularly required to keep me and their peer group briefed on business cases and environmental developments. They help me to keep my finger on the pulse of the ever-changing marketing environment in often interesting and creative ways. To them I owe a debt of gratitude, but with a disclaimer of any implied entitlement to a percentage of the royalties!

How to use your CIM workbook

The authors have been careful to structure your book with the exams in mind. Each unit, therefore, covers an essential part of the syllabus. You need to work through the complete workbook systematically to ensure that you have covered everything you need to know.

This workbook is divided into ten units. Each unit contains the following standard elements:

Objectives   tell you what part of the syllabus you will be covering and what you will be expected to know having read the unit.

Study guides   tell you how long the unit is and how long its activities take to do.

Questions   are designed to give you practice – they will be similar to those you get in the exam.

Answers   give you a suggested format for answering exam questions. *Remember* there is no such thing as a model answer – you should use these examples only as guidelines.

Activities   give you the chance to put what you have learnt into practice.

Exam hints   are tips from the senior examiner or examiner which are designed to help you avoid common mistakes made by previous candidates.

Definitions   are used for words you must know to pass the exam.

Extending activity sections   are designed to help you use your time most effectively. It is not possible for the workbook to cover *everything* you need to know to pass. What you read here needs to be supplemented by your classes, practical experience at work and day-to-day reading.

Summaries   cover what you should have picked up from reading the unit.

A glossary is provided at the back of the book to help define and underpin understanding of the key terms used in each unit.

UNIT 1

The organization and its environments

In this introductory unit you will:

- Examine the diversity of organizational types.
- Distinguish the various environments of the business.
- Consider how the marketer should adapt and respond to change.
- Assess the relative abilities of different businesses to respond to environmental change.

By the end of this unit you will:

- Appreciate the strengths and weaknesses of different types of organization.
- Become aware of the interrelationships between an organization and its environment.
- Be able to classify the complex variety of external influences.

Covering the introductory part of the CIM syllabus this first unit of the Sales and Marketing Environment Workbook will provide you with a framework and organizational setting within which you may explore the dynamic interrelationships between businesses and the various environments in which they operate. The material is straightforward but of critical importance to an understanding of subsequent units, since it provides a foundation upon which the others are built.

Since the sales and marketing environment is broad and ever changing it is essential that you constantly work to relate the course material to current developments. Acquire the habit of 'scanning' the quality press for up-to-date articles, reviews and surveys relating business to its environments. Supplement this by tuning in weekly to a serious news analysis programme on TV or radio. As you will see under 'Examination hints' later in this unit, you will need to be prepared for broad questions which test your grasp of the evolving marketing environment.

I would expect you to take 2–3 hours to work through this first unit and suggest you allow around 4–5 hours to undertake the various activities suggested. These are very important since examiners will expect you to relate understanding to application. Besides your notepad and writing equipment you will need the following to complete this unit:

- Annual reports of two or three large public limited companies (plcs)
- Newspaper cuttings
- Any available feedback or group discussion notes

This first unit will also help you to familiarize yourself with the approach and style of our workbooks. It has been developed to ensure that you acquire not only the knowledge necessary for examination success but also the skills to apply that knowledge both in the examination and in your work as a professional marketer. You will find the boxed panels clearly signposted to help you practise, evaluate and extend your knowledge and these will be used throughout this workbook so that you can manage your own learning in terms of both pace and depth.

STUDY TIPS

Start as you mean to go on in the organization of your study materials. From the very beginning of the course it is sound advice to:

- Use file dividers to index broad topic area notes.
- Add relevant materials, activity output, articles and clippings.
- Summarize related articles which may provide current examples for illustrating examination answers. The examiner *will* expect this!
- Cross-reference to other sections of the file since questions may address more than one part of the syllabus.
- Incorporate past questions, examiner reports, model answers and revision notes when available.
- Edit and summarize into bullet points for easy memorizing.

In this way your file sections will be complete and facilitate ease of revision prior to the examination.

The importance of the marketing environment

The CIM defines marketing as:

> ...the management process which identifies, anticipates and supplies customer requirements efficiently and profitably.

This focuses attention on the importance of the marketing environment for practitioners and students alike. Identifying and anticipating customer requirements is impossible unless the organization looks outward from itself, to understand its external environment and the implications of changes taking place on its current and future profitability. Few businesses can afford to adopt a 'production orientation' and fail to respond to the evolving opportunities and threats in its marketplace.

QUESTION 1.1

List the elements of the external environment you consider most important to the marketers' understanding of:

(a) Its potential customers
(b) Its potential profitability

Provide *four* different examples of external factors where you feel 'change' seems fastest.

Probably your initial thoughts were of existing and potential markets. The changing tastes and preferences of customers, their disposable incomes and the price and availability of substitutes will clearly be important, as will the size, strength and numbers of competitors. Less obvious are the changes in the broader environment which influence these market conditions. Demographic changes alter the population of various market segments while tax adjustments affect their purchasing power. Cultural and technical developments may exert even more powerful influences on the longer-term supply, demand, profitability and life cycle of different goods and services. Rising concern with the green environment, for example, has caused many businesses to modify their product offerings and methods of production.

No organization, whether small or large, public or private, profit or non-profit making can afford to ignore its environment. As the strategist H. I. Ansoff observed,

> the firm is a creature of its environment. Its resources, its income, its problems, its opportunities and its very survival are generated and conditioned by the environment.

Societal concerns are often translated through the legislative process to impact on the freedom of business to manage. The marketer must always therefore be aware that the environment reflects the pressures from a range of interested groups to which a positive response may be called for. It is also the domain of actual or potential competitors, and is consequently ignored at the organization's peril.

Large firms, particularly multinationals, may be able to exert greater influence over their business situation but small firms may have the advantage in responding to the need for change more flexibly.

> **DEFINITION 1.1**
>
> A *multinational* has operations in many host countries, but control and decision making remains in the parent country. The worldwide annual turnover of companies such as Exxon (Esso) and General Motors exceeds the gross domestic product of many of the smaller West European countries.

Before exploring the nature of this environment and the marketer's approach to it, we need to study the different forms of business organization involved in the economy.

> **QUESTION 1.2**
>
> Can you identify a named example of each of the following forms of business organization?
>
> *Legal form*   *Your example*
>
> - Sole trader
> - A partnership
> - A cooperative
> - A limited company
> - A public limited company (plc)
> - A nationalized industry
> - A municipal/local authority enterprise
> - A franchisor
> - A multinational
> - A quango
> - A holding company

The purpose of organizations is to bring together people with common interests in a systematic effort to produce goods and services. We all come into contact with organizations when we buy goods, attend lectures, deposit funds or go to the doctor's. Your list of examples should reflect this *diversity*. Whatever the form or purpose of the organization it will have common characteristics such as:

- A framework of written or tacit rules (e.g. articles of association)
- A decision-making hierarchy (e.g. AGM, board of directors, the MD)

- A record of proceedings (e.g. minutes of meetings)
- A means of coordinating efforts and resources to determine what and how to produce, in what quantities and using what channels of distribution.

These matters are explored in the CIM workbook *Effective Management for Marketing* while we are concerned with the types of business organization and their environment.

Business classifications

As marketers, we need to understand the diversity of business:

- Each address potential customers in different ways due to their differing objectives, strengths and weaknesses.
- Each are buyers and sellers in their own right.
- The implications for competition, growth and innovation vary with each.
- Their relative importance is changing with the growth in small businesses and self-employment, a shrinking public sector and the rising importance of entrepreneurial non-profit makers such as charities.

To understand the diversity of business we must first classify the various types and form a framework for understanding their characteristics.

The formal and informal economy

An economy may be thought of as being made up of three parts: the public sector, the private sector and the informal economy.

The public sector

This comprises all those activities involving provision of goods and services by the state. Revenue to finance these is raised by:

- Taxation on the rest of the economy
- Fees and charges or
- Government borrowing.

These resources are then allocated to the various spending departments who plan provision according to government objectives rather than market forces. The state has taken responsibility in a number of areas where provision by the private sector was not seen as adequate or appropriate. *Public goods* such as defence, law, order and emergency services comprised one major category while *merit goods* such as health, education and other social services provided the other. A number of other industries might come into the domain of the state for a variety of reasons including: strategic considerations, natural monopolies; job preservation and national security.

In post-war Britain direct government expenditure has accounted for 20–25 per cent of GDP although this has fallen recently with the privatization of many businesses. The government has also sought to introduce market disciplines into its remaining activities through various initiatives to make public services accountable to their users (e.g. hospital trusts, local management of schools and compulsory competitive tendering for local authority services). The public sector organizations who provide marketable goods and services are seen in Figure 1.1.

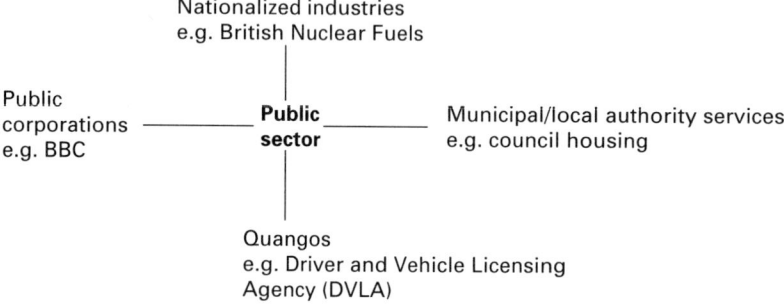

Figure 1.1 Public sector organizations providing marketable goods and services

Match the terms with their correct definitions:

- GDP (gross domestic product)
- Natural monopoly
- Privatization
- Merit goods
- Public goods
- Quango

1. Can be provided by the private sector but concern for equity and whether sufficient would be provided, leads to public provision.
2. A good or service which cannot be priced accurately and therefore cannot be efficiently supplied by the private sector. Consumption by one person does not reduce supply for others (e.g. TV signals/street lighting). No consumer can be excluded even if they refuse to pay (e.g. public health) and no-one may abstain from consumption (e.g. defence). All consume equally but have no incentive to pay for what must be provided in any case.
3. A quasi-autonomous non-government organization is neither an elected nor a private business organization, but has executive or administrative authority to implement or advance government policy. The marketer is likely to encounter large numbers of such bodies (e.g. Office of Fair Trading, Advertising Standards Authority).
4. A firm that can satisfy all the market demand, but still has unexploited cost savings. Competition would duplicate expensive resources.
5. Measures the output in any one year arising from economic activity.
6. The transfer of ownership of 51% or more of shares in a nationalized concern to private hands.

Note GDP is not adjusted for taxes, subsidies or capital used up in the production of the output. Furthermore, if net income from overseas activities were added it would become GNP or gross national product. This is an important concept and the marketer will see many references to it in the quality business press.
(**See** Activity debrief at the end of this unit.)

Scan a quality paper/or periodical for the term GDP or, better still, if you have access to CD-ROM identify the usage of the term in newspaper reports and summarize the context in which it is used.

Hint: look particularly at reports of economic growth.

Prepare a summary report on the activities of two quangos which affect your business and/or the marketer.

Hint: Locate them from the directory and phone for details.

The private sector

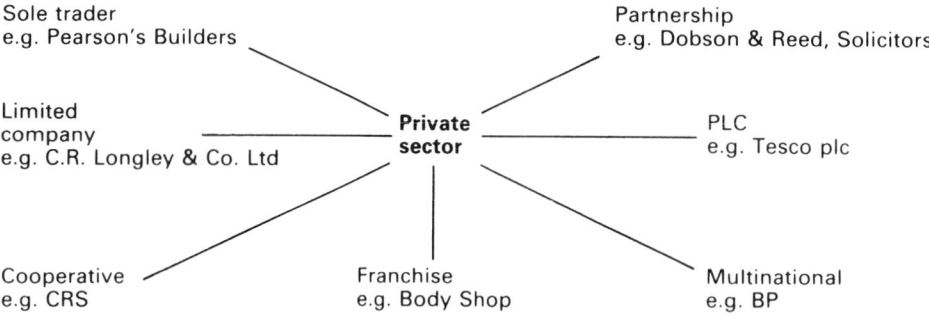

Figure 1.2 Elements of the private sector

This sector accounts for the majority of domestic output and exports. It also produces most of the investment goods. Resources are privately owned and businesses compete to satisfy consumer wants and needs. Most are profit motivated and decide on what and how to produce by identifying and anticipating market demands, on the one hand, while combining and converting resource inputs efficiently, on the other. As you can see in Figure 1.2, a number of different trading organizations may be identified and we will explore their strengths and weaknesses below.

The informal economy

The activities of the public and private sectors constitute the formal economic activities of a country and their combined output is measured by GDP. However, three other sectors should be recognized and understood by the marketer. These are shown in the Figure 1.3.

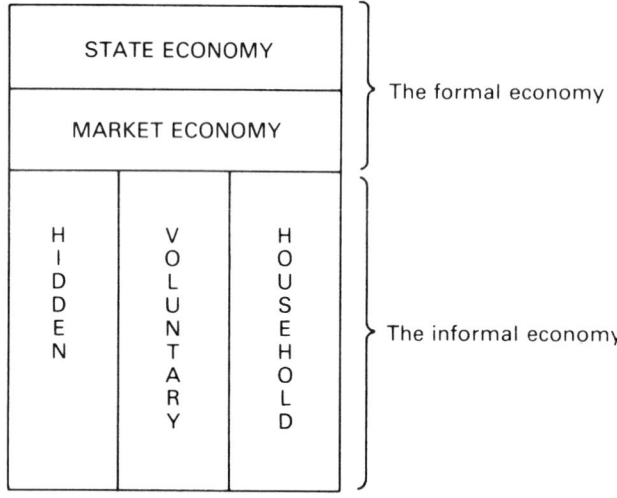

Figure 1.3 The formal and informal economies

The *household* economy includes the unpaid domestic services of wives and mothers (e.g. childcare, cooking and cleaning). This economy has undergone significant changes in recent years with women's liberation and increasing employment in the formal economy.

Do-it-yourself activities are also undertaken here and gardening, property improvements, maintenance and repair have increased rapidly. None of these activities are, however, counted in the GDP statistics since no market transactions occur.

The *voluntary* economy includes those services undertaken by individuals and organizations, for which no money payment is involved. They are performed out of friendship or as acts of charity focused on the most needy in society. As such, they satisfy important needs and generate considerable social welfare but are not counted in the statistics. Charities are controlled by the Registrar of Charities and attract tax concessions. In Britain their trading activities have been reflected in the increasing presence of 'charity shops' on the high street. As such, they constitute an element of choice and competition with established retailers.

The *hidden* or black economy involves transactions and activities which are 'undeclared' for tax purposes. Moonlighting workers perform services outside their normal work for cash in hand and no questions asked! The marketer cannot afford to ignore this economy in terms of either hidden purchasing power or as low-cost competition. Small and medium businesses in the formal economy paying tax and national insurance, charging VAT and conforming with legislation may be at a considerable disadvantage compared to so-called 'cowboy operators'.

Estimated to account for as much as 10 per cent of GDP, this economy tends to grow with self-employment, high taxation and unemployment. Other elements of this hidden sector include pilferage, fiddles and outright illegal activities such as drug dealing and stolen goods. A new crackdown on tax avoidance and evasion was announced in the 1996 Budget targeted on this shadowy economy.

Brainstorm the implications of the trend towards more working wives for

- Retailers
- Food suppliers
- Household appliance manufacturers.

Why has DIY increased and which businesses are most affected by this 'self-service' trend. Can you think of 'business opportunities' that have arisen from this?

Is the hidden economy growing or shrinking? Justify your answer.

(**See** Activity debrief at the end of this unit.)

Another important way of classifying business is according to the sector it operates in. The government has a comprehensive framework which places businesses into classes, groups and activities as part of its annual measurement of national output. Table 1.1 gives an indication of the significant changes in the relative importance, in terms of employment, of different sectors over a comparatively short period of time.

The primary sector includes agriculture, fisheries and forestry. Industrialization brought about a dramatic decline in its share of employment as seen in the shift of the 60 per cent across the chart. By the start of this century the majority were employed in industry which included manufacturing, energy and construction, but again this had fallen considerably by 1981 as service employment became dominant. Manufacturing had already shrunk to under 20 per cent of employment in 1996 and some, like Professor Stonier in his book '*The Wealth of Information*' predict a fall to as low as 10 per cent by early next century.

Table 1.1 Percentage sectoral change in employment patterns over time

Sector/Time	1801	1901	1981	2010	2041
Primary	60		4		
Secondary		60		10 est.	
Tertiary			60		
Quaternary					60

The quaternary sector involves personal rather than business services (e.g. health, education, leisure and other personal services). This may represent the areas where humans have a comparative employment advantage over computer-based technology in the next century.

- Draw up a list of sales and marketing employment specialisms which you consider will continue to exist as job opportunities in the year 2010 and those that will not, due to computer-based developments.
- When you next visit your local convenience store or hairdressers ask the proprietors about the advantages and drawbacks of being a sole trader. Compare this with your expectations arising from reading the following sections.

> - Why do you think professional people and building contractors prefer partnerships to sole trader status? Check your answer the next time you have dealings with them.

The legal form of trading organizations
Sole trader

Characteristics
- Oldest type, simplest to form
- Unincorporated
- Ownership and control in a single person
- No separate legal existence – business = individual
- No disclosure of information bar to tax authorities.
- No limit on employees
- Farming/personal services/building/retail

Merits	*Disadvantages*
Minimum formalities/privacy	Unlimited liability for any debts
Complete control/no consultation	Raising capital difficult: own funds/plough back/family
Highly motivated/single-minded	Specialized and risky – banks view
Least costly to form	Jack of all trades /narrow outlook
Close to customers/employees	Depend on health/lack continuity
Flexible/attend to detail	Self-exploitation – work long hours
Niches where limit to market	Competition from large/small
Exemption from legislation/VAT	Lack management skills
Personal satisfactions – status	No-one to share burden

Of around three million businesses in Britain today, 97 per cent employ less than 20 employees (equivalent to one third of total employed outside government). Small firms and the sole trader are the predominant form in terms of numbers but not in terms of contribution to total output. However, all firms employing less than 100, outside government, now account for over 50 per cent of turnover, up from 40 per cent in 1979.

Found in sectors where entry barriers are low and capital requirements limited, few sole traders would be defined as entrepreneurial. Perhaps 10 per cent of the total might fall into this category and even here their inventiveness is not always sufficient to produce innovation. They will be weak compared to well-resourced companies. Limited capital restricts their growth while excessive competition often requires hard work and long opening hours just to survive. Their social and economic lives tend to merge, and while they are motivated by self-interest they also bear all of the risks. They are often under pressure from larger businesses e.g. according to *Verdict*, the share of specialist food retailers fell from 10.5 to 6.5 per cent between 1989 and 1996.

It is difficult to know the precise number of such enterprises since they merge into the hidden economy.

Partnerships

Characteristics
- Unincorporated
- Two or more in common with a view to profit
- No more than 20, bar certain professions
- Form an agreement or are bound by 1890 Act
- Unlimited liability and jointly liable
- Share management/profits/losses
- No legal personality

Merits	*Disadvantages*
Able to raise more capital	Unlimited liability unless 'Limited' – still must be at least one partner fully liable

Pool expertise/mutual support /funds	Lack of legal identity – dissolves if death/ disagreement = expense/trouble
More chance to specialize	Potential disagreements
No corporation tax on business	Frozen investment

This form is much more attractive to the professions where capital requirements are limited in many cases and codes of conduct limit the risk of financial malpractice. Legal formalities are few and privacy is high. However, recent high profile and costly legal settlements involving poor financial advice given by accountancy firms to corporate clients has caused at least one of the largest (KPMG) to opt for the company form. For most other businesses the company form is much more attractive.

Registered company

Characteristics
- Incorporated, separate legal entity – enter contracts etc.
- Confers various rights and duties
- Members contribute capital and own shares
- Dominant form
- Liability limited to amount invested or guaranteed

Public company (plc)	*Private company (Ltd)*
Two or more members	Minimum two / £100 authorized capital
£50,000 and two directors	One director plus a Secretary
Offer shares to the public	Offence to offer shares to public – friends OK
Requires Business Certificate before trading/borrowing	Trade once incorporation certificate received
	Typically family business

A registered company has a number of duties and must also submit to the Registrar of Companies:

- *Memorandum of association*: regulates external affairs/protects investors and suppliers/ states name, liability, objectives and scope of business
- *Articles of association*: regulate internal administration
- *Statutory declaration of compliance* with the relevant Act
- *Independently audited annual accounts and directors report* (smaller firms of less than 50 employees provide a summary only)

Duty of care and trust on all directors

Public companies must also hold an AGM and comply with Stock Exchange regulations

Merits	*Disadvantages*
Separate legal entity	Special and double taxation
Limited liability of owners	Complex/costly to form
Greater financial capability	Disclosure requirements
Easy transfer of ownership	Government regulations
Able to fund innovation	Inflexibility of size
	Impersonality

Many companies hold shares in other enterprises which they may have formed or acquired. If these exceed more than 50 per cent of the voting rights the business is termed a *holding company*. Such holdings may sometimes form a pyramid, with the *ultimate* holding company having overall control.

Keep your eye on the company section of a quality newspaper (e.g. *Financial Times*) for a company seeking plc status and offering shares for sale to the public. Read the preamble to the Offer and list the advantages of this course of action to the business. What are the potential drawbacks?

In undertaking this activity you might reflect on several factors:

- The ability to raise considerable amounts of capital is the main attraction of the plc but what about the 'costs' of raising funds this way?
- What are your feelings about the degree of scrutiny required by the Companies Act?
- Does a quotation on the Stock Exchange force the business to think short term rather than long term as some commentators suggest?
- Why have some public companies decided to buy back their shares (e.g. Virgin Group, the Bodyshop)?
- Doesn't going public make you vulnerable to a takeover and what if the 'Offer' flops?
- Why have increasing numbers chosen 'Unlimited company' status since the law allowed exemption from filing accounts (i.e. financial affairs are kept private)?

Cooperative

Characteristics

- 1844 Rochdale pioneers in retailing
- Governed by Industrial and Provident Societies Act
- Worker ownership/control but falling numbers/mergers
- Limited liability but one member, one vote
- Self-help not profit maximizing via management committee
- Equitable distribution of dividend *if a surplus is made*

Comment

A significant but declining force in grocery retailing (food share fell from 7.6 to 6.1 per cent between 1990 and 1996) in the face of competition from the better-managed and more focused multiples, the CRS has been forced to merge and specialize in other niches. There are other worker cooperatives among farmers and craft workers but these are not organized under the same Act. They tend to establish in times of recession or rapid structural decline in the industries concerned. Producer coops doubled in the 1980s but suffer weaknesses in attracting managers of the right calibre and raising capital for large-scale ventures. The Scott Bader Commonwealth, a chemical concern, is the most-quoted industrial example with an interesting constitution which includes among other things; a limit of 350 employees per unit, a maximum remuneration spread of 1:7 and no dismissals.

Franchising

Characteristics

- Franchisor sells the right to market a product under its name to a franchisee
- Separate entities but interdependent businesses
- Rapid growth especially retailing (e.g. Tie Rack)
- Ready-made opportunity for an entrepreneur with capital wishing to minimize risks of a new venture (90 per cent survive beyond three years)

ACTIVITY 1.5

- Identify a franchise business and a 'manager'-run outlet of a national company in your locality.
- Observe the quality of service in the two outlets
- Assess the relative strengths and weaknesses of the two
- Consider *why* franchising has become such an important form of business organization and *what* makes it so customer orientated.

In undertaking this activity take account of a 'typical' agreement:

Franchisor agrees to	*Franchisee agrees to*
Provide business format/initial training	Pay an initial sum to franchisor
Supplies of product and quality control	Pay a percentage of profit to franchisor
Promotional support (e.g. advertising)	Buy supplies of product from franchisor
	Maintain standards laid down

The public services
The public corporations

- Publicly owned, controlled and accountable via Ministers to Parliament
- Separate legal entities created by Statute or Royal Charter (e.g. Royal Mint)
- Boards of management appointed by ministers
- Financed from revenue raised or central government funding
- Designed to be commercially independent but subject to ministerial control
- Intended to secure long-term strategic objectives and control of the economy
- Lack of competition and conflicting objectives led to inefficiency
- Susceptible to pressure group activity, especially trade unions

The regulated plcs

- The bulk of the nationalized industries were privatized during the 1980s
- They were sold:

    Direct to the public (e.g. BT) or to management/employee buyouts (e.g. National Freight Corporation)
    To other companies (e.g. Rover to British Aerospace and subsequently to BMW)
    In parts (e.g. British Rail hotels)

- Those remaining are either unprofitable or unsalable (nuclear) or ideologically difficult (Royal Mail)
- The transfer of ownership to private shareholders was justified under:

Political factors	*Economic factors*
Reduced role of the state	Achieve efficiency improvements
Deregulation of the economy	Increased competition and choice
Encourage shareholding democracy among customers	Pressure on management to become marketing orientated
Enable worker share-ownership	Improve industrial relations
Provide freedom to manage	Exploit new opportunities
Cut borrowing (PSBR) and taxes	Supply side rises in productivity
	Cut costs

- The creation of private monopolies in water, electricity, gas and telecoms was counterbalanced by new regulators with considerable powers to enforce efficiency gains and improvements in service. Recent public concerns that some regulators have become increasingly influenced by the regulated (e.g. OFWAT, OFLOT) have, however, resulted in an enquiry by the Greenbury Committee on public standards.

Local authorities

Services provided by local government include, among others, fire and police, road maintenance, consumer protection, recreation, environmental health and education. They are managed by elected councillors through full-time professional officers. As in the rest of the public sector, they have been subject to radical structural and operational changes over the past decade. Central government control has increased, but authorities have been encouraged to forge mutually beneficial links with local business communities. Exposure to market forces through compulsory competitive tendering has transformed the council officer role into that of a 'facilitator' rather than a direct provider of local services.

Visit one or more of the following and explain what steps a local authority could take in introducing a 'marketing orientation' into:

- Its library services
- Sheltered accommodation for the elderly
- Planning controls

Competitive tendering for the provision of local authority services such as refuse collection, street cleaning or vehicle maintenance involves the submission of a tender, meeting or exceeding stated service specifications, providing assurance on standards and priced competitively. What would be the contribution of the marketing department in achieving success with such a tender?

The business as a resource converter

All the forms of organization discussed above are seeking, as Peter Drucker observed, *to make resources productive*. All organizations, irrespective of their specific objectives, have this as their common goal. Inputs, as seen in Figure 1.4, are drawn in from the environment and converted in time, place or form to create utility, value and satisfaction for the ultimate consumer.

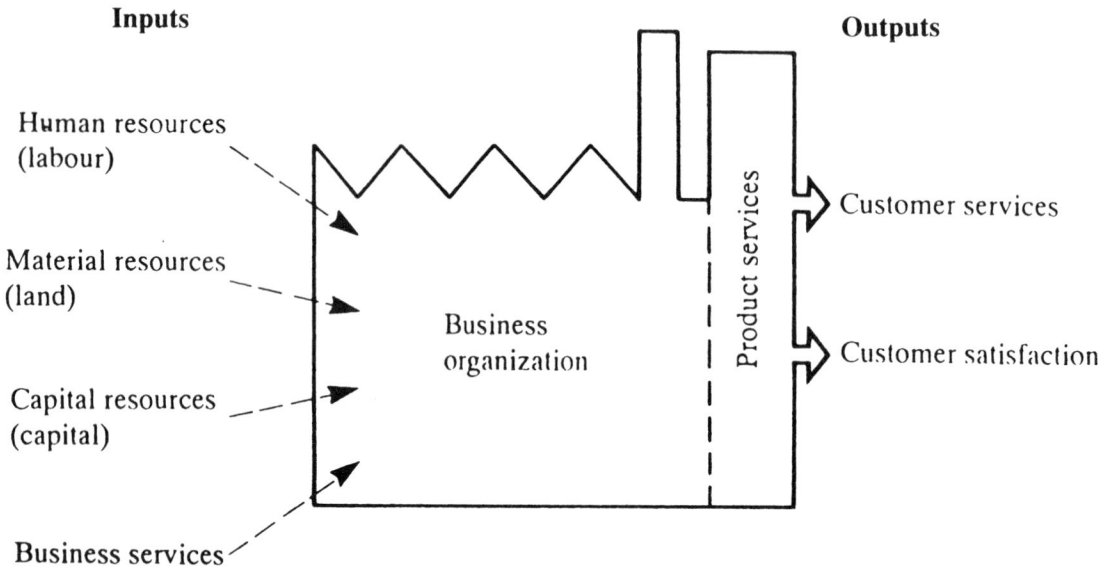

Figure 1.4 Business as a resource converter

In modern business, productive inputs are diverse and often complex entities in themselves, drawn from an interrelated global economy. The traditional economic classification of land, labour and capital is therefore simplistic. The human resource an organization requires may embody numerous skills, enterprise, creativity and an ability to adapt to changing circumstances.

Capital resources are often high technology and very specialized. They include not only buildings, equipment and transportation but also financial inputs to lubricate the process of resource conversion in advance of actual sales. Business services are important inputs as more and more firms contract-out provision of transport, catering, market research, etc. to focus their resources and attention on their core conversion activities.

ACTIVITY 1.6

Select a sales or marketing resource and explain the process of making it productive.

The resource providers may also be viewed as stakeholders in the business. This idea will be developed further in Units 2 and 4, where organizations are viewed as a coalition of stakeholders and it is the role of management to achieve a workable balance between the claims and interests of these groups. Shareholders, as the owners of the business, would seem to qualify as stakeholders but in practice this term is reserved for other providers of inputs:

- Employees
- Management themselves
- Suppliers

- Creditors
- Local community
- Distributors
- Customers

There is a considerable potential for conflict of interest between these groups. Higher wages for employees may conflict with shareholder profits or result in higher prices which upset customers. Local community concerns for health and safety may increase costs, reduce competitiveness and jeopardize jobs.

If any stakeholder considers they are not receiving sufficient return they may withdraw their contribution to the organization. For example, if customers no longer feel a product is value for money they will buy elsewhere. If workers consider their remuneration too low they will change jobs and their contribution will be lost.

Balancing these partly conflicting stakeholder expectations while achieving objectives of growth, market share and profitability is not easily achieved, not least in times of rapid change. *Internal marketing* is now widely recognized as an essential part of any manager's role. Implementation and fulfilment of business strategies requires that managers identify groups of internal as well as external stakeholders and market their plans to them.

The micro-environment of the organization

The environment of business has never been so complex and challenging as it is today. Marketers more than ever before are finding themselves confronted by increasing pressures and demands which they must seek to understand and respond to. To assist you in dealing with the threats and exploiting opportunities involved, a classification is required of the persons, groups, trends and often turbulent events that occur, external to the firm's boundaries. You need a grasp of the big picture and the role of your organization and yourself within it.

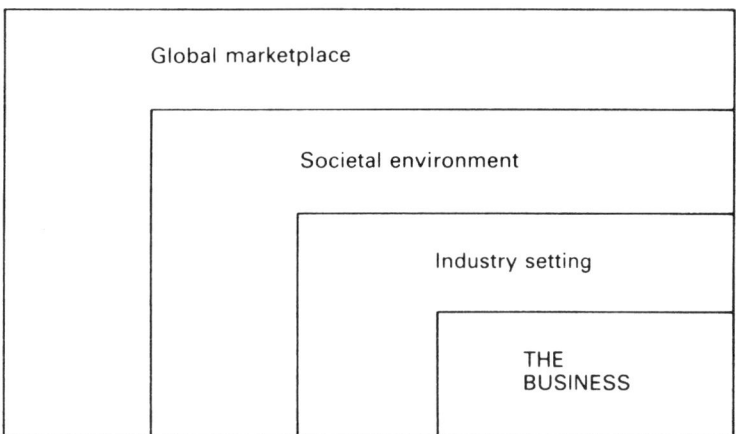

Figure 1.5 The environmental framework

Figure 1.5 provides a possible classification. The lines do not imply a solid separation and the influence of each seeps through into the business. Within a society all businesses face a common political, economic, social and technological environment, although any one factor will often impact differently according to the size and situation of the firm.

> Take a typical workday of a sales or marketing executive and log occasions and actions which link your organization to its environment.
>
> **Hint:** This should include items on news bulletins and in the local papers.

ACTIVITY 1.7

The micro-environment includes those stakeholders which have the closest and most direct relationships with the business. As can be seen in Figure 1.6, it consists of households, organizations and forces having significant effects on the marketing organization.

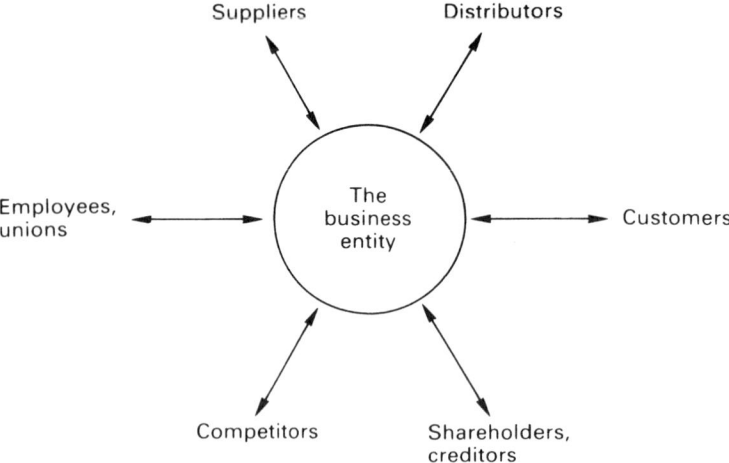

Figure 1.6 The micro-firm environment

Suppliers

No firm can supply all its own needs. Materials, components, fuel and a host of business services are necessary inputs. Suppliers are a critical link with the environment, a source of cost and also of possible partnership. A vehicle producer may have hundreds of suppliers but, as the arrows in Figure 1.6 suggest, it is a two-way dependence. Firms such as these are dramatically reducing their number of suppliers but demanding, in return for long-term contracts, total quality, just-in-time delivery, research and design support.

Dependence on one or two suppliers, however, has considerable risks, just as it is risky for the smaller business with only one or two customers. Any action or decision may have critical consequences.

It is essential that you achieve a sound grasp of these basic environmental concepts. They will occur frequently as part of different questions referring to the environment.

Competitors

These are the exceptions in the micro-environment in that they threaten rather than contribute to the survival of the business. As we will explore in a later unit, the reality of competition may be in the form of hundreds of similar rivals, as in corner-shop retailing or catering, or a handful of powerful multinationals, as in pharmaceuticals or oil refining.

The relationship is again two-way in that while competitors can constrain the achievements of the business, the marketing department can also shape and influence the competitive environment. As can be seen in Figure 1.7, business has the discretion to adjust its marketing mix as conditions change. The truly marketing-orientated company will ensure that its strategies, plans, tactics and responses will be decided not in a vacuum but with careful reference to its changing threats and opportunities.

Customers

All businesses, as the marketer knows full well, have customers as the final link in the input–output chain. The idea that they are stakeholders is less familiar, although the choice of withdrawing their stake or not will determine the success or otherwise of the enterprise. The business will naturally be concerned with all the influences affecting that choice. *Distributors* must also be considered where the firm does not sell directly to the consumer. Their power and position may be significant not least in respect of retailer brands which may be promoted aggressively at the expense of manufacturer offerings. Tying in distributors may provide a competitive edge over rivals.

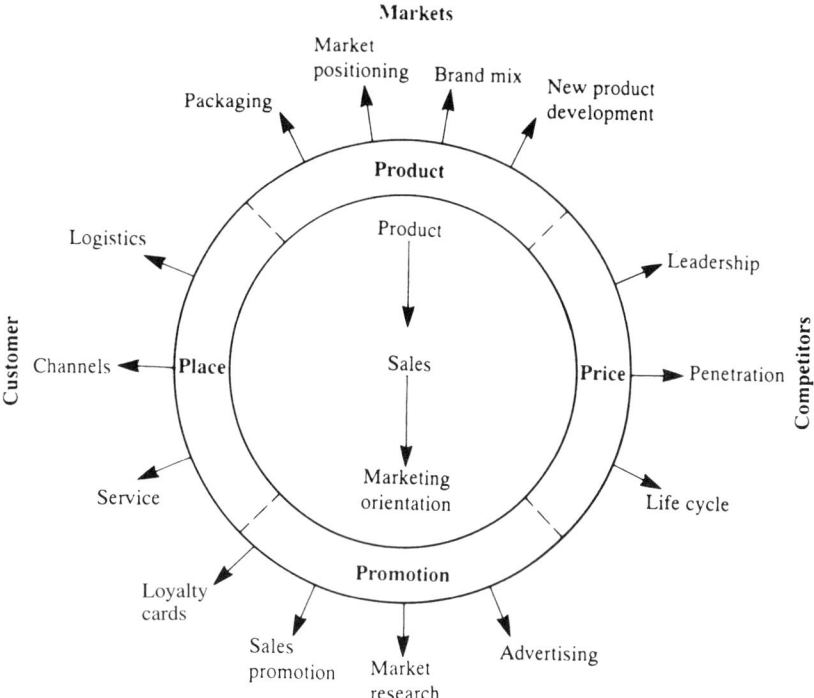

Figure 1.7 The marketing set

Shareholders and creditors

Shareholders provide the longer-term capital while creditors such as banks provide short- and medium-term funds. They can affect the business through the sale of shares or withdrawal of credit. Small businesses are particularly vulnerable to the latter in times of recession while institutional shareholders, such as pension funds, are becoming more active in their scrutiny of public company management.

Employees and unions

Most businesses have employees who contribute their time and skills for monetary and other rewards. They form part of the wider society and reflect the values and beliefs found there. They are clearly affected by company activities, including harmful ones, but again the effects are two-way. They can unionize, adversely affect productivity, leave or have equally positive effects on company fortunes. The decline in trade unions has clearly affected the freedom of many firms to manage but so too has increased legislation on health, safety, employment and pollution.

> Taking a business with which you are familiar, identify and rank its five most important suppliers, distributors, competitors, customers and creditors. What marketing mix does it employ to:
>
> - Retain and motivate its distributors?
> - Secure a competitive edge over its rivals?

The macro-environment

The wider environment (Figure 1.8) over which the organization can exert little influence is often referred to by the acronym PEST. The inclusion of a regulatory framework of laws, standards and customs converts the acronym to SLEPT while the addition of ethics and environment converts it to STEEPLE. These provide compartments into which we can sort the various trends, events, threats and opportunities which occur in the environment.

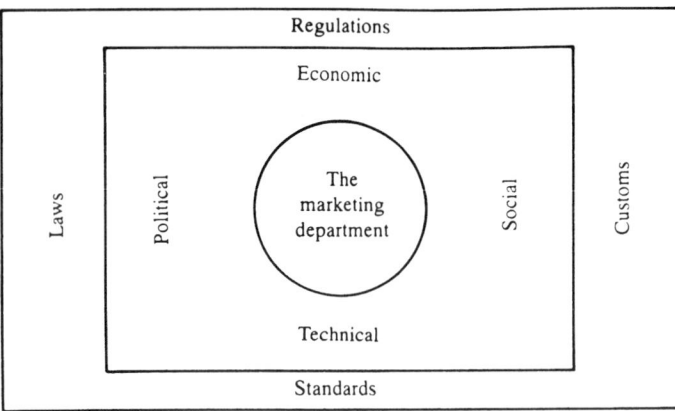

Figure 1.8 PEST factors and the regulatory framework

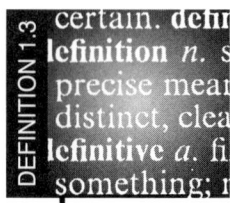

Match up the following terms:

- Customs
- Laws
- Standards
- Regulations

1 Prescribed qualities and performances to which products must conform.
2 Rules or orders governing various business operations and procedures (e.g. health and safety).
3 Long-established business practices and modes of customer behaviour (e.g. half-day closing).
4 Enactments established by government authority.

(**See** Activity debrief at the end of this unit.)

Units 5–9 will consider each of these macro-environments in detail, but we may conclude this unit with just a brief mention of each.

Political

The role and impact of the state on business extends far beyond the making of laws. The size of the public sector was mentioned earlier and all its organizations affect businesses whether as suppliers, customers, policy makers or regulators. The philosophy of the government in power sets the climate for business and a change of party in office can significantly alter the thrust and direction of all aspects of their policies.

Economic

This is closely linked with the political environment, and economic policies to achieve government objectives will impact on the costs, prices, competitiveness and profitability of businesses. The business pages of the quality press are therefore required reading for the serious marketer since an understanding of the key economic indicators provides the necessary information for anticipating developments in the marketplace. The economic horizons of businesses will vary greatly, as seen in Figure 1.9.

Many sole traders compete wholly in local markets and are therefore only interested in the local economy. However, the conditions experienced here will often have cascaded down from conditions in the world economy, which in turn influence national economies and regions within them. The importance of international factors has increased in recent years with the development of trading blocs, single markets and the successful conclusion of the GATT talks. The implications of European Monetary Union and a single currency currently confront Britain's politicians and businesses alike. Businesses who are reluctant to search out the opportunities presented by these developments may soon find their profitable niche markets exposed to new competition.

Figure 1.9 The four horizons

'*Prepare a regular business environment brief*'
Produce a summary of the main events and developments affecting a business of your choice over the past week. Use the elements in your micro- and macro-environment as your headings.

Many companies appoint an executive to collate such information on an on-going basis in order to build up a moving picture of change in their environment. Perhaps you could organize weekly briefs in your CIM classes.

Social

This is perhaps the most difficult environment for the marketer to identify, evaluate and respond to. It includes changes in population characteristics, educational standards, culture, lifestyles, attitudes and beliefs. The way we think, live and behave is the outcome of complex cultural conditioning by family, friends, school, church, work and the various media. It conditions who decides what we buy, where and when we buy it, whether we use credit or cash. Social and demographic change may often appear to change slowly, yet their impacts are likely to far outweigh the consequences of political decisions over the longer term. The trends towards lower and later births and the corresponding ageing of the population, for example, will generate massive changes over time in patterns of work and spending.

Technical

This environment is characterized by accelerating rates of change in the means, methods and knowledge that organizations utilize in the supply chain. It is the primary means by which the production possibilities of society and the productivity of scarce resources can be expanded, enabling more wants to be satisfied. It also constitutes threats to those organizations that fail to innovate new and better products and processes.

The lead time between invention, innovation and market introduction has shrunk significantly with the application of computer technology, while the development of telecommunications has combined to make the global economy a reality. All businesses face the challenges implied but only the more alert, flexible and proactive, such as Microsoft, 3M and Sony, will translate them into opportunities and profit.

Summary

In this unit we have seen that:

- Business ignores the environment at its peril.
- Marketers have a key role in identifying environmental change.
- A diversity of business organizations exist in a mixed economy.
- The strengths of one form are often the weaknesses of another.
- An informal economy exists alongside the formal.

- Businesses have a number of primary stakeholders and these make up its micro-environment where influence is two-way.
- Businesses must also account and respond to opportunities and threats in its wider environment over which it has no control.

Activity debrief

There have been many different activities suggested in this unit and many of a practical nature. It is important that you undertake these and compare the outcomes with what the workbook has suggested. As you will have realized, some of the questions were intended to get you thinking about the subject matter in the sections that followed.

The answers in matching the definitions were:

1.2 – 5, 4, 6, 1, 2, 3.
1.3 – 3, 4, 1, 2.

In *Extending activity 1.1* you should have considered implications from the employment and marketing side. For example, the increasing numbers of working wives is filling the gap left by declining numbers of school leavers. (Women are expected to account for 46 per cent of the workforce by 2006 and contribute the majority of employment growth, according to the 1997 *Social Trends* report.) This allows flexible staffing using part-time hours but demands changes in personnel policy as a result. Working wives alter the times of peak shopping hours and increases the demand for convenience and frozen foods.

Examination hints and specimen questions

The material in this unit covers about 10 per cent of the syllabus. Specific questions or part questions will be posed from time to time on the characteristics and relative merits of different types of organization. These may also be linked to topics covered in the next unit.

A grasp of the various environments of business is fundamental to the whole syllabus. The activities requiring you to monitor and think about the various aspects of the marketing environment will frequently form a question in their own right and possibly related to your home country. They will also provide the necessary background to addressing the compulsory question.

1   (a)   Distinguish clearly between public, private and voluntary sector organizations and provide an example of each. (8 marks)
    (b)   Select either the public or the voluntary sector and discuss the changing role and importance of marketing within it. (12 marks)
                                                         (CIM Marketing Environment paper, December 1995)

2   You have been asked to address a small conference of young sales executives on the subject of: Setting up in business – the legal form of enterprise.

    Prepare a series of overhead projector slides for this presentation outlining the comparative merits of the different forms for small business start ups. (12 marks)
    Given the failure rate amongst new business start ups, how important will a sales background be to success? (8 marks)
                                                         (CIM specimen Selling Environment paper 1994)

Hints: Indicative content and approach

Note: the marking scheme will always be flexible to accommodate a variety of teaching approaches and national contexts. You must, however, seek to respond within the spirit of the question by addressing it specifically and in a focused manner. Using the following guidelines and your understanding of Unit 1, plan out and answer the question in the 30–35 minutes you will have under examination conditions.

Question 1(a)
- Be sure to *distinguish* between the terms, e.g. public is state owned and controlled as distinct from private ownership and decision making.

- Provide at least one good example, e.g. charities in the voluntary sector, such as Oxfam or Save the Children.
- Don't mistake public and private *sectors* for public and private *companies*.
- *Briefly* define and distinguish each term, since mark allocation is likely to be 3 for a good definition, 3 for relevant example(s) and 2 for quality of distinction.

Question 1(b)
- Select carefully since more in-depth discussion is required.
- Don't repeat material from part (a).
- Divide attention equally between changing role (6 marks) and importance of marketing (6 marks).
- Focus on *changing* role, not just current role, for top marks.
- Set the importance of marketing in the context of the changing role, e.g. public sector shift to marketing and customer orientation.

UNIT 2

Organizations and their objectives

In this contextual unit you will:

- Examine different organizational objectives.
- Define the concepts of stakeholders and social responsibility.
- Explore the factors influencing the size of organizations.
- Consider how business responds in organizational terms and the role of marketing within the structures adopted.

By the end of this unit you will:

- Appreciate the diversity of organizational objectives.
- Understand how the goals and nature of organizations can and do change.
- Be able to evaluate the case for and against the adoption of a socially responsible stance towards an organization's stakeholders.
- Become aware of the strengths and weaknesses of different structures in accommodating change in the environment.

This unit is primarily concerned with the organization. It is looking at the objectives organizations seek to achieve and how these interrelate with its environment. Objectives will not be set without reference to external opportunities and constraints, and, as was seen in Unit 1, they will not be achieved without the necessary inputs drawn from the environment and the outputs supplied to it.

In order to achieve its objectives an organization must organize its resources effectively and formulate policies to assist efficient implementation. While it would appear that setting these objectives is an 'internal process' the reality, as we shall see, is often very different.

This is an area where you should be able to relate to your own experience of organizations. Working through the unit's content is expected to take around 3 hours but the activities may take up to twice this time if you undertake them thoroughly. The unit covers around 10 per cent of the syllabus, accounting for two-thirds of the Organization section. It is suggested that you:

- Open a file section under the heading of 'Organization'.
- Combine materials from this unit with that on types of organization from Unit 1.
- Store notes here on each of the activities and add to them as material becomes available.
- Scan the annual reports you were asked to obtain in unit 1 for information on their objectives.

- Obtain a written statement of your own organization's objectives and those of your department.

Organizational objectives

Organizations exist to pursue objectives. They provide direction and a sense of purpose. You should try to distinguish between a number of terms often used in this area:

- *Business purpose* This is the broad role defined for business by society (e.g. to manage scarce resources efficiently and effectively to maximize the society's welfare).
- *Business goals* These provide a broad sense of direction to organizational activities. Often used interchangeably with objectives, they normally have a longer time horizon. Goals are future outcomes to achieve (e.g. to become the leading consumer marketing company in the Far East).
- *Business mission* A fundamental statement defining the place and purpose of the organization's existence within its environment. Unique to the business, it usually refers to its primary market/product/technology.
- *Business vision* The ability to imagine or foresee the future prospects or potential for the organization (e.g. Coca-Cola, 'always be within an arm's length of desire').
- *Business values* Moral or ethical standards applied in the pursuit of business objectives (e.g. quality, honesty, customer satisfaction, etc.).
- *Business objectives* Targets or ends to be achieved in order to fulfil the goals and mission of the organization.
- *Strategies* These are large-scale programmes involving interaction with the environment in order to achieve objectives (e.g. become least-cost supplier in the market in order to achieve No.1 position).
- *Plans* These are the means devised for implementing strategies.

EXTENDING ACTIVITY 2.1

Study the following mission statement:

The University's mission is to serve the needs of industry, commerce, the professions and the community as a national and international institution which enables students to reach their full potential by providing a wide range of educational opportunities within an excellent learning environment.

The University aims, over the period of the plan:

- To increase opportunities by providing an expanded portfolio of courses, more flexibly available, to a greater number of students.
- To enable all its students to reach their potential in becoming highly qualified, creative, constructively critical people, able to contribute to the improvement of the human condition.
- To maintain a first-class environment for learning through the provision of high-quality staff and facilities, the pursuit of excellence in teaching, scholarship and research, and the commitment to a caring, friendly culture within which students are offered a stimulating, broadly based learning experience.

(University of Huddersfield Corporate Plan 1992–1996)

You may notice that typical mission statements are made up of a number of components as follows:

1. *Customers* Who are our customers?
2. *Products/services* What is our major product?
3. *Location* What is our main market?
4. *Technology* What is our core technology?
5. *Philosophy* What are our beliefs/aspirations/values?
6. *Objectives* What economic objectives are we committed to?
7. *Strengths* What is our competitive edge?
8. *Concerns* Attitudes to employees and social responsibilities.

- Use this framework to draw up a mission statement for your own organization or one with which you are familiar.
- Compare and contrast the above mission statement for an educational institution with one for a business.

(**See** Activity debrief 1 at the end of this unit.)

In the first part of this unit we will focus on organizational objectives in more general terms before considering how organizations can most effectively translate them into action. In Unit 1 we studied the diversity of organizations across the business, public and voluntary sectors. In a mixed economy it is not surprising that the nature of objectives will vary. We may identify a number of orientations:

Organization	*Primary orientation*
Private business	Profit
Cooperative	Members' returns
Public corporation	Public service + profit
Social service	Public service
Interest group	Member self-interest

As we shall see, however, the actual objectives pursued by any one organization may be both diverse and complex. They will also be subject to considerable influence by the environment.

ACTIVITY 2.1

- List the main objectives you consider would be pursued by a competitive business. Your own organization would be ideal.
- Now list your own personal and career objectives.
- How do your objectives relate to those of the business?

Do they conflict? Or
Are they complementary?

- What are the objectives of the sales and marketing department in the business? Do they conflict with those of the business as a whole?

You will probably have put profit at the top of your business objectives list, but how many others could you think of? What about basic survival as a motive or the desire for growth? Did you think about the personal objectives of those who actually decide the strategies and allocate the resources in business? These might diverge from the interests of the shareholders.

What of your own goals? Do these include such things as a high and rising salary, plenty of perks, promotion, job security and a satisfying job? If so then perhaps your ambitions would not be best served in a business pursuing maximum profits.

What of your marketing department? Is not its inclination to build sales and market share even at the expense of profitability? Should it be constrained by the financial director in this regard or is it the 'right' objective? Clearly, there are a number of difficult questions to be addressed here so we must approach it step by step.

STUDY TIPS

Don't just accept at face value what you read in a text or a newspaper. Think through what is said, carefully and logically. Do not be afraid to have your own opinion, but be prepared to justify it to others. Critical awareness of the subject matter is something that is welcomed by the examiner but usually only evident among excellent candidates. Make the investment this needs in 'thinking' and 'discussion' time. It will repay handsome dividends.

Survival

This is a basic drive in all businesses and relates to the needs we have as individuals for security and the satisfaction of our economic wants. The jobs of management and workers depend on it, and this can lead to considerable sacrifices being made in times of economic hardship. The Japanese in particular are renowned for their willingness to accept cuts in salary and redouble efforts to restore corporate fortunes.

In Unit 1 we saw that many sole proprietors would continue in business even at the cost of exploiting themselves and family workers. The directors of public limited companies will also be aware of the need to avoid the possibility of a hostile takeover bid. These often lead to the removal of top management, especially where the bid arose due to their underperformance in the eyes of shareholders. The press frequently reports examples, such as Hilton Hotels' $6.5 billion hostile bid for ITT who own the prestigious Sheraton chain.

Society is faced with the reality of scarce resources relative to its needs and wants. It therefore requires that these are managed effectively and is prepared to see businesses fail so that their resources are released for use by the more competent managers.

Businesses must justify their use of resources over and over again if they are to survive and avoid possible takeover or liquidation. This means that they must make a profit!

> **EXAM TIP**
>
> The need to survive is a fact of life for all candidates enrolled on professional courses like CIM! Viewed at the outset, the syllabus and the workbook look like big mountains to climb. So always apply the Chinese proverb – many small steps make a giant stride!

Profit and profit maximization

This is the most-quoted business objective, although, strictly, it is more a motivation than an end in itself. It does, however, provide a *measurement system* for assessing business performance. Profit maximization implies that businesses seek to make not only a profit but the maximum possible profit through time. Profit, as shown in Figure 2.1, is the difference between revenue and cost.

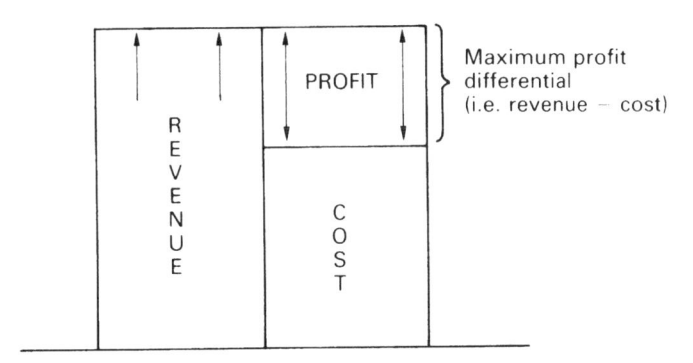

Figure 2.1 Pursuit of the maximum profit differential

Businesses are viewed as rational and self-interested in their decisions, seeking to allocate resources so as to maximize this profit differential by:

- *Supplying those goods that consumers most wish to buy*   Profit and marketing-orientated firms will carefully research customer needs, anticipate their changing preferences and supply whenever the addition to total revenue exceeds the change in costs.
- *Combine resource inputs to produce planned output at minimum possible cost*   Business will not satisfy consumer wants to gain revenue irrespective of cost. They will cease to supply further units when additional cost exceeds the price received. At this output they will ensure that factor inputs are combined so as to produce at least cost.
- *Responding quickly to changes in supply and demand conditions*   If consumer tastes change or input prices alter then it will profit the firm to adjust the marketing mix or production methods accordingly.

EXAM TIP

Maximizing is a principle to apply to your CIM studies and examinations. You must aim for maximum understanding from your available study time, and that is where this Butterworth-Heinemann Workbook series is so useful in concentrating and centralising the knowledge you need in one source.

You must also maximize your marks from answering the right questions in the required manner. Again, the activities and specimen questions contained in these workbooks are the ideal means to achieve this end. So do not settle for under-performance. Be a 'smart' student and use your workbook to the full!

The pursuit of maximum profit therefore answers two of the basic economic problems arising from scarcity:

1. What to produce and in what quantities and
2. How to produce them

It also provides a dynamic growth incentive to the business system. As can be seen in Figure 2.2, business has the incentive not only to produce efficiently to satisfy existing preferences but also to:

- Innovate new and improved products that enhance value for money for consumers and revenue for the firm
- Invest in research and development of more efficient methods of production to reduce costs.

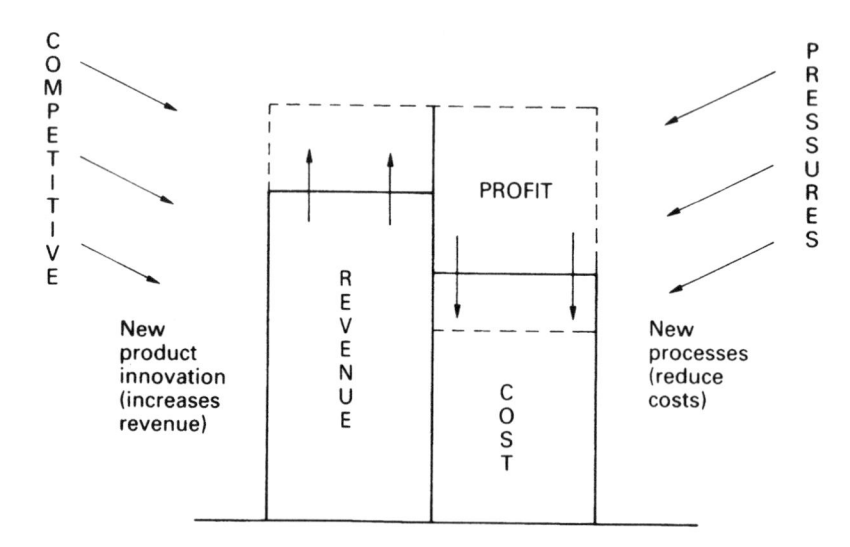

Figure 2.2 The carrot and the stick to profit maximization

Maximizing profit would appear to promise an ideal allocation of resources by rewarding those businesses that produce and market the right goods, in the right quantities, using the most efficient methods and ploughing back resources into producing economic growth through new products and better methods.

ACTIVITY 2.2

- Taking a business with which you are familiar, list practical suggestions which, if implemented, would improve profitability.
- Review the suggestions on your list and consider this question: Why has the business not already taken steps to exploit this extra profit potential?

- Is the profit objective/motive strong enough, by itself, to produce the outcome mentioned above?

What if businesses were content with just modest profits or decided to pursue other objectives? What if they are run by salaried managers, who stand to gain nothing from extra profit, rather than the shareholders? What if they are production-orientated and are not concerned with the consumers' real needs? These possibilities can only arise in the absence of *full and free competition*.

When competition is very strong, firms must market what consumers demand, otherwise their competitors will, reducing market share and threatening the very survival of the business. Firms must be efficient, otherwise they will be undercut by lower-cost rivals. They must provide excellent service because the consumer is sovereign in such a situation.

No firm, no matter how profitable, can afford to stand still. Much of the profit earned has to be ploughed back into new product development and improved methods if the firm is to retain a competitive edge. Customers will not give a second thought to a badly managed business, which will go bankrupt or be taken over by firms better fitted to manage the resources e.g. Facia Group, second largest retailer chain into receivership in March 1996.

Business therefore appears to be very much a treadmill when competition is strong. Even if an innovative business succeeds in making extra profits, this will merely attract new competitors into the market to erode away the rewards. However, as we shall now see, the scope for pursuing other objectives will be much greater where market imperfections exist or large firms dominate.

> **QUESTION 2.1**
>
> If managers are rational and they have the choice between making either 'maximum possible profits' in the short term or just modest profits, can you think of any sound business reasons why it might be sensible to choose the latter?
>
> (**See** Activity debrief 2 at the end of this unit.)

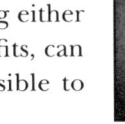

Market share

Observation suggests that many businesses seek to maximize sales *subject to a profit constraint*. There may indeed be a positive correlation between profit and market share, but beyond a certain point extra share may only be 'bought' at the expense of profit. Prices and margins will be trimmed or extra promotional expense incurred. So long as sufficient profit is made to keep shareholders content, then management may see an advantage in the stability and security of a dominant position.

Japanese exporters have been accused of pursuing this objective in the short run in order to drive out domestic competitors prior to raising prices and profits in the longer term. *Long-run versus short-run profits* is an important consideration. It is suggested that many quoted British companies are under considerable pressure from 'the City' to deliver buoyant short-run profits even at the expense of longer-term investment. Japanese and German companies, by contrast, are able to give greater emphasis to the long run due to the support of shareholding banks.

> **QUESTION 2.2**
>
> How would sales and marketing differ between a business looking for short-run profit and one seeking long-run profit?
>
> Think about the different emphasis in the marketing mix as well as the nature of long-term marketing investment payoffs. What sales and marketing strategies will produce long-run profitability?

Business growth

> **QUESTION 2.3**
>
> What are benefits to management of a growing company?
> Identify a fast-growing company and determine the primary cause of the growth.

While growth and profits may be positively related, again after a certain point this will cease to be the case. The rapid growth in out-of-town grocery superstores appears to be a case in point. Alternatively, growth may require takeovers and acquisitions and these may prove unsuccessful, especially if they represent diversification into unfamiliar areas. It will also put pressure on the scarce management resource.

Growth is, however, attractive for a number of reasons:

- It is easier to resolve conflicts between stakeholders.
- It provides opportunities for promotion and job satisfaction.
- It increases market power and management status.
- It raises morale in general.

Management objectives

If management is not under severe competitive pressure, it may decide to *satisfice*. That is, it will produce satisfactory performance and profits. Where there is a *separation of ownership from management* there is no automatic incentive for professional management employees to maximize profits for shareholders.

The organization may operate with what is termed *organizational slack*. This is the difference between the cost level which would maximize profits and actual costs. These excessive costs would finance a number of 'unnecessary expenditures', for example;

- Buy market share
- Management perks
- Pet projects
- Excess staff assistants

> **QUESTION 2.4**
>
> Can you identify slack in your organization?
>
> How does management respond to a downturn in sales?

> **ACTIVITY 2.3**
>
> Scan the papers for a business or public sector organization facing adverse change in its environment and look for evidence of efforts to reduce organizational slack.

The idea of slack then suggests that management may choose to have their own satisfactions as an objective. They will manage the business so as to maximize their security, income, status, power and job interest. They can also take in the slack without threatening core activities and programmes in times of adversity.

The existence of slack has underpinned government efforts to improve productivity in a range of public services. Lack of competition, the absence of a profit incentive and powerful stakeholder groups led to an accumulation of slack in health, education, local authorities, nationalized industries and the civil service.

Public sector organizations are intended to maximize benefits to society given a budget resource constraint. To eliminate pursuit of self-interested objectives and reduce budget deficits the government, you will recall from Unit 1, has:

- Deregulated markets
- Introduced internal markets
- Made services client-driven
- Introduced citizens' charters – setting service standards
- Insisted on compulsory competitive tendering
- Weakened the power of trade unions
- Attracted better-calibre managers.

As the objectives have become more customer-orientated in the public sector so the nature of these organizations have been transformed. The skills of the marketer have also come to the fore in the quest for more focused customer benefits.

> **EXAM TIP**
>
> Have you given any consideration to the examiner's objectives? Is it to pass only a certain proportion, for example?
>
> In fact the examiner's objective is to bend over backwards to pass as many students as possible *but only* if they meet the CIM *professional standard*. Employers must have faith in what a CIM qualification stands for, and it is in your long-term career interests to see that this is maintained. So be well prepared, it *pays* to meet the standard required.

What causes the goals to change?

To understand how business goals change we must understand how they are formed. The board of directors are responsible for deciding objectives and formulating policies to secure their effective achievement. The managing director is appointed to implement policy while non-executive directors are often invited onto the board of public companies to provide an external dimension to formulating objectives.

Objectives provide a focus for the organization and a sense of unity. They also provide motivation for management and staff if used effectively. The organization must periodically review its objectives primarily to account for change in the environment. Larger organizations may adopt corporate planning to formalize this process.

> Corporate planning is the continuing process by which the long term objectives of the organization may be formulated and subsequently attained by means of long term strategic actions.
> (G. A. Cole)

Strategic objectives are set in functional areas of the business for up to 5 years ahead and summarize where the business intends to be by that time. More specific and quantifiable tactical objectives roll forward from year to year (e.g. increase sales of product *X* by 25 per cent).

> **EXAM TIP**
>
> Another objective of the examiner is to complete the marking with the minimum of headaches. An examiner-friendly script is therefore required, one that is legible, clear, well set out and expressed in an easy-to-understand semi-report style format.

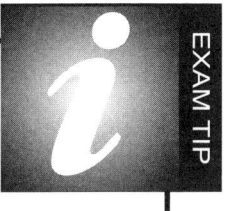

In reviewing objectives the organization will account for current performance and assess strengths and weaknesses in *key result areas*. According to Peter Drucker these include:

- Market standing
- Innovation
- Profitability
- Management performance
- Worker performance and attitude
- Public responsibility.

It will also scan the external environment for opportunities and threats. When the organization adapts to this external environment it will impact on its *effectiveness* whereas when it adapts its internal structure and organization it will impact on its *efficiency*.

Stakeholder pressures

> QUESTION 2.5
>
> *Review questions*
> Review the section in Unit 1 on the business as a resource convertor and consider the following question:
>
> - What would an organization *without stakeholders* look like?
>
> (**See** Activity debrief 3 at the end of this unit.)
>
> *Review activity*
>
> - Taking either your college or business, identify its stakeholders and divide them into *direct* and *indirect* groupings.
> - Select a stakeholder from each group and examine the nature of their relationship with the organization you have chosen.

Stakeholders may be defined as any group or individual who can affect or are affected by the achievement of the organization's objectives. Since they have a stake, a legitimate interest in the business, they can influence objectives. Management cannot hope to operate in isolation but must seek to satisfy their stakeholders' legitimate expectations if they are to contribute value in return.

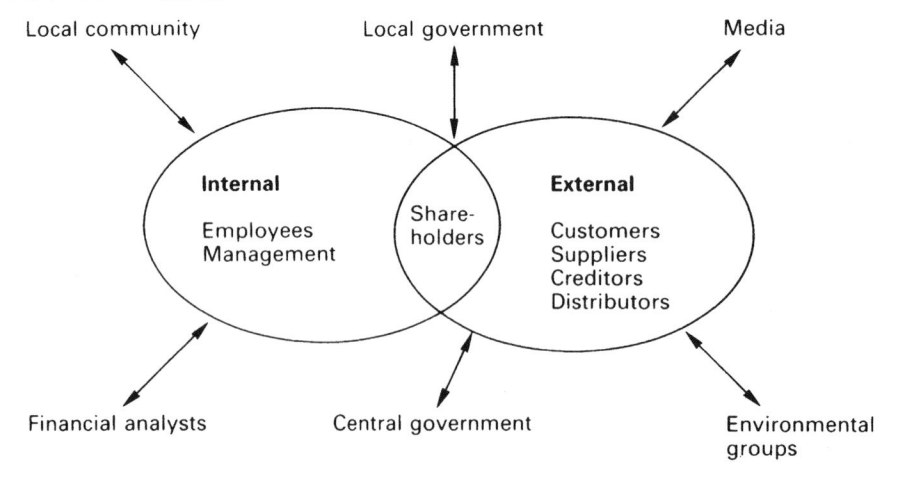

Figure 2.3 Internal and external stakeholders.

Direct or connected stakeholders are closely related to the core economic functions of the business. Together with the pressure exerted by competitors, they can change the goals and nature of the organization unless managed effectively.

Stakeholder	Pressure exerted
Shareholders	Delegate decision power to board but recent increase in activism over remuneration and appointments. Selling shares is the real threat as a falling share price attracts takeover predators.

Employees	Absenteeism, turnover, low morale, media leaks, unionization, poor productivity.
Customers	Reduce purchases, buy from competitors, organize boycott, complain to other potential customers, press for legislation
Creditors	Limit credit, withdraw credit, cut credit rating, charge higher rates.
Distributors	Stock and promote competing brands/own-label, integrate backwards, delay payment.
Suppliers	Supply competitors, reduce priority, limit trade credit, poor-quality service, integrate forward

> **EXTENDING ACTIVITY 2.2**
>
> In the light of the above consequences of *failing* to attend to the interests of direct stakeholders, suggest how a business can best ensure that their contributions remain positive and add value.
>
> **Hint:** One way of doing this might be to draw up a 'code of good practice' for each stakeholder.

Indirect stakeholder groups are not directly engaged in the business operations but can exert influence on and be seriously affected by their activities. A few of these are listed below for each group. Can you think of others?

- *Local government* Interested not only in the investment, jobs, prosperity, tax revenue and prestige the organization generates locally but also on its compliance with relevant legislation, planning requirements, etc.
- *Communities* Concerned with property values, quality of life, jobs and prosperity, congestion, links with local schools and charitable activities. Can protest, mobilize the media, obstruct planning applications, etc.
- *Financial analysts* Assess past/future performance in financial and broader terms. Downgrade where suspicious of unethical behaviour and highlight undervalued assets/possible takeover. They have the ear of the shareholders.
- *Media* Can seriously enhance or damage the public image of the business. They publicize issues and corporate achievements and form a line of communication from the organization to the local/national community.
- *Central government* Make, interpret and enforce laws, monitor compliance, levy taxes and implement economic policies. They also provide infrastructure, spend, protect, subsidize, rescue and restructure. The organization may seek influence through trade associations, lobbying, provision of information, joint projects and even political donations.
- *Environment groups* Trend until recently of rising membership and public concerns but clamour for more jobs and improved competitiveness together with the government's desire to cut red tape and regulations may actually reduce environmental pressures on firms, particularly in times of economic recession.

> **QUESTION 2.6**
>
> In what sense are you a stakeholder in CIM and how might you seek to influence the organization?

Stakeholders will have differing and often conflicting viewpoints on the organizational objectives to be pursued. It is not surprising therefore that statements of objectives are frequently vague and generalized. The objectives clause in the Memorandum of Association is deliberately broad so as not to limit development and provide maximum flexibility for management. There will be a *hierarchy of objectives* rather than a single focus, and these will cascade down through the various functional areas of the business. Many may implement *management by objectives* (MBO) as a means of linking goals with planning and management at all levels. Managers commit themselves to achieving certain objectives and are appraised and rewarded according to their success in doing so.

The concept of social responsibility

To what extent do you believe that business should have responsibilities to the rest of society? Should they incur extra costs in protecting the environment? Is it right that they sponsor community projects? Is it proper if their employment practices far exceed the requirements laid down by law? These are important questions which involve consideration of business values and ethics.

Business ethics are the standards of behaviour and conduct applied by managers in carrying out their business. Examples of business ethics would include the following:

- Obey the law, e.g. profit only the overriding objective given minimum legal compliance.
- Respect for individuals, e.g. part of Marks & Spencer's mission is to treat employees well.
- Above all, do no harm, e.g. Body Shop's concern for sustainable development.
- Tell the truth, e.g. product recalls where defects are discovered.

Ethical businesses obey the spirit as well as the letter of the law and often operate well in excess of minimum legal requirements, e.g. ethical retailers such as the Cooperatives (CRS) developing a Code of Practice to govern sourcing from poorer nations.

What is social responsibility?

Social responsibility is acceptance by an organization of obligations to protect and improve the welfare of society as well as its own interests. Stakeholder concerns, other than those of the shareholders, are accounted for and action goes beyond the minimum requirements of the law. Action is voluntary and may involve net cost and therefore the sacrifice of net profit.

Milton Friedman, the American market economist, argues that business is there *to maximize returns to shareholders*. This and competition ensures that society's scarce resources are most efficiently utilized. Its primary and only responsibility is as a wealth producer and allocator of these scarce resources. There is no such thing as a free lunch, Friedman maintains, and any avoidable costs incurred in pursuit of social objectives will inevitably be at the expense of one stakeholder or another, i.e.:

- Shareholders, if profits are reduced
- Customers, if prices have to be increased
- Employees, if jobs are lost or wages constrained
- Communities, if local plants have to be closed

Social responsibility blurs management accountability and reduces competitiveness, not least with other countries, he argues. It also requires that business assumes authority in social areas where they have limited competence and where issues should rightly be left to the state.

EXTENDING ACTIVITY 2.3

- Where does your government stand on this issue? Consider, for example, why the Conservative Party opposes the Social Chapter of the Maastricht Treaty, while the Labour Party supports it.
- List any areas where your organization acknowledges social responsibilities. What is its justification and what (if any) is the net cost?
- How would you convince your board of directors that social responsibility is the key to achieving competitive advantage?

Society's view of the role of business has changed as economies have prospered. The narrow role expressed by Friedman is no longer accepted by many commentators, who suggest that it is a fallacy that business can prosper or even exist without due regard to broader social concerns. They argue the following:

- Sanctions will be applied if stakeholder interests are ignored.
- Societal concern may represent enlightened self-interest since bad publicity damages sales, employee morale and corporate reputation and vice versa.
- Laws, as the expression of society's wishes, lag behind current attitudes and expectations, so compliance with minimum standards is insufficient.
- Social responsibility can be profitable (e.g. by materials recovery, recycling and energy conservation).

> **ACTIVITY 2.4**
>
> Can you think of how social responsibility might be profitable in
>
> - Health and safety standards for consumers?
> - Positive discrimination in favour of recruiting female marketers?
> - An ethical code of practice for fair dealing with suppliers?

- Management is a leadership group with the capabilities and resources to create a better environment for both society and for business.
- Business has concentrated economic power and control over global resources. It must be accountable for the 'responsible' exercise of this power. Being efficient and profit-motivated is no longer sufficient, and business must account to its stakeholders for how products are produced, used and disposed of, how profits are distributed and their contribution to society.

> **QUESTION 2.7**
>
> In fulfilling the needs of society for jobs and rising living standards it has been argued that business cannot divorce wealth creation from the means of producing it and the consequences for stakeholders. Our way of life must be *sustainable* into the future and there is clearly more to human welfare than additional goods and services, however efficiently they are produced. Society gives organizations their charter to exist, so if they diverge from fulfilling its wider purpose or behave irresponsibly, the charter may be revoked.
>
> But – is social responsibility a luxury that only large organizations with monopoly power can enjoy?

The factors affecting organizational size

We have already considered a number of influences affecting organizational size in Unit 1. The main factors will now be outlined and the responsiveness of differently sized organizations to environmental change assessed. Limitations on size include:

- Legal form (e.g. span of control possible for a sole trader)
- Ability to raise capital
- The fundamental limit of the market/niche size
- Where the service provided requires attention to detail
- Preferences of owners and employees for a human scale of enterprise
- Available technology offers no advantage to scale.

> **DEFINITION 2.1**
>
> What is a small firm? While it may be easy to define a very small firm, it is not easy to draw the line with medium and large-scale organizations. Textbook definitions are often arbitrary e.g. less than 200 employees (manufacturing) or a value of turnover (retailing). Perhaps you have thought of more commonsense criteria such as:

- The owners have effective control and manage the business.
- They and employees live near the business.
- It is small relative to others in the market/industry.
- It has limited power to influence market conditions.

Large numbers of small businesses are formed each year by people attracted by the prospects of financial independence and often encouraged by a whole battery of government incentives and supports. Governments are well aware of the fact that small firms employing less than ten employees now account for around 90 per cent of all new jobs, while those employing over 1000 are net shedders of labour, especially in recession. Of 3 million small firms beginning in a typical year, however, only half of the new ones starting up will have survived five years on. Lack of capital, expertise, competition and personal problems account for most of the casualties.

Factors promoting growth in the size of the firm

1. *Growth in the market*   Unless the business grows at least at the same rate it will lose market share.
2. *Cost advantage*   If output increases more proportionately than the required inputs as productive capacity rises, the business secures increasing returns to scale. Figure 2.4 shows the fall in unit costs as economies of scale are exploited. Unless the firm operates at minimum economic scale (MES) it will have such a cost disadvantage that it will be unable to compete effectively, no matter how well managed its operations. The main economies of scale may be classified as follows:

At plant level
- Technical economies

At the level of the firm
- Marketing economies
- Supply and purchase economies
- Financial economies
- Managerial economies
- Risk-bearing economies

At the level of the industry
- External economies
   of concentration
   of information
   of disintegration

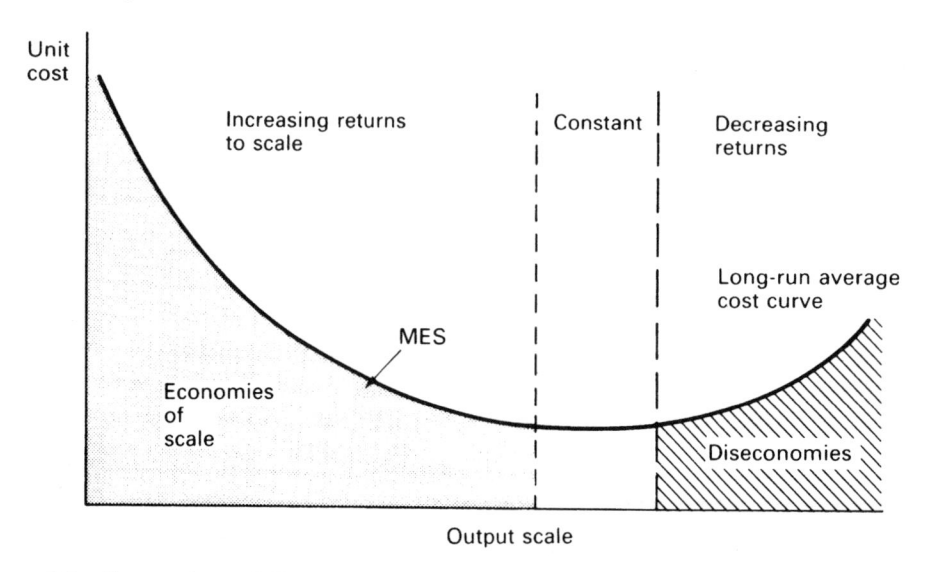

Figure 2.4 Economies and diseconomies of scale

> **EXTENDING ACTIVITY 2.4**
>
> Using your experience and library resources find another example for each of these categories of scale economy. Technical economies can be broken down into the following:
>
> - Economies of increased dimensions, e.g. warehouse construction
> - Economies of balancing, e.g. successive steel processes
> - Economies of superior technique, e.g. robot welders
> - Economies of lengthened production runs, e.g. paperback books
> - Economies of experience and the learning curve, e.g. airliners, housebuilding
> - Economies of stocks and spare capacity, e.g. airlines.
>
> Can you apply these and others you discover to justify the likelihood of falling unit costs and increasing sales effectiveness in an expanding marketing department?

It can be seen in Figure 2.4 that beyond a certain scale, unit costs start to rise. This introduces the possibility of diseconomies of scale as an organization grows. This, as we shall see in the final section of this unit, alerts management to the need for organizational effectiveness if the benefits of size are not to be lost. Examples of diseconomies may be:

- *Technical* A highly specialized operation is vulnerable to a downturn in activity, causing costs to rise steeply.
- *Managerial* Increased size brings problems of coordination, communication and motivation.
- *Marketing* Falling production costs may be more than offset by higher distribution and promotional costs, not least where competitors retaliate to avoid loss of market share.
- *External* The bidding up of factor input prices plus congestion and other negative environmental impacts.

> **EXAM TIP**
>
> Any new course of study is hard going at the beginning. You do not know the terminology and you have studied too few pieces of the overall jigsaw to be able to see the overall picture unfolding.
>
> However, remember that the more pieces you fit together, the easier it gets, not least because you move down your learning curve. Each question and activity you attempt provides experience you can apply to advantage when you address the next. So keep on going and develop some learning momentum!

3 *Monopoly motive* growth by the takeover of competitors not only provides scope for economies it also reduces competition and doubly improves profitability.
4 *Security and market power* J. K. Galbraith suggests that firms pursue growth in size to protect themselves from hostile takeovers and to secure some control over their environments. The costs and risks involved in developing new products today are so high that firms attempt to control their inputs, the market and even the consumer.

> **ACTIVITY 2.5**
>
> In his books such as *The New Industrial State* and *Economics and the Public Purpose* Galbraith went so far as to suggest that big business was attempting to *create dissatisfaction in the minds of consumers* by bombarding them with broadly based promotional activity which encouraged them to replace existing products with successive generations of 'new and allegedly better products'. Can you think of any examples which may support Galbraith's thesis? Can you provide a positive defence against what is clearly an attack on the contribution, values and social responsibility of modern marketing methods?

5 *Technological requirements* Mass consumption in a world of global specialization requires mass production. The only practical means of meeting most of the high consumption needs of large populations is through large-scale operations. Public and merit goods, provided equitably on a national scale and to uniform standards, require large bureaucracies.

The rapid growth of the multinational owes much to the technology that makes centralized strategy, planning and control possible. On the other hand, it is the versatility and flexibility of microprocessor-based equipment which now allows smaller concerns to compete on a more equal footing with the large ones.

There is a tension between the drive for size and market power, on the one hand, and the nimbleness of small businesses in adapting quickly to change in the environment on the other. The large firm has the capital, resources, management capacity and operational structure to exploit market opportunities and diffuse the benefits of innovation rapidly and on a global scale. However, as the recent experiences of corporate giants such as IBM and General Motors have demonstrated, they are often victims of their own success which inhibits radical transformation and new patterns of thought in the face of technological change.

> **EXAM TIP**
>
> Remember the course you are studying is first and foremost about the *environment*. Do not be tempted to answer questions in sales or marketing terms alone.

Small firms, by contrast, are better able to identify the threats and opportunities in their environment; are willing to take advantage of them and respond flexibly, but are often unable to mobilize the resources necessary to exploit them quickly enough. Most technical break-throughs come not from the well-financed research centres of dominant firms but from small and medium enterprises (SMEs), often in other industries unrestricted by accepted ideas. Large firms have responded by developing organizational structures which overcome their weaknesses and encourage adaptive and entrepreneurial behaviour within a well-resourced framework.

> **DEFINITION 2.2**
>
> Match up the following definitions:
>
> - Entrepreneur
> - Intrapreneur
> - Change agent
> - Champion
>
> 1 A risk taker and creator of new enterprises.
> 2 An individual with a fresh perspective who acts as a catalyst in helping the organ-ization find new solutions to old problems.
> 3 One who believes in the value of an idea or approach and supports or advances it in the face of numerous possible obstacles and opposition within the organization.
> 4 Individuals who are encouraged to fulfil entrepreneurial roles within a large organization.
>
> (See Activity debrief 4 at the end of this unit.)
>
> **Note:** The entrepreneur and his or her equivalents have been viewed as the vital spark that has ignited the economic engine ever since the Industrial Revolution. Resources are little use in themselves unless they can be creatively and innovatively combined to generate new and improved products and processes. The economist J. A. Schumpeter viewed the entrepreneur as both a positive and a disruptive force which:

- Kept existing businesses on their toes
- Broke up the old economic order by innovating change
- Created wealth through new factor combinations to better serve the market.

Internal organizational structures

Professor Charles Handy sees the management task as:

- Defining and fulfilling the organization's purpose through people, structures and systems
- Within the environmental constraints
- By adapting to change and
- Maintaining a suitable balance between the often-conflicting pressures at work both in and outside the organization.

If a plan is the route map to the objective desired, then organization is the mode of transport for reaching that destination, the means of translating intentions into effect.

Beyond a certain size the total business task must be broken down. Considerable benefit can be achieved from specialization and the division of labour. There is, however, a limit to any manager's span of control over subordinates and roles must be structured to ensure effective coordination, communication and control.

Activities may be grouped in a number of ways to achieve this outcome:

- By function
- By division
- By product
- By region
- By market or customers served
- By project (matrix form)

(M-form or self-contained where each division has its own functional specialists).

Organizational charts may be drawn to reflect these groupings and the distribution of power and authority. Figure 2.5 shows the typical functional structure and a summary of its strengths and weaknesses while Figure 2.6 shows the less familiar matrix form.

> **EXTENDING ACTIVITY 2.5**
>
> Using a text such as G. A. Cole's *Management Theory and Practice*, draw charts for the other forms of organization mentioned above and summarize their strengths and weaknesses. Into what category does (1) your work organization or (2) your college fall? How responsive are they to environmental pressures for change? Suggest any situations where a matrix organization would be effective and comment on the likely role of the marketing function. (**See** Activity debrief 5 at the end of this unit.)

```
                        Managing director
        ┌──────────────┬────────────────┬──────────────┐
   Operations      Marketing       Human Resources   Financial
    Director        Director          Director        Director
                       │
              ┌────────┼────────┐
            Sales   Marketing  Advertising
            Admin.  Research
```

Strengths
- Full utilization of specialist expertise
- Coordinate to serve whole organization
- Opportunity for careers and advancement

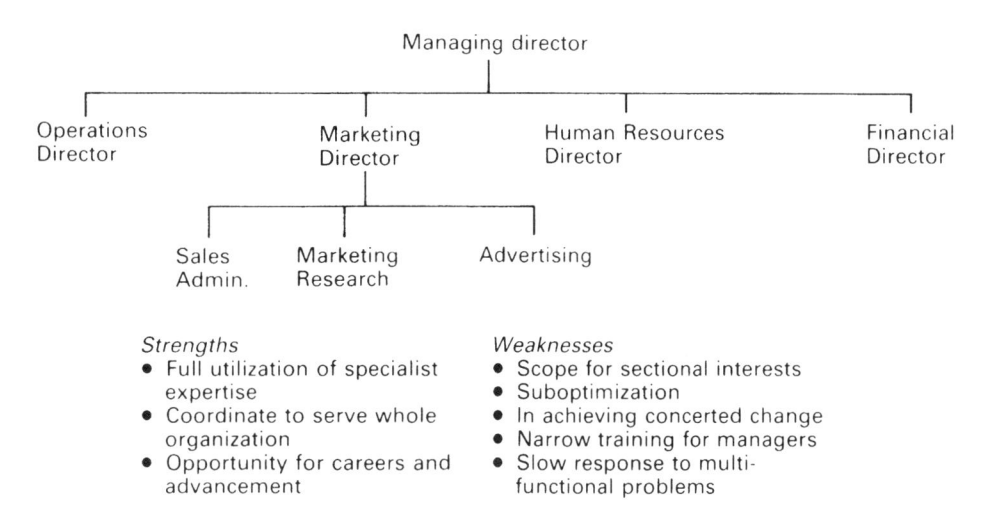

Weaknesses
- Scope for sectional interests
- Suboptimization
- In achieving concerted change
- Narrow training for managers
- Slow response to multi-functional problems

Figure 2.5 The functional organization

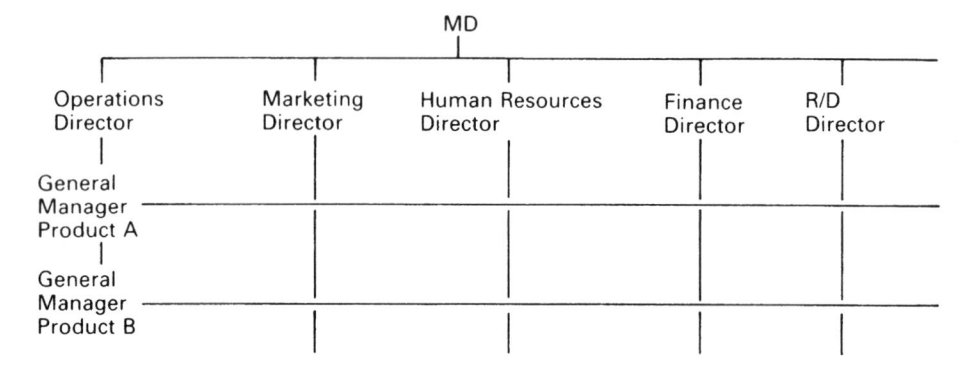

```
                              MD
      ┌───────────┬───────────┼───────────┬───────────┐
  Operations   Marketing  Human Resources Finance    R/D
  Director     Director     Director     Director   Director
      │           │           │             │          │
General ─────────────────────────────────────────────────
Manager
Product A
      │
General ─────────────────────────────────────────────────
Manager
Product B
```

Strengths
- Improved environmental monitoring and fast response to change
- Decentralized decision making
- By combining functional and project forms it achieves lateral and vertical communication
- It combines efficiency and flexibility
- It is client-focused and emphasizes the contribution of functions

Weaknesses
- Complex and costly
- Overemphasis on group decision may slow response
- Divided authority
- Divided loyalties of team members

Figure 2.6 The matrix organization

Future organization

Large organizations are under increasing global competitive pressure to become leaner, meaner and generally more innovative and responsive in the face of environmental change. A number of trends may be identified which are transforming the organization of such businesses:

- *Delayering* Reducing the number of levels in the organizational hierarchy. This speeds the flow of information to the top and decisions to the bottom of the chain of command.
- *Downsizing* Middle managers are stripped out of the organization and those who remain take over their duties, assisted by more effective information systems.
- *Outsourcing* Businesses focus on core activities and competencies while contracting third party operations to undertake peripheral activities.
- *Empowerment* Decision-making power is delegated to subordinates often operating in teamworking situations with day-to-day tactical matters determined without reference to higher authority.
- *Demerger* Reversing earlier trends towards conglomerate strength, Thorn-EMI, ICI-Zeneca, TransCo-British Gas and Hanson's four-way demerger is a vote for manageable focus.

An example of downsizing and restructuring may be seen below, where a large grocery retailer introduced the second structure as a means of delayering, improving communication and teamworking, and realizing staff savings. On the other hand, it increased the workload, hours and possible stress for a number of the managers involved. A loss of status and pay also made it unpopular with the managers affected by the reduction from six to four management levels.

The role of marketing in organization structures

There are three fundamental classifications of business focus:

- Production orientation
- Sales orientation
- Marketing orientation

Each has implications for the organizational structure adopted and the degree to which it is outward-looking. As business evolves from an inward-looking focus on production efficiency through greater sales awareness to comprehensive operational emphasis on anticipating and

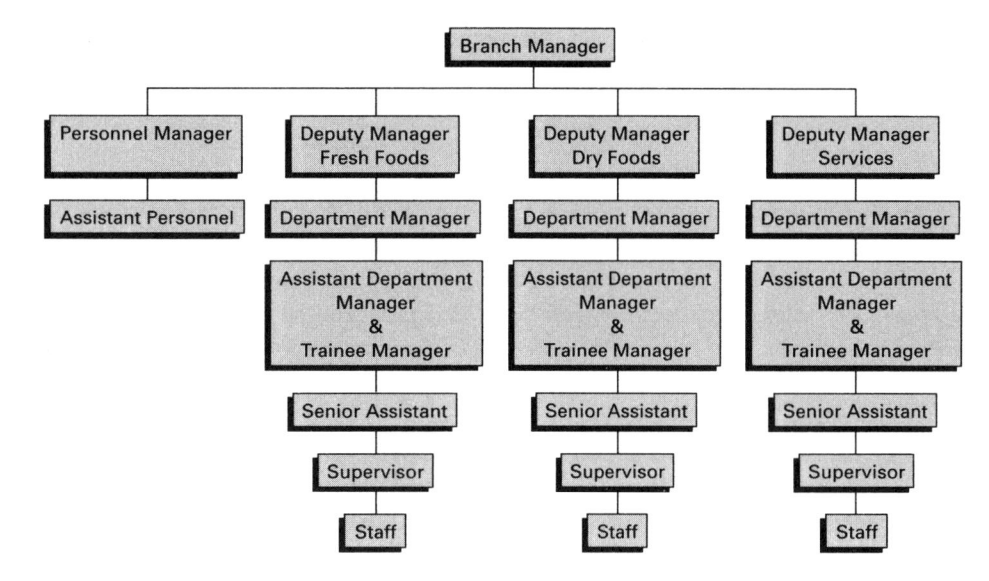

```
                        ┌─────────────────┐
                        │ Branch Manager  │
                        └────────┬────────┘
        ┌────────────────┬───────┴────────┬────────────────┐
┌───────────────┐ ┌───────────────┐ ┌───────────────┐ ┌───────────────┐
│Personnel Mgr  │ │Deputy Manager │ │Deputy Manager │ │Deputy Manager │
│               │ │ Fresh Foods   │ │  Dry Foods    │ │   Services    │
└───────┬───────┘ └───────┬───────┘ └───────┬───────┘ └───────┬───────┘
┌───────────────┐ ┌───────────────┐ ┌───────────────┐ ┌───────────────┐
│Asst Personnel │ │Dept Manager   │ │Dept Manager   │ │Dept Manager   │
└───────────────┘ └───────┬───────┘ └───────┬───────┘ └───────┬───────┘
                  ┌───────────────┐ ┌───────────────┐ ┌───────────────┐
                  │Asst Dept Mgr  │ │Asst Dept Mgr  │ │Asst Dept Mgr  │
                  │ & Trainee Mgr │ │ & Trainee Mgr │ │ & Trainee Mgr │
                  └───────┬───────┘ └───────┬───────┘ └───────┬───────┘
                  │Senior Asst    │ │Senior Asst    │ │Senior Asst    │
                  │Supervisor     │ │Supervisor     │ │Supervisor     │
                  │Staff          │ │Staff          │ │Staff          │
```

Structure 1 is the basic Branch Structure for most retail outlets.

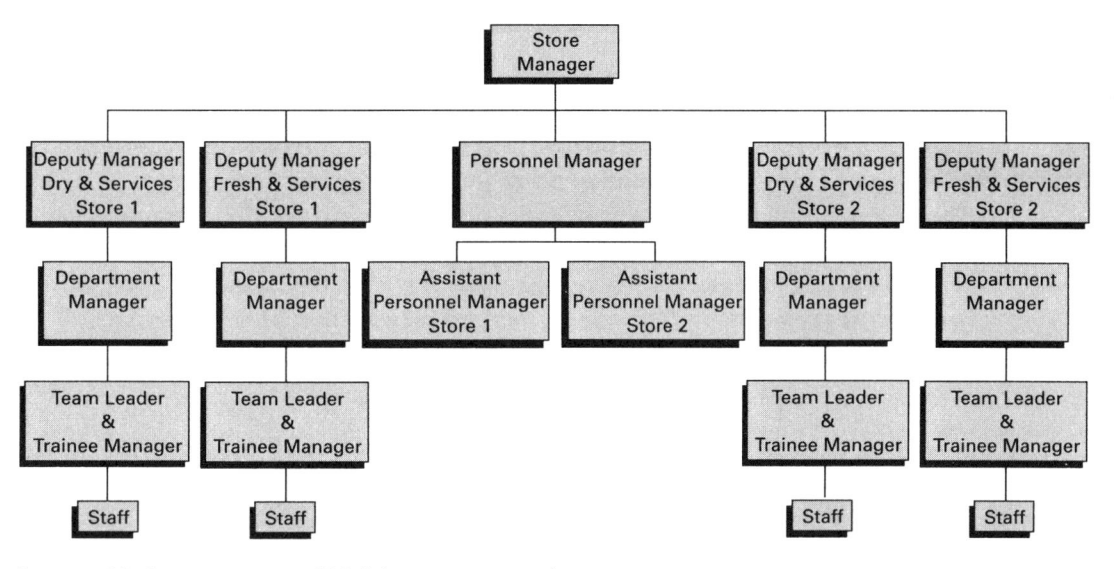

```
[Store Manager]
├── Deputy Manager Dry & Services Store 1 → Department Manager → Team Leader & Trainee Manager → Staff
├── Deputy Manager Fresh & Services Store 1 → Department Manager → Team Leader & Trainee Manager → Staff
├── Personnel Manager
│     ├── Assistant Personnel Manager Store 1
│     └── Assistant Personnel Manager Store 2
├── Deputy Manager Dry & Services Store 2 → Department Manager → Team Leader & Trainee Manager → Staff
└── Deputy Manager Fresh & Services Store 2 → Department Manager → Team Leader & Trainee Manager → Staff
```

Structure 2 is the new structure which links two stores together.

Figure 2.7 An example of downsizing and restructuring (*Source: USDAW Journal*)

satisfying changing consumer requirements, so the organizational structure must adapt to facilitate it.

> **QUESTION 2.8**
> What is the orientation of your own organization or college?
> Justify your answer.

Aim	*Form*	*Orientation*	*Focus*	*Marketing role*
Profit via minimum production cost/good design	Functional	Production	Operations/ finance	Negligible
Sales volume with profit constraint	Functional/ product divisions	Sales	Sales and Promotion	Sales support only

37

| Profit by satisfying customer needs | M-form/ matrix | Marketing | Coordinated organizational response to customer needs | Central |

Where *production orientation* prevails the emphasis is on design and operations management. Technical or finance specialists will tend to dominate the hierarchy in which the sales function will be minor with no representation on the board. Examples are found in niche markets where demand far exceeds supply (e.g. Morgan cars) or in the public services like education and health before recent efforts to break their monopoly. The latter tended to be bureaucratic, dominated by professionals with little incentive to inquire into or respond to the real needs of their captive consumers.

In the absence of a seller's market and where competition is increasing, businesses soon learn that producing efficiently is not enough. A natural reaction was to focus on salesmanship and promotion to overcome consumer resistance. The sales director would gain equal status with operations and finance to ensure volume and market share.

EXAM TIP

What orientation are you going to adopt in the examination?

- A technical orientation, where all your attention goes into getting the information down *you* feel is appropriate?
- A selling orientation with lots of gimmicks to try to convince the examiner you know what you are talking about but without that ring of confidence?
- Or a marketing orientation where you focus on what the examiner (i.e.) the customer really wants – a clear answer focused on what the question requires.

A *sales orientation*, however, gave no real thought to the needs and requirements of the final customer. The requirement was not just to change the name of sales to the marketing department but also to focus the efforts of the whole organization to this end. A *marketing orientation* is now recognized as a survival condition in a competitive and rapidly changing environment. As T. Levitt observed:

> Selling focuses on the needs of the seller, marketing on the needs of the buyer. Selling is preoccupied with the seller's need to convert his product into cash; marketing with the idea of satisfying the needs of the customer by means of the product and the whole cluster of things associated with creating, delivering and finally consuming it.

ACTIVITY 2.6

A marketing orientation places the customer at the centre of the whole organization's attention. With this in mind, make a list of desirable organizational characteristics that would achieve this.

Taking an organization of your choice, design an organizational form that would place it close to its customers.

(**See** Activity debrief 6 at the end of this unit.)

The main difficulty confronting a business wishing to achieve a marketing orientation is the change in organization and culture implied. Functional divisions within the business create potential barriers, preventing a cohesive response to customer needs. Unless there is drive and strong leadership from the top to establish the philosophy throughout the organization they will fail to pull together, reverting instead to narrow departmental interests. If the organization is unable to get its own internal act together it is unlikely to respond successfully to environmental change.

Summary

In this unit we have seen that:

- Business objectives are varied and reflect different motivations.
- Objectives pursued must reflect market constraints and stakeholder interests.
- There is an important distinction between maximizing and satisficing behaviour.
- Objectives may change as a result of stakeholder pressures.
- Social responsibility is increasingly expected as public perceptions of the role of business change.
- Big is best for mass markets but small appears to be increasingly beautiful, not least for employment prospects!
- A marketing-orientated organization structure is the key to effective achievement of objectives in an environment of rapid change.

Activity debrief

1   *Mission statement*   Unless the adoption of a mission statement changes organizational behaviour, it has little value. Yet its absence is like being a traveller without a destination with no way of determining progress. Organizational objectives must therefore be formulated which enables progress towards them to be measured.

   A mission statement should differentiate the organization from others and establish its individuality, if not its uniqueness. As such, it defines what the organization 'wishes to be' and provides a unifying concept which both enlarges its view of itself and brings it into focus.

   It should be relevant to all the direct stakeholders and motivate their commitment. Accordingly, it needs to excite and inspire, encouraging participation through a shared vision. Do your mission statements meet these criteria?

2   *The case against profit maximization*   Management may think twice about making as much profit as possible if:

- It involves taking high risks.
- It attracts new entrants to the market.
- It leads to an anti-monopoly investigation.
- It encourages wage demands which are unsustainable in the long term.
- It creates rising dividend expectations among shareholders.
- It is at the expense of sales and market share.
- It prejudices customers who perceive the profit as resulting from high prices and will turn to alternatives once available.

3   *Question 2.5*   A Self-sufficient monastry?
4   *Definition 2.2*   The answer sequence was: 1, 4, 2, 3.
5   *M-form divisional organization*

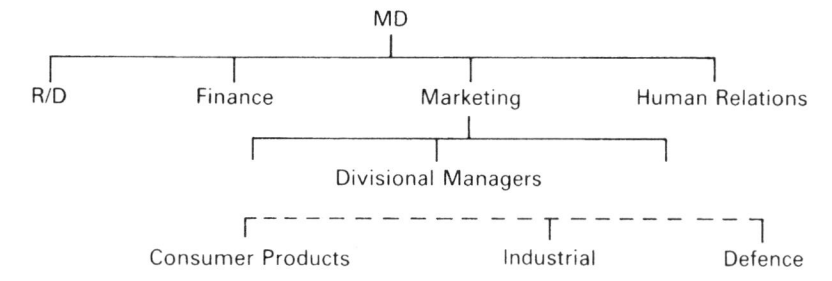

```
                        MD
        ┌──────┬────────┼────────┬──────────────┐
       R/D   Finance  Marketing   Human Relations
                        │
               ┌────────┼────────┐
                  Divisional Managers
        ┌────────────────┬───────────────┐
   Consumer Products   Industrial      Defence
```

Figure 2A

Strengths
- Operational autonomy within defined corporate strategy
- Fast response to environmental change
- Simple coordination across functions

Weaknesses
- Duplication of resources in divisions
- Competition between divisions
- Limited sharing
- Dual responsibility to operational (divisional) and strategic (HQ)
- Less in-depth expertise

- Focus on customer needs
- Broad general management training
- Conflict between divisional/corporate goals

6 *Marketing orientation and organizational characteristics* The need to be close to the customer, sensitive to change in the environment and coordinated to ensure quick response throughout the organization would require:

- Marketing representation at main board/MD level
- A flat decentralized structure
- Delegation of decision to those closest to the customer
- Open communications internally and externally
- Profit-centred general manager structure for coordination of all functions
- Integrated Management Information System (MIS)
- Customer service philosophy promoted by the organization

Examination hints and specimen questions

Since the marketing environment links the organization with external constraints, opportunities and threats, it is not surprising that organizational issues frequently arise in examinations. Two of the compulsory questions in the June 1996 paper concerned this unit, for example. The content of this unit covers 10 per cent of the total and much of the Organization section, but its significance is much wider. You may be expected to relate any aspect of the syllabus to your college or organization, to which some of the material covered above may be relevant.

Openness to the environment and the adoption of a marketing orientation reflects a business philosophy, a way of approaching the customer in particular and the environment in general.

1 (a) Prepare a short report outlining the main reasons why businesses of different sizes exist. (12 marks)
  (b) Are there any relationships between the size of the business and the market in which it operates? (8 marks)
  (CIM Marketing Environment paper, June 1995)

2 See Question 2 in the December 1996 paper.

Hints: Indicative content and approach

Question 1(a)
- This is *not* a question on the legal forms of enterprise.
- Adopt a report format, but focus on findings.
- Keep it short (12 marks = 18–20 minutes), providing an outline only.
- Main *reasons* include size/limit of market segment; nature of technology required; ease of company formation, entry and exit; degree of risk involved; importance of choice and differentiation.
- Provide appropriate examples of small, medium, large and global businesses.

Question 1(b)
- Alternative approaches are possible here.
- Relate to market structure (see Unit 3), e.g. perfect competition = small firms, oligopoly/monopoly = large firms.
- Relate to availability of economies of scale. These are substantial for large firms.
- Relate to markets: mass, niche, speciality, consumer and industrial.

Alternative Selling Environment question – illustration only

2 Using an industry you are familiar with:

  (a) Identify the primary and secondary stakeholders, justifying why you consider some more important than others. (10 marks)
  (b) Taking *two* of the groups identified in (a), outline the role of the sales person in creating consistent, profitable sales for the company whilst balancing the interests of these stakeholders. (10 marks)
  (CIM Selling Environment paper, December 1995)

UNIT 3

The competitive environment

OBJECTIVES

In this critically important core unit you will:

- Examine the nature of the competitive process.
- Relate the increase in size and decrease in number of firms to a spectrum of market imperfection.
- Consider the main market models and their relevance to sales executives and marketers.
- Undertake a structural analysis of an industry.

By the end of this unit you will be able to:

- Identify the strategies available to improve profitability.
- Predict competitive behaviour in different market structures.
- Assess the role and function of intermediaries and suppliers and the growing importance of relationship marketing.
- Appreciate the implications of industry structure for the organization.

STUDY GUIDE

This unit is the most analytical one in the book. It is concerned with the micro-environment of the organization and deals with the aspect which impacts continuously on most businesses – *the competition*. It is the aspect that the marketer is most concerned with on a day-to-day basis and therefore has most experience of. You must remember, however, that you will be examined primarily on your understanding of the competitive market environment. The application of marketing to alter or respond to changes in this environment is normally the secondary part of any question posed.

Much of the content in this unit is economic, and you will find it useful to refer to economic texts such as *Economic Theory and Marketing Practice*, by Hatton and Oldroyd (Butterworth-Heinemann Marketing Series) for a more detailed and in-depth coverage. The examiner will, however, be looking only for an appreciation of the competitive environment and its impact on the organization.

This unit accounts for 10 per cent of the syllabus, but it represents a very important segment of the external environment. Subsequent units, which consider other environments, have most of their effects on competitive relationships. You will find that you will spend more time working through this unit since you will have to read and reread some of the sections. The activities should take less time since you will be able to readily relate the material to your organization and work experience. Together they should take around 8 hours.

It is suggested that you:

- Open a new file under the heading Competitive Environment.
- Subdivide this into five sections: industry competitors, potential new entrants, suppliers, intermediaries/distributors and substitutes.

- Ask your marketing director if you can scan the executive summary and conclusions of a recent industry analysis consultancy report. Alternatively, use inter-library loans to obtain a copy of a report on an industry that interests you (e.g. Economist Intelligence Report on the car industry).
- Study the annual reports for references to competitors.

The nature of the competitive environment

It is important that the marketer acquires a knowledge of market structure and the competitive environment in order to:

- Understand the nature of the competitive process and how key variables can be manipulated to advantage.
- Recognize the market structure the organization operates within and the strategies available to it.
- Identify market conditions, changes in them and their implications.
- Ascertain the limits to freedom of action that particular market structures impose.
- Assess the sources and significance of monopoly power.

QUESTION 3.1

- What do you consider would be the conditions necessary to create the most intense degree of competition imaginable?

You may wish to think of this in terms of setting up a business in an area of your choice. Try to come up with the worst possible scenario you could face. Do this before you read any more of the unit.

- Can you think of any markets where this degree of competition is approached? If you are struggling to think of examples, why is this?
- Can you also think of the conditions necessary for an organization to have the highest degree of monopoly power possible. Again, are there any realistic examples?

Probably the most likely condition you suggested was a *large number of competitors*, especially if they were all supplying nearly identical or *homogeneous products*. Rational customers would be indifferent as to which firm's product they bought, especially if there were no hidden extras like *transport costs*. There would have to be no firm large enough to influence market price or frictions arising from *government interferences* (for example, subsidies or taxes). To make the nightmare complete we would include *perfect knowledge* and *freedom of entry* into the market whenever conditions caused profits to improve.

In this situation, typically dominated by firms which are small relative to the overall market, price will be set by the forces of industry supply and demand. Customers buy solely on the basis of price, making firm's *price takers* at the level set by market forces. As can be seen in Figure 3.1, individual firms face a horizontal demand curve.

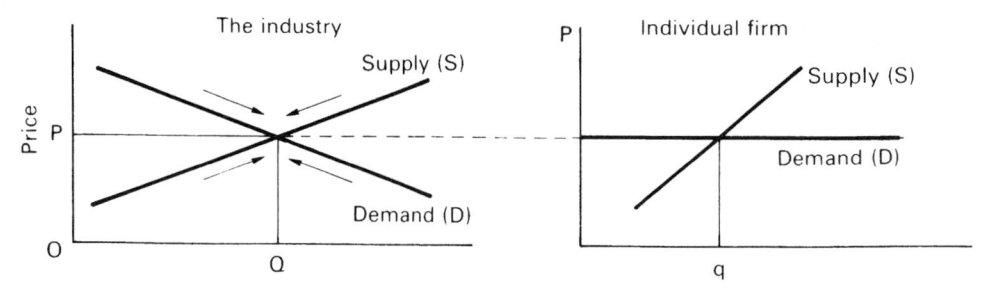

Figure 3.1 Equilibrium for the industry and the firm

Equilibrium price will be established at the intersection of demand (D) and supply (S). If the actual price was more than OP there would be *excess supply* in the market since firms would like to supply more at this price than customers demand. Firms and customers would continue to bid down prices until the excess was eliminated. Similarly, any price below OP would create *excess demand*, putting upward pressure on the price. Note that as the price rises towards OP it is discouraging demand, on the one hand (see the arrow) and encouraging businesses to supply more, on the other, until the two are brought into equilibrium.

> **EXTENDING ACTIVITY 3.1**
>
> Study Chapter 4 of *Economic Theory and Marketing Practice* and familiarize yourself with the basic idea of supply and demand theory. This is a very useful tool of analysis for the marketer to master. Make sure you are familiar with the following:
>
> - The factors/conditions which determine quantity demanded and supplied to a market
> - The distinction between a shift and a movement along a demand curve
> - The rationing function of price
> - The effect of changing conditions on price and quantity
> - The marketing implications.

If the firm tries to set a price above OP it will sell nothing at all. It must sell at the going price, but, being small, it is able to supply all it can effectively produce at this price (i.e. the market price) without affecting its level.

> **QUESTION 3.2**
>
> - What can you predict about the likely level of profit for firms in such a situation?
> - What would happen if there was an improvement in the market environment in this industry? Suppose there was a rise in demand (represented by a rightward shift of the curve) due, say, to a rise in disposable incomes. How would profits be affected (a) initially, (b) as time went by?
>
> (**See** Activity debrief at the end of this unit.)

Examples of competitive markets are very difficult to find because reality is very different to this extreme of *perfect competition*. There is no need for physical contact between buyers and sellers *but* information about what is going on in the market must be easily and continuously available. Stock markets, foreign exchange and world commodity markets make the best examples, although with government interventions these are rarely perfect. One example more familiar to marketers is the product which has become a 'commodity' as it enters late maturity in the product life cycle. A saturated market and knowledgeable repeat buyers will make successful differentiation extremely difficult and costly, producing a price taker situation.

> **ACTIVITY 3.1**
>
> You have been appointed as consultant to a small manufacturing concern currently operating in a very competitive market environment. Based on your knowledge of competition and observations of more profitable firms and industries, suggest five basic strategies which could improve profitability.

The other extreme to intense competition is known as *pure monopoly*. The most powerful *monopoly* would be:

- A sole supplier of the good or service
- Supplying goods for which there were no available substitutes
- Protected by barriers to new entry
- The supplier of a necessity.

Any potential examples of such pure market power would tend to be owned or regulated by government (e.g. tobacco or water services). A sole supplier of illegal drugs in a particular market would fit the bill with addicts prepared to beg, borrow or steal to finance their habit and the monopolists' profits. The demand curve in this case would be vertical, reflecting the fact that no matter how high the price, demand would be unchanged. Taking the example of a premier football club season ticket, draw such a demand curve for yourself and think about what happens to total revenue as price is increased.

Note also that the marketer is seeking to create the equivalent of an habitual good in the mind of the customer through extensive branding. Promotional activity seeks to steepen the demand curve, allowing premium prices to be charged with little loss of sales.

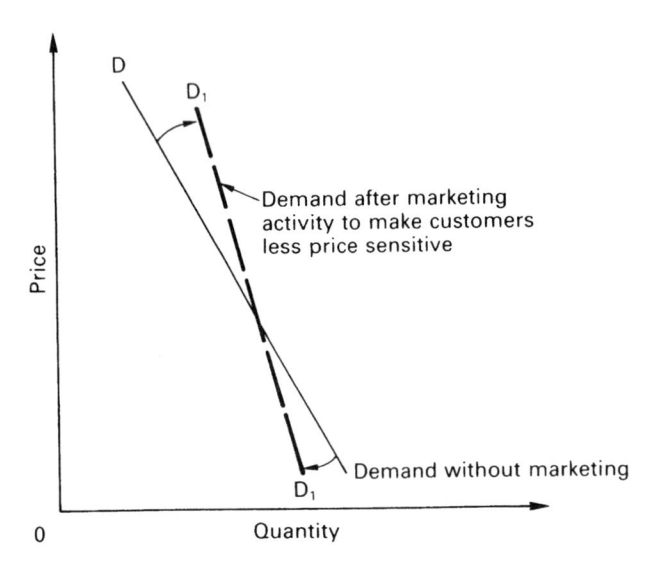

Figure 3.2 The impact of marketing activity on demand

Strategies available to the competitive firm

Faced with the prospect of only normal profits, any business in a competitive market will rationally seek out means of improving them. Much of the drive, dynamism and product diversity associated with a competitive economy derives from this motivation. We can analyse alternative market structures in the context of this drive for superior profitability. The strategies to consider are:

1. Cost minimization
2. Form a cartel or association
3. Differentiate your product
4. Merge with or take over competitors for size and market power
5. Establish barriers to entry
6. Innovate continuously.

If any of these strategies 2–6 are successful, the business will achieve an element of monopoly power. In practice, this will mean that it now faces a down-sloping demand curve, allowing prices to be raised without losing all its customers.

This may be seen in Figure 3.3. The steeper the demand curve, the greater the net improvement in revenue when premium prices (P_2) are charged. Since fewer units are sold (Q_2), causing total costs to fall, overall profitability will improve substantially.

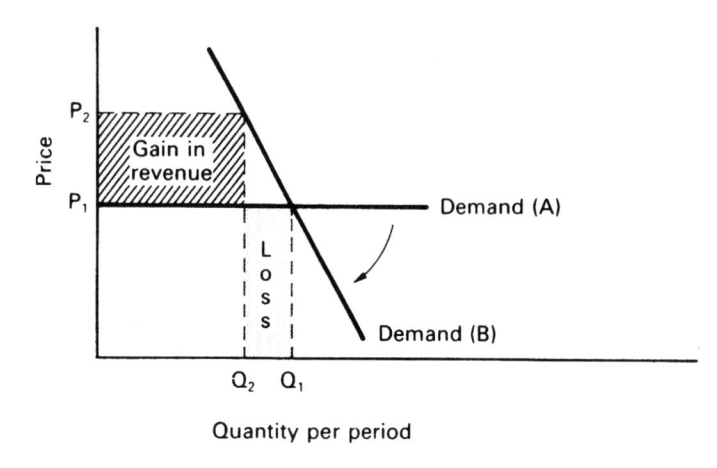

Figure 3.3 Revenue implications of a down-sloping demand curve

Cost cutting

Cutting costs is a reflex action for most managers, but the question should be posed as to why have they not realized these economies already. In practice, the pressure of intense competition would have ensured that all steps had already been taken to guarantee least-cost operation given existing knowledge. This is more an option for businesses possessing monopoly power and organizational slack e.g. newly privatized rail companies.

Cartels

A cartel, if successful, would become the sole supplier to the market. Output could be restricted and market price and overall profitability would rise. The existence of restrictive practices legislation (see Unit 5) has ruled most forms of collective agreement illegal but cartels still appear to operate clandestinely in some industries (e.g. concrete/PVC) and internationally (e.g. OPEC (oil), IATA (airlines) and De Beers (diamonds)).

All cartels, however, are subject to instability in the longer term:

- Internal dissension over the allocation of quotas necessary to restrict supply and justify the higher cartel prices
- Incentive for any cartel member to exceed quota for higher profits. This raises supply, making it harder to sustain the price
- Internal policing is essential plus control over market entry
- New producers operate outside the cartel at slightly lower prices, forcing increasing excess capacity on cartel members.

> **ACTIVITY 3.2**
>
> Consider the gondoliers of Venice. What enables them to charge such high prices for a glorified boat-ride? How do you think they manage to maintain these prices over time? Is clever marketing the explanation?

Product differentiation

The marketer's natural response to competition forcing down profit levels is to mobilize the marketing mix to differentiate the product either by specification or in the minds of the consumer. The dimensions of possible differentiation are, of course, immense:

- *Product* Permutations of the *core, tangible* (e.g. design, quality, packaging) and *augmented* product (e.g. brand name, delivery, after-sales service).
- *Price* Credit and payment terms may vary, as could allowances and trade-in values.
- *Promotion* To support the differentiation (e.g. sales force, advertising).
- *Place* Offers opportunities through location adopted, coverage and, most importantly, service provided.

EXAM TIP

> Have you considered the advantages of 'differentiation' for your own examination script? An examiner is faced with marking scripts, literally into hundreds, all answering the same questions. How are you going to make yours stand out?
>
> What you require is a premium product which catches the examiner's eye at the outset. See the final section of this unit for some hints in achieving this effect.

Businesses will therefore segment the market in the search for a profitable niche which they will then service with a product combining the optimum blend of characteristics that are clearly differentiated from those of close competitors. Those that satisfy customer needs and wants most effectively will earn *excess profits*. The seller, in effect, obtains a monopoly of the branded product and, due to the successful differentiation, is able to charge a higher price and still retain customers who 'prefer' the product. But what will happen next, given this situation?

QUESTION 3.3

> Can you think of local examples where small firms innovated product or service offerings which were quickly imitated by rivals or new entrants? (**See** Activity debrief at the end of this unit.)

The profit associated with successful differentiation will attract imitation from both existing firms and new entrants in the longer term. Normal profits will be the most that can be earned, but consumers benefit as the imitation enables rapid diffusion of superior product and service ideas. New entry will reduce demand for existing firms and *excess capacity* will result. Any attempt to fill this capacity by cutting prices or additional promotion will add more to cost than to revenue, producing losses.

This market structure is known as *imperfect competition* and provides an effective means of competing for increased market share, resting on customer preferences rather than random selection among identical suppliers. It is underlain by the diversity of consumer tastes, incomes, attitudes and characteristics. Sellers must discover the qualitative mix which satisfies the needs of the target market and make the most of the product's unique individuality or selling points before the competition arrives.

Merger and economies of scale

We saw in Unit 2 that average costs will fall whenever the potential to exploit economies of scale exist. If unit costs can be reduced relative to market prices then excess profits will result. Firms will seek to reduce unit cost to the minimum level possible by increasing their size until all economies are exhausted. One method of doing this is to take over competitors. Operations can then be rationalized and resources fully utilized. A further advantage is that there is one less competitor to contend with e.g. British Airways and American Airlines.

ACTIVITY 3.3

> Lloyds Bank merged with the TSB (Trustee Savings Bank) in December 1995. What economies of scale might be exploited here? Do you think any other motives were involved?

Barriers to entry

All the strategies considered above suffer from the weakness that any profit improvement obtained is only short term. The dynamics of competition ensure that forces are set in motion to eventually return profits to normal. One strategy to delay or prevent this is to build barriers against the new entry which undermines the extra profitability. This is the foundation of *effective monopoly power*, defined as: the ability to earn excess profit over time.

A number of barriers can be identified:

- *Natural* The limit of market size. A village shop may have an effective monopoly because there is only enough trade to support one outlet. Entry of a competitor would cause losses to be made by both.
- *Legal* A state monopoly is protected by statute (e.g. Royal mint). Licences, trademarks, patents and copyrights also provide protection.
- *Absolute cost advantages* The entrenched firm secures control over critical inputs such as prime sites, expertise and long-term contracts with suppliers. It also establishes its reputation with the clientele and ties up key distribution channels. Its accumulated knowledge of the market and experience with the technology will give it an important advantage over new entrants using the same operational processes.
- *Economies of scale* Increase the initial cost and therefore the risk of market entry. The minimum economic scale (MES) may be in terms of capital equipment (e.g. a microprocessor plant costs £1 billion) or research and development expenditure (e.g. drugs) or promotional expenditure (e.g. detergents).

> **EXAM TIP**
>
> Are you remembering to think of at least one or two more examples for each one cited in the text? The examiner is going to be more impressed with your orginal examples, rather than re-reading his/her own!

Other considerations include:

- *Deliberate action to restrict or discourage entry* The monopolist may use its excess profit base to undercut or buy out any new entrants before they become established. Competitively priced 'fighting' brands may be retained for this purpose. Alternatively, the firm may expand capacity to pre-empt entry or use product proliferation to deny profitable market positions for competitor brands. It may also illegally seek to enforce exclusive dealing on its suppliers and distributors and so deny them to entrants. One final tactic to consider is *limit pricing*, where the monopolist restricts price levels to just below the level which would prove profitable for new entry.
- *Expected entry impact deters competitors* Where a new entrant has to enter at a large MES the extra supply onto the market will reduce price and profitability for all concerned. The new entrant will also tend to bid up the price of resource inputs, raising costs and so reducing the incentive to enter.

The monopolist protected by entry barriers will face a down-sloping industry demand curve. Output will normally be lower and costs higher than under competition. One exception is the *natural monopoly*, where unified provision exploits large-scale economies and competition would bring wasteful duplication and exhorbitantly higher costs (e.g. rail track networks or power lines).

> **QUESTION 3.4**
>
> How many more natural monopolies can you think of?

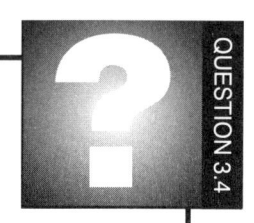

A monopoly protected in this way may be able to exploit its market power more fully if it uses *discriminatory pricing*. This arises where the product or service is sold at two or more prices that do not reflect proportional differences in costs of supply.

It may take a number of forms:

- *By customer* e.g. trade and retail prices
- *By product* e.g. different brands of dog food
- *By place* e.g. opera house stalls and balcony
- *By time* e.g. peak and off-peak utility rates

The conditions for successful discrimination may be summarized as:

- The market must be segmentable
- The segments must exhibit different intensities of demand
- Those paying a lower price cannot resell to those forced to pay higher prices
- There is little chance of competitors underselling you in higher-priced segments
- The cost of segmenting and policing is less than the additional revenue accruing
- The practice should not breed customer resentment.

Businesses, especially smaller ones, may also suffer from this practice. It can only occur however where competition is imperfect, although it does not always follow it will arise in such circumstances.

> **QUESTION 3.5**
>
> Why is price discrimination more likely to be found in the service sector? List some representative examples.
>
> Ignoring higher transport costs, why does distance and national frontiers enable businesses to practise price discrimination?
>
> In the light of the decision by British Telecom to cut its 9 a.m.–1 p.m. peak rate in March 1994, suggest examples of changes in the competitive environment leading to the erosion of discriminatory pricing practices.

Innovation

Continuous innovation is the only strategy that, if successfully implemented, would ensure the firm excess profits over time. New products that more effectively satisfy customer needs and wants will increase profits as will cost-saving processes and technologies. However, only by ploughing back profit into maintaining technological or design leadership can long-term profits be ensured. Competitors will seek to enter the market and imitate the innovations, but they will always be aiming for a *moving target*.

Such innovation will also be of benefit to consumers since by making more effective use of existing resources and focusing on improved value for money products the production possibility curve will shift outward, as seen in Figure 3.4.

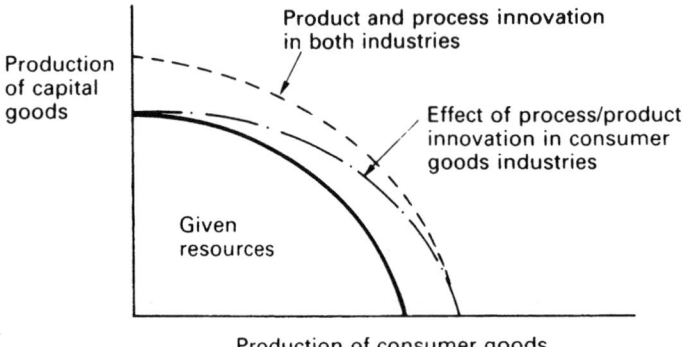

Figure 3.4 Innovation and the production possibility curve

> **EXAM TIP**
>
> An examination question in this area will often state 'in the context of an industry example, explain . . . .'. Make sure you know an industry example inside out, and preferably your own.

The market structure which generates most innovation might be thought to be perfect competition. However, as we have seen in Unit 1, small firms are undercapitalized, making it difficult to exploit inventions. Monopolies, on the other hand, have control of the market, no competitors to imitate the development, but no real incentive to write off existing investments to make way for the innovation. The best 'climate for innovation' would be offered by a combination of large, well-resourced firms and a considerable degree of competition. This would drive the introduction of the innovation and provide the finance to diffuse its benefits rapidly into the market. Such a market structure exists and is known as *oligopoly*.

> **QUESTION 3.6**
>
> Is the company you work for in an oligopoly market structure? Is the college you attend in an oligopoly? Is the bank you use an oligopoly?

If the number of firms operating in a market falls to a small enough number for their decisions to depend on their assessment as to the reactions of competitors then oligopoly prevails. The term means *competition among the few*, and is the typical market structure in economies such as Britain. It arises where a small number of large firms control a high proportion of total sales to the market.

Since each firm accounts for a large slice of the market any substantial change in the market share of one firm, whether achieved by lower prices, product innovation or successful advertising, will adversely affect the shares of competitors. The activities of 'popular' national newspapers often provide an interesting case study of such a market. Firms will watch each other very closely, producing a tension in the market between the *desire to compete* and gain sales at the expense of competitors, on the one hand, and the *desire to collude* in order to limit mutually damaging competitive activity, on the other.

> **ACTIVITY 3.4**
>
> *Seller concentration* is defined as the degree to which production or sales for a particular market is concentrated into the hands of a few large firms. With this definition in mind calculate a *five-firm concentration ratio* for your own industry (i.e. add up the market shares of the five largest firms). Alternatively, look up a Mintel report on an industry of your choice.

The key features of this market may be summarized as:

- High concentration with the balance often held by a tail of small firms
- The demand curve faced is uncertain because it is dependent on how rivals react
- The market outcome is not predictable when oligopolists have multiple competitive options available to them.

For example, if one of the oligopolists cuts its prices, another may follow suit, or it may cut its prices by more or less than the first firm. Alternatively, it may choose to do nothing, or respond with a large promotional campaign, or launch a new brand.

EXTENDING ACTIVITY 3.2

Refer to Chapter 8 in *Economic Theory and Marketing Practice* on how firms make their pricing decisions. This provides analysis of all the market structures we have been discussing. Look particularly at Figure 3.5 below (Figure 8.12 in the above book). Consider the following tactics and suggest how they would affect the demand curve shown:

- Price leadership
- New product development
- Collusion
- Promotional expenditure

(**See** Activity debrief at the end of this unit.)

Watch the press for large firms announcing price increases (e.g. cars, bank interest rates, petrol) and then look for their competitors' reactions. Do they follow suit, or not, and if so how quickly?

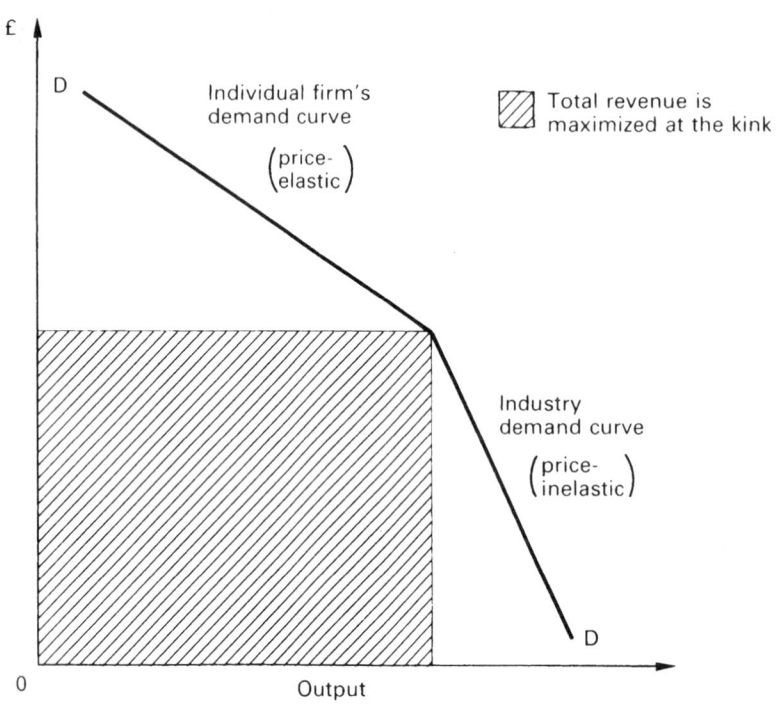

Figure 3.5 The kinked demand curve of the oligopolist

However, a number of generalizations are possible:

1. Oligopolists tend to avoid the use of price as a competitive weapon. They are termed 'sticky' because:
   - If price is cut relative to competitors it is assumed that they will follow suit to avoid loss of market share. Sales volume therefore rises less than proportionately and total revenue falls.
   - If price is raised, they will not follow suit, leading to a large loss of market share and sales revenue.
2. Non-price competition, promoting carefully differentiated branded products, is preferred.
3. There is a tendency to occasional price war when a restructuring of market shares is in progress.
4. Collusion is an attractive option but normally illegal (e.g. sixteen European steel producers were fined heavily in 1994 (£79 million) for price fixing in steel beams. British Steel alone was fined £24 million. Note also the collapse of the Net Book Agreement and pressure being applied by Asda supermarkets on over-the-counter medicines.

5   Price leadership often occurs to reflect underlying cost changes (e.g. retail petrol, tobacco, car and beer prices).

Summary

We have seen that competitive activity involves more than the price variable. Choice between alternatives is the key as firms compete on service, innovation and non-price variables. Large firms tend to predominate in monopoly and oligopoly structures due to the importance of barriers to entry in which economies of scale figure importantly. Smaller firms are the product of more competitive structures although profitable niches can be found in most markets.

The models considered so far, while providing some predictions of competitive response, only consider other firms within the market. More complete analysis requires account to be taken of certain other groups in the micro-environment.

> **EXAM TIP**
>
> As you will appreciate, this is not an easy unit and you must read and re-read sections to fully absorb their meaning. It is the same with examinations, where the key to success is in reading the whole paper, and each question very carefully before attempting an answer.

Structural analysis and market power

Businesses earn profit by being more successful than competitors in creating and delivering value to the customer over time. Real success demands that the business:

- creates value for money
- achieves a competitive edge in delivering that value
- operates efficiently.

The profit potential of the industry will be determined by the balance of supply and demand for the product in the short run and industry structure in the long run.

Michael Porter, in his books *Competitive Strategy* (1980) and *Competitive Advantage* (1985), provided a five-forces model of industry structure. This is summarized in Figure 3.6.

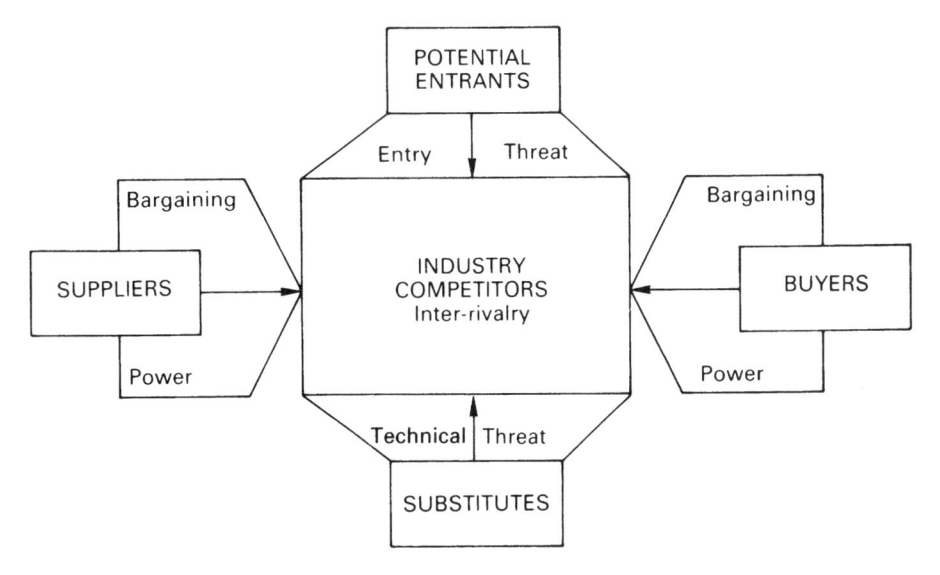

Figure 3.6 The five forces model. (Adapted from M. E. Porter, *Competitive Strategy*, The Free Press, 1980: © The Free Press/Macmillan)

All marketers must seek to understand the nature of their competitive environment if they are to exploit and profit by it. They must assess what is driving the competition in the industry and recognize that the collective strength of these five forces will set the present and future degree of market rivalry. This will determine the profit potential of the industry although each firm within it will seek to position itself so as to exploit maximum competitive advantage.

> **QUESTION 3.7**
>
> Use five-force analysis to match perfect competition and pure monopoly to two of the following combinations:
>
> 1. Intense inter-rivalry, high threat of entry, high buyer and supplier bargaining power, strong threat from substitutes.
> 2. Limited inter-rivalry, high threat of entry, low buyer and supplier bargaining power, weak threat of substitutes.
> 3. No inter-rivalry, no threat from substitutes or entry, no buyer or supplier bargaining power.
> 4. Intense inter-rivalry, weak threat from substitutes and entry, low buyer bargaining power, high supplier bargaining power.
>
> (**See** Activity debrief at the end of this unit.)

Unlike market structure models, this approach provides marketers with a framework for analysing the complexity of their own industry situation. The approach is less rigorous but perhaps more useful in understanding the effect of structural and environmental change over time.

The intensity of inter-rivalry

Rivalry, as we have seen, can range from non-existent (monopoly) through gentlemanly (oligopoly) understandings to cut-throat (price war) competition. Porter identifies the variables which determine the degree of this rivalry:

- The rate of industry growth – the less there is, the greater the rivalry
- Use of specialized facilities and high fixed costs – strong resistance to loss of sales
- The extent volatility of supply and demand produces intermittent over-capacity (e.g. a new hotel opening in a locality)
- The extent of product differentiation, brand loyalty and switching costs for customers transferring to competing products
- The number of firms and their relative size
- The diversity of corporate cultures (e.g. presence of foreign firms)
- What is at stake (e.g. specialist producers dependent on one product or market)?
- The cost of leaving the industry (e.g. contractual commitments).

> **ACTIVITY 3.5**
>
> Take each of the above variables and think how they are related to the intensity of rivalry. Using your own industry or one with which you are familiar, rate each factor in its contribution to rivalry (i.e. low to high) and come to an overall conclusion.

The threat of substitutes

An industry is a group of firms producing goods or services which are close substitutes for each other. In practice, the nature of substitutability is complex and a galaxy of widely differing offerings compete for limited discretionary purchasing power which can only be spent once at any point in time. Package holidays compete with conservatories and new computer systems with upgrading the transport fleet.

The threat may materialize in many forms; for example, different materials, an alternative technology or a new distribution channel. Vinyl records, for example, have been partly replaced by cassettes, which in turn have been substituted by compact discs which are now threatened by digital mini discs. Factors affecting this threat are:

- The relative *price–performance* ratio of the substitute (e.g. glass compared to metal or plastic containers)
- *Switching costs* for customers to the substitute (e.g. switching from coal- to gas-fired equipment or from branch to home banking)
- Buyer willingness to search out substitutes.

The rule of thumb to apply here is the higher the price and excess profitability, the greater the incentive to search for and develop substitutes.

The threat of new entry

We have already discussed the nature of entry barriers and the consequences of entry at minimum economic size. The bidding up of input prices, additional capacity and the likelihood of strong competitive reaction from incumbent firms means that such action is seldom undertaken lightly. The threat will range from the minimal, where barriers to entry are substantial, to very high (e.g. nuclear fuel reprocessing), where barriers are virtually non-existent and entry occurs whenever more than normal profits are earned by existing firms (e.g. fast food outlets).

> **ACTIVITY 3.6**
>
> Refer back to the section on barriers to entry and under each heading (e.g. economies, access to inputs and channels, switching costs, learning effects, cost advantages, etc.) rate your industry on threat of entry.
>
> When was the last time a new competitor entered your industry? How did existing firms react? Was it successful and if so, why? What was the origin of the entrant?
>
> New entry into oligopoly markets is not as frequent as you might think due to the high barriers. The main threat comes from *cross-entry* by a well-financed business in an adjacent industry or one using similar processes and distribution channels. Takeover by a foreign company of an existing firm, to provide a base for future growth in market share, is another possibility.

The bargaining power of suppliers

Where the relative power of suppliers is considerable and their behaviour aggressive, the rate of profit in an industry will be squeezed. However, an ability to establish some corresponding control over supplies will strengthen the hand of businesses in the industry. The main factors determining relative power are as follows:

- The degree of supplier concentration relative to the industry
- The degree of substitutability between the products of rival suppliers determines whether the buyer can switch to alternatives
- The switching costs involved in doing this
- The dependence of suppliers on maintaining large volumes of sales
- The importance of being unimportant – the lower the cost of the supplies as a proportion of total cost, the higher the bargaining power
- The threat of forward integration by suppliers (i.e. they may establish their own production facilities in the industry).

> **EXAM TIP**
>
> The best way of ensuring that you really understand what an examination question is trying to get at is to *underline the key words*, break it up into the relevant parts, identify the context and establish the precise format required.

The bargaining power of buyers

Buyer power will tend to reduce profitability although the ability of individual firms to develop specific arrangements with distributors and/or customers may prevent this. Buyer power depends on two main factors:

1 *Price responsiveness* The responsiveness of the buyer's purchases to a change in the relative price is, in effect, price elasticity of demand. This is determined by such things as:
   - The importance of the product as a proportion of the total purchases of the buyer
   - The emphasis given by the buyer to product differentiation and branding
   - The profitability of the buyer, which may dull price sensitivity if substantial. Alternatively, buyers may be under pressure to cherry-pick for best value for money, while others give precedence to availability, delivery and quality.
2 *Buyer leverage* a number of factors also affect this:
   - *Buyer concentration and size.* The five largest grocery multiples provide an excellent example of this with nearly 50 per cent of total sales.
   - *Volume and the importance of purchases* to the seller
   - *Practicality and costs of switching to alternative suppliers* for the buyer
   - *Knowledge of the market and information available to buyers*
   - *Existence of substitutes*
   - *Threat of backward vertical integration*

> **EXTENDING ACTIVITY 3.3**
>
> A useful group activity to reinforce your grasp of Porter's five-forces model is to consolidate the activities above into a full industry analysis. Select your own or a representative industry and go through all the factors listed above under the five headings and evaluate them in turn. You will find it useful to interview key people within your organization (e.g. purchasing manager, sales and marketing executives). Other sources could include trade associations, the trade press, market intelligence reports, the business press and company sources.
>
> It is very important that you apply this model and not just content yourself with 'learning' the factors. It is a much more challenging and useful exercise to 'really understand' what drives the profitability within an industry.

The role and function of intermediaries and suppliers

The final section of this unit is concerned with relationships in the supply chain and the increasing importance of *relationship or partnership marketing*. Any business, unless it is vertically integrated throughout its entire operations (e.g. tobacco from plantations to sales kiosks), is part of a supply chain (Figure 3.7).

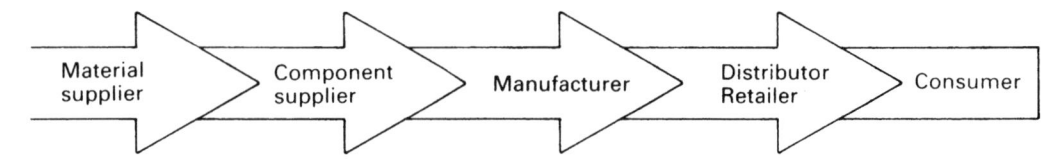

Material supplier → Component supplier → Manufacturer → Distributor Retailer → Consumer

Figure 3.7 A business supply chain

There is clear interdependence in this chain since none can prosper without the input or output of the other. Each benefits from the advantages of specialization in focusing on their own core business in order to gain from trade and exchange with the others in the chain. They all form part of the others' micro-environments and each can be viewed as a stakeholder.

Porter's analysis, however, suggested that profitability partly depended on the relative bargaining power of the parties. This might lead to the natural conclusion that it is in the best interests of buyers and suppliers to use their bargaining power to the full to secure the best possible price.

The emphasis here is on the *transaction* rather than on the *relationship* with the supplier or customer concerned. Attention is focused on the single contract and the short run rather than the prospects for repeat business in the long run. There is, therefore, very limited contact or commitment on behalf of the supplier or the intermediary.

The relationship is *competitive* and suppliers and distributors would change frequently in what is known as a zero-sum game, i.e. if one side wins the other, by definition, loses. The firm will play one supplier off against another to achieve lower prices, but this would frequently be at the expense of assured quality, delivery and service.

In recent years, however, many companies have moved towards much more *cooperative* relationships, forging ever stronger links between otherwise independently owned businesses in the supply chain. The aim is to achieve a win–win outcome based on partnership, as in the case of Marks & Spencer and its dedicated suppliers.

The impetus came partly from academic writers such as Peter's and Waterman, who suggested in their book, *In Search of Excellence*, that the best-managed companies got close to their customers, and partly from the demonstration effect of Japanese companies in their single-minded drive for *total quality*.

> **EXAM TIP**
>
> A quality answer earns an 'excellent' mark. Jot down what you consider to be the ingredients of a quality answer and compare them with the points made in the final unit.

Japanese companies such as Toyota and Sony are at the summit of a complex hierarchy of primary suppliers who in turn contract to second-tier suppliers and so on down the pyramid. Relationships are long term, secure and mutually beneficial often being cemented by cross-shareholdings. Any changes to specifications are by negotiation rather than unilateral action or a move to a rival substitute.

Pursuit of concepts like zero defects and just-in-time (JIT) stock control has made closer relationships essential. This may take the form of electronic data interchange (EDI) between members of the chain, where each can interrogate the other's internal information systems. The supplier may maintain staff permanently on the customer's site to ensure co-ordination, service and the required performance standards. In the extreme, a plant may be purposely located adjacent to the customer to guarantee alignment of quality, service and JIT delivery. The satellite plants that have formed around the Nissan and Toyota assembly operations in Britain are good examples of this tendency.

Businesses have then been able to sharply reduce the number of suppliers with whom they deal. This process has perhaps gone furthest in motor components, where single-sourcing has become the norm in some areas.

The growing importance of relationship marketing

Relationship marketing can be considered in the context of the micro-environment and stakeholders. It represents the impact that marketing has on relationships not only with customers and suppliers but also on actual and potential employees, government agencies, financial and other groups. It also seeks to integrate customer-orientated marketing with total quality across all the functional areas of the business and customer service.

IKEA, one of the world's most successful multinational retailers, operates as a global organization using subcontracted manufacturers from all over the world. Close relationships allow the company to keep costs between manufacturers and customers as low as possible and fulfil their vision of creating a better everyday life for the majority of people.

> **EXTENDING ACTIVITY 3.4**
>
> Relationship marketing could be the key development of the decade according to Christopher, Payne and Ballantyne in a book of the same name published by Butterworth-Heinemann. It covers the concept in much greater depth than can be considered here and includes

> a number of highly relevant case studies. Use these as the background for considering whether your organisation is 'transactions based' and the steps required to secure competitive advantage from building relationships based on quality and service.

Instead of concentrating on trying to recruit new customers this approach stresses 'keeping' the customers and suppliers you already have by building strong relationships with them, making them, in effect, trading partners. By successfully conforming to customer perceptions of required product quality and service they will effectively become part of the sales force by generating new customer business through referrals. The Insurance Service, for example, a company providing direct car insurance, offers discount bonuses to formally recognize those customers who refer friends and acquaintances.

Christopher, Payne and Ballantyne see the following factors as central to relationship marketing:

- A focus on customer retention
- An orientation towards product benefits rather than product features
- A long-term view
- Maximum emphasis on customer service
- High customer commitment and contact
- Total quality philosophy throughout the organization

They see the marketer's role as one of achieving the *best match* between the controllable internal marketing mix and the largely uncontrollable external environment. As can be seen in Figure 3.8, success will be a function of the degree of match obtained.

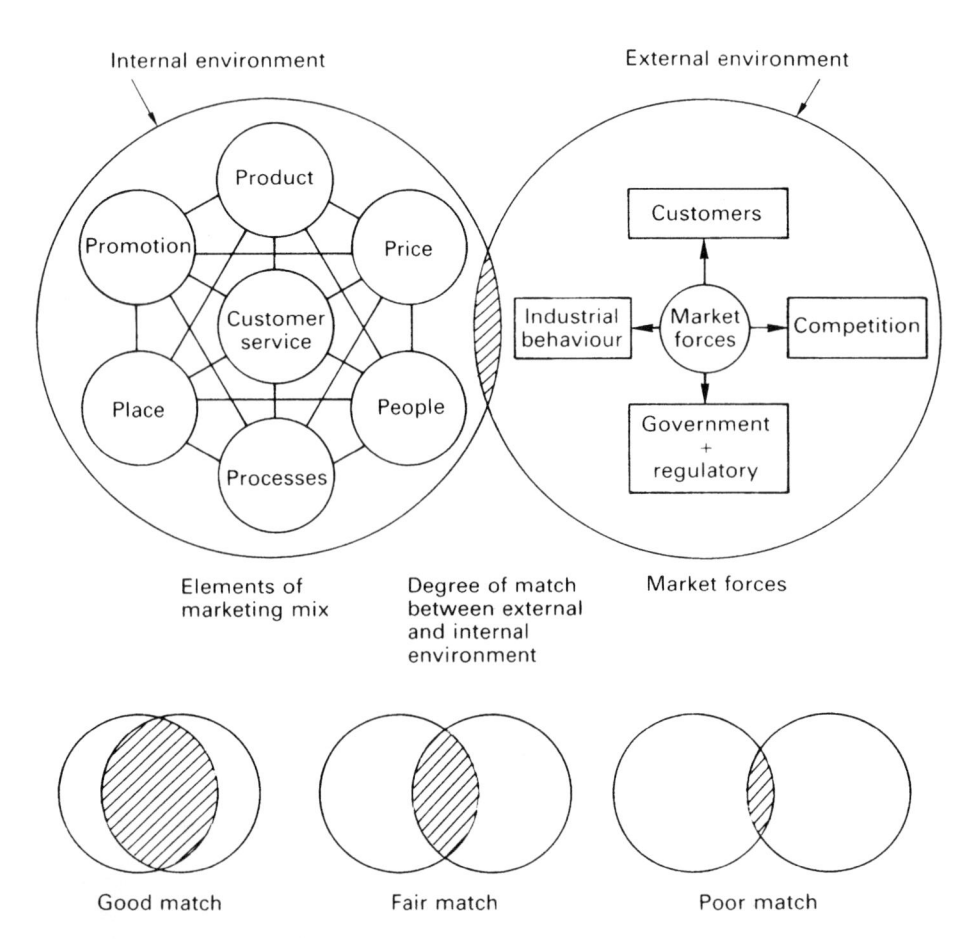

Figure 3.8 The marketing programme as a matching process. (From Christopher, Payne and Ballantyne, *Relationship Marketing*, Butterworth-Heinemann)

> **ACTIVITY 3.7**
>
> Based on what you have read about relationship marketing, draw up a contract of mutual responsibilities between a company of your choice and a representative supplier and distributor.
>
> Think about new product development and product specification, quality-improvement initiatives, information systems, training and coordination, exchange of ideas, flexibility, cost reduction and mutual obligations (e.g. scheduled orders and scheduled deliveries).
>
> Note that the philosophy is one of continuous cooperation, partnership and coalition between otherwise separate businesses. Mutual trust is the basis for mutual profitability in designing, developing, producing and delivering the product or service.

The clear message from this analysis is the importance of monitoring change in this turbulent environment, adjusting the mix to exploit opportunities and closing any gaps between customer expectations and actual provision. This is particularly important in industrial and service markets, where building interactive relationships between all the stakeholders should be seen as critical. Also, for businesses with products in maturity or late maturity stages of the product life cycle customer service may be the only means of achieving an edge over rivals. The scope for manipulation of the elements of the marketing mix are very limited in this situation.

Under the pressure of two intense recessions and the demonstration effects of foreign multinationals, expectations have been changing. Businesses cannot afford to be anything but professional and demanding of their suppliers. Equally, they must seek a competitive advantage with customers/distributors by building a close relationship with those they judge will be future industry winners.

Summary
In this unit we have dealt with the following important aspects:

- The nature and implications of competition at its most powerful in perfect competition, to its near-absence under monopoly conditions.
- The tendency towards just normal profits in markets and the strategies available to businesses to achieve improvement on this outcome.
- The fact that large firms tend to exert some degree of market power in comparison to most smaller concerns, where more intense competition tends to prevail.
- The importance of marketing initiatives in shaping the profitability of the firm. Branding and product differentiation are important means of increasing the inelasticity of the demand curve, so justifying premium prices without substantial loss of sales.
- Oligopoly was discussed in some detail with a particular focus on the interdependence typical of this market structure.
- A full appreciation of competitive forces was given by Porter's structural analysis. This provided a practical framework for assessing the intensity of competition within a market and changes over time.
- The developing importance of relationship marketing was considered in the context of suppliers and customers. The need to build mutual trust and support in the supply chain is increasingly vital in the context of rising quality expectations among customers and the need to share and make effective expensive research and development resourcing.

Activity debrief
Questions 3.2 The intensity of competition will ensure that firms will only earn a *normal profit*. This is the level of profit that is just sufficient to keep the firm in the activity in the long run. We saw in Unit 1 that sole proprietors will often continue in business at very low levels indeed. The greater the risks and enterprise required, the higher this profit requirement will be.

As seen in Figure 3.9, an improvement in demand conditions shifts the demand curve to the right and causes market price to rise to OP_2. The firm will therefore gain windfall profits as it expands output. Each extra unit produced will be adding more to revenue (marginal revenue) than to cost (marginal cost) causing excess profits to be made. Marginal costs will rise with increasing production due to diminishing returns, overtime payments, higher wastage rates etc. limiting output to OQ_2.

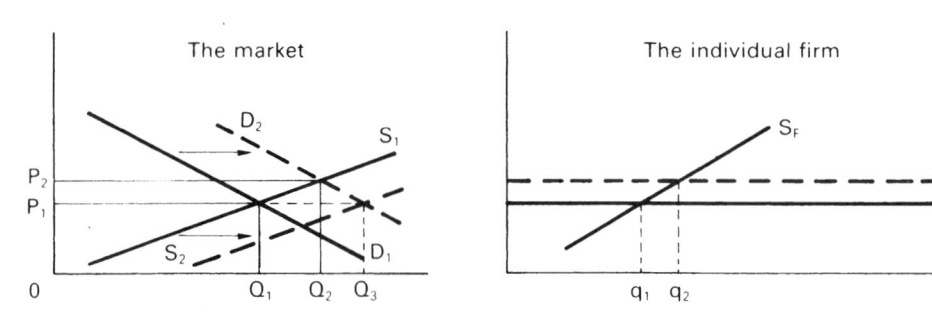

Figure 3.9 The results of an improvement in demand conditions

New firms would be attracted by these profits, and though it would take time eventually the supply curve would shift out to the right (S_2) as this extra output came onto the market. Price would fall (back to P_1) and profits would be forced back to normal levels.

Question 3.3 examples could include longer opening hours for convenience stores, fast-food deliveries, store-interior formats.

Extending activity 3.2 A *price leader* removes the kink if all firms follow immediately. The largest firm or the one most sensitive to supply and demand pressures normally acts as leader. If the others do not follow, the leader will be forced to cut prices again, making it unwilling to perform the role in future.

New product development is the most effective means of competing in oligopoly since it cannot be quickly imitated. This is why this structure promotes fast rates of process and product innovation. The firm's demand curve becomes more inelastic.

Collusion means a cartel causing the kink to disappear leaving the industry demand curve. *Promotional activity* makes the firm's demand curve steeper/more inelastic. However, the firm must beware of sparking off a promotional war.

Question 3.7 Perfect competition is best described by number 1 while pure monopoly is represented by number 3.

Examination hints and specimen questions

The importance of this section of the syllabus has already been emphasized. It is a critical environment that confronts virtually all organizations in some way or another. It is also the bread-and-butter concern of the marketer. The examiner has a variety of question options available. These range, as the specimen shows, from Porter's analysis, to comparison of different market structures, to the competitive/cooperative relationships between a business and its suppliers or distributors.

You must demonstrate not just an understanding of the theories and analysis discussed in the unit but also an ability to relate to your own or a representative industry. You must be very clear as to the contribution of the marketer to shaping marketing forces and sustaining better than normal profitability over time.

1 (a) You have been asked by your marketing director to provide a brief report analysing the profitability of your industry.
Selecting an industry of your choice, identify the key elements of its structure and summarize the five forces which determine its long-run profitability. (12 marks)
 (b) Append your recommendations on the strategies a company could adopt in order to maintain or improve profitability. (8 marks)
(CIM Marketing Environment paper, June 1995)

2 (a) 'Suppliers and intermediaries are important stakeholders in the micro environment of the business.'
Explain the evolving role and functions of these stakeholders in the marketing oriented businesses of the 1990s. (12 marks)

(b) With examples, comment on the growing importance of relationship marketing in this regard. (8 marks)

(CIM Marketing Environment paper, June 1995)

3 (a) What do you understand by **two** of the following terms:
   (i) Contractual relationship
   (ii) Relationship marketing
   (iii) International relations
   (iv) Public relations
   (v) Environmental interrelationships (12 marks)
(b) Discuss the importance of 'relationships' to the marketer and briefly comment on how good relationships are best achieved with consumers. (8 marks)

(CIM Marketing Environment paper, June 1996)

Hints: Indicative content and approach

Question 1(a)
- Adopt a brief report format addressed to the marketing director.
- Be careful to select an industry, e.g. grocery retailing, not a company.
- Define profitability (normal and excess) and distinguish long run from short run.
- Identify key elements of structure: number of firms, interdependence, nature of product, freedom of entry, etc., related to your industry choice.
- Only a summary of the five forces is required – Porter's not SLEPT!

Question 1(b)
- Credit will be given for appending your recommendations to the report.
- Briefly outline possible strategies: product differentiation to steepen demand curve; cartel; merger and acquisition for cost economies and minimization; focus; continuous innovation.
- This is a broad question allowing specific or general strategies to be developed.

Question 2(a)
- Define the meaning of marketing oriented business.
- Define the stakeholder concept but focus on suppliers and intermediaries.
- Divide the remaining time between role and function.
- Excellent answers will demonstrate how these are evolving/changing in the 1990s.
- Reference to relationship versus transaction marketing is required and mention should be made of forces which are promoting closer ties, e.g. quality and customer orientation.

Question 2(b)
- Refer to the matching of internal and external environment.
- Provide examples, e.g. Japanese supply chain, TQM, JIT, single sourcing.
- Increasing pace and cost of new product development demands cooperation.
- New computer technology allows effective interaction, e.g. EDI.

Question 3(a)
- Select only two terms, each worth 6 marks or 15 minutes' writing time.
- Emphasis is on 'relationships' and understanding their importance.
- Plan out your answers to 3(a) and 3(b) at the outset if you select part (ii) and/or (iv) so as to avoid overlap.
- Focus on environmental meaning of the terms *not* marketing or PR.
- (ii) involves all stakeholders, not just customers.

Question 3(b)
- Concentrate on 'importance' in terms of benefits and significance.
- Discussion suggests some critical comment, negative as well as positive.
- Brief practical comments required in second part, e.g. loyalty cards.

UNIT 4

The organization and its 'publics'

OBJECTIVES

In this broad-ranging unit you will:

- Recognize the variety of 'publics' interested in the organization.
- Review the significance and operation of pressure groups.
- Consider the steps to be taken by a socially responsible business in its dealings with these publics and pressure groups.
- Appreciate the role of marketing and internal marketing in communicating effectively with these publics.

By the end of the unit you will be able to:

- Apply the philosophy of relationship marketing to other stakeholders or publics relevant to the organization.
- Assess the potential impacts of particular groups such as consumerists and environmentalists.
- Follow an action checklist in responding to relationships with any of the publics which have significance for the business.

STUDY GUIDE

This is a wide-ranging unit which considers the diversity of an organization's many publics. It is a development of the stakeholder concept introduced in Unit 1 and developed in more depth in Unit 2. You should therefore refresh your understanding of direct and indirect stakeholders and the pressure they can bring to bear on the organization. The potential for conflict of interest between stakeholder groups was another important theme considered.

Organizations, especially large ones with market power, are in a position to respond positively to the influence exerted by these various stakeholder groups. Most of this influence is a direct response to the impact such organizations have on publics far beyond the corporate base. However, as in the efficient allocation of scarce resources, so management will be aware that it can only afford to do so much, and must prioritize according to the pressures and their likely impacts.

This aspect of the syllabus ranges across all the stakeholder publics. While we have space to consider only one or two in some depth, you must try to keep abreast of developments in them all. The examiner may focus on one public in particular or may test your knowledge of their collective importance to the organization. It is at these stakeholders that the vast majority of marketing communications are directed. The customer is the main target, of course, but marketers will also be keen to influence and persuade other groups such as employees, investors, political decision makers and the broader community.

This unit should take only 2 hours to work through thoroughly, with a further 3 hours for the extending and other activities. As in previous units, you are advised to:

- Open a new file under the heading 'Stakeholders, the firm's many publics'.
- Subdivide this file into five sections on: responsibilities to direct stakeholders, responsibilities to indirect stakeholder publics, pressure group activities and methods, the management of stakeholder pressure and marketing to its publics.
- Open subsections in the first two for each stakeholder group and build up information and clippings on these. Pay particular attention to the consumerist and environmental lobbies.

Stakeholders: analysis of an organization's many publics

The days when organizations could safely 'mind their own business' are no longer! The behaviour of companies and the managers that run them, like politicians, have become everybody's business nearly all of the time. Pressure groups are exerting two types of pressure:

1. *Legislative*, which will be the concern of the next unit, and
2. *Ethical*, which seeks to change business objectives, policies and behaviour in various ways.

For example, large firms should pay smaller ones more promptly, top executives should set an example in their remuneration practices and all businesses should employ a higher proportion of women and minority groups in senior positions.

The stakeholders of any organization are unique but may either threaten and challenge its objectives and operations or support them. It is therefore vitally important that the business 'knows its stakeholders', since from knowledge comes the power to deal with them effectively.

The political importance of stakeholders has also been emphasized by Tony Blair, the Labour leader, in a speech to Singapore business leaders. His idea of a 'stakeholder economy' mirrors many of the points made below.

> **ACTIVITY 4.1**
>
> Draw up a 'stakeholder map' for yourself as an individual. Who has a legitimate stake in you and your objectives? What are their interests and what is the nature of the relationship between you? How do you have an impact on these stakeholders? How could they potentially have an impact on you?
>
> Knowing your own personal stakeholders provides an insight into the importance of such knowledge to an organization. It also may help you assess your current position in both work and life in general. How do you cope with the pressures these stakeholders may seek to put on you? Do you try to play one off against another? Do you know how they are likely to respond to any major initiative you are considering? Can their response affect the intended outcome?
> (**See** Activity debrief at the end of this unit.)

The seven steps in stakeholder analysis

1. Which publics are important to the firm's operations?
2. Are they increasing or decreasing in importance?
3. How strong are company–stakeholders relationships?
4. What is the impact of corporate actions and operations on these publics?
5. What actual or potential impact could they have on the business?
6. What are the interests of each relevant public?
7. Which groups pose a threat and which an opportunity?

Which publics?

Each business should map out its own unique set of stakeholder publics. Not all of the general categories we identified in Unit 2 will be relevant to all businesses. This is particularly the case with the indirect categories. The 'set' will vary according to whether the business is small or multinational, in manufacturing or services, commercial or public sector. The weight and significance of each stakeholder will vary as will the strength of the relationship.

> **QUESTION 4.1**
>
> Compare and contrast the stakeholder relationships for a large national company and a small local business.
>
> Are the direct stakeholders (customers, suppliers, employees, owners/creditors) the same? Is the relationship different, and if so, why does the smaller concern have the advantage in developing a sound basis to them?
>
> What about indirect stakeholder publics – government, consumer and environmental groups, unions, other businesses, community groups, the media and analysts?
>
> Can you list all of the publics/groups in each of the above categories who are relevant to an organization of your choice? This should not be too difficult, but it is the important first step in analysing their potential impact on the organization you have selected.

Within each main stakeholder group there will be subcategories that need to be identified and appraised. The local community, for example, may break down into a number of subgroups each with their own specific interests or causes which might impact on the business:

Residents – central, suburban and outlying
Other businesses – utilities, manufacturing, transport/services
Council taxpayers
Schools and colleges
Farmers and horticulturalists
Civic associations
Churches, charities and good causes
Heritage groups
Environmental groups – subdivide into groups concerned with noise, congestion, emissions and effluents
Visitors and transit road users

When subgroups are listed under the other main stakeholder headings it becomes clear that a medium-sized or large nationally based organization will be confronted with a diversity of publics. Resource constraints of time, management and finance mean that these must be screened and prioritized on a regular basis not least because their strength and potential impact will change over time. Company decisions involving such matters as closures, new processes, redeployments, logistical changes and expansion of facilities will also raise its profile with particular publics at particular times.

What are the stakeholder interests?

One possible way of classifying stakeholders would be to divide them into those supporting the objectives of your business and those opposed to them. This is too simplistic, however, since business strategies can be deployed to form alliances or understandings with groups such as Friends of the Earth to achieve mutual objectives. This may allow a competitive edge to be achieved in the marketing of such joint initiatives to interested publics.

> **EXAM TIP**
>
> You must be prepared for exam questions that adopt a non-standard format. The examiner will be particularly concerned to see if you can apply some of the different formats for communicating information you will have dealt with in your Business Communications syllabus.
>
> You should therefore practise communicating information in a number of forms (for example, lists, summaries, presentation slides, reports, briefs or structured prompts).

Business must therefore understand the interests and objectives of its key publics and seek to satisfy these within the framework of its own goals. Stakeholder interests may be classified as:

Single-cause group
Simpler to deal with
Less concern for other stakeholder interests

Multiple-interest group
Need breadth and expertise
Room for compromise/negotiation
(e.g. Local authority)

Social cause
Benefit accrues to society
Qualitative/relate to values
Often intangible benefits

Economic vested interest
Benefit accrues to the group
Can quantify costs and benefits
Language business can understand

While it is very difficult to measure such aspects as visual amenity, wildlife protection, equal opportunities for minority groups and comprehensive product information they are often as, or even more, important than clear-cut economic self-interest issues.

Local interests
Focus on a specific operation
Train local management to handle
Be aware of possible escalation

National/international interests
Focus on industry operations
One company may be used as a 'demonstration effect'

ACTIVITY 4.2

- List the key stakeholder publics for your organization.
- Classify their current demands on your organization under the following headings:

    Legitimate demand   *Debatable demand*   *Doubtful legitimacy*

- Rank each demand on a scale of 1–5 according to how strongly the stakeholder group holds it. Add a + or a – if the strength is expected to increase or decrease over the next 12 months.
- Rank each demand in terms of its probable impact on the organization's image. This should range from 5– for a severe impact on key publics to 5+ for a large positive impact.

This exercise analyses the relationship between each stakeholder and organization of your choice. For each you should assess the *direction of effect* (are company operations impacting on the group or vice versa?), the *strength of the impact* (if unaddressed how might goodwill, sales, shareholder relations etc. be affected?) and the *likely time scale of the impact* (is immediate management action required?).

How should management and the marketer respond?

The marketing response will be considered in more detail at the end of this unit, but it is appropriate at this point to consider some of the general issues in dealing with this complex of publics.

We saw when considering social responsibility in Unit 2 that where a business is sensitive to the interests of its publics it is more likely to react effectively to change in its marketing environment. Issues are more complicated than internal operations and more long term in their impact.

Conflicts of interests between its stakeholders as well as with company objectives are also more frequent. Returns on efforts to manage these consistently are increasing, however, and trust built up through a record of 'public' service is an asset and an investment to protect. Customers are discouraged from consuming brands where *negative publicity* arises and insensitivity in one area can cancel positive efforts elsewhere.

> **QUESTION 4.2**
>
> Can you think of some recent 'negative publicity' for your or any high-profile company? If not, scan the newspapers until you have a number of relevant examples on file.
> **Hint:** Shell, Perrier, Yorkshire Water, Prudential.

The stakeholder planning and policy-making process should involve:

- A framework of stakeholder analysis outlined above
- Review of current policies towards stakeholder groups
- Establishment of a stakeholder monitoring system
- Identify scope for competitive advantage through 'reputation'
- Implement mechanisms for achieving change
- Measure and review progress.

The organization must decide its fundamental responsibilities and develop a policy towards each stakeholder based on the values it considers important. Priorities must be established to ensure that limited resources are not spread too thinly. It should logically focus first on current and prospective legal obligations towards stakeholders.

Due to the slow working of the legislative process and political manifestos, companies have advance warning of such developments. Organizations, or their trade associations, must therefore monitor proposed developments, both in the UK and in the European Union, very carefully, since they may wish to influence its detailed formulation in their own interests.

Second, the organization will wish to consider its moral responsibilities and where it stands on these (and relative to its competitors). In these, as well as with projected legislation, it will wish to concentrate its attention where the likely impacts on its business are greatest. Investment, in other words, should be in respect to publics which are most important to the company and achievement of its objectives. Is the action to be taken going to help both the company and the stakeholder group concerned?

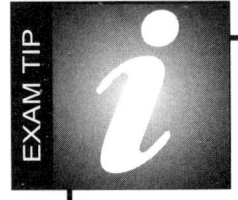

> **EXAM TIP**
>
> There is always a strong temptation in a time-constrained examination to start writing as soon as possible, especially when those about you seem to have done so already. It is more than likely, however, that such candidates will be writing unstructured answers which do not address what the question requires, and certainly not in a logical sequence.
>
> As any effective marketer will tell you, it is the planning that goes into a campaign that is the secret of its success. The same is the case with exam questions. Understanding what the customer (i.e. the examiner) wants and then spending four or five minutes to plan how best to effectively satisfy these wants is what produces the excellent pass. Writing it out in a form the examiner can comprehend is merely the mechanics of the process.
>
> You should develop the habit of jotting down *trigger word plans* for all the sample exam questions in this workbook. Each 'word' represents an idea or factor you will introduce into the essay. Just one word will remind you of the idea and it ensures that you will not omit to include it at the appropriate point in your answer.

As Figure 4.1 suggests, any organization (let us say a grocery retailer) is confronted by a seemingly endless procession of stakeholder issues in whose crossfire it threatens to be caught. It is important that the organization does not over-react to these issues since they can be double-edged. Politically correct behaviour, not least in the area of sexual harassment and the promotion of women into senior managerial positions, may also rebound if the result is a steep rise in the turnover of company trained male managers. Performance against intended objectives must be measured and assessed. Every effort should be made to frame objectives in such a way that progress towards them can be estimated.

Animal testing	Minority recruitment	Solvent abuse
Women managers	Sunday opening	Sponsorship
Passive smoking	Part-time contracts	Organic foods
Employee share-ownership		Political donations
Alcohol sales	MARKS & SPENCER	Rain forests
Environmentally friendly supply sourcing		City-centre decline
Use of recycled material	Diet and health	Product labelling
Third World sourcing	Irradiated food	Land use/parking

Figure 4.1 Real-world stakeholder issues

The methodology of marketing has a role in many of the stages discussed above. Understanding the needs of the various publics and their legitimate demands on the organization requires the equivalent of a segmentation analysis. Each group can be evaluated in terms of its needs and wants, expectations and concerns. Market research methods can be used to gain understanding of their interests and objectives.

The effectiveness of company policies towards stakeholders may also be assessed using surveys and panels. Marketing communication and persuasion is required to target representative 'influencers' or champions among these publics and secure their ongoing contribution to the organization. Just as the marketer must reach both the target market and the individual consumer within it, so account must be made for the individual employee, shareholder and member of the community as well as the stakeholder groups as a whole.

> **QUESTION 4.3**
>
> What is your own personal role in maintaining the good reputation of your business? Think about this question in terms of your behaviour both at work and outside work.
>
> Refer back to Activity 4.1 above when you identified your own personal stakeholders. Are there similarities to your behaviour in building your own personal reputation?
>
> Do your own ethical standards match those of your organization? What options do you have if there is a mismatch?
>
> (**See** Activity debrief at the end of this unit.)

Pressure groups

Characteristics of pressure groups are as follows:

- They are subsections of the population organized on the basis of *specific common interests or attitudes.*
- They exert pressure on people, organizations or government for their *own special purpose.*
- They seek to *influence* the context of government decisions.
- They do not seek election to government office and *are not political parties* (e.g. Green Party).
- They exercise pressure both for the purpose of securing favourable decisions and for preventing undesirable ones.

We have already made the distinction between a *sectional or interest group*, whose membership is based on the performance of a specific economic role, and a *promotional or cause group*, who are bound by shared values or attitudes and seek to promote a particular issue or prevent an adverse outcome. The latter may be formed to fight a specific issue and then disband when it is won or lost.

> **ACTIVITY 4.3**
>
> List the pressure groups you have belonged to and classify them into the two groups above. Do the same for the following: Chambers of Commerce, the Mothers' Union, Campaign for Real Ale, British Medical Association.
>
> (**See** Activity debrief at the end of this unit.)

Examples of sectional pressure groups include trade unions, the Consumers Association, trade associations and businesses themselves. The Trades Union Congress (TUC) and Confederation of British Industry (CBI) are representative organizations. Promotional groups are very numerous and have expanded rapidly in recent years. They fall into several groups:

Welfare   Age Concern, RSPCA, Action on Smoking & Health (ASH)
Recreation   National Cyclists' Union, Ramblers Association
Cultural   Citizens' Advice Bureau, Lord's Day Observance Society
Environmental   Conservation Society, Noise Abatement Society, AA
Political   Tenants associations, Campaign against Racial Discrimination
International   Oxfam, Anti-Apartheid movement, Save the Children Fund.

Pressure groups are the activists of the stakeholder publics considered so far. They are the means through which the individual can be heard on important issues by joining forces with like-minded people whether locally or nationally. Groups can arise to fight factory or hospital closures, unacceptable business practices and motorway proposals (e.g. A30 tunnellers). They will usually use all means at their disposal to achieve their objectives:

- *Complain* (e.g. to the local media)
- *Inform and persuade* those likely to be affected
- *Debate and challenge* at local meetings
- *Lobby and petition* local MPs and Parliament
- *Canvass and opinion form* among stakeholder groups
- *March and demonstrate* outside the factory gates
- *Demand and negotiate* action and concessions from the company

> **ACTIVITY 4.4**
>
> Identify an issue of importance to business, such as Sunday trading, the route of the high-speed rail link, the sharp curtailment of government road spending, the nuclear fuel reprocessing plant at Sellafield or a topical/local equivalent.
>
> Map out the protagonists in the issue and classify them according to whether they are sectional or cause groups, where they stand on the issue, their respective interests and what they stand to gain or lose.
>
> Monitor their activities and strategies under the headings mentioned above and try to identify others (e.g. alliances, leaks, infiltration, bribery, opinion forming, misinforming and blackmailing).

The formal channels through which pressure groups function are:

- *Pressure through government*   Formal pressure may be applied when the group is invited to give evidence to, for example, Royal Commissions, Committees of Inquiry, Select Committees and other quasi-non-government organizations such as the Monopolies and Mergers Commission or the Office of Fair Trading. Government departments will also consult directly with recognized and responsible pressure groups to sound out views on proposed legislation. Input at the initial drafting stage is an important advantage, although all may comment once a 'Green Paper' has been issued for discussion. Governments cannot legislate effectively without consultation with interested parties, and these are part of the routine relationships it maintains.

- *Pressure through parliament* Pressure groups will seek to recruit sympathetic MPs to their cause. MPs will be concerned with any matters affecting their constituencies and re-election prospects and are therefore susceptible to particular issues and causes. Businesses often employ professional lobbyists to identify and mobilize such support for their interests. MPs can introduce private members' bills and ask parliamentary questions to publicise a cause, but this is normally much less effective than pressure exerted through government ministers and departments. The need to disclose earnings arising out of representation may also constrain such pressures.
- *Pressure through public campaign* Educational and propaganda campaigns can be mounted to move public opinion in the longer term. Attention in the short term will tend to focus on raising public and stakeholder awareness and seeking to mobilize them against a specific threat. The typical means here include public meetings, demonstrations, petitions, newspaper advertisements and exposure in the media in general. This has been relatively successful in the case of drink-driving, for example, but less certain in the current campaign developing against fast urban driving.

The consumerist movement

The consumer movement had its origins in America during the late 1950s when commentators like Vance Packard and Ralph Nader began to alert consumers to the fact that businesses were concerned more for their own profits than customer or environmental welfare. Nader's book, *Unsafe at any speed* successfully challenged the might of one of the world's largest multinationals, General Motors, and signalled the birth of consumerism.

In Britain, its development was slower. The publication and interest in the Consumers Association's *Which?* reports, comparing the relative performance and merits of rival brands from the users point of view, served notice on the ancient maxim 'caveat emptor' (let the buyer beware), replacing it with 'caveat vendictor', (let the seller beware). There is little wonder that the reduced willingness of customers to suffer in silence coincided with more proactive companies adopting a marketing orientation towards these increasingly aware stakeholders.

> **ACTIVITY 4.5**
> Visit your local reference library and request back copies of recent *Which?* reports or their equivalents in your own country. They should be conveniently bound into yearly volumes. Using these as your reference data, report on the main areas of current interest to the consumer movement.

There is no one accepted meaning of the term 'consumerism'. Some of the suggested definitions are as follows:

- The search for getting better value for money
- A social movement seeking to augment the rights and powers of buyers in relation to sellers
- Anything consumers say it is.

Consumerism is clearly a force within the environment designed to aid and protect the consumer by exerting legal, moral and economic pressure on business. It has evolved over time and as the following chart suggests it means different things to different consumer groups:

Early causes	*Later causes*	*Future causes?*
Unfair pricing tactics	High credit costs	
Fraud and deceit	Promotion of superficial values	
Lack of competition	Designed obsolescence	
Deceptive advertising	Deceptive packaging	

Unsafe/junk products Product labelling
Lack of product information Price/quantity/value for money
Poor service Ecolabelling and claims
Pressure selling tactics 'Free' goods offers
Misleading warranties Junk promotional literature
Poor-quality products Complex technology products
Exploiting the poor/young User-unfriendly instructions
Limited means of redress Poor value extended warranties
Refusal of refunds Easy credit-card availability
Unsolicited marketing

> **QUESTION 4.4**
>
> In the light of the above lists and your survey of recent *Which?* reports, what do you consider will be the future 'causes' of the consumerist movement?
>
> How might a marketing-orientated organization exploit your perceptions and obtain a competitive advantage over its rivals?

Right of safety	Right to be informed
Right to be heard	Right to choose

Figure 4.2 Consumer rights

In 1962 US President John Kennedy laid the foundation to consumerism by proposing the four basic rights set out in Figure 4.2:

- *Safety* The right to protection against the marketing of any products which are hazardous to life, especially where hidden dangers may be involved. Products such as pharmaceuticals, cars, household appliances, insecticides and foods have been the source of many customer-related accidents and a major spur to consumerism.

  The long-term implications of food additives, irradiated foods, E-coli bacteria and the transfer of BSE from cattle to humans are four topical examples of such concern. Safe alternatives do not always cost more and may provide an edge for companies in the marketplace. However, where extra cost is involved, as in fire-retardant furniture foam, or fully effective air bags and ABS (electronic vehicle braking systems), competition often prevents concerted action in the interests of greater safety. However, note the marketing consequences of the Transport Research Laboratory impact tests on seven popular European 'super-minis'. Though the methods were disputed, those vehicles warranting 3 stars benefitted significantly in media terms. European carmakers claim they must undertake 450 tests to comply with 47 EU design directives applying to each vehicle.

- *Information* The right to protection from fraudulent, deceitful and grossly misleading information and to be given the necessary facts to enable an informed decision to be taken. This is an important role for consumerists and an area which impacts directly on the ethics of marketing departments. The consumer is a generalist lacking the expertise, the time and often the inclination to acquire the product knowledge necessary to make an informed purchase.

Reliance for comprehensive and comprehensible information is therefore placed on the marketer in respect of advertising, promotional copy, personal selling, packaging, guarantees and service contracts. Time share, insurance and packaged holiday companies, for example, still seem to inhabit the lower reaches of the pressure sell and 'small print' jungle!

> **EXAM TIP**
>
> Remember you are a consumer as far as the CIM and your college are concerned. You have a 'right' to expect a relevant syllabus, an applied approach, comprehensive information on examination requirements and feedback on performance.
>
> Make sure you take advantage of your consumer rights and do not forget to read and carefully file each copy of *Tactics*. There is no better source of up-to-date customer information.

- *Choice* The right to variety and a competitive service at a fair price. The customer should have the information and opportunity to make an objective selection and be able to distinguish between me-too and 'real' competition in promotional offerings.
- *A hearing* The right to express dissatisfaction over poor service and substandard product performance. Consumers should have easy-to-navigate channels for airing their grievances and receive full and sympathetic consideration. The need for legal process and an external policing mechanism will be examined in the next unit, when fair trading statutes are considered.

Consumerist responses to those businesses which sought to exploit them have included individual refusal to buy, collective boycotts, lobbying and media campaigns through 'Watchdog' television programmes. Consumer power has always suffered from diffusion arising from the variety of calls on available buyer purchasing power. Agitating over dissatisfaction with a low value or infrequently purchased good or service is often judged a waste of time and effort. This probably explains the resort to legislation rather than place reliance on voluntary codes of practice.

Business initially viewed the consumer movement as a threat which created extra costs of compliance and inhibited their freedom of operation. Marketing-orientated organizations, however, soon learnt to listen to what consumers really required and found acceptable in terms of good business practice.

Consumers vote with their money and, given acceptable choices, will shop elsewhere. Better to accept the challenge of consumerism and take constructive steps to address the problems before the competition does it for you!

> **QUESTION 4.5**
>
> **The impact of customer power and green marketing**
> Read the following extracts from the *Financial Times* and consider the questions posed:
>
> Green consumerism has the briefest of histories in Britain, but there are signs that it is entering a new phase, one in which businesses will have to take greater care to substantiate their claims before wrapping their products in a green label.
>
> The government too has signalled that it is losing patience with manufactures who plaster their wares with unjustifiable claims of eco-virtue in an attempt to cash in on the environmental bandwagon. They support a European Community labelling scheme that would require products to be independently vetted before they could carry an eco-label.
>
> Pressure from environmental groups like Friends of the Earth and consumer organisations such as the Consumers Association, has already forced many companies to review their marketing approach:
>
> - Rover cars quickly withdrew its mistaken claim that an unleaded model was 'ozone friendly'.

- BP contravened Advertising Standards when they claimed their Supergreen petrol offered 'no pollution of the environment' simply because it was lead free.
- General claims to be environmentally friendly misleadingly applied to specific products which are not neutral in impact have been challenged by Consumer groups, e.g. Sainsbury's own green label.
- Varta cadium free battery labels were revised, after criticism, to 'environmentally friendlier', recognising that an absolute standard for such a product was currently impossible. Market share rose from 4 to 15 per cent.

Such efforts by companies at self-regulated labelling is a half-way house to a statutory scheme. This will take time, however, since the Environment Department will only introduce an eco-label after agreement on an EC-wide system.

News reports also claim responsibility for the algae blooming in the Adriatic lies partly with the phosphate residues from detergents. The Soap and Detergent Industry Association, however, points out that Italian detergents do not even contain phosphate! They are concerned about confusion in the consumer's mind over the relative merits of 'allegedly green' labels. The rapid emergence of phosphate-free brands like Ecover, Ark and Bright White has challenged the market domination of Unilever and Procter & Gamble. Their market is threatened by the rising tide of consumer belief that products which make no overt claims to be 'green' are to be deemed harmful.

New product labels claiming 'no chlorine bleach', for example, are misleading since such ingredients are used in *no* fabric washing powders in Britain. Biodegradable is another term much used for marketing advantage yet this is also a legal requirement for all domestic detergents. However, as the market leaders are well aware, once a simple, apparently reasonable proposition is implanted in the mind of the consumer, it can be almost impossible to uproot.

More recently, steps have been taken to 'Green' the recently concluded GATT agreement with focus particularly on trade in products from origins where environmental legislation does not meet 'recognised' standards. This may pose a further threat to some of the rapidly developing economies of the Pacific Rim.

1. In what sense can green consumerism be both a threat and a potential opportunity for the marketer?
2. How would you advise companies such as Procter & Gamble and Unilever to counter the threat to their 80 per cent combined market share, posed by these allegedly eco-friendly detergents?
3. Visit two competing major supermarkets and compare and contrast their policies on eco-labelling. Are their claims responsible, or misleading to the consumer?

4 Update the GATT/WTO position on environmental standards. Are these a potential non-tariff barrier to protect Western markets from the emergent Asian tigers? Assess the implications for your country and industry.

(**See** Activity debrief at the end of this unit.)

EXAM TIP

You must get as much practice as possible at answering questions based on newspaper articles. The compulsory question worth 40 per cent of the marks will typically follow this format. You must remember, however, that the examiner is testing not your specific knowledge of the article in question but your ability to relate it to your overall knowledge of the marketing environment.

A typical question is reproduced at the end of this unit, but you will see that the questions only use the article as a *context*. They ask you to relate concepts or terms mentioned in the article to your broader knowledge and understanding of the syllabus.

Summary

Consumerism has provided many customer-orientated businesses with an opportunity to make product strengths and socially responsible marketing a source of competitive advantage. It is a well-established feature of the marketplace and will remain so while ever there is scope for opportunist sellers to mislead and confuse the consumers. Its concerns now extend far beyond consumer protection to issues such as pricing, design obsolescence and, increasingly, the environment. Marketers must therefore respond positively to the interests of this fundamental stakeholder group.

Environmentalism

There are an estimated 1400 environmental pressure groups in Britain alone. Demands they are making range over the following:

- Conservation of resources
- Re-use, redesign and recycling of products
- Energy saving
- Elimination of non-eco-friendly products
- A slowing of economic growth
- Protection of the natural environment and endangered species
- Animal rights

QUESTION 4.6

How many environmental pressure groups can you list? How would you classify these different groups?
(**See** Activity debrief at the end of this unit.)

Clearly such demands imply economic and financial costs for business, potential redundancies and higher consumer prices. Despite a cyclical pattern to such pressures and some decline recently they are likely to increase rather than diminish with time. Some industries are more likely to be targeted than others but none are immune. Those most recently in the firing line include aerosols, agriculture, airlines, animal testing, chemicals, fertilizers, motorways, oil tankers, plastics, pulp and paper, refrigeration, tobacco, tourism, toxic waste and water.

QUESTION 4.7

1. Take each of the industries listed above and suggest the environmental issue that has placed them in the firing line.
2. What responses have businesses in these industries made that you are aware of?
3. What other industries, not mentioned above, would you include as high-profile targets for environmentalists?

(**See** Activity debrief at the end of this unit.)

A number of possible threats arise if a business ignores its environment:

- The corporate image deteriorates in the eyes of stakeholders
- Customers may prefer alternatives they perceive as less harmful
- Shareholders may prefer to invest in ethically sound companies
- Recruitment and retention of quality staff becomes more difficult
- Unnecessarily strict legislation enacted due to failure to act
- Loss of community support, harder attitude from authorities
- Increasing competitive disadvantage to proactive rivals
- Cost penalties – higher energy bill, insurance, legal claims

ACTIVITY 4.6

In the light of the potential threats outlined above, make a case to your board of directors stating the potential benefits of becoming a more environmentally aware company.

Suppose the board is persuaded by the force of your arguments but asks you for guidelines to ensure that this new philosophy is adopted throughout the company. What would you suggest?

(**See** Activity debrief at the end of this unit.)

We will return to the natural environment in Unit 9 of this workbook, but before concluding this section on environmentalism, two final aspects should be mentioned: first, the importance of size and second, the business response required to such pressure groups.

Small businesses normally face more intense competition and are less likely to have the resources to commit to achieving environmental standards in excess of those required by legislation. On the other hand, they will be owner-managed and do business in localities where they live. Such business people have traditionally filled many civic posts in the local community and may sacrifice profit to maintain their reputation and standing in this and other respects. Larger firms, in comparison, will be well resourced and have a higher national profile. They will be more aware of developments with regard to the industry and its environment and are more likely to participate in government and other initiatives to bring about improvements.

On the other hand, they are often in a position to relocate production activities to other parts of the world where legislation is less stringent. Small firms will find it less easy to justify the cost of meeting new environmental management standards such as BS 7750, although there are increasing pressures on suppliers to adopt these, irrespective of size.

EXAM TIP

The compulsory question counts for 40 per cent of the total marks on the paper. Given that the paper is 3 hours long, this means you should spend 40 per cent of the time on it, i.e. 1 hour 12 minutes. If this compulsory question has four parts to it, then you should be allocating just 18 minutes per part. The question paper will tell you if the parts are worth different mark values, but typically they will be the same.

At 18 minutes per part it is very important that you keep to the time allowed. What examiners find, all too frequently, is candidates who spend too long on parts they happen to know a lot about at the expense of one or two of the others on which they have time to write very little at all. Do not be tempted to fall into this trap. Spend roughly the same amount of time on each and give the examiner something to mark even in those parts where you are less confident.

The response

The final question is, how should the business respond to pressure from environmentalists, or any of the other publics, for that matter? We have already seen that the organization must prioritize since it has insufficient resources to deal with all pressures. It must assess which pressures are significant and offer the greatest likelihood of impact on the business. The response may be framed in very simple terms, but each option requires considerable management effort and time to make it effective:

- Listen to them
- Consult with them
- Liaise with them
- Work with them
- Support them to work for you
- Oppose them

Take your own organization (if appropriate) or one of your choice which is in the environmental firing line. Select an environmental pressure group currently concerned with the consequences of this company's operations and think through all the above options in practical terms. How would you go about listening, consulting, liaising, etc. and why might their support provide the marketing department with a competitive advantage?

As you scan both the newspapers and promotional packaging look for examples of cooperation between companies and pressure groups (e.g. Tidy Britain Group on cans of soft drinks, Automobile Association recommendation of car safety products).

Conclusions on pressure groups

Pressure groups and their relationship with governments will be dealt with in Unit 6. At this point we can conclude that pressure group activity and influence is increasing and becoming better organized and more professional in their approach to both government and target companies. They are now much more adept at marketing their causes and highlighting the deficiencies of companies towards their stakeholder groups.

Green consumers guides and the Friends of the Earth green 'con' awards are just two examples of potentially damaging copy for a business's reputation. To minimize such risks a company must establish and apply values and beliefs conducive to a sustainable business. It must be aware of the threats as well as the considerable opportunities of enhancing its reputation in the eyes of stakeholders through effective and well-managed policies towards the environment. Unilever and the World Wildlife Fund for Nature, for example, recently agreed a sustainable standard for fish products with a special logo if from accredited fishing grounds.

Communicating with its publics: the role of sales and marketing

The organization has a number of communication channels available to relay messages to its publics:

The promotional mix
- Advertising
- Sales promotion
- Publicity – public relations
- Personal selling

to which may be added:

- Internal marketing
- Relationship marketing

Communication is the process of establishing a oneness of thought between the sender and the receiver. A business wishing to communicate effectively with its publics must tune its channels to operate on the same wavelength. The marketer is competing for the attention of stakeholders who are being blasted with rival messages from all sides. The communication must be encoded into a visual, printed or spoken message and transmitted through a TV commercial, newspaper advertisement, poster or letter to the receiver who then decodes it. To check the message has been received and the intended meaning understood, the marketer must monitor the outcome and act on the feedback obtained.

Marketing communication using the promotional mix is well understood by the marketer as a means of establishing links with the buying public. It is also recognized that the total product offering, or bundle of satisfactions within the augmented good or service, are the means of retaining the contribution of the consumer and securing the mutual achievement of one another's goals.

> **ACTIVITY 4.7**
>
> Consider the appropriate promotional mix to communicate most effectively with the following stakeholders:
>
> - Shareholders
> - Local community
> - Environment group
>
> Will this vary according to the size of the business concerned?
>
> Find examples of companies using price, product and place to communicate the company's social responsibility stance and values on stakeholder issues (e.g. incentives to re-use/recycle packaging; purchase secures company contribution to a worthy cause; product features – use of recycled materials).

The characteristics of the product or service itself provides numerous cues to the various publics and represents the litmus test of an organization's real commitment to its stated ethical values. The design, fuel economy, inherent safety, recyclability, packaging economy, durability and so on are revealing indicators of a company's focus on its publics. The promotional mix raises awareness and reinforces perceptions of a good business image or, alternatively, seeks to ensure that it is not undermined.

Ensuring that your organization is one that stakeholders want to do business with involves some obvious and basic steps:

- Ensure systems are in place to listen to the publics
- Ensure systems are in place to respond to them and make the necessary things happen.

With customers, for example, most organizations have three points of direct contact:

- The point of sale
- Servicing or repair
- Complaints

The key at each stage is to demonstrate that the company really cares about the customer. This will only be convincing if the company and its employees actually do care. Smile training is not therefore sufficient and the product supplied must, first and foremost, be fit for the customer's purpose. Showing that the company cares might also be effectively signalled by:

- A director responsible for customer service and requiring that performance is regularly monitored
- Staff who are fully trained and expertise always available to handle customer queries
- Decisions to resolve customer problems being taken closest to where they originate by staff with the power to resolve them.
- Complaints being treated as an opportunity, providing focus for locating where performance can be improved and competitive advantage gained
- A published customer service policy, and any code of practice adhered to is independently audited
- Customer involvement in direct feedback, through panels and suggestion schemes, for example.

The Citizen's Charter initiative launched in Britain in early 1991 is an example of seeking such improvements in public services. Progressively improving published standards will lead to customer compensation when the organization fails to achieve them, as in the case of rail services.

> **EXAM TIP**
>
> Questions on this part of the syllabus are most likely to require some explanation of a concept such as stakeholders, publics, social responsibility and then some evidence that you can apply it in a marketing context. It is therefore important that:
>
> - You prepare outline marketing responses to deal with stakeholder groups such as described above.
> - You find examples to illustrate the ideas you suggest.

Public relations

'Public relations practice is the deliberate, planned and sustained effort to establish and maintain mutual understanding between an organization and its publics.' This definition by the Institute of Public Relations clearly recognizes the plurality of publics to be addressed. Its central objective is to establish meaningful communication between the organization and its stakeholders with a view to building mutually beneficial relationships and resolving any conflicts of interest. The intention is to establish a consistent and clearly defined corporate identity that its publics can relate to. The term 'corporate image', however, seems to be at odds with a responsible business of substance.

To be effective, all aspects of the business must be in tune with this identity. Its policies, management style, staff behaviour and operational activities must all consistently reflect it, if public perceptions are to respond positively.

Internal marketing

This is an area which can contribute to the achievement of consistency in corporate identity although its main aim is to improve service quality within the organization. Internal marketing seeks to apply the principles of marketing to the internal transactions between members of the same organization.

The key is to encourage staff to view themselves both as suppliers to certain members of the organization and as customers to others. In this they are trained and rewarded to respond to a common set of goals and objectives. Any organization with a mission to serve its various publics will then achieve a comprehensive customer orientation coordinated throughout all functions and departments.

> **ACTIVITY 4.8**
>
> Apply this idea, of each department being the customer or supplier of the other, to your own organization.
>
> - How would this customer orientation affect the activities of:

> Research and development
> Production departments
> Finance functions
> Training department
> Building services
>
> - Compare what happens now with your suggestions.
> - What must the organization do to implement internal marketing?

You may already have seen a similarity between this approach and relationship marketing. The achievement of quality improvement and effective customer service requires that staff are all pulling together in the same direction. Communication is clearly critical to success and to the reduction of conflict between functional departments. It also requires commitment from the highest level and an open management style if staff are to be mobilized to cooperate across defined boundaries.

If the organization is to communicate effectively with its publics it must pursue the unity of purpose required through both internal and relationship marketing. This will, if successful, enable a consistent customer orientation and a coherence between its internal and external marketing efforts.

Summary

In this unit we have seen that:

- The organization must understand its stakeholders and the pressures they seek to apply.
- In a resource-constrained business, stakeholder interests and pressures must be analysed and prioritized before action is taken.
- That action by the organization involves a number of steps, including establishing its own values and giving priority to legal obligations.
- Pressure groups are increasing in importance and can be classified as interest or cause groups.
- Pressure groups can employ a number of means and channels through which their pressure may be brought to bear.
- Consumerism has become a force for companies to reckon with, especially as the causes pursued have broadened out from just narrow consumer protection issues.
- One of the important current issues for consumers relates to the claims and counter-claims of marketers regarding the eco-friendliness of their offerings.
- The scope of environmental concerns and the specific threats posed to businesses are potentially serious (e.g. Perrier water – benzene traces; *Exxon Valdez/Sea Empress* – tanker spillage; meat products and BSE).
- The constructive response is not necessarily to confront and oppose pressure groups but, where possible, to understand their interests, listen to their point of view and work toward a common solution.
- The organization must coordinate and focus the deployment of all its resources and expertise to achieve the necessary orientation towards its customers and publics. All aspects of the marketing and promotional mix must be mobilized to maximum effect supported by an evolving philosophy built on internal marketing.

Activity debrief

Question 4.3 You are an ambassador for your company and your appearance, attitude and views will colour the perceptions of others to it. Whenever you come into contact with customers or other stakeholders your behaviour will positively or negatively affect their preconceptions.

If your ethical standards (i.e. regarding how people treat one another, what you believe in and think is right) conflict with your organization's view of acceptable behaviour then you may:

- Move to a more sympathetic organization
- Try to change organizational ethics
- Adapt your beliefs and conform to the organization's
- Try to avoid situations where conflict arises

Question 4.5 Environmental consumerism is a threat where it allows your market to be penetrated by allegedly eco-friendly alternatives. Consumers may perceive your own product as unfriendly merely because it does not make claims to the contrary. It is an opportunity for new entrants or smaller firms since it sidesteps product-proliferation strategies based around traditional product values.

To counter this threat, the companies must either try to communicate to correct the misinformation associated with the so-called eco-friendly labels *or* press for tighter legislation on labelling *or* develop and promote own brand alternatives.

Question 4.6 Environmental groups could be classified as local, national and international; by type of impact (e.g. Noise Abatement Society or National Society for Clean Air).

Question 4.7 Aerosols – CFCs/ozone layer; agriculture – fertilizer runoff; airlines – energy, noise, ozone; chemicals – effluent, spillage; paper – energy, greenhouse effect; refrigeration – CFCs and disposal; tobacco – health, passive smoking; Tourism – areas of natural beauty; toxic waste – leaks, accidents, health.

Other industries coming into the firing line might include biotechnology – genetic implications; transport – congestion, safety and accidents; pharmaceuticals – dependency and ethical considerations.

Activity 4.1 Your map should have included some of the following: parents, lecturers, boss, colleagues, religious leader, neighbours, peers, friends, spouse, etc. You impact on these in any number of ways, but notably how you allocate your time, your activities, attitudes, values and reactions. They may impact on you in terms of financial and time pressures, various social demands and requirements.

In considering the second part of this activity think of an issue or objective and map their likely responses and your responses to them.

Activity 4.3 Sectional interest – Chambers of Commerce, British Medical Association. Cause/promotional – CAMRA and the Mothers' Union

Activity 4.6 Potential benefits include enhanced reputation for companies at the leading edge (e.g. Body Shop or Norsk Hydro – the Norwegian chemicals, paper and energy company which was first to use independent environmental auditing); attracting a new market segment of environmentally concerned consumers; cost savings through recycling or improved energy efficiency.

Guidelines for implementation might include:

- Apply from product conception through to final disposal
- Responsibility of staff at all levels
- Build achievement of environmental objectives into the reward structure of the business
- The business should not knowingly do harm to the environment
- The business should behave as a custodian of resources for future generations.

Examination hints and specimen questions

The first question below is an example of a *compulsory* question of which there is one on every CIM paper. Your tutor has already been advised of the importance of this question, reflecting as it does the breadth of the syllabus. This means that you will normally have to draw material from different elements of the course in order to answer all parts of the question successfully.

It has been suggested that you practise interpreting news clippings of this type and relating them to relevant parts of the syllabus. I suggest that you read quickly through the clipping once and then read the questions very carefully. Underline key words and remember that you only have, say, 15 minutes for each part after reading time so *stick closely to what the question asks for*!

Now reread the clipping more slowly using a coloured marker pen to highlight sections relating specifically to the questions posed.

1 Compulsory question

People's interest is fickle but rising

Opinion polls suggest that most people's concern for the environment is a little fickle and strongly influenced by media coverage.

When times are good the economy is growing, people worry about the fate of the planet and future generations. When recession looms or an international crisis blows up, green worries are shoved aside by more immediate concerns about personal security.

But polling suggests that something more fundamental happened in the late 1980s. A substantial proportion of the population – about a fifth – have had their environmental consciousness raised permanently and have changed their lives.

The changes made by these 'green activists' may not appear profound. They may have joined a pressure group, begun recycling bottles, cans and newspapers, switched to lead-free petrol. But they are starting to take the environment into account in everyday decisions. Green issues will affect what they will buy, where they holiday, and how they vote – even if it is not for the Green Party. The activists tend to be younger, better educated and more affluent than average.

Source: *Independent*, 10 September 1991

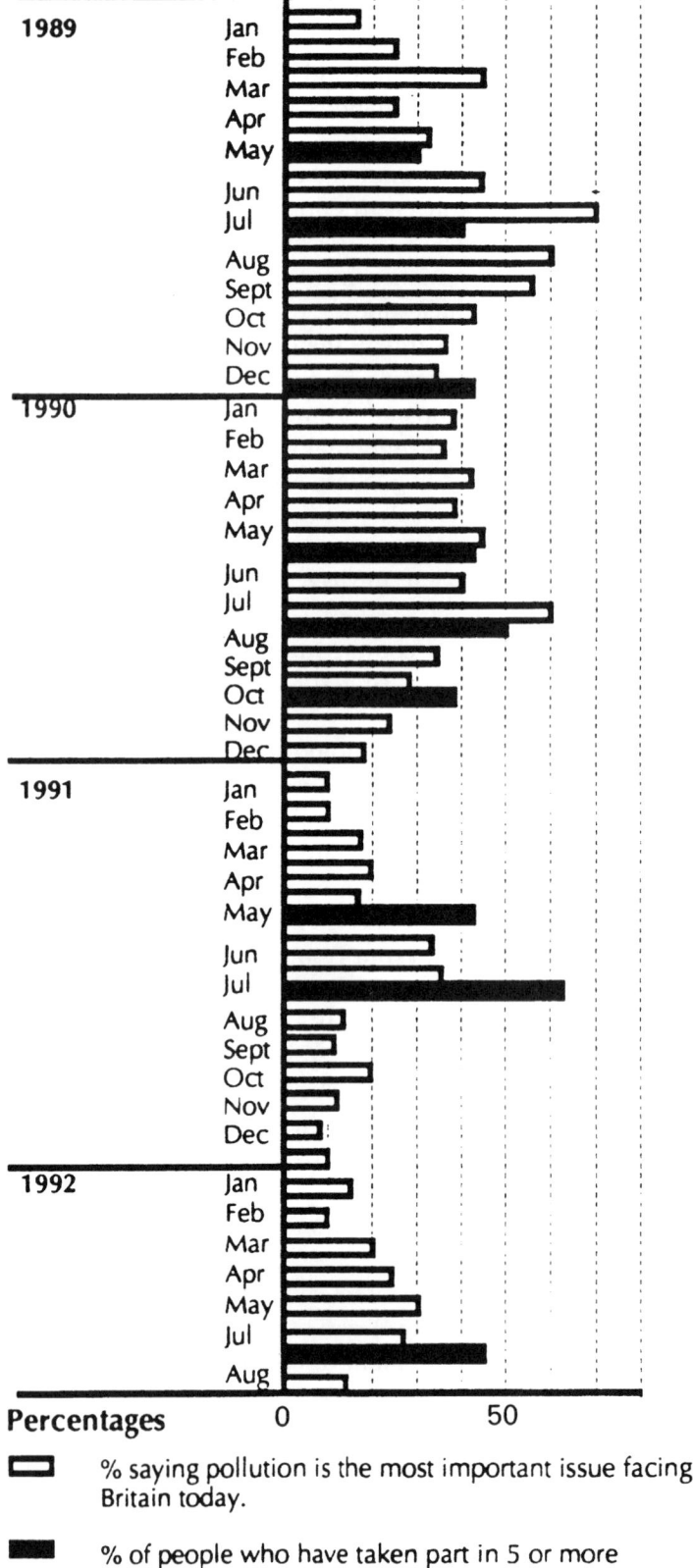

☐ % saying pollution is the most important issue facing Britain today.

■ % of people who have taken part in 5 or more environmental activities in the last year or two.

Look very carefully at the chart and be sure to understand what the two types of bar mean. How many years of information are provided? Are there enough to show a full business cycle? Is the pattern of the two types of bar chart the same? Is there a seasonal pattern in the figures?

One final warning: are you watching the time? With 10 minutes to study the clipping and plan your structure and just an hour to answer three or four parts you will have to get on with it. You might even consider doing the three optional essays first to avoid the danger of spending too long on this question.

1 (a) What do you understand by the business cycle and does it reflect the patterns shown in the accompanying chart? (10 marks)
   (b) Suggest reasons why business concern for the environment should not depend on the stage of the business cycle. (10 marks)
   (c) Giving appropriate examples, explain what you understand by the term 'pressure group' and briefly discuss how business should respond to them. (10 marks)
   (d) If green issues affect buying decisions how should the marketers respond? (10 marks)

(CIM specimen paper 1994)

2 (a) In the context of your country's political system, discuss the role, and methods of operation of pressure groups. (12 marks)
   (b) Taking **either** consumerists **or** environmentalists, identify the relevant pressure groups and assess their recent effectiveness in bringing about change in marketing practice. (8 marks)

(CIM Marketing Environment paper, December 1995)

Note also Question 3 at the end of Unit 3 which refers to public relations and relationships.

Hints: Indicative content and approach

Question 1(a)
- Define the business cycle and draw a diagram showing stages and turning points (Figure 7.5).
- Cycle duration 4–5 years or 9–10 years so insufficient data.
- Relate the 1989–90 economic boom to peak environmental concern.
- Relate the 1991–92 recession to primary concern with unemployment.

Question 1(b)
- Trend is one of rising concern.
- Ratchet effect of legislative enactments.
- Social responsibility should not vary with the cycle.
- Proactive approach means systematic action now!

Question 1(c)
- Define sectional and cause pressure groups.
- Provide two relevant examples of each.
- Monitor, screen, listen, consult, liaise, support, etc.

Question 1(d)
- This question is testing your understanding and ability to apply what you have learnt to marketing practice.
- Provide examples where green issues have affected buying decisions, e.g. ozone-friendly aerosols, dolphin-friendly tuna, real fur coats, recyclable products – BMWs, paper and so forth.
- Relate marketing response to market research, product development, segmentation analysis and marketing communication.

Question 2(a)
- Do provide a brief context of your country's political system.
- In Britain's case, relate to democratic, first-past-the-post, five-year system.
- Pressure groups to allow individuals/groups to exert influence between elections.
- Define pressure groups and divide time between role and methods.
- Emphasize pressure through Government and Parliament.

Question 2(b)
- Select according to your ability to answer the specific question, not your general knowledge overall.
- Cite only the main pressure groups in your country – three or four should suffice.
- Cite examples of changes in marketing practice in recent years.
- Be sure to discuss how far this was due to 'pressure'.

UNIT 5

The regulatory environment

OBJECTIVES

In this unit, which explores the interface between the organization and the legal environment, you will:

- Examine how the legal environment impacts on the organization.
- Appreciate the essential features of a very complex aspect of the sales and marketing environment.
- Recognize at a general level the constraints, limits and also opportunities the law represents.
- Understand the legal relationships and obligations between the different members of the micro environment.

By the end of this unit you will have:

- A raised awareness of current legal issues.
- Distinguished between different forms of regulation.
- Briefly explored the areas of legislation most relevant to the marketer and the organization.
- Assessed legislation as a legitimate means of achieving society's objectives.
- Identified when to seek legal advice and what questions to ask.

STUDY GUIDE

This unit will first consider general issues concerning the legal framework within which the organization must work. This will involve such matters as the role and objectives of law and regulation; the methods available; an outline of the legal system; the costs and benefits of compliance as well as the impacts involved on business and society.

Relevant areas of the law will then be studied taking British statutes as examples. Students from Asia, Africa, Europe and the Caribbean should understand that they may refer to their own legal system when examples are cited in examinations. Different countries have different legal traditions and systems. Even in Britain the law applying to England and Wales is different in many respects from that applying in Scotland.

You should also note that the examiner will not expect a detailed or definitive knowledge of the law. An appreciation of general principles and their application in the business context is what is important. Legal issues are, however, becoming increasingly important in business, not least in the area of sales and marketing. A marketer must know when to seek legal advice and understand it sufficiently to ensure that the right questions are posed. Remember, lawyers are primarily concerned with the finer points of the law and are in an advisory capacity. Final decisions balancing commercial as well as legal considerations rest with the marketing and other directors.

This unit completes the micro environment and accounts for just under 10 per cent of the weighting. It is a fairly straightforward part of the syllabus but one that will be relatively unfamiliar to you. While it is shorter than previous units and should take only 2 to 3 hours to read and reread thoroughly, it is very important that you put the required effort into the activities to reinforce your understanding. These will take another 3 to 4 hours and it is suggested that you:

- Open a new file under the heading 'Regulatory environment'.
- Subdivide this into one main section under the heading Common and Statute Law and another headed Other Forms of Regulation.
- The first section should have a number of divisions including the main areas of law covered: contract, consumer protection, etc.
- Consult your legal department (if your company has one) for information on legal issues of current interest.
- Scan the newspapers for at least one or two examples or applications of each type of regulation. Summarize what you read to no more than a paragraph length so that it is usable in an examination.

The legal background

Legal issues and cases involving businesses are regularly in the news. Seldom a week goes by without mention of such things as a copyright infringement, an advert being withdrawn, an out-of-court settlement for negligence, a new law governing video nasties, a case of insider dealing or a fine imposed by a government inspectorate. Law was initially based on a concept of natural justice and parties to a transaction were treated as equals. Each party looked to their own best interest and suffered the consequences of their own poor judgement. Consumers were faced with the reality of 'caveat emptor' (let the buyer beware). The growing power and size of businesses relative to individual consumers, however, made this untenable, and pressure grew for legal protection which tilted the scales by increasing the rights of buyers and the duties of sellers. As mentioned in Unit 4, 'caveat vendictor' (let the seller beware) became the operating principle.

> **QUESTION 5.1**
>
> How does the law influence or affect you during a typical working day? This may not be directly, unless you get a speeding ticket! But how does it affect your day indirectly?
> (**See** Activity debrief at the end of this unit.)

The regulatory framework

The framework of law is the product of both legal and political influences. An independent judiciary are responsible for the interpretation of common law. These are broad, comprehensive principles based on ideals of justice, fairness and common sense. The term 'common' means that it applies to all subjects. The way that common law is interpreted and applied changes over time through the effect of legal judgments. When made by the High Court, the Appeal Court or the Law Lords they become precedents which must be applied by lower courts such as Crown or Magistrates' Courts. Such judgments adapt the law to reflect current attitudes and values within society. One recent judgement awarded damages to asbestosis sufferers who had grown up in close proximity to the plant manufacturing the product. This exposed the company to substantial liabilities arising from potential claims from other victims.

Governments introduce new laws in the form of statutes in order to implement their political manifestos. These Acts of Parliament reflect political philosophy as well as a growing pressure from society on government to regulate undesired activity or behaviour. This arises partly out of need, but also from the various stakeholders in the form of pressure group activity and vested interests.

The resulting increase in parliamentary workload has forced governments to concentrate on 'enabling Acts', delegating authority to government departments or local authorities to fill in and administer the details. These are issued in the form of statutory instruments, regulations and bye-laws.

These authorities are normally responsible for the following roles:

- Rule making and their interpretation
- Standards setting (e.g. emissions, food and hygiene)

- Inspections – usually unannounced spot checks due to complaints
- Enforcement – various sanctions from fines to closure.

> **ACTIVITY 5.1**
>
> Scan quality newspapers for articles on legal issues relating to business. Look particularly for cases involving an impact between business and its stakeholders. Comprehensive coverage of legal changes may be found in the *Monthly Digest of Current Law* which should be kept by large libraries.
>
> Remember to open a file section for these cuttings and classify them into various types: contract law, consumer law, competition law and employee legislation.

Following entry into the European Economic Community in 1973, Britain became subject to the legal provisions of the Treaty of Rome. The laws and regulations deriving from the European Commission and Council of Ministers apply throughout the European Union. Directives require implementation by member states superseding national laws. They affect business, particularly in the area of competition policy, where fines of up to 10 per cent of turnover may be levied. The European Court of Justice is now the final court of appeal in legal cases.

Role and objectives of regulation

Regulation involves a delicate process of balancing the diverse and often conflicting interests of the the various stakeholders involved. Some of these may be summarized as follows:

- Governs exchanges between parties, the foundation stone of the market economy.
- Ensures a level playing field between individuals and companies.
- Counterbalances the economic power of business.
- Settles disputes between stakeholders.
- Denies market access to certain groups (e.g. alcohol to children).
- Balances the rights of the individual company with the collective rights of wider society.
- Prohibits certain goods or activities (e.g. hard drugs/pornography).
- Seeks to prevent abuse without imposing excessive regulation.
- Governs what business can and cannot do.

Unfortunately the law is a relatively blunt weapon in the achievement of such objectives, not least because society's attitudes and concerns can often change rapidly whereas the law tends to lag behind. There is a limit to what Parliament can amend or enact each year and many worthy legal bills fail to become law because of lack of parliamentary time. The activities of the media and pressure groups such as the Consumers Association and Citizens' Advice Bureaux have, however, made consumers more aware of their rights and more willing to initiate action to seek redress. Interestingly, a recent *Which?* report suggested that many clients of solicitors were given inaccurate and misleading advice as well as substantial price discrepancies. The Law Society for its part criticized the researcher's methods as 'unethical' for not revealing their true identities during the investigation. Attitudes have changed dramatically in recent years with much more demanding expectations of the 'service' consumers believe they have a right to expect from business. Not all this pressure on business to deliver the 'proper' goods comes from the law alone as Figure 5.1 shows.

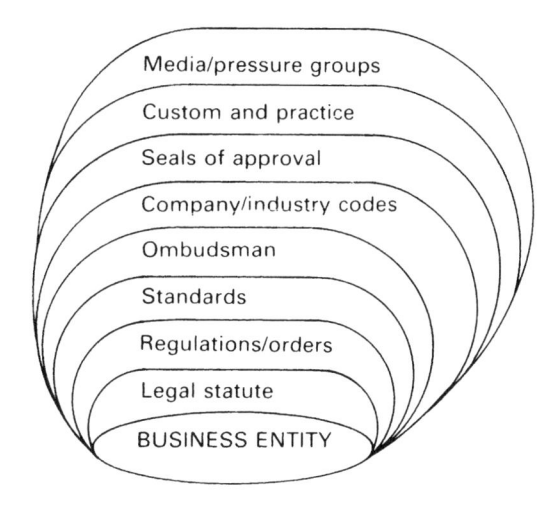

Figure 5.1 Regulatory pressures on business

> **DEFINITION 5.1**
>
> Match up the following terms to the definitions below:
>
> - Caveat emptor
> - Caveat vendictor
> - British Standards Institute
> - Code of practice
> - Legislation
> - Statute
> - Ombudsman
> - Seal of approval
>
> 1. Let the seller beware
> 2. The process of making laws
> 3. Voluntary guidelines to encourage desirable modes of behaviour
> 4. Let the buyer beware – no legal obligation to notify defects
> 5. A quango established to set product safety/quality standards
> 6. An official appointed to investigate individual complaints of maladministration (e.g. as in banking)
> 7. Law laid down by government legislation
> 8. A mark, given by an expert, to confirm or guarantee a product.
>
> (**See** Activity debrief at the end of this unit.)

The government is therefore responsible for the establishment, updating and operation of the legal framework. The law provides a means by which it can constrain business activities by defining the powers and responsibilities of owners and management. Conservative governments in Britain, however, have sought to curtail the amount of regulation in recent years. They have launched successive campaigns to reduce bureaucracy and red tape especially where it impacts on smaller businesses. They have also deregulated a number of industries, such as telecommunications and coach services, in order to increase competition and release the latent potential for productivity improvements where slack and inefficiency had accumulated. On the other hand, they have found it necessary to establish a large number of quangos to regulate and oversee operations. It has also been claimed that the UK introduced 294 new regulations between 1992 and 1995 compared to 116 from the EU. To exemplify these extra legal bodies let us take the regulation of broadcasting:

ADVERTISING STANDARDS AUTHORITY
Origins: Set up in 1962 by the UK advertising industry to keep its own house in order and counter the need for legislation.
What does it do? Ensures that everyone who commissions, prepares and publishes advertisements complies with the industry's British Codes of Advertising and Sales Promotion. Carries out research, issues advice to the industry, and, in 1994, handled 8,661 complaints from members of the public. 2,677 were pursued, and 1,611 upheld.
Members: the ASA is made up of the Committee of Advertising Practice, comprising representatives from various trade associations, and the ASA Council. This council comprises 12 people from differing academic backgrounds to adjudicate on complaints.

BRITISH BOARD OF FILM CLASSIFICATION
Origins: Set up as the British Board of Film Censors in 1912. Became the British Board of Film Classification in 1985, when Parliament made the body responsible for dealing with the problem of so-called video nasties with the passing of the Video Recordings Act (1984).
What does it do? The Board views submitted films for cinema and video release and classifies them according to the current rating system (U, PG, 12, 15, 18), making cuts if necessary. Between 6 and 7 per cent of films are cut, either to conform to the certificate requested by the makers, or to the requirements of the law.

INDEPENDENT TELEVISION COMMISSION
Origins: Set up with the passing of the Broadcasting Act in 1990, replacing the IBA and Cable Authority.
What does it do? Licenses commercial television services in the UK, terrestrial and cable/satellite. Regulates services with a code of practice on programme content, advertising, sponsorship and technical standards, and has a range of penalties for failure to comply. Has a duty to ensure a wide range of services is available, that they are high quality and appeal to a variety of tastes and interests. Also ensures fair competition. Reports on complaints about programmes and adverts, dealing with issues of content and scheduling, are published monthly. In 1995, out of 3,432 complaints about advertising, 57 were upheld wholly or in part.

BROADCASTING STANDARDS COUNCIL
Origins: Established in 1988, and became a statutory organisation under the 1990 Broadcasting Act.
What does it do? Although it has statutory powers in the handling of complaints, its role is advisory, not regulatory. Its remit extends to the portrayal on television and radio of violence, sexual conduct and matters of taste and decency, including bad language, treatment of disasters and issues of stereotyping. Also conducts audience research to determine attitudes. Received 2,838 complaints in 1994, and reached a finding on 1,492 of them; 20 per cent of those were upheld wholly or in part.

Source: The Sunday Times (adapted)

QUESTION 5.2

What do you understand by the term 'red tape'? Survey different departments of your business for examples of this phenomenon but try to distinguish between that created directly by the government from that arising due to business procedures designed to ensure compliance.
(**See** Activity debrief at the end of this unit.)

There is something of a pendulum effect operating with regulation since fresh societal concerns regarding certain business activities will bring calls for the government *to do something about it*! The costs of regulation and ensuring compliance must be balanced with the benefits to stakeholders and society of the legislation in question. Some of the drawbacks of regulation include:

- The extra costs of purchasing and installing required equipment; training staff to conform to standards; recording, reporting and taking action where deviations arise.
- Conforming to legal requirements (e.g. tighter emission standards) adds to business costs and reduces competitiveness with overseas rivals.
- Conforming to safety standards (e.g. testing required on new pharmaceutical products) delays introduction and returns so deterring investment and innovation.
- Complicated regulatory procedures may form a barrier to entry against smaller companies.
- Employment or environmental legislation may drive businesses to locate in Third World countries, taking jobs, investment and potential exports with them.
- Legal and insurance costs – fines and adverse publicity.
- Reduced consumer choice – loss of the right to buy as we wish.

Note: Small companies are much harder hit by regulations. Compliance costs will be a much higher proportion of total cost, they lack form-filling expertise and the time involved is a diversion from the sole trader's real business. Since small firms tend to be single-product or single-market operations, regulation is more likely to affect the whole business than in a large multi-product concern.

> **EXAM TIP**
>
> Questions on the regulatory environment may be concerned with the effects of particular aspects of the law (e.g. consumer protection) but often they will focus at least in part on the impact of the law on the activities of the salesperson and marketer. You may also be asked to give examples of recent legislation to support the points you make.
>
> It would be advisable therefore to have thought through exactly how the law has its impacts and find appropriate examples from your own country's legislation. Figure 5.2 provides an outline of the relevant areas.

While many businesses complain that they cannot compete fairly or profitably with current or proposed legislation, others cannot seem to compete without it, pressing the government for tariffs and quotas or longer periods of patent protection for the products they develop. Suppliers of branded goods, such as Coca-Cola and Nescafé for example, are seeking stricter regulations to stop retailers using 'me-too' packaging for their own-label products.

Clearly, legislation can be double-edged, in some cases making markets more competitive while in others creating new entry barriers. Industry will be well advised therefore to actively lobby for workable legislation when the government proposes change.

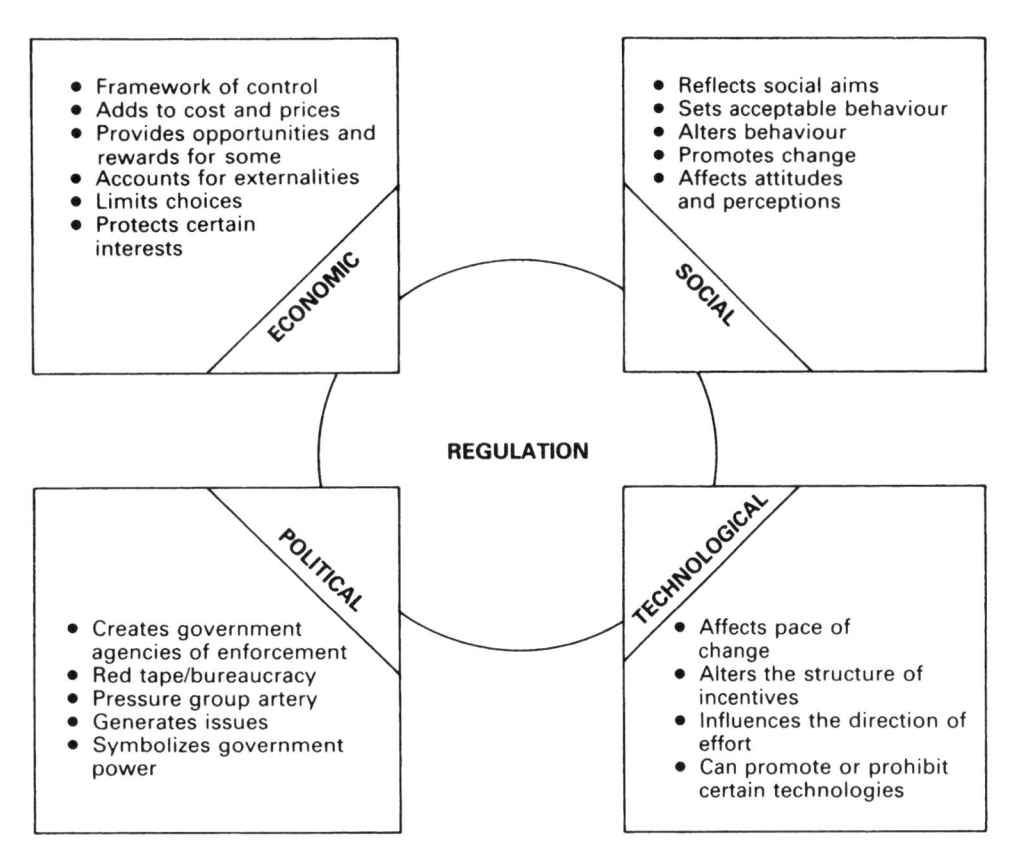

ECONOMIC
- Framework of control
- Adds to cost and prices
- Provides opportunities and rewards for some
- Accounts for externalities
- Limits choices
- Protects certain interests

SOCIAL
- Reflects social aims
- Sets acceptable behaviour
- Alters behaviour
- Promotes change
- Affects attitudes and perceptions

POLITICAL
- Creates government agencies of enforcement
- Red tape/bureaucracy
- Pressure group artery
- Generates issues
- Symbolizes government power

TECHNOLOGICAL
- Affects pace of change
- Alters the structure of incentives
- Influences the direction of effort
- Can promote or prohibit certain technologies

Figure 5.2 Macro environment impacts on the regulatory framework

Positive impacts

- *Facilitates desirable social change* Legislation in the areas of equal pay, equal opportunities and sex discrimination have underpinned increasing female participation rates in the labour force and rising proportions in higher managerial positions.
- *Corrects market failures* Legislation to deter restrictive practices and the exercise of monopoly power produces workable competition to the benefit of consumers in the form of lower prices and wider choice.

- *Encourages further knowledge* New environmental standards encourages research into problems like the greenhouse and ozone effects.
- *Reassurance of the public at large* The introduction of more stringent vehicle tests, for example, reduces safety concerns and improves emission standards.

It should be noted that the beneficial impacts of regulation are both difficult to measure and more likely to be understated. Business will also be more inclined to measure the costs of compliance and to a much greater degree than society will be inclined to calculate the benefits.

> **QUESTION 5.3**
>
> How are different areas and functions of the business affected by the law? Use the following chart to think about this question, the factors to the right are stakeholder groups while the ones on the left are functional aspects of the business. Think of a statute or regulation that applies to each.
>
> Product design — Customers
> New product development — General public
> Promotion — BUSINESS — Other businesses
> Information systems — ENTITY — Employees
> Operations — Local authority
> Transportation — Shareholders
>
> (**See** Activity debrief at the end of this unit.)

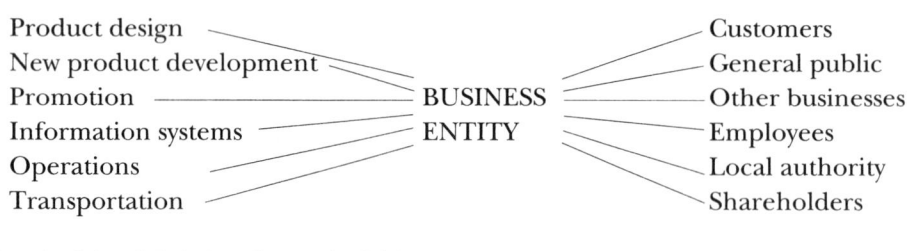

Relevant legislation and appropriate action

The relevant legislation which impact on the business in general and the marketer in particular may be seen in Figure 5.3.

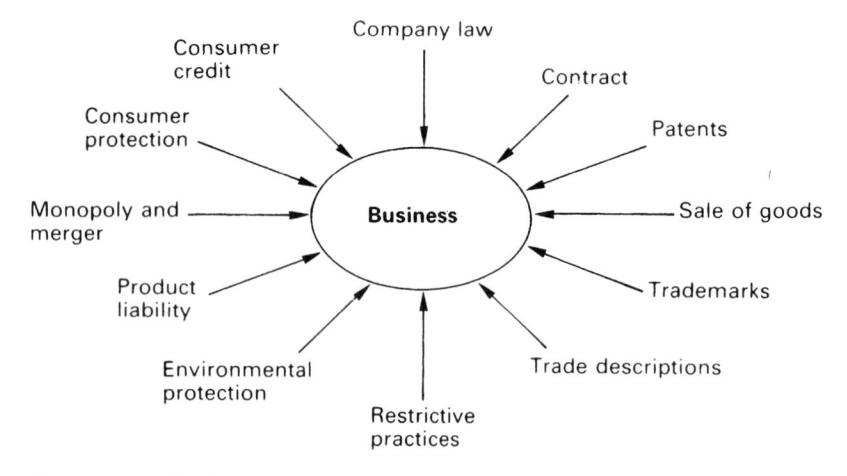

Figure 5.3 The impact of legislation on a business

Management needs to formulate a coherent policy in respect of legal matters. Primarily it must seek to avoid liability under the various laws and regulations that affect it. This means establishing policy guidelines in all affected areas to ensure that at least minimum standards are attained. It also requires a policy regarding whether to take legal action against others and if so in what circumstances. This may involve competitors infringing patents, for example, or bad debts, or even a libel action against environmental activists maligning the company product, as in the case of MacDonald's.

In all but the simplest of cases a business should hire professional legal advice and representation. The law is extremely complex, not least where precedents are involved. Solicitors may deal with out-of-court advice and small claims, such as recovery of bad debts in the Small Claims Court. Barristers may be required for higher courts and specialists will probably be retained where highly technical matters are concerned. Larger companies will tend to have legal departments who will be well versed in the interests and affairs of the business. Smaller concerns will normally use an independent firm of solicitors as and when needed.

> **EXAM TIP**
>
> We are now on Unit 5, which means that on its completion you will have undertaken half the syllabus.
>
> Have you attempted any of the sample examination questions yet, including those at the end of the workbook? *Or* did you think you could safely leave it until later? If the latter is the case, think again and attempt the questions set while the material is fresh in your mind. This also means you can come back and review your effort later in the light of further knowledge, ideas and, most importantly, confidence in the subject.

A number of considerations will need to be accounted here:

- The expensive nature of legal actions
- The effect of actions on the company image
- Longer-run interest in ongoing business relationships may incline companies to live and let live rather than resort to law
- Business contracts may therefore be deliberately drawn up to include means of resolving any disputes that arise between the parties: the use of mediators or arbitrators to resolve disputes is an example of this
- Regulatory agencies may be content with assurances from an offending company that standards will be met in future
- Voluntary codes may be preferred to regulation and legal processes. These are standards of practice all businesses in the industry are expected to follow. They are difficult to enforce and may be replaced by law if widely ignored or flouted. Reporting standards in the British press are governed by such a code and have been much criticized recently
- Industrial Tribunals are semi-judicial bodies used for cases of unfair dismissal, discrimination and related matters. To avoid liability in such cases a business must ensure that it meets all its obligations by establishing the required internal policies and procedures and monitor their operating effectiveness (e.g. verbal and written warnings prior to dismissal of employees)
- Smaller companies are often exempted from certain legislation because of the high costs of compliance (e.g. employee protection).

> **ACTIVITY 5.2**
>
> Use your local reference or college library to research and assess the operations of the Advertising Standards Authority or its equivalent in your own country. List the advantages and drawbacks of voluntary codes. What sanctions does the authority possess? Where and why have they taken action recently? What does this tell you about their ethical position? Can you find examples of other codes of practice?

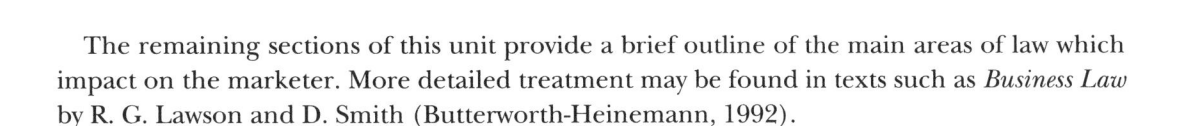

The remaining sections of this unit provide a brief outline of the main areas of law which impact on the marketer. More detailed treatment may be found in texts such as *Business Law* by R. G. Lawson and D. Smith (Butterworth-Heinemann, 1992).

Legislation and contractual relationships

Contract law is the legal cornerstone regulating exchanges between buyers and sellers. Without a contract there is no direct relationship between the parties and hence no rights and obligations. A contract, in effect, exchanges promises. The buyer may promise to pay a certain sum of money in exchange for a specified product or service.

The basic legal assumptions originally involved here were freedom and equality of contract. Buyers had the right not to buy the products on offer, but in the spirit of fair competition it was their responsibility to negotiate the best deal possible for themselves when deciding to buy.

A contract comprises a number of elements, including:

- *Offer* Unlike an invitation to make offers, this is a definite offer by word or deed to be legally bound on the stated terms. It can be withdrawn before acceptance and may be terminated, but only in circumstances such as rejection by the intended buyer, lapse of time or death. One interesting application is the case of priced merchandise in a shop window. This is legally interpreted not as an offer at the price stated but as an invitation to the customer to make an offer which the seller can reject. It is customary in Britain for buyers to accept the ticketed price without bargaining or question. Should the item have been mistakenly underpriced, however, the shop is under no obligation to sell. This may however, under certain circumstances, be construed as a criminal offence under Part III of the Consumer Protection Act 1987.

> **ACTIVITY 5.3**
>
> Try to make some time to study the 'terms and conditions' attached to goods or services supplied by your company and compare them to the elements outlined here. Alternatively, study those you have to sign when making a major purchase.

- *Acceptance* This must be unconditional, involving no new terms and must occur within a reasonable time period. Acceptance by the person or company to whom the offer was made must normally be communicated by word or conduct. For the contract to be valid, agreement between the parties must be voluntary and genuine. In the event of misrepresentation or duress the contract will be deemed legally void. In the case of fraudulent or negligent misrepresentation damages may be sought.
- *Intent to create a legally binding contract* Most commercial contracts make this assumption.
- *Consideration* English law normally requires that something of value is exchanged for a contract to be enforceable. In commercial terms this would normally involve cash or other goods. The seller is then legally obligated to fulfil the contract.
- *Capacity* Parties to a contract must have the capacity to make one for it to be binding. Possible exceptions include minors, intoxicated adults and those claiming to be of unsound mind. Certain contracts are unenforceable against minors by statute, as in the case of non-essential goods supplied on credit. Outside suppliers acting in good faith are also protected when entering contracts with companies which lie outside the latter's 'objects clause'. This is legally termed *ultra vires.*
- *Legality* Contracts are deemed illegal if they contravene existing statute or common law (e.g. are in restraint of trade).

> **QUESTION 5.4**
>
> In the light of the points made above consider the following:
>
> - A customer in a retail electrical store cannot believe his good fortune at finding a good-quality personal stereo with a price ticket of just £9.99p. The sales assistant claims there has been an error and the actual price is £29.99p. Where does the customer stand?
> - A company having rung round alternative suppliers for a more competitive price without success, contracts to buy £100,000 of steel girders. What is its position when it reads in the newspaper that suppliers are being prosecuted for operating a cartel?
> - What are the contractual procedures followed by your company? Do they conform to the elements listed above or do other principles apply? What are these principles?
> - What is the legal situation of those providing services in the informal economy?
> - What are the remedies available for breach of contract?
>
> (**See** Activity debrief at the end of this unit.)

The main remedies include injunctions and award of damages. Companies must, however, weigh the desirability of such actions very carefully. Any award made will be to compensate the injured party for damages but no more than that. If no actual loss has occurred, only nominal damages are likely and all reasonable steps must be taken to mitigate (minimize) the extent of the damage sustained.

A small painting and decorating company, for example, is confronted by difficult judgements where a customer challenges an invoice by claiming that the work done was not performed as specified or agreed. If the sums involved are small, is it worth the time and effort involved to take the case to court? Given the highly technical issues involved in judging whether a contract has been satisfactorily completed, is the risk of an adverse judgment worth the considerable legal costs involved? Finally, what of the impact on the image of the company if it is seen to be taking its customers to court over relatively trifling amounts, not to mention the need to retain the goodwill of large customers in the longer run?

> **EXTENDING ACTIVITY 5.1**
>
> An effective method of extending your knowledge of the special difficulties confronting the sole proprietor or small business is to talk to them directly. Undertake a personal survey of a cross-section of such businesses that you have dealings with and ask them to outline their three legal headaches.
>
> Try to ensure you also survey businesses that provide contracted services to larger concerns. In the light of your findings consider if the law has a role in helping to resolve the problems you have found.

Legislation, fair trading and the consumer

This section deals with consumer protection, with the next being concerned with restrictive practices between companies to the detriment of the buyer. Since 1955, both of these areas of law have grown incrementally in their impact on the marketer, through a progression of superseding legislation culminating in the Food Safety Act 1990. The pressures, bringing a move away from the legal presumption that the consumer was king, and assumed equal to enter contracts with suppliers on the basis of independent judgements of product quality or description, included:

- The increase in the size and power of businesses and the sophistication of the marketing techniques they could deploy provided them with a comparative advantage relative to consumers.
- The ability of consumers to make objective purchasing judgements in the context of increasingly complex and technical products.
- Mainly passive consumers meant that prices and products were set on the supplier's terms. Consumers, in any case, did not have the knowledge or expertise to bargain effectively.
- Available civil law remedies were not widely known to consumers and implied potential risks and high legal costs.
- The activism of interest groups such as the Consumers Association.

> **EXAM TIP**
>
> If you are an overseas candidate for the CIM examination you have the option of relating answers concerning legal environment questions either to UK legislation, as outlined in this unit, or to that of your own country. It is important in the latter case to familiarize yourself with the equivalent legislation in your own country.
>
> The ability to compare and contrast the two within the context of general principles is the best of both worlds, of course.

The factors influencing the ability of the consumer to make informed judgements may be seen in Figure 5.4.

Figure 5.4 Factors influencing the consumer's judgement

Since the Fair Trading Act 1973 the British consumer has enjoyed the protection afforded by the Director-General of Fair Trading (DGFT), in effect a 'consumer watchdog'. His or her role is to gather information on the activities of suppliers, identify those detrimental to consumers and recommend action to be taken. This covers terms and conditions of sale, selling and promotional methods, packaging and supply as well as payment methods.

A permanent Office of Fair Trading (OFT) provides a pool of expertise and experience in consumer affairs and represents a considerable deterrent to dishonest traders. As a statutory body it can deal with suspected abuses as they arise and prosecute actions against persistent offenders on behalf of the public. Local authorities are responsible for most of the day-to-day enforcement of consumer protection legislation and their knowledge in areas such as weights and measures, trade descriptions and trading standards are complementary.

> **ACTIVITY 5.4**
>
> Contact or visit your local trading standards office in order to get an insight into their activities in your area. It may be possible for one of their officers to visit your college and talk about current issues. Your tutor may be able to arrange this.

The areas where consumers require positive assurance of the good faith of suppliers are outlined below with the main corresponding legislation relating to it:

Assurance on labelling and description of goods
- Trade Descriptions Act 1968
- Weights and Measures Act 1985
- Food Safety Act 1990

It is a criminal offence to falsely describe goods or services offered for sale. This applies to physical features and fitness for purpose. Similarly, prices must not be misleadingly stated (e.g. sale goods must have been offered at a higher price over 28 continuous days in the previous 6 months). Price displays are now covered in Part III of the Consumer Protection Act 1987 and the Code of Practice for Traders set up under it.

For suppliers to defend themselves against such actions they must show that they have taken all reasonable steps to prevent the occurrence of such an offence and that it arose due to a mistake, accident, third party, information supplied or some other cause beyond the firm's control.

The other Acts govern how food can be stored, described and sold. Quantities and contents in prepackaged foods must comply with the stated amount:

Assurance on quality and expected performance
- Sale of Goods Act 1979
- Supply of Goods and Services Act 1982

Goods supplied must be as described by the vendor and of merchantable quality. This means fit for the purpose bought for with due regard to price, description and any other factor (e.g. a second-hand good could not be reasonably expected to conform to the same standards as a new one). Any consumer contract clauses intended to limit liability in this respect are void under the Unfair Contract Terms Act 1977.

The 1982 Act extends similar protection to services whereby consumers have a right to expect that these will be carried out with reasonable care and skill, within a reasonable time and at the agreed price, or at a reasonable charge where none was previously agreed.

> **EXAM TIP**
>
> Remember that examination questions will be testing your general appreciation of the legal environment and its impact on the marketer. Make sure you concentrate on grasping the basic principles involved and do not worry about exact legal jargon.
>
> Under exam conditions you will not have the time or space for more than a few notable examples to support the broad points you make.

Assurance of safety
- Consumer Protection Act 1987
- Medicines Act 1968
- Poisons Act 1972

These Acts regulate the sale of dangerous goods in terms of availability, packaging and labelling. Retail chemists, for example, must be under the supervision of a registered pharmacist.

Restraint of objectionable sales promotion
- Broadcasting Act 1990
- Food Safety Act 1990

Controls on advertising are to be found in a number of laws. False statements in adverts are an offence under the Trade Descriptions Act while the Broadcasting Act devolves executive power to the Independent Television Commission (ITC). Its 'voluntary' code evolves to reflect changes in public attitudes towards issues such as drink and tobacco advertising. Health warnings on cigarettes are the result of voluntary agreements between the government and the industry concerned, while the ban on poster cigarette adverts within a mile of schools is the work of the Advertising Standards Authority and its British Code of Advertising Practice. Similar bodies exist for commercial radio and cable advertisements.

Under the Control of Misleading Advertising Regulations 1988, the DGFT may seek an injunction (i.e. court order) from the High Court to prohibit false or misleading advertisements. Such systems are intended as a 'backstop', used only when other methods have either failed or are not swift enough in effect. Some actions have been taken, however, in respect of nutritional and weight-reducing claims made by certain foods, marketed as 'green' or slimming aids.

EXTENDING ACTIVITY 5.2

Contact your local office of the Citizens' Advice Bureau and ask for leaflets published by the Office of Fair Trading giving information on industry codes of practice.

Assess the provision of these codes in the light of President Kennedy's consumer rights of safety/information/choice and being heard as discussed in Unit 4.

Relaxations in the ITC Code has led to previously restricted products such as condoms and sanitary products being advertised at adult viewing times. Conduct a small survey on the views of both sexes among your peer group on this issue and report on changing social attitudes and values. Consider what has been the impact on competition in these markets.

Assurance on fair payment Terms   Consumer Credit Act 1974

This Act provides comprehensive protection and enforcement on consumer credit and hire agreements not exceeding £15 000. As with much of this legislation, it does not apply to corporate transactions. The main provisions include:

- Tight control of credit advertising
- Required disclosure of the real interest rate (the %APR) and total to be paid in credit sales or loans
- Agreements signed away from trade premises may be cancelled later, thus reducing the effectiveness of high-pressure sales techniques employed in the home. Licensing of traders also helps here
- Ensuring that the debtor is made fully aware of the transaction and its cost as well as their rights and liabilities (e.g. the right to repay debt early)
- A 'cooling-off' or cancellation period will apply if the credit agreement is drawn up away from the business (e.g. at home)
- The Director-General is responsible for overall supervision and enforcement.

QUESTION 5.5

In the light of recent scandals over misleading selling of pension policies and endowments, up-front commissions and so on, what is the appropriate response to recent surveys suggesting that 30 per cent of life insurance policies are *terminated within 2 years* at considerable financial loss to the consumer?

(**See** Activity debrief at the end of this unit.)

While consumers' awareness of their rights has increased as a result of the above legislation, considerable ignorance and lethargy still remains. Consumers often have neither the time nor the inclination fully to exercise their existing rights, especially where small-value purchases are concerned. On the other hand, suppliers are more likely to implement the letter of the law rather than risk their reputation or the wrath of the enforcement agencies. The legislation has successfully removed outright dangerous products from the market (although concerns were raised recently over firework accidents) and out-lawed dubious methods such as pyramid selling and mail order trading of unsolicited goods.

Since the customer now has the option of settling a dispute directly with the supplier concerned or going directly to the authorities, it has forced even reputable companies to review and formalize their trading standards. Companies like Marks & Spencer who have prospered by guaranteeing quality, no-quibble exchanges and refunds, must now codify their excellence in practice. They may also be forced to resort to law to counter adverse media coverage, as in the allegation in early 1996 of the use of under-age labour by one of their Taiwanese suppliers. Mitsubishi also lobbied the US Equal Opportunities Agency after allegations that they had turned a blind eye towards sexual harrassment in their plants.

Voluntary industry codes are both encouraged and monitored by the authorities. Tailor-made to the needs of the industry concerned, they can be effective if membership is conditional on compliance. They also may provide a marketing edge to participating companies where the customer looks for a mark of service or quality assurance.

> **ACTIVITY 5.5**
>
> Use the information you obtained on codes of practice to draw up a model for one of the following sectors:
>
> - Estate agents
> - Holiday companies
> - Legal services

One final question to consider is whether the consumer is now overprotected. Certainly from the marketer's point of view there has been a marked increase in legal and pressure group constraints on what can and cannot be done. The legislation is unlikely to be reversed but it can be viewed *positively* in defining the areas within the boundaries of the law and voluntary good practice where the firm has '*freedom to market*':

- It has the right to market any good or service given compliance with health and safety requirements.
- It has the freedom to price products provided it does not conspire or discriminate.
- It has discretion in the marketing and promotional mix adopted providing it does not mislead or misrepresent.

Laws therefore represent freedoms as well as constraints; rights as well as obligations.

> **QUESTION 5.6**
>
> The tobacco industry has been under considerable pressure in recent years arising out of the habitual nature of consumption and its links to cancer, heart and respiratory diseases:
>
> - If there is a proven link to these diseases why, given a rising trend of consumption among younger age groups, has not smoking been made illegal?
> - Why do major retailers, who profess to be socially responsible, continue to sell such products?
> - What is the legal position regarding smoking in public places? Why does the prevalence of no-smoking areas vary between public buildings, offices, shops and restaurants?

Legislation and competition

We saw in Unit 3 that firms facing intense competition might seek to form cartels as a means of restricting output and raising prices and profitability. This was even more likely in oligopoly where a small number of large firms producing very similar products might find collusion far more rewarding than rivalry. Large firms, including those that monopolized their industry, might also abuse their power and position to discourage potential entrants.

While all these actions would be to the disadvantage of the customer, legislation governing such restraint of trade has been introduced more with a view to promoting more effective use of resources and to support a belief in the virtues of workable competition.

1. *Restraint of trade* Most agreements in English law must not involve terms that restrict or prevent a person from doing business. Exceptions include where the seller of a business or an employee agrees not to set up in competition within a given area or period of time. Whether the insider knowledge of a member of the marketing team joining a rival firm could be so restrained is, however, a moot point. Another exam-

ple is where a business agrees to restrict its suppliers in exchange for an advantageous supply contract. Commercial agents (i.e. independent sales or buying agents) cannot, however, be restricted for more than two years after the termination of an agreement.

> **EXAM TIP**
>
> As you can see, the legal environment can get fairly complex. However, if you have the kind of mind that can grasp this subject matter, then there is often a big marks payoff. Legal environment questions are more likely to have a 'right' answer, compared with more discursive questions, enabling you to hit the jackpot with a focused response.

2 *Restrictive practices* Legislation to curb monopolies and agreements between companies, which had grown up in the adverse trading conditions of the 1930s, was introduced soon after the Second World War. It was consolidated by legislation introduced in the 1970s.

Fair Trading Act 1973
- Extended coverage to restrictive agreements in services and those involving the exchange of information
- Monopolies and Mergers Commission (MMC)
- Director-General of Fair Trading took overall control

Resale Prices Act/Restrictive Trade Practices Act 1976 Competition Act, 1980
- Cover agreements on prices, recommended prices, terms, areas/businesses supplied and so on

Example The MMC may outlaw the practice of 'recommended retail prices' following investigation of the retail consumer electronics market. This found that the prices of products such as TVs and videorecorders varied little between competing stores. Discount retailers also claimed they experienced difficulty in obtaining supplies. Manufacturers such as Sony and Panasonic protested that the similar prices were evidence of the high degree of competition.

- Agreements must be registered
- Agreements are presumed to be against the public interest unless the parties can justify it to the Restrictive Practices Court
- Eight gateways can be used including protection of or benefits to the public, protecting jobs or export earnings or to countervail competition or monopoly.

Example Medicines but not books, following the withdrawal of major publishers from the Net Book Agreement in 1995. The attempt by Asda supermarkets to cut the price of vitamin products, however, was met with legal action by manufacturers. However, the supermarket is to continue its campaign against this agreement.

- Must not 'on balance' be detrimental to the public
- Enforcement of minimum retail prices on distributors was also outlawed in the Resale Prices Act. Withholding supplies with a view to coerce was also prohibited

Example Withholding supplies of perfumes to cut-price multiples like Superdrug was allowed by the MMC

- 1980 Act empowers the DGFT to investigate seemingly anti-competitive practices and refer them to the MMC if assurances are not forthcoming. The DGFT also referred two agreements regarding televising premier league football to the Restrictive Practices Court in early 1996.

OFT to probe used cars

By John Griffiths and Robert Rice

Used-car dealers are to be investigated by the Office of Fair Trading following a big rise in the number of complaints about second-hand cars.

Sir Bryan Carsberg, director-general of fair trading, said yesterday that the inquiry would focus on the Motor Code of Practice, a voluntary code operated by the Retail Motor Industry Federation and the Society of Motor Manufacturers and Traders.

Complaints about second-hand cars have risen from 51,000 in 1988 to 64,000 last year. Half concerned defects and about a third misleading statements.

The federation, whose 12,500 members represent the bulk of the franchised retail motor trade, last night promised full co-operation with the inquiry on ways of improving the working of the code.

It also called for the government to consider licensing all motor traders. Doing so could help bring under control what it described as thousands of 'Arthur Daley' garages outside the membership of either the SMMT or the federation.

Mr Geoff Dossetter of the federation, while acknowledging the existence of some offenders in the 'official' trade, insisted that the vast majority of complaints were made against the unfranchised 'lower end' of the motor trade.

The code was last changed in 1990 from requiring pre-sale inspection of second-hand cars against a checklist, to a system of after-sale inspection and the use of warranties.

Sir Bryan said the rise in complaints suggested this change might be causing confusion among dealers. But it was also possible that general knowledge about the application of the code was poor.

The inquiry would concentrate on finding ways of remedying the code's defects, he said.

Mr Stephen Locke, Consumers' Association director of policy, said the inquiry was very welcome, if long overdue. 'Consumers have been hoodwinked, misled and conned for too long,' he said.

There were many areas of concern, the most serious being the practice of 'clocking' and the handling of writeoffs. The Consumers' Association looked forward to playing a constructive part in the inquiry to ensure a better deal for consumers, he said.

Sir Bryan expressed concern that consumers were paying too much for new cars because of huge discounts given to commercial fleet buyers, and that their servicing costs had been pushed up because of the relative insensitivity to price of company car owners.

The federation said it had long shared Sir Bryan's concerns about new cars. According to Mr Alan Pulham, director of the National Franchised Dealers Association, which forms part of the federation, such discounts add as much as £1,000 to the cost of new cars bought through dealers. Discounts can be up to 40 per cent on sales of 200,000 or more new cars a year sold directly by manufacturers.

(*Financial Times*, December 1993)

1. Visit a reputable franchise garage and obtain a copy of the code of practice. Examine what it has to say about defects and misleading statements.
2. Make a case for and against the use of licensing. Be sure to consider the possible effects on competition.
3. Is the high price of new cars for consumers evidence of price discrimination, buying economies, collusion or what?

Monopolies and merger legislation

Both the Secretary of State and the DGFT (but not mergers) have powers to refer a case to the MMC. The legal definition of a referable monopoly is a 25 per cent market share while anti-competitive behaviour is broadly specified as any practice which distorts the operation of market forces. Where proposed mergers involve assets in excess of £30 million or would create a legal monopoly or add to it they may be referred. A recent example (December 1996) is the referral of tour operators and travel agents in order to examine ownership links and the practice of giving discounts only if insurance cover is purchased.

The MMC may just report or will make recommendations. The final decision, however, rests with the Secretary of State, who has been known to overrule MMC recommendations. This is particularly likely when the benefits of greater size are thought to offer increased international competitiveness. A reverse example concerned the go-ahead given to PowerGen and National Power to take over the Midlands and South distribution companies respectively. Ian Lang, the then Secretary of State, blocked both bids on the grounds of reduced competition.

If the Secretary of State decides to act, he or she may ask the DGFT to obtain appropriate undertakings or lay an order before Parliament prohibiting continuation of the practice. Orders are enforced through trading standards officers and offences are punished under criminal law.

QUESTION 5.7

State five ways in which the DGFT is active in the protection of consumers. (**See** Activity debrief at the end of this unit.)

The promotion of free competiton between member states of the European Union is fundamental to the success of the Single Market and its legislation therefore overrides national legislation. Relevant sections include:

- Article 85: prohibits all restrictive agreements affecting trade between member states which prevents or distorts competition.
- Article 86: relates to abuse of a dominant market position.
- Articles 92–94: forbid government subsidies to firms or industries which distort or threaten to distort competition.

Directives have also been introduced governing such matters as ingredients in food and the introduction of sell-by dates. UK law has yet to come into line with EU law and its tough fines of up to 10 per cent of domestic turnover for illegal anti-competitive agreements.

ACTIVITY 5.6

Monitor the quality press for examples of decisions by the Secretary of State as to whether to refer a monopoly or merger proposal to the MMC or not. Note the reasons that are given for the decision in question. Recent examples include:

- Bass and Carlsberg Tetley – to refer
- Independent and Mirror Group Newspapers – not to refer
- Lyonnaise des Eaux and Northumbrian Water – to refer
- Lloyds Bank and TSB – not to refer
- British Airways and American Airlines – not to refer
- GEC and VSEL – to refer but DTI overturned MMC decision against merger

Other areas of legislation and the marketer

1. *Patents* This is a right given to the inventor to reap all the rewards accruing over a specified period, normally 20 years. Application must be made to the Patents Office and be covered by the Patents Act 1977. To qualify, the invention must be novel and go beyond the current state of the art. A European Patent Office has also been established as a cost-effective means of achieving coverage across member states.
2. *Trade marks* Of considerable importance to the marketer who has invested heavily in a particular brand name, the Trade Marks Act provides exclusive rights to registered marks (words or symbols). Infringement may lead to an injunction and damages.
3. *Product liability* Where a manufacturer can be shown to be under a duty of care to the customer (i.e. to avoid acts or omissions that could reasonably be expected to harm) then a breach resulting in damage may be judged negligent.

A 1985 directive on product liability was enacted as Part I of the Consumer Protection Act 1987. Producers, including importers into the European Union, are liable for product defects. A defect exists if the safety of the product 'is not such as persons generally are entitled to expect'. Damage to property as well as death and personal injury are covered by the Act, although each case is considered on its merits and not with hindsight.

Factors considered include the product purposes that are marketed, any warnings or instructions and what constitutes reasonable usage. The courts will also seek to balance the benefits of use of the product against the risk(s) involved.

One important defence is where the state of scientific and technical knowledge at the time was not such that the producer might have been expected to have discovered the defect. The European Commission is, however, seeking a modification of this defence and it did not prove effective in the recent asbestosis case brought against Turner & Newall plc.

Summary

In this unit we have dealt with important aspects of the legal environment for marketers. They have included:

- A brief outline of the regulatory framework.
- A recognition that the law provides an evolving framework within which commercial activities can take place in a fair but effective manner.
- An underlining of the tension between the needs of business to innovate and deploy resources efficiently over time and the health, safety and equitable treatment of various stakeholders.
- Mention of quasi-legal means of regulation such as codes of practice.
- Account of the possible economic costs of regulation and competitive implications when licences, patents and other potential barriers to entry are involved.
- Considerations a business must have before legal proceedings are initiated.
- The relevant elements for the marketer to be aware of in respect of the law relating to contract, consumer protection, competition and other important areas.

Activity debrief

Definition 5.1 4, 1, 5, 3, 2, 7, 6, 8.

Question 5.1 This might include the requirement for public liability insurance, laws governing the use of public transport, road traffic laws, health and safety at work, employment protection law including discrimination, unfair dismissal, sexual harassment and equal pay. If you go shopping then a whole battery of legislation will apply if you feel unreasonably treated.

Question 5.2 Excessive, unnecessary and often complicated formalities involved in government regulations.

Question 5.3 Design (environmental standards), development (patents), promotion (trade descriptions), information systems (Data Protection Act), operations (health and safety), transportation (lorry sizes/tachographs), customers (sale of goods), public (public liability), businesses (agency agreements), employees (employment protection), local authorities (planning) and shareholders (Companies Act).

Question 5.4 The first case is an invitation to offer and the retailer is not under a legal obligation to sell (although it may be a criminal offence). The second case is restrictive trade practice and the contract is void. The other two questions concern alternative principles of trust, and reliance on 'the handshake' to seal an agreement. Where the agreement is between private individuals 'caveat emptor' applies.

Question 5.5 With such a high rate of terminations it begs the question that many policies were sold to people for whom they were not suitable or really wanted. You might therefore consider that much more and clearer information should be given to potential customers, including the likelihood and cost of early cancellation. Consultation with the industry to ensure workability would probably be advisable.

Question 5.7
1. He or she receives information on potentially harmful business activities from various sources and can refer them for investigation by the MMC or the Consumer Protection Advisory Committee (CPAC) as appropriate.
2. He publicizes consumer rights.
3. He actively encourages industry associations to introduce and progressively improve codes of practice.
4. He can obtain assurances from or injunctions against persistent offenders or publishers of misleading advertisements.
5. He can propose new laws to the independent CPAC who then reports to the Secretary of State.

Examination hints and specimen questions

Given the number of questions on the paper as a whole, you cannot guarantee that a full question will always come up on this aspect. There is a strong likelihood, however, that it would form at least part of a question should this be the case. The examiner will be aware that candidates come from different legal backgrounds and will set questions accordingly. The focus is much more likely to be on general principles and the impact on marketing than on specific legislation. Since the examiner also has the option to set a question which asks candidates to relate to their own country's legal position, care must be taken to become knowledgeable in this area.

It has not been possible in this short unit to consider all possible aspects of the legal environment. Employee legislation and the law relating to commercial agents has been neglected, for example. You must therefore make the effort to add to your file any information you find relating the legal environment to marketing.

1 (a) In light of recent legislation in your own country, assess the extent to which the position of consumers compared to business has improved. (12 marks)
  (b) Provide a checklist for your brand manager to ensure that a new product complies with the main consumer legislation in force. (8 marks)
  (CIM Marketing Environment paper, June 1995)

2 (a) Prepare arguments, for and against, greater control being exercised over business and marketing practices by government. (12 marks)
  (b) Using an appropriate example, evaluate the virtues and drawbacks of using voluntary codes of practice to regulate business activity. (8 marks)
  (CIM Marketing Environment paper, June 1995)

Hints: Indicative content and approach

Question 1(a)
- Set this in the context of your national legislation or you will lose marks.
- Recent legislation would mean 10–15 years.
- Detail is not expected, just the context.
- Focus on consumer legislation.
- Excellent answers will concentrate on 'assessing' the degree of improvement.

Question 1(b)
- Use a checklist format with boxes to signal compliance or otherwise.
- Select a suitable product, e.g. foodstuff, medical or electrical.
- Does it have a use by/sell by date? ✔
- Does it list ingredients and additives? ✔
- Does it have comprehensive instructions for use, health warnings, etc.?

Question 2(a)
- This is a debate question relating to regulation.
- The focus is for and against 'greater' control.
- Provide illustrative examples from both general business and marketing practice.
- You could adopt a theme such as 'environmental friendliness'.
- Refer to the sections on regulation.

Question 2(b)
- Set in the context of an appropriate code, e.g. Advertising Standards, Personal Investment Authority, Chemical Industries Responsible Care.
- Provide arguments for and against.
- Remember to evaluate the case for voluntary codes.

Compulsory Marketing Environment question – illustration of relevant parts only

(a) Write notes on **two** of the following pairs of terms from the article and comment briefly on their relevance to the marketer:

(i) Office of Fair Trading and Monopolies and Mergers Commission.
(ii) Restrictive trade practices and market power. (6 marks each)
(b) Prepare two slides:
Clearly depicting the regulatory environment for Unilever, or a large company of your choice, in respect of:
(i) Competition.
(ii) Fair trading and the consumer. (10 marks)

(CIM Marketing Environment paper, June 1996)

UNIT 6

Forecasting the macro-environment

OBJECTIVES

This unit introduces the important macro-environment of the business. Subsequent units consider the economic, social, technical and natural environments in more depth while in this one you will:

- Recognize the critical importance to an organization of monitoring change in its macro-environment.
- Understand the nature of the PEST environments and their potential impacts or influences on the marketer.
- Appreciate the concept of the environmental set and its relevance to corporate strategy.
- Become aware of the main sources of data on the macro- and micro-environment.
- Consider the relevant dimensions of the political environment.

By the end of this unit you will be able to:

- Undertake an identification and assessment of environmental threats and opportunities facing an organization of your choice.
- Develop alternative scenarios of the future.
- Access and assess relevant data on the environment of business in a time- and cost-effective manner.
- Consolidate your knowledge of the political environment.

STUDY GUIDE

This unit provides the framework for a section of the syllabus accounting for 45 per cent of the total. It is primarily concerned with the importance of monitoring, understanding and interpreting changes in the wider environment. The main elements of the macro-environment were briefly defined in the second part of Unit 1 and you should refresh your memory of this before reading on.

Although this is, in a sense, an introductory unit to the ones that follow, it is also a fertile source of possible questions on the examination paper. Questions may be posed on your general understanding of the macro-environment not least because of its importance in the development of marketing strategy. Another area is that of information sources, which, given their importance to the marketer's ability to monitor a changing environment, will form the basis of questions from time to time. As you will see from the sample questions, these may be related to any particular aspect of the macro-environment.

The June 1995 paper also contains a question on the environmental set concept which is to be considered in this unit, while the June 1996 paper explicitly questions your knowledge of forecasts and scenarios. So despite the first part of this unit being relatively short, do not underestimate its potential importance in examination terms.

I would expect you to work through the unit material in 3 hours but the activities could take more than double this, depending on whether you are able to cooperate with a group to spread the work. As was stressed in Unit 1, it is vital that you seek to relate your work to up-to-date and relevant examples and applications. I hope by now you *have* acquired the habit of scanning the quality press for these, since the examiner will expect and give credit for your knowledge of *current* developments as befits a student of the sales and marketing environment!

Your file on the micro-environment should be fairly substantial by now and still expanding as you add relevant clippings and cases. It is therefore time to open a new file devoted to the macro-environment:

- Divide this file into six sections; Introductory concepts and information needs, Political/legal, Economic, Social, Technical and Natural.
- Determine what environmental information is currently gathered by your organization
- Consult Chapters 11 and 14 of *Economic Theory and Marketing Practice* published by Butterworth-Heinemann for further background on this unit.

The importance of monitoring the environment

Marketing, as we have already learned, is actively concerned with anticipating and then responding positively to changes occurring in the external environment. It is these generally uncontrollable forces in the macro-environment that create a succession of potential threats and opportunities for the business.

Unlike the micro-environment, these broad political, economic, social and technical trends and changes do not directly impact on day-to-day operations. They are, however, extremely important in shaping the competitive situation and the actions and perceptions of relevant stakeholders.

How many businesses do you know that can afford to be purely production orientated in the 1990s? Ever since the dawn of the industrial era, *change* has been the predominant and enduring feature in both industry and wider society. The marketer is actively involved in the shaping and changing of consumer tastes but such effects are nothing compared to the evolving influences of education, the media, peer groups and travel.

It is also likely that the twentieth century will be best remembered for technological achievements that have put astronauts on the moon, transformed communication and automated industrial processes. Satellites, computers and supersonic aircraft have produced a 'global village' where events on the other side of the world are known earlier than those in a nearby town. Business must therefore be constantly alert to new processes and technology, to possible substitutes and, increasingly, competitive threats.

> **QUESTION 6.1**
>
> Can you think of any businesses that face *static* market conditions? This implies no change in both consumer tastes and the state of technical knowledge.
> (**See** Activity debrief at the end of this unit.)

'But tomorrow always arrives, it is different and then even the mightiest company is in trouble if it has not worked on its future.' This quotation by Peter Drucker underlines the reality of continuous change in modern societies. Size is no automatic defence against the forces of change, indeed, of the companies listed in the *Financial Times Top 100* twenty-five years ago, only half still remain there today. Those missing have fallen victim to a number of misfortunes such as:

- Acquisition by another firm
- Spectacular failure
- Poor relative performance
- The state forced to take ownership

Clearly, the larger business must stay on its toes to survive changing circumstances, although the weight of its bureaucracy may make this difficult. Smaller businesses may have the flexibility to adapt more effectively, but only if given access to sufficient resources. Both must recognize that they are on the equivalent of a moving conveyor, they must move fast just to stand still as tastes, technology and competitive forces alter.

> **ACTIVITY 6.1**
>
> It was mentioned above that since 1972 half of the largest firms operating then no longer exist. Conduct some research among relevant groups and individuals to build up a picture of what life was like twenty-five years ago. You will be surprised at the differences!
>
> Try to find out as many dimensions as possible regarding life at work, at home, leisure activities, living standards, type of goods and services. What kind of things that we take for granted today were not available? What product or process technologies were not available or even thought of?
>
> (**See** Activity debrief at the end of this unit.)

Although *change* is the characteristic feature of industrialized societies, its pace and complexity also appears to have increased. The 1950s and 1960s, for example, while still experiencing change, were relatively stable and predictable. In Britain, economic growth was continuous and fluctuated within narrow limits. Unemployment and inflation were relatively low and steady and a high degree of social consensus prevailed. Political parties had similar agendas and both technological and market changes were manageable. The oil crises of the 1970s replaced this comparative calm with turbulent, complex and often dynamic interactive change which has continued ever since. This is even more the case in Asian economies such as Hong Kong, where rapid growth is compounded by critical political uncertainties.

In Britain such change exposed previously sleepy market sectors to considerable threats since familiarity with previously established conditions had led to complacency. Similar effects have been felt more recently with privatization and deregulation, the Single European Market, the GATT agreement, European Monetary Union, and so the list goes on. In dynamic and complex market environments the marketer's aim must be to understand the future rather than rely on the patterns of the past. Any organization wishing to be consistently successful in the future must:

- Scan their environment
- Identify those forces relevant to the organization/its industry
- Respond to threats and opportunities by implementing strategies
- Monitor the outcome of planned action
- Continue to scan their environment

The scope for environmental forecasting may be seen in Figure 6.1.

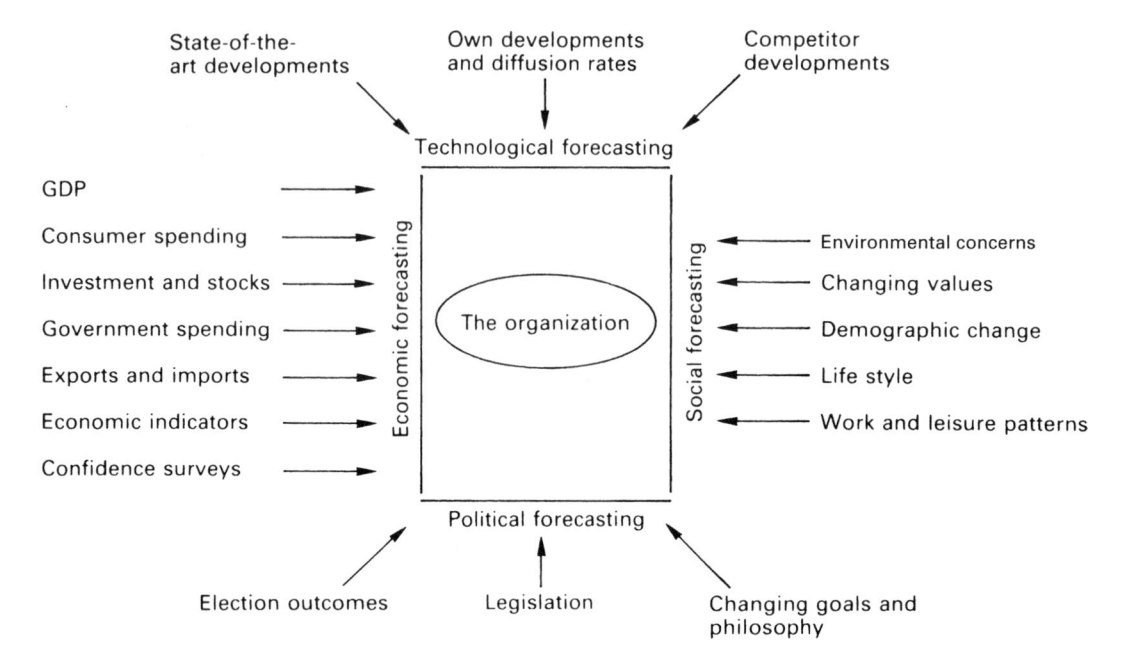

Figure 6.1 The scope for forecasting

> **EXAM TIP**
>
> The format of the CIM examination paper suggests that the final question may be of a similar type. The June 1995 paper required that candidates discussed two macro-environmental terms from a choice of four. The second section required a practical application of one of the terms in the environmental set to a company of your choice.
> (**See** End of this unit for the full question.)
>
> If this pattern is repeated then you are advised to practise relating PEST elements to everyday/internationally common industries, sectors or companies. Retailing, transport, financial services, tourism and so forth could be possibilities.

The key problems

Since the determinants and resulting shape of the future market for a product may be significantly different from the past, most forecasting techniques that rely on historic information and the projection of past and current trends will tend to be misleading. Even highly sophisticated forecasting based on computer models, as used by the UK Treasury, has been prone to considerable error. One cynic suggested that economists had successfully forecast nine of the last five recessions!

The long-awaited green shoots of recovery in 1991/1992, for example, took 18 months longer to germinate than predicted and led to the resignation of the Chancellor of the Exchequer and a record widening gap between government expenditure and revenue of £48 billion in 1994. The long-term consequences of the sharp tax rises then required and the persistence of the 'feel bad' or at best 'feel insecure factor' implied a change in government at the next election. Such are the potential consequences of bad forecasts and any business must address the following problems:

- *Which are the right forecasts?* There are often a variety of independent economic forecasters, but how can a business know which to rely on in advance?
- *How significant are the different trends?* Think about this question in reference to green consumer attitudes. Are concerns strengthening or tending to ebb and flow with recession and boom?
- *How long before a pattern of events become a trend?* Is teleworking or working from home via a computer/communications link with your employer a trend yet or not?
- *Where are the turning points?* Many aspects of life have rhythms, not least sales patterns, where seasonal or cyclical movements occur. The important requirement here is timing of the upturn or downturn. Failure to anticipate and prepare for it will result in either lost sales or unsold stock, depending on the error.

> **QUESTION 6.2**
>
> 1. Why must a business forecast?
> 2. When must a business forecast?
> 3. What must a business forecast?
>
> (**See** Activity debrief at the end of this unit.)

- *Which are the discontinuities?* This is one of the most difficult areas to forecast since it implies a reversal or even disappearance of a trend. The significant shift from cheap to dear energy caused by the OPEC cartel in the 1970s was a discontinuity. A change in government with a very different economic philosophy can also have this effect. The demise of the nuclear family (2 adults + 2 children) as the norm is another.
- *What is the pace of change?* Knowing the direction of change is one thing, but knowing the speed of its development is the key to an effective response. Who predicted the frightening pace of contraction in the British coal mining industry? From 170 deep mines employing 175 000 people in 1985 to just seventeen operational pits

employing a mere 11 000 in early 1994. Suppliers and local traders who failed to anticipate this and adjust will also have suffered the consequences.

> **QUESTION 6.3**
>
> Identify three strong patterns or trends in a market of your choice which you consider will reverse or discontinue up to the turn of the century. Give reasons for your choice.

Many distinctive trends have reversed or discontinued in recent years. The power and significance of trade unions has declined greatly, house prices have fallen while inflation in general has decreased to negligible rates not seen for over twenty-five years. With falling birth rates Britain's youth culture has also given way to an affluent ageing one.

Disagreements over the answers to the key problems outlined above produces very different views of the future with no guarantee as to which will turn out to be the most accurate one. The possible business responses to such forecasting problems are as follows:

- *Abandon all forecasting pretensions* This would be a naive response to such difficulties. Every action involving plans or preparations for tomorrow requires some forecasting to be effective. The essence of managerial decision making involves forecasting future conditions. Even day-to-day operational decisions, involving a much shorter time horizon than strategic decisions, require a clear view of the future if such matters as stock levels, sales targets or advertising budgets are to be effectively set.
- *Concentrate on short-term adaptive planning* If the further the manager peers into the future, the murkier the view becomes, then this is a great temptation. Focus on the year ahead but establish a flexible management system that allows rapid adaption to environmental change. This may be possible for some businesses in relatively static markets, but what about a water company, a telecommunications supplier or a pharmaceutical business? A new reservoir must be planned over ten years ahead, while technological change is so rapid in telecommunications that a reaction strategy, no matter how effective, would come far too late. The drug company must be planning its product life cycles in the knowledge that testing and verification procedures will take a decade. All companies considering acquisition, modernization or diversification must forecast the medium- and longer-term future, if only in broad terms.

> **EXAM TIP**
>
> Remember that the examiner may set the question in the context of your business communications skills. Instead of a straightforward essay question you may be asked to prepare a brief or write a report. Read the question carefully, and if this is the case then follow the instructions given. Remember *up to 15 per cent* of the marks *may* be awarded for presentational effectiveness.
>
> If a report is required then the format would normally include:
>
> - Title
> - Summary
> - Contents
> - Introduction
> - Findings
> - Conclusions
> - Recommendations
>
> *Do not get carried away* with the format, however, and forget to answer the question itself which counts for at least *85 per cent of the marks*. Set the points out clearly and break up the text using lists of short, key points rather than long sentences.

- *Improve the quality of conventional forecasts* Forecasts normally refer to objective, quantitative techniques which seek to extrapolate or project historical data into the future. The problem is not a lack of the necessary statistical techniques but rather the quality and availability of the necessary data. As with computers, the principle of garbage-in garbage-out applies and the resulting projection will only be as good as the input. Sophisticated statistical methods such as multiple regression, moving averages and exponential smoothing will be of little value if the data collected is suspect. Be warned by the wry response to the question 'why did God create economists?' – answer, 'To make weather forecasters look good!'

DEFINITION 6.1

Match the following terms to the definitions:

- Demand function
- Depth interview
- Multiple regression
- Moving averages
- Exponential smoothing
- Probability

1. Best estimate of the outcome of each decision alternative.
2. Unstructured, usually face to face and intended to elicit meaningful information from a respondent.
3. A technique used to calculate the explanatory value of a number of independent variables affecting a dependent one.
4. The factors that determine the quantity demanded of a good per period of time.
5. Change in the average of, say, sales values over a number of time periods, by adding the most recent value and dropping the earliest in the series.
6. When weights used in the averaging process decrease progressively for values further into the past.

(**See** Activity debrief at the end of this unit.)

- *Use the combined view of experts (Delphi technique)* This is a subjective and qualitative technique relying primarily on human judgement rather than statistical method. They are essentially intuitive techniques, deriving, from the expert's blend of knowledge, experience and judgement. The experts may include academics, consultants, relevant stakeholders as well as key directors in marketing, operations, finance and non-executive board members. Each may make an independent forecast of sales, for example, or respond to an initial prediction. These may be fed back for further comment in the light of each expert's contribution. The resulting forecast reflects the collective 'informed view' of those who are in the best position to judge developments. The consensus achieved will 'smooth out' extreme views and should carry credibility with those who use it. Unfortunately it is a time-consuming process and therefore costly in the expert's time. It may also fail to capture the possibility of radical change due to a similar mind set of the experts involved.

EXTENDING ACTIVITY 6.1

It is said that decisions should be taken closest to the customer affected. It is also suggested that the day-to-day operative knows most about the process involved. In the light of this, conduct a Delphi study within the sales force of your company with a view to forecasting sales on a product-by-product basis. Alternatively, survey the expert views of counter/shelving and support staff in your college library on improving customer service.

List the *advantages* of using the sales force to build up forecasts.
List the *weaknesses* of this approach.
(**See** Activity debrief at the end of this unit.)

- *Use judgemental analysis to identify a desired future* We all engage in goal-orientated planning if we wish to progress in life. It is a relatively successful approach so long as the world around us remains relatively stable and predictable. A young boy or girl who decides that becoming a renowned doctor is their goal will plan to get good GCSE grades, particularly in maths and science so they can progress to 'A' level, where good results are required if they are to gain entry to a university with a record of excellence and so on toward their goal. The organization may also map out its future towards a desired goal given the current environmental landscape. Lack of perfect foresight, unexpected obstacles and changing conditions might force changes in direction along the way, but the goal is clear and an outline map is better than no map at all!

> **ACTIVITY 6.2**
>
> Have you identified your desired future and made a map?
>
> The fact that you are reading this workbook suggests that you have given some thought to your future, but have you really planned it out?
>
> - Where do you want to be in five years' time?
> - Where do you want to be in ten years' time?
> - Where would you like to be at the peak of your career?
> - What do you need to do to ensure that you reach these milestones?
> - What are your personal and intellectual strengths?
> - What are your areas of weakness?
> - Are these going to inhibit you from achieving your goals?
> - If so, how are you going to remedy them and when?
> - What qualifications, skills and experience will be necessary?
> - Where are the gaps and when and how are you going to fill them?
> - Is your job leading somewhere you want to go?
>
> The list could go on, but the important thing is to try to control your own future and not drift along on a hope and a prayer. The environment will change and the unexpected will occur but a future-orientated plan provides a framework for successful adaption.

- *Use scenarios* These are alternative views of the future and have been developed by organizations such as Shell to assist prediction in uncertain times. The best way of understanding scenarios is by comparing them with quantitative forecasts:

A scenario	*A forecast*
A description of the future based on mutually consistent groupings of determinants.	A statistical synthesis of probabilities and expert opinion.
Says here are *some* of the key factors you have to take into account and this is the way they could affect your business.	Accounts relevant factors to yield *the best answer* – what is most likely to happen. This tends to *dictate final decisions.*
Designed to be considered with other scenarios – it is valueless on its own.	Stands alone.
A tool to assist understanding. It forms the backdrop to decision making, not an integral part of it.	Intended to be regarded as an *authoritative statement.*
A means of placing responsibility for planning decisions on the managers concerned.	A means of removing much of the responsibility for the final decision – managers tend to rely on the central forecast
Essentially qualitative.	Fundamentally quantitative.

Forecasts are therefore based on the belief that *the future can be measured and controlled*, whereas scenarios are based on the belief that they cannot be. Shell warns all corporate planners that the forecasts they know, love and rely on are based on this fallacy. It likens decisions based on them to pursuing a straight line through a minefield, and views much economic and business theory as a 'pretend world' in which people act as if they had knowledge where it can not exist. Planners seek firm answers and optimum solutions, as if uncertainty and change can be assumed away.

> **ACTIVITY 6.3**
>
> Identify key variables in the PEST environment and vary your assumptions about them in order to produce two alternative futures for the year 2002. Variables might include such factors as the outcome of the next general election, the stage of the economic cycle, demographic trends, trade factors and so forth.
>
> You should also use the same exercise to produce two alternative industry scenarios based on the key variables operating in the specific market concerned. You may wish to label the scenarios to reflect the view of the future they suggest (e.g. business as usual or rapid recovery).

The environmental set

Every organization faces a set of environmental factors over which it may have some influence but seldom any direct control. Small or large, public or private, manufacturer or service organization, they all operate in the context of a shifting set of what are, in effect, potential threats or opportunities. The set that concerns any specific business will, however, be individual to its own particular circumstances and situation. It will also change over time as the elements in the set shift in relative importance and actual impact upon the business.

The board of directors must ensure that they monitor changes in their set and rank the elements in terms of likely impact on the business. The set is a vital stating point for environmental assessment and SWOT analysis providing the basis for formulating a strategic response.

> **ACTIVITY 6.4**
>
> Obtain the three most recent annual reports of a public limited company of your choice by writing to/or phoning the company secretary or visiting a main reference or college library with a strong business section. Paying particular attention to the chairman's and managing director's reports, identify the main opportunities and threats for the company. Observe any change in importance attached to these set factors over the period covered.

1996

- Lack of 'feel good' factor (1)
- Domestic competition (2)
- Rising input prices (6)
- Manufacturer
- Falling interest rates (5)
- Impending election (4)
- Falling exchange rates (3)

1997

- EMU concerns e.g. customers relocating. (8)
- Rising exchange rate (1)
- Post-election policy changes (2)
- Union militancy (7)
- Manufacturer
- Increased interest rates (3)
- Environmental legislation (6)
- Skill shortages (5)
- Buoyancy in domestic consumer spending (4)

Figure 6.2 Environmental set for a large manufacturer, 1996 and 1997

The set of the business in Figure 6.2 changed significantly even in one year.

- The lack of feel good factor was the most important set element in 1996 for this manufacturer due to its dampening effects on volumes and trigger for more intense domestic competition. By 1997 recovery in the economy had displaced this with concern over *export competitiveness* as the pound rose strongly. This was compounded by *developing recession in its main European markets*, particularly Germany and France, as they struggled to meet the criteria for EMU.
- *Rising interest rates* had become a concern in 1997 due to fears that they might dampen recovery by adversely affecting consumer confidence and spending. As with exchange rates, a turning point was experienced between 1996 and 1997 signalling changed conditions.
- Rising input prices in 1996 reflected worries about reviving inflation and signs of labour militancy in the car industry. These continued into 1997 with particular focus on emerging *skill shortages* in key areas.
- *Environmental worries* were exercising directors' minds in 1997, not least in respect of progressively tightening emission and environmental management standards. EU packaging standards requiring tighter and tighter recycling percentages were of concern, whereas proposals to bring UK 38-tonne truck limits into line with EU 44-tonne practice promised savings.
- The Single European Market (SEM) had become an operational reality by 1994 but the impacts and opportunities had so far been found disappointing and less than expected causing it to disappear from the 1996 set. However, concerns over impending *European Monetary Union* in 1999 and Britain's probable opt-out were rising in 1997. A high proportion of the manufacturer's exports would be affected by the introduction of the Euro. This would also raise the issue as to where capacity ought to be located. Toyota, the car manufacturer, had already signalled its concerns to the government.
- *Post-election policy changes* ranked number two in 1997 due to the spring election. This ranking was underlined by numerous early policy initiatives as the new Labour government 'hit the ground running.' However, it would be in the following budget that these would mainly be crystalized, not just in terms of tax rises, e.g. VAT rises would be of particular concern to the manufacturer, but also expenditure priorities. Economic management might be expected to be tightened due to the reluctance to raise interest rates in the pre-election period and underlying inflation trending above its 2.5 per cent target for the end of the Parliament. Labour had pledged to build a new constructive relationship in Europe but this would include signing up to the Social Chapter.
- Rising input prices in 1996 had reflected concern over sharp rises in oil and other material inputs. In 1997 the concern became more generalized due to the *rise in sterling*. Fortunately the manufacturer will have hedged its forward currency requirements in the short term but continued sterling strength would soon force sharp price rises.

> **ACTIVITY 6.5**
>
> Produce a current environmental set either for your own organization or the one you chose in Activity 6.4 above.
>
> Rank the elements you identify and consider their significance:
>
> - 12 months ago
> - In 12 months' time
>
> Which of the elements you have considered are opportunities and which are threats? If you have mainly selected threats, why is this? Can the threats you have identified also be looked at as opportunities?

The set for a public sector organization reflects very different managerial concerns (Figure 6.3). Factors affecting the income of the authority are clearly important although their nature has changed between the two years.

1996

- Green issues (6)
- National election outcome (1)
- Union militancy (5) — Local authority — Local economy (2)
- Private finance initiative opportunities (4)
- Central government policies, e.g. business rates and spending cap (3)

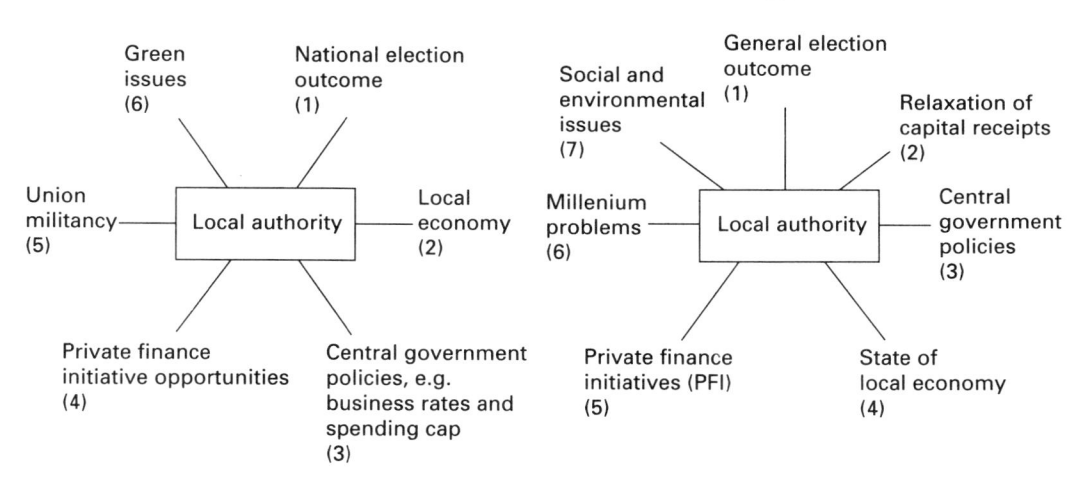

1997

- Social and environmental issues (7)
- General election outcome (1)
- Relaxation of capital receipts (2)
- Millenium problems (6) — Local authority — Central government policies (3)
- Private finance initiatives (PFI) (5)
- State of local economy (4)

Figure 6.3 Environmental set for a local authority, 1996 and 1997

- The *outcome of the general election* dominated the early part of 1997 since it influenced not only the outcome of the May local elections, and therefore the distribution of power in the town halls, but also the national party in power. This was of particular significance to Scotland and Wales where devolution of decision-making power was at issue.
- *The state of the local economy* is important in terms of expenditure and income. Depressed conditions reduces income from business taxes while increasing spending on social services. Certain authorities will be beneficially impacted by the expenditure of National Lottery funds in the years up to the millennium, while others will continue to attract overseas direct investment to boost activity. Recovery has impacted more on the South East of Britain than in the North due to the subdued state of manufacturing.
- *Government policies* to transform authorities from 'providers' into 'facilitators' of local services have required many of them to be put out to tender against private companies. Others are expected to operate as profit centres raising income from fees. The aim has been to achieve provision from the most cost-effective source and realize best value for money for local taxpayers. The spending cap has created considerable difficulties, particularly for relatively deprived councils. Sheffield, for example, is contemplating further redundancies and faces the cost of resolving safety problems with its hi-tech tram system. A change in government policies may allow councils the opportunity to resolve such problems without resort to higher council tax or job losses.
- Local authorities anticipate that a Labour government will allow them to *spend accumulated receipts from the sale of assets* such as land and council houses. This would enable them to undertake overdue capital expenditures and relieve the squeeze on their finances. An alternative is to develop more partnerships involving PFI.
- *Social factors* are always important to local authorities responsible for education, housing and other social services. There have been considerable changes in birth and death rates, marriage patterns and household types to which authorities must respond. Metropolitan authorities have lost population while the 'shires' and East Anglia have gained. Ethnic groups are growing fastest and councils such as Bradford must respond to changing needs or face resulting community pressure.
- *Environmental issues* continue to be important and authorities are under pressure to strike a balance between the need for new economic development and a desire for an improving environment. European Union funds have often supported projects in this area. One specific issue which has come to the fore in 1997 is the realization that up to 4.5 million new homes will be required over the next 20 years to cater to the changing household structure (i.e. single person). Authorities must identify suitable land for development and pressure groups are already mobilizing as in West Sussex where the Council for the Protection of Rural England aims to block greenfield development.
- The *millenium problem* concerns up to 40 per cent of all computers which are not programmed to distinguish between the 20th and 21st centuries. Local authorities are faced with considerable costs to reprogram their older systems.

- One new factor in 1996 was *rising militancy* among workforces whose pay had been limited by central government to a rise of 1.5 per cent per annum. This was significantly below the rate of inflation. However, the pre-election period has seen more generous, although staged, settlements. A post-election pay explosion could quickly see this factor back in the set!

Further sets could be developed to represent the major influences to be accounted for by businesses in financial services, import–export, retailing, construction and so forth. As seen above, though, the elements will vary and a threat for one organization may be an opportunity for another. Private security firms (Group 4, for example), are seizing the opportunity provided by the government in privatizing low-security prison facilities. CIM, who are potentially threatened by a Malaysian policy to reverse its large services deficit by encouraging foreign universities to set up campuses, have taken the opportunity of setting up a branch there as well as in Singapore.

> **QUESTION 6.4**
>
> Which functional areas of the business will be most affected by environmental set factors and which will be least affected?
> How will the research and development function be affected?
> What can the business do to influence elements in its set?
>
> (**See** Activity debrief at the end of this unit.)

The main sources of environmental data

Organizations that have the ability to sense environmental change and be proactive in their response to it tend to perform better than those that lack it. It often signals the need for organizational change and reformulation of marketing strategy, but there is no guarantee of the appropriate response taking place in time. This vitally depends on the quality of the information systems available to the business and the extent of management's understanding of the complex and often-interacting changes taking place in the external environment.

'To manage a business well is to manage its future, and to manage its future is to manage information' (M. Harper, Jr).

As Figure 6.4 shows, any business needs an integrated internal and external information system to provide the means for dovetailing organizational and marketing developments with environmental change.

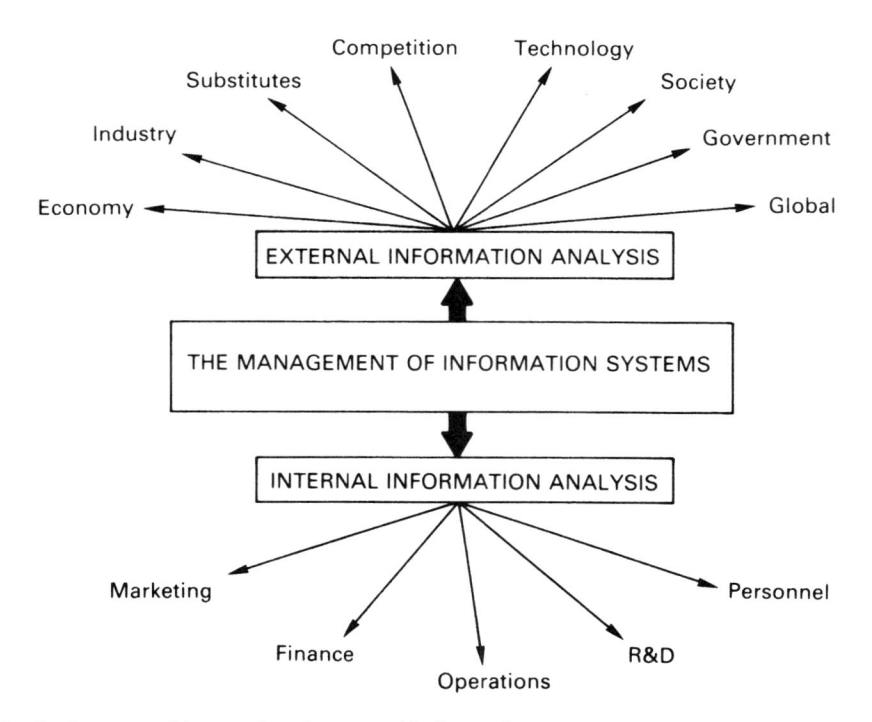

Figure 6.4 An integrated internal and external information system

Internal and external information systems

There are two main categories of existing information:

- *Internal data* gathered in-company as a result of operational activities (e.g. employment, cost and sales figures)
- *Secondary data* gathered from external sources (e.g. government statistics, published surveys, etc., see Figure 6.5).

Business information needs:
- Company reports, e.g. Companies Registration Office
- Quality press, e.g. *Financial Times*
- Business periodicals, e.g. *Management Today*
- Trade magazines, e.g. *Computer Weekly*
- Academic journals, e.g. *European Journal of Marketing*
- Government statistics, e.g. *ONS* (Office for National Statistics) *Annual Abstract*
- Directories, e.g. *Kompass*

Figure 6.5 Secondary data for a business

A third source of information is *primary data* commissioned specifically to fill knowledge gaps left by the much cheaper alternatives above.

> **EXAM TIP**
>
> The examiner will always give credit to candidates who not only make a relevant point in answer to an examination question but can also cite the source. Since sources of information are an explicit part of the CIM syllabus, you would be well advised to link different information sources to different sections in your file.
>
> For example, what sources would you use in analysing the competitive environment? Which are relevant in keeping in touch with population changes and the identification of new niche segments?

What kind of information is required?

Many different types of information are required, depending on the decisions to be taken. Examples of the more important types include:

Competitors
- Prices, discounts, credit terms, etc.
- Sales volumes by segment, product, region, distribution channel
- Market shares
- Promotional activities, catalogues, distributor incentives
- New product development, expansion plans, changes in personnel
- Financial strength and relationships with key stakeholders

Similar information is required on suppliers, distributors and potential entrants into the market.

Industry
- Sales volumes by product, segment, region and country
- Sales growth and seasonal/cyclical patterns
- Production capacities, levels, plans and stock positions
- Technical change and investment plans

Economy
- Main economic indicators – inflation, interest rates, vacancies
- Business confidence indicators – capacity utilization, investment
- Labour market changes
- National income, output and expenditure patterns
- Government taxation and spending plans

Similar factors could be identified in other areas of the PEST environment underlining the diverse nature of information requirements in modern business today. In an environment of rapid change, where time and delay can cost a company dearly, the ability to obtain a clear and accurate picture of developments can provide the firm with a distinct competitive advantage. Information is power, but to achieve this requires a knowledge not just of key sources of information but also of how to access them quickly and resource effectively.

> **EXAM TIP**
>
> News analysis is one means of assessing the importance of current environmental issues. Since editors only have limited space they must make critical choices as to what and what not to include. They will therefore tend to include subjects that are of current and future concern but exclude those they identify as 'yesterday's news'.
>
> One method of defining whether an economy is coming out of recession, for example, is to track the number of references to it in the quality press over time. As this index declines so the economy must be picking up, since writers and editors no longer see articles on it as 'news'.
>
> The conclusion must therefore be to keep your finger on the pulse of environmental change by scanning the news media regularly.

Internal sources

Many questions can only be answered by reference to internal records. The strengths and weaknesses of the business may be identified in this way, although this must be assessed relative to competitors. To be useful, however, this must be gathered in a form that is accessible, accurate and relevant to the forecast or evaluation required. The flow of information through a business should be analysed systematically to achieve these objectives.

> **QUESTION 6.5**
>
> The sales and marketing department is the primary interface between the business and its customers. What information should it generate? Suggest three key pieces of information from each of the following:
>
> - Management accountant
> - Purchasing department
> - Operations
>
> (**See** Activity debrief at the end of this unit.)

Published material

Such sources are seldom used regularly or systematically by business decision makers. The diffuse nature of many of the sources shown in Figure 6.5 makes collection, classification and distribution to interested managers an expensive and time-consuming process. The government is one of the main producers of primary data, published through the re-named Office of National Statistics (formerly CSO).

Published business information sources

Some larger organizations delegate a junior executive to undertake this task and circulate a regular summary to appropriate staff. Organizations such as McCarthy and Extel also grew by providing information on specific companies in a readily referenced format. However, while the value of such information in informing decisions has been recognized by perceptive marketing executives and planners, their use has been haphazard and on a need-to-know basis only.

> **ACTIVITY 6.6**
>
> The key skill for the sales executive and marketer to develop is to know *what information is available* on a particular issue and, most importantly, *where to find it*. Published material is available on most topics and is far cheaper than undertaking primary research.
>
> You *must* familiarize yourself with the operations and opportunities within a modern business library. Visit the best one in your locality and familiarize yourself with the following:
>
> - The index system – usually a computerized database enabling you to interrogate by subject, author, class number, etc.
> - The inter-library loans system allowing you to access material not held in the library itself. All you require is the title, author, publisher and date.
> - Electronic databases – these are often based on CD-ROM systems for easy use and linked to printers so that you can obtain a hard copy.

Trade sources

The usual means by which managers keeps informed of both internal and external developments, in many cases, is through the grapevine. They establish and build *networks* of information sources which can be drawn on when the need arises. Regular conversations with colleagues, customers and other stakeholder contacts provide a moving tapestry of events supplemented with such things as sales records and consultancy reports. Much of the material gathered from the sources in Figure 6.6 will be sifted, cross-referenced and assimilated on a day-to-day basis.

Figure 6.6 Trade sources and networks

Information at your fingertips

Keeping an ear to the ground (or, more likely, to the phone or the internet!) in this informal way may not always be effective in times of rapid change. The information may either come too late or not become available to the decision maker who requires it. The volume of potentially useful data appears boundless, and as it expands from year to year, the need to manage it more effectively becomes more pressing. Excellent companies must work more smartly if they are to survive, and this raises demand for better-quality information to support decisions.

A changing economic structure has also shifted the emphasis in favour of knowledge-intensive sectors such as financial services, retailing and high-technology industries. Small firms similarly add to the demand for value-added information services from government and consultancies.

Mass markets are also fragmenting into specialist niches as tastes become less standardized and predictable. Sophisticated marketing information and analysis is, however, required if businesses are to take advantage of the opportunities presented.

The explosion in business-focused information is a reflection of these forces. Sources range from new national newspapers such as *Sunday Business* to more than 3500 business-to-business magazines. Collectively, such sources are termed the 'business press'.

> **EXTENDING ACTIVITY 6.2**
>
> If you are part of a wider college group then a useful exercise to extend your knowledge of available information sources is to compile an *information booklet*. If you divide up the task and each cover a handful of references this should be manageable.
>
> The objective is to identify key sources of information on the environment classified under various headings and summarize in a short statement their location, ease of access, content, application, ease of use and 'star rating'.
>
> The categories might include, sources on companies; on industries; on the economy; on wider society; on international markets and developments; on trade media; business environment texts, etc.

On-line business information

An efficient information system must be able to programme information into the 'corporate memory' of organization members in much the same way as a computer. The objective is to make the information accessible and usable by the relevant decision maker when required. The power and flexibility of networked computer database systems now offer this capability and can support the more 'human' networks mentioned above.

Databases are revolutionizing management information systems. A database is simply a file of information in electronic form providing ease and speed of access and manipulation. On-line means that the database is stored on a remote computer but can be accessed directly by business users through phone lines. Real-time systems mean that they are constantly being updated with new inputs of information while CD-ROM systems are millions of pieces of information stored on compact discs, updated on a regular basis (e.g. monthly) and accessed flexibly by the computer. The rapid development and take-up by business of fax machines and intelligent printers is also expanding the potential of such information sources by providing hard copies to remote locations when required.

Some of the main types of databases currently available include those shown in Figure 6.7. Computers can therefore offer the solution to many of the marketer's problems. By keying in a competitor's name, for example, such systems can search out all available published material.

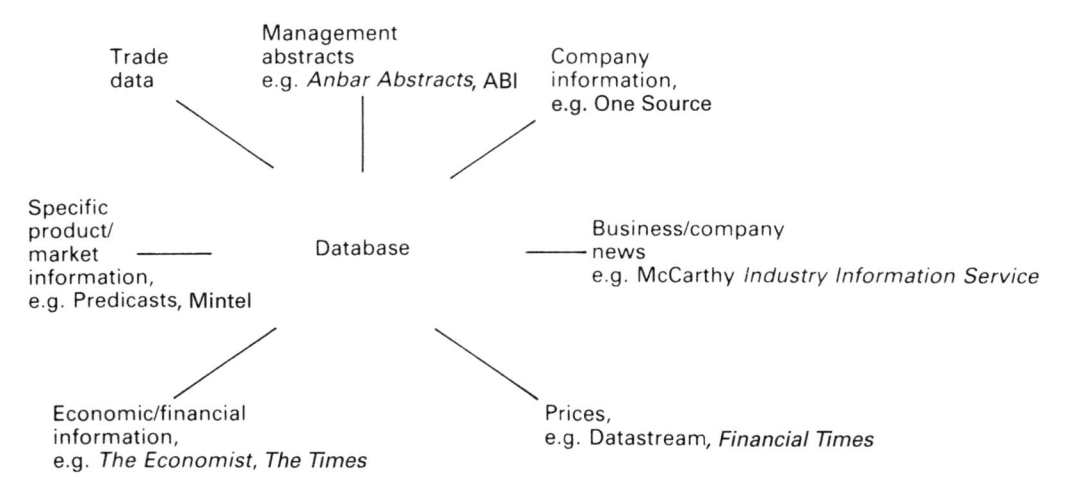

Database sources (Figure 6.7):
- Trade data
- Management abstracts, e.g. *Anbar Abstracts*, ABI
- Company information, e.g. One Source
- Specific product/market information, e.g. Predicasts, Mintel
- Business/company news, e.g. McCarthy *Industry Information Service*
- Economic/financial information, e.g. *The Economist*, *The Times*
- Prices, e.g. Datastream, *Financial Times*

Figure 6.7 Relevant database sources

> **QUESTION 6.6**
>
> List the types of information on competitors which will *not* be available in published sources. What other methods are available for obtaining information in the areas you have identified?
> (**See** Activity debrief at the end of this unit.)

Computers combined with communications technologies are generating a wealth of readily transmitted business information available at rapidly falling costs. Global knowledge brings global competition as Asian companies assess the competitiveness of Western markets as a prelude to exports or direct entry.

The benefits of on-line searching compared to traditional methods may be summarized as follows:

On-line features	*Benefits*
Speed in searching	Time-saving
Selectivity in searching	Quality data
Flexibility in searching	Comparative data
Interactive searching	Flexible scope
Data manipulation	Usable statistics
Up to data	Best available data
User-friendly	Will be used
Charge on actual use	Economic access
Professional methodology	Competitive edge

With information of particular importance to the marketer, areas of business database application should include:

- Market research
- Marketing plans
- Marketing presentations
- Sales force coordination
- Market analysis
- Sales analysis
- Customer communications

One final word of warning in regard to computer databases as a panacea for marketing solutions. There is a considerable *learning curve* involved in the effective use of such systems and many commercially available databases are expensive to subscribe to for any but the largest company. It is also the case that the most important information, namely that relating to future plans and developments, is not available even on real-time systems.

> **EXTENDING ACTIVITY 6.3**
>
> As a final exercise in this area of information sources and their interpretation by the sales executive and marketer you should undertake a *competitor analysis*. Taking your own company or a selected plc, select one of the main markets it competes in and identify its main local, national and international competitors using directories such as *Kompass*.
>
> Gather and summarize information on these companies using sources such as the Companies Registration Office, Extel and Datastream. Trade sources should also be used for 'insider' assessment of competitor strengths and weaknesses. Trade association statistics and an interview with the research officer would be particularly useful.
>
> You need to establish a framework of criteria by which to compare and contrast the companies – think of what aspects are most important here. You will certainly want to assess their product and its positioning, pricing, promotional mix, unique selling propositions and distribution channels.
>
> Present your report to the marketing director or your college tutor for their assessment.

The political environment

This unit will be concluded by a summary review of one of the least predictable aspects of the macro-environment. The political environment might produce a variety of emotions ranging from apathy to outright cynicism, but it is one that marketers ignore at their peril, since its impacts on business activity are both numerous and potentially damaging.

National and European legislation and the decisions of public authorities have an increasing influence on business activities and must be monitored carefully to:

- Alert management to impending legislation
- Mobilize efforts to represent stakeholder interests to the legislators
- Develop awareness of the intentions of those public bodies that can make decisions affecting business operations
- Identify likely changes arising out of electoral shifts
- Assess the implications of political manifestos and the evolving convictions and philosophies of the party and ministers in power.

The government also controls the macro-economic framework and its decisions affect both its position as a major customer of the private sector and the political distribution of the tax burden. Business has a collective interest in the relative burden of business taxes and rates as well as trends in the size and composition of government spending on goods and services. These will be examined in more detail in Unit 7.

The public sector itself has undergone a fundamental transformation in recent years with policies of privatization, deregulation and the contracting-out to private tender of more and more local authority and civil service functions. The conviction politics of Margaret Thatcher based on the values of private ownership and an enterprise culture have, however, been modified in the 1990s by the 'responsible' capitalism of John Major and its attendant social charters. Blairism seeks a partnership of private initiative and responsible public enterprise to promote the welfare of all members of society.

DEFINITION 6.2

Match up the following terms with their definitions:

- Privatization
- Deregulation
- Enterprise culture
- Social charter
- Party manifesto
- First past the post
- Electoral cycle

1. The candidate with the most votes cast in an election is the winner, irrespective of the distribution of votes to other contenders.
2. Removal of rules and requirements restricting competition.
3. A programme of intended policies if successfully elected.
4. A 4–5 year pattern of stop - go economic activity.
5. A climate that encourages and approves self-reliance, entrepreneurship and individual wealth creation.
6. Transfer of 50 per cent or more of the voting shares to private hands.
7. Published performance standards for customer service in public sector organizations.

(**See** Activity debrief at the end of this unit.)

The political framework

Political systems are located along a spectrum ranging from totalitarianism to popular democracy. The main features of these two systems are outlined below:

Totalitarianism	*Democracy*
Power concentrated in single leader of the ruling party	Universal suffrage
	Periodic free elections
Official ideology rules	Freedom of speech/media
Repression of opposition parties	Open political competition
	Pluralistic – power spread
Central direction/command	Majority rule/minorities are protected and equal under the law
Government controls media	
Minorities persecuted	Pressure groups free to lobby between elections

Political power is the ability to bring about change through influencing the behaviour of others. All organizations are affected by politics because people have different views, ideals and interests. Disagreements naturally arise over such matters as objectives to be pursued, decisions to be made and, perhaps most importantly, resources to be allocated. These must be resolved, otherwise conflict would result and organizations and indeed society would cease to function effectively. Political stability arises out of the identification and resolution of disputes through a mixture of authority, enforcement and compromise.

Political stability is important, not least to investors who wish to minimize their risks. Multinationals, for example, were reluctant to invest in Britain during the labour unrest of the late 1970s and early 1980s, while the Tiananmen Square incident in Beijing in 1989 had serious repercussions not only in China itself but also in Hong Kong and other adjacent territories.

QUESTION 6.7

What are the areas and issues where 'politics' are involved in:

- The sales and marketing department?
- Relationships between marketing and finance?

What sources of information should the marketer consult to keep a finger on the political environment pulse? Are there more cost-effective means of keeping abreast of national and supra-national legislative developments?
(**See** Activity debrief at the end of this unit.)

The political process is outlined in Figure 6.8 and is based on the British system. It is, however, applicable in general terms to most democratic market economies.

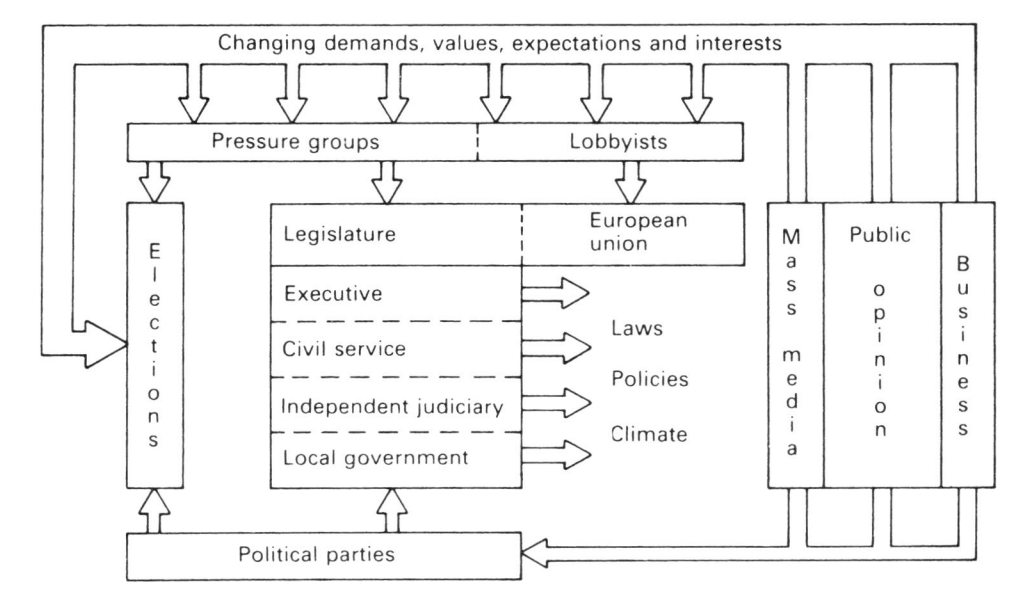

Figure 6.8 An outline of the British political system

The main features of this process will be explained in turn together with the implications for business and the marketer. The inputs into the political system originate in wider society and arise out of their changing attitudes, perceptions and demands. These will be diverse and conflicting and tend to coalesce around support for alternative party manifestos at election time, e.g. lower taxes, devolution of power to the regions, more education spending, etc. Political parties seek to differentiate themselves from their rivals, but also appeal to a sufficiently wide constituency as to gain election to government.

Elections are the ultimate democratic control over government and provides the electorate with an opportunity to pass judgement on performance. It is also an opportunity to judge the 'promises and proposals' of the opposition. Fear of defeat at the next general election should encourage account of the public wishes.

QUESTION 6.8

Since voters are very much like customers as far as political parties are concerned, what advice would the sales executive or marketer offer to the election campaign manager of:

- The party currently in office?
- The main opposition party?
- A Green party looking to establish a base in Parliament?

(**See** Activity debrief at the end of this unit.)

Britain has a first-past-the-post electoral system which produces a number of characteristics:

- A simple majority of seats contested gives one party the power to form the government.
- No post-war government has ever won a 'majority' of votes cast.
- Smaller parties do not see their proportion of the vote reflected in seats won.
- Three party elections involving Labour, the Liberal Democrats and the Conservatives have resulted in the majority of the electorate voting against the latter but splitting the opposition vote.

This appears unfair but elections are held to produce governments. There has also been considerable resistance in Parliament to a more proportional voting system, despite the fact that Britain is out of step with the rest of Europe. The key question is whether a strong and effective government is what is wanted or a more representative one.

QUESTION 6.9

Summarize from a business point of view the case for and against electoral reform.
(**See** Activity debrief at the end of this unit.)

The main concern of business is for a minimum of instability arising out of political decision making, a dependable planning horizon and a positive climate in which to operate. With Conservative governments in power since 1979 there has certainly been continuity of policy, even when the sense of direction has sometimes been lacking. However, the landslide election of a Labour government may again cause discontinuity. Some policies will be reversed, institutions abolished and legislation amended to reflect New Labour political philosophies despite assurances to the contrary. Business must ponder the implications of Tony Blair's cabinet implementing their pledges, or not, as the case may be. 'New Labour's Ten Pledges' are:

- To increase the proportion of national income spent on education.
- To reduce the proportion spent on the welfare bills of social failure.
- To cut spending on NHS bureaucracy and increase it on patient care.

- To reduce the number of long-term unemployed and cut the number of jobless youngsters by more than half.
- To halve the time it takes young offenders to get to court.
- To keep government borrowing and inflation within low targets.
- To keep the promises Labour makes on tax.
- To reduce class sizes in primary schools and raise school standards.
- To devolve power to Scotland, Wales and the regions of England.
- To build a new and constructive relationship in Europe.

This discontinuity creates uncertainty for business, especially if the party in power is changed frequently. Similar discontinuity may face the people of Hong Kong after June 1997 although much political energy has been invested in assuring smooth transference of power, so limiting adverse business and popular reaction.

The electoral cycle

The other source of political instability is the tendency for elections to 'influence' business cycles. Governments know that reducing taxes and increasing spending as an election approaches will create a temporary sense of well-being. Disposable income rises, as does employment and business activity. This will be short-lived since prices also tend to rise, as do imports, and action will have to be taken to reverse the resulting inflation and trade deficit. However, since there will be a lag before such effects are felt, the government may well win re-election and be in a position to apply the economic brakes. These can then be released as the next general election approaches. This may explain the reluctance of the Chancellor to raise interest rates prior to the election despite strong pressure from the Bank of England.

One final point to note is that an adversarial two- or three-party system does tend to widen the credibility gap between politically nurtured expectations, on the one hand, and actual performance of the economy, on the other. It is as well that the marketer takes with a pinch of salt the ideals and objectives advertised and promoted by the various parties in general and the government in particular. Politics is said to be the 'art of the possible' but this sometimes has a habit of being less than expected!

ACTIVITY 6.7

The sales executive and marketer should always be aware of the political agenda. Governments issue their plans annually in the Queen's speech (or your national equivalent) while party manifestos are published in the run-up to an election.

You should scan the contents of these when they become available to assess their implications either directly through proposed legislation or indirectly on stakeholder groups.

Central government

Parliament is the supreme legislative authority in Britain. Although private members (of Parliament) can propose bills the vast majority that become law are government sponsored or supported. The marketer should understand the origins of new laws and how businesses might influence their form and content:

Stages	Influence
1 *Origin* Popular issue, committee of inquiry recommendation, election pledge, pressure group, government initiative, to close loopholes.	Trade association may press for legislation
2 *Green Paper* Government puts ideas on paper for discussion	Monitor and contribute if industry interests are to be affected
3 *White paper* Government sets out definite proposals	Comments from parties affected will be accounted/included

Note: It is vitally important that business views on proposed laws are made clearly and persuasively at this time. If legislation is inevitable, then business must ensure that it is workable and no unintended disadvantageous side-effects result. Emotional legislation in response to a public outcry is to be avoided through active lobbying.

4 *Draft bill – first reading*
5 *Main debate – second reading*   MPs can be lobbied to speak in support
6 *Committee stage*
7 *Report stage — to full House of Commons*
8 *Final debate and amendments – third reading*   Last opportunity to lobby support
9 *To House of Lords – process repeated*
10 *Possible reference back to Commons*
11 *Royal Assent – the law is enacted*

The process is long and complicated, placing a limit on how much legislative business can be completed. Virtually all government-sponsored bills become law although the opposition can use delaying tactics. Case law, in contrast, evolves through independent judicial decisions and is not susceptible to influence by business, although the right of appeal exists.

> **EXTENDING ACTIVITY 6.4**
>
> The ability of business lobbies to influence legislation which affects them is considerable. The spirits industry in 1996, for example, was able to persuade the Chancellor to reduce the duty by 4 per cent but was unable to prevent concerns over the attractions of alcopops to underage drinkers forcing a 40 per cent rise in duty. The tobacco lobby convinced Conservative ministers to vote against the EU directive banning all forms of advertising (now reversed by Labour). The motor industry lobby campaigned successfully to remove special taxes on new cars. The farm and defence lobbies are other notable examples.
>
> Select either a current Green or White Paper, or a recently enacted piece of legislation affecting a strong business lobby and compare the original proposals with the final legal form. Try to identify why and how the lobby was effective. Draw up a list of groups for and against the legislation.

Pressure groups were discussed in some detail in Unit 4, where it was concluded that from a pluralistic view they are a good thing. They represent a channel through which individuals and groups can make their views known to governments between elections. They are much more important than political parties in terms of membership and represent numerous, overlapping and competing influences within society.

Pressure group effectiveness requires *commitment, cohesion, organization, resources* and *strategic positioning*. Ministers who decide government policies need pressure groups. They often have a statutory duty to consult and require advice, information and feedback of views and reactions from those affected. They favour those groups with the ability to deliver on bargains and compromises made and who provide support in return. They also need co-operation in the implementation and administration of new laws.

> **EXAM TIP**
>
> Both the sales and the marketing environment are large syllabi and diverse subjects of which to keep abreast. So, on the principle that two heads are better than one, why don't you pool resources with a fellow student and actively compare notes and ideas? Your combined strengths will produce synergy (1 + 1 = 3) and help to reduce the overall workload.

Businesses are strategically well positioned to obtain political support when Conservatives are in office but less successful when Labour rules. It should be noted, however, that effective pressure group activity tends to stimulate the development of counter-pressure. Countervailing action between rival groups and coalitions limits the influence of any one grouping. Ministers will also be in a position to play one group off against another!

The professional lobbyist

Lobbying may be defined as influencing members of the legislature and soliciting their votes. For pressure to be effective it must be exerted *where and when the decisions are being made*.

The value of professional lobbyists to a business are as follows:

- *Monitoring* — an early-warning service on forthcoming legislation
- *Interpreting* — the implications of draft bills
- *Identify* — MPs/ministers with a special interest in your issue
- *Inform* — MPs/decision makers about (your) industry developments
- *Prepare* — background briefs and cases for busy MPs
- *Coordinate* — constituency 'protest' letters to MPs
- *Advise* — the business on strategy and tactics to adopt.

While there is little likelihood of stopping proposed legislation, the lobbyist will be seeking to persuade ministers and senior civil servants to *think again on details, clarify ambiguity, gain assurances and secure legislation the industry can live with*!

The media

Public perceptions and public opinion are clearly important inputs into the political process. The climate the government seeks to create through its policies and laws is an equally important output intended to positively influence these opinions. If successful, the public will be more likely to re-elect the government concerned.

The mass media, including press, radio and television, are important influences on these perceptions and opinions. They supply awareness of political issues and scrutiny of government behaviour and performance. As with pressure groups, they can influence decision makers and their policies through their campaigns. Investigative journalism in particular can have serious impacts on business as well as politicians. For example, the Malaysian embargo on British exports in 1994 was a direct reaction to press reports in *The Times* and the cash-for-questions exposé prompted a radical overhaul of Parliamentary privilege.

Public relations is an equally important aspect of marketing management and special skills are required to create and maintain mutually beneficial relationships with the media. It is a two-way relationship based on principles similar to those between a minister and a pressure group.

> **EXTENDING ACTIVITY 6.5**
>
> If you were contacted by the local media requesting an interview regarding an issue arising over the marketing of a new product how would you respond and what would you say?
> (**See** Activity debrief at the end of this unit.)

Local government and other government agencies

Brief mention should be made of other dimensions of government with which the marketer might interact. Supra-national bodies, like the European Union, whose powers may supersede national governments will be dealt with in the final unit. Much closer to home are local authorities to whom businesses, both large and small, will have to make representations from time to time. If a problem area is within local government jurisdiction it is usually politically inappropriate to seek redress centrally. Local politicians are protective of their independence and often represent opposition parties and policies. The appropriate decision-making authority has therefore to be identified and lobbied, as in the case of central government.

Local government in Britain has undergone radical change in the last ten years. Their powers to set business rates, raise taxes independently and decide expenditure totals have all been constrained by central government actions such as spending caps. Setting of national standards in education and other social services have also limited local autonomy. In previous units we have learnt that local government officers are now service facilitators rather than direct providers because of the requirement on them to also offer contracts out to competitive bidding.

This has made local authorities much more marketing orientated in pursuing value for money services for their ratepayers. Formerly 'free' services, such as libraries and leisure centres, are now run on a more commercial basis. Consumer needs are identified and services provided priced and promoted in order to cover costs and make a contribution to council funds.

Apart from bidding for council contracts in street cleaning, parks maintenance, refuse disposal, etc., there are also opportunities for working jointly on projects combining civic improvement and commercial development. Local authorities are important stakeholders since they decide planning applications, control the supply of school leavers and provide a variety of inspectorates that impact on local business. It is an aspect of the environment, therefore, where the business should build positive and mutually beneficial relationships.

> **ACTIVITY 6.8**
>
> Local authorities produce Economic Development Plans. Contact your local planning office and arrange to view one. Consider whether any of the proposed developments represent threats of opportunities for your business.
>
> List the ways in which your business could get its views heard locally.
>
> (**See** Activity debrief at the end of this unit.)

One final area to note is that of government agencies and other quasi-government bodies. The intention of the current government is to transform much of the civil service into executive agencies. These will be free from day-to-day control by ministers and therefore able to focus on the achievement of long-term performance objectives. Some will also be privatized. If the experience of previous privatizations is a guide then this will underpin a significant rise in both marketing and competitiveness in the areas concerned. Such agencies are unelected, however, and this has raised questions over their independence and accountability. This has led to a Code of Practice for making such public appointments and the appointment of auditors to seek out malpractice.

Summary

In this unit we have seen that:

- It is crucially important to monitor change and for the organization to be specifically aware of its environmental set.
- There are problems in making accurate forecasting when the environment is turbulent but scenarios can provide management with alternative views of the future.
- Marketers must draw on internal and external sources of information. Computer databases now offer the potential for selective analysis of particular environments when required.
- The political process is complex but pressure points are available to business lobbies at central and local levels.
- The political environment is a source of potential instability for business especially at election times, when outcomes are uncertain.
- The media play an important role in setting the political agenda. The influence of lobbyists is less readily detected but of greater importance to business interests.

Activity debrief

Definition 6.1 4, 2, 3, 5, 6, 1.
Definition 6.2 6, 2, 5, 7, 3, 1, 4.
Question 6.1 Few examples. Craft industries, personal services (e.g. funerals and nursing homes).
Question 6.2 Forecasts are necessary whenever resource decisions affecting the future (e.g. investment in plant and equipment, new product research and development, etc.) require a view to be taken of future supply and demand conditions. Factors affecting supply and demand must be forecast, which in effect means all relevant factors in the micro- and macro-environments.

Question 6.4 Marketing and sales most affected, perhaps administration and after-sales least affected. R/D affected by the technical and competitive set factors. It can use the marketing mix.

Question 6.5 Sales volume by product, product group, region, channel and market segment. Intelligence reports on competitor prices and promotion, strengths and weaknesses. Assessment of own promotional mix effectiveness. Accounts provide data on cost of sales, debtors, overall sales analysis by customer, variances. Purchasing provides assessment of supplier reliability, stock control and availability, service levels. Operations provide order status, completion dates, production capacity.

Question 6.6 Information on strategies, product developments planned promotions, future intentions, likely reactions. Methods range from industrial espionage to debriefing former employees to questioning associated stakeholders.

Question 6.7 Think about office politics and positioning for promotions and perks. Departmental conflicts arise over resources and priorities. The quality press and periodicals like *The Economist* and *Newsweek*. Trade associations and lobbyists.

Question 6.8 Think in terms of product positioning, 'value for voting' and differentiation (of manifestos and policies, i.e. clear blue water between the parties).

Question 6.9

Case for	*Case against*
Coalition government produces continuity of policies	Allows a strong government to take bold initiatives
Avoids short-term focus on the next election	Coalitions lead to compromise
	Too many small parties
Moderate consensus policies avoids the extremes	Government more susceptible to pressure groups
Avoidance of extreme swings in government enables planning	Strong link MP – constituency

Activity 6.1 No calculators, no colour TVs, no unemployment, no equal status for women, etc.

Activity 6.8 A business person could stand for the council, cooperate with initiatives, be a member of a Training and Education Council, establish relationships with local schools and colleges, etc.

Extending activity 6.1 First-hand experience of customer base. Realism if believed to feed into budgets and targets but may corrupt if bonus payments related to them. Too close to market.

Extending activity 6.5
- Don't be rushed – no obligation to give interview there and then!
- Don't start an interview until you know why, why *you*, who is calling, which paper, how long, what's wanted
- Don't do it there and then – phone back
- Gather your thoughts – take advice
- Prepare a statement if you are suspicious of their motives
- Don't answer leading or hypothetical questions
- Keep it short and to the point. Be polite and positive
- Don't make off-the-record comments.

Examination hints and specimen questions

The importance of this area of the syllabus has been outlined earlier. The specimen question is a long one and you must *read it very carefully* to ensure that you understand what the examiner requires. As you will see, it combines a knowledge of elements in this unit and the next since its focus is macro-economics. Once you have attempted to answer it within the 30 minute time constraint turn to end of Unit 7 and compare it to the first question posed.

1. (a) You have been asked to prepare a presentation on: 'The collection and assessment of macro economic data'
   (b) Write a series of structured prompts for use in this presentation outlining sources of information you would recommend and why. (10 marks)

Briefly summarize the economic situation in your country using such information under appropriate headings. (10 marks)

(CIM specimen Marketing Environment paper 1994)

2 (a) What do you understand by **two** of the following terms:
- Secondary stakeholders
- The macro environment
- Social responsibility
- The environmental set (10 marks)

(b) Using any company of your choice, produce and justify an environmental set. You should include and rank at least five factors in your set. (10 marks)

(CIM Marketing Environment paper, June 1995)

Hints: Indicative content and approach

Question 1(a)
The main sources of macro economic data would include:

- Government statistical sources
- Independent forecasting groups
- Bank reviews and forecasts
- Employer association surveys (e.g. CBI leading indicators)
- Quality newspaper coverage
- Databases
- Other sources such as trade associations, chambers of commerce.
- These should be set out in the prompt form requested in the question.
- The 'why' aspect would involve discussion of the source's availability, cost, timeliness, accuracy, specificity and comparability.

Question 1(b)
- The second part of the question is in what is likely to be a frequent format.
- This requires the candidate, who may be from Singapore or Trinidad, to relate their knowledge of the environment to their own national circumstances.
- This underlines the importance of keeping abreast of developments across the board in your own economy.
- The last part of this question will be discussed at the end of the next unit when you will have mastered the economic environment.

Question 2(a)
- Make sure you only attempt two parts.
- Avoid attempting such a question if you know the answer to the first part but can only guess at the second (as many candidates who had not studied this workbook did!)
- Don't spend too much time on the first part – only a concise summary is possible and required for 5 marks. Define them, produce one or two examples and briefly explain their role, function and importance.

Question 2(b)
- Be sure to use a company context – your own or a high profile one from a sector you are familiar with.
- Include five factors (5 × 2 marks) but for full marks you must rank them in terms of actual/potential impact on the company.
- Rising interest rates, for example, could be justified if the company is highly geared or dependent on credit sales.

Marketing Environment – test question
(a) Distinguish between a scenario and a forecast. (6 marks)
(b) Using a bullet point format, provide:

(i) One scenario based on the assumption that your government wins the next election.
(ii) One scenario based on the assumption that the main opposition party wins the next election. (10 marks)
(c) Identify **two** important marketing implications of either scenario (i) or scenario (ii).
(4 marks)

Hint

Attempt this question having read this unit but also the policy section of Unit 7. It is a challenging question and requires you to understand the policy differences between the two parties and how these would impact on the marketing environment. Note that only 5 marks are available per scenario so only a limited number of bullet points need be provided.

UNIT 7

The macro-economic environment

OBJECTIVES

In this fundamental unit you will:

- Understand, in basic terms, the workings of the economy and the role and objectives of government in influencing it.
- Recognize the use and limitations of economic indicators.
- Identify the nature of the business cycle and its significance for business decision making.
- Appreciate the issues of current importance in macro-economics.

By the end of this unit you will be able to:

- Evaluate measures of economic activity and living standards.
- Understand the conflicts in achieving macro-economic objectives.
- Assess the likely effects of alternative economic policies.
- Evaluate the varying impacts and implications for marketers in different types of organization.

STUDY GUIDE

The economic environment is one area where we all have first-hand experience. Not only do we read the newspapers and listen to items on television or radio, we also feel the direct impact of economic events such as rising taxes at budget time, a falling exchange rate or a pay freeze. However, a little knowledge is said to be a dangerous thing, and we need to set our day-to-day experience within a framework of understanding as to how the economy works.

Macro-economics is about the *aggregate* behaviour of consumers, businesses and governments. Concern is with the general or average price level rather than the prices of individual products, and interest focuses on the output, income and spending of society in total. The rate of economic growth is also of central importance as are cyclical fluctuations around this trend.

Despite the wide focus on aggregates and a very limited ability to influence them, all businesses must take very careful account of this environment. Decisions on capital investment, the timing of a new product launch or hiring and firing, for example, will need to be set against the general economic background. Unanticipated movements in interest or exchange rates can quite literally convert expected profit into loss.

The economy is a complex system and the marketer who can master the diagnosis of current economic problems and anticipate the direction of policy changes will possess a considerable edge over rivals. An 'economic way of thinking' as regards this aspect of the environment is therefore a useful attribute for you to develop!

This unit requires careful reading since you must understand rather than memorize the subject matter. Allow yourself at least 3 hours to read and reread its contents. Further reading to support your studies and assist in tackling the questions and activities can be found in *Economic Analysis and Marketing Practice* by Hatton and Oldroyd, Chapters 15–21.

Subdivide your macro-economic environment file into subsections on: Measurement of economic performance; Macro-economic objectives; The Business Cycle; Economic policy and relevant indicators (divide this into Fiscal, Monetary, Physical and Supply side policies) and Management implications.

This is an area where there is no shortage of information so you will have to be selective in what you file. Your goal is to be able to provide an outline economic assessment of your own country, assess and give examples of economic policy impacts on business and marketers and finally evaluate how a business should respond in varying economic circumstances.

This unit will consider only the national economy. The impact of external trade and payments will be taken up in the final unit.

A model of the economy

To understand how the macro-economy works you must think in terms of 'flows' between households and businesses, banks and governments. These flows are composed of either incomes or expenditures, and circulate around the economic system. If we start our model with households and firms, we can see in Figure 7.1 that households, as the *owners* of productive resources, receive a flow of income from firms who employ them to produce goods and services.

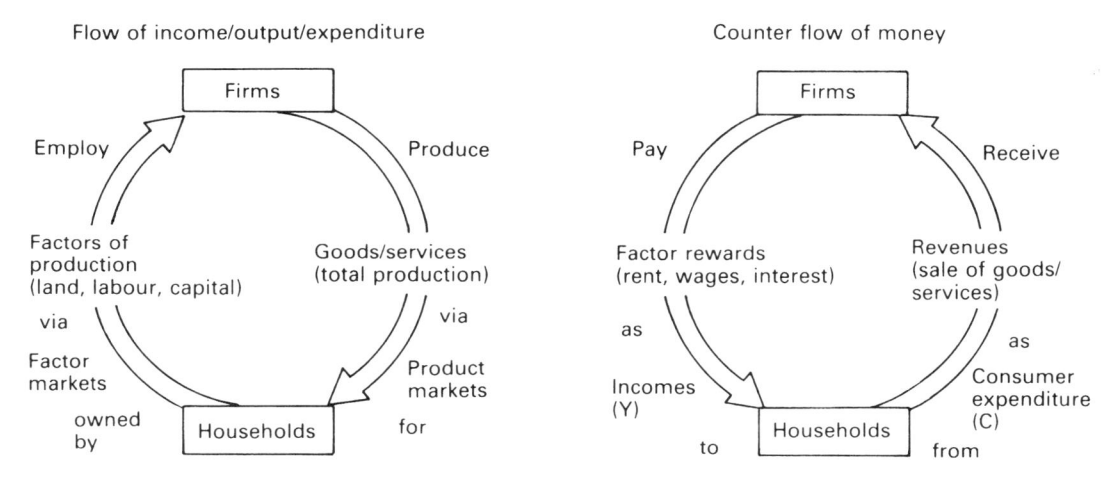

Figure 7.1 The circular flow of economic activity

The households use this income (i.e. wages, salaries, rents, interest and distributed profit) to purchase goods and services from firms. This flow of expenditure is demand for the products of the firms and the revenue received meets the cost of inputs for the next round of production. In this simple model all income is spent and the flow continues period after period.

> **EXAM TIP**
>
> This syllabus replaces one on economics in the old scheme. Since we are now considering all aspects of the environment, you will not be expected to understand economics to the depth required previously. An *appreciation* of economics is what is now expected and there will be no requirement to reproduce detailed analysis.

In reality, of course, households would probably save a portion of their income. Consider the effect of this on the circular flow. Imagine it as a flow of liquid spending power for which an equivalent flow of real goods and services is produced and which in turn provides employment for available resources. As we can see in Figure 7.2, it is a *leakage* and the level of the flow will fall while savings continue to be made out of income received.

```
              ┌─────────────┐
         ┌───▶│ Individuals │───▶ Savings
         │    └─────────────┘        (S)
         │                 │
        (Y)               (C)
         │                 │
         │    ┌─────────────┐
         └────│    Firms    │◀──┘
              └─────────────┘
```

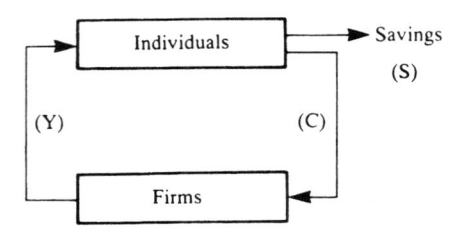

Figure 7.2 The effect of savings

You will probably argue, however, that since a fall in household spending forces firms to cut back production and because of lower revenues hire fewer resources and pay out less income, so the newly unemployed will spend their savings, channelling demand back into the flow.

QUESTION 7.1

What will the households still in employment save as they see unemployment rise and fear that perhaps they may be made redundant next?

Can you now explain what economists call 'the paradox of thrift'?

- Think about your younger days and what you were encouraged to do with presents of money.
- Think also about the opportunity cost of consumption today compared with investment and more consumption tomorrow.

(**See** Activity debrief at the end of this unit.)

Of course, the above situation is simplistic, since savings are normally not just withdrawn from the flow and hoarded but are deposited in financial institutions where interest may be earned. These funds are normally then borrowed by either other households or firms and respent in the circular flow restoring equilibrium as seen in Figure 7.3.

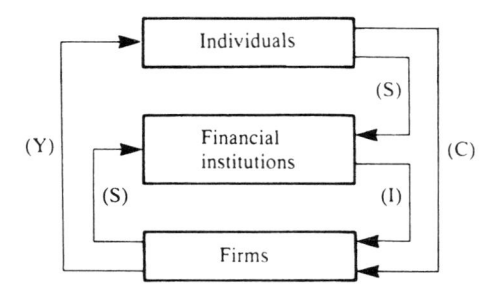

Figure 7.3 The effect of investment

Investment is known as an *injection* into the flow and creates demand for the producers of plant, equipment and supplies. However, is there any guarantee that sufficient aggregate demand will be forthcoming to sustain production at the desired level? Those who decide to invest are often different people from those who save, i.e. the savings leakage may not be exactly balanced by the investment injection.

QUESTION 7.2

Can you think of a mechanism that might bring savings and investment to equality at the equilibrium level? Do you think this mechanism will work quickly and effectively?

What is the condition for equilibrium or stability in the flow?

(**See** Activity debrief at the end of this unit.)

To complete our model and make it realistic we introduce flows to the government and the rest of the world (Figure 7.4). Households pay taxes on income and also expenditure and these are leakages from the flow. Similarly, spending on imported goods and services is demand for the output of foreign firms. Government spending and exports, on the other hand, are injections of purchasing power into the flow.

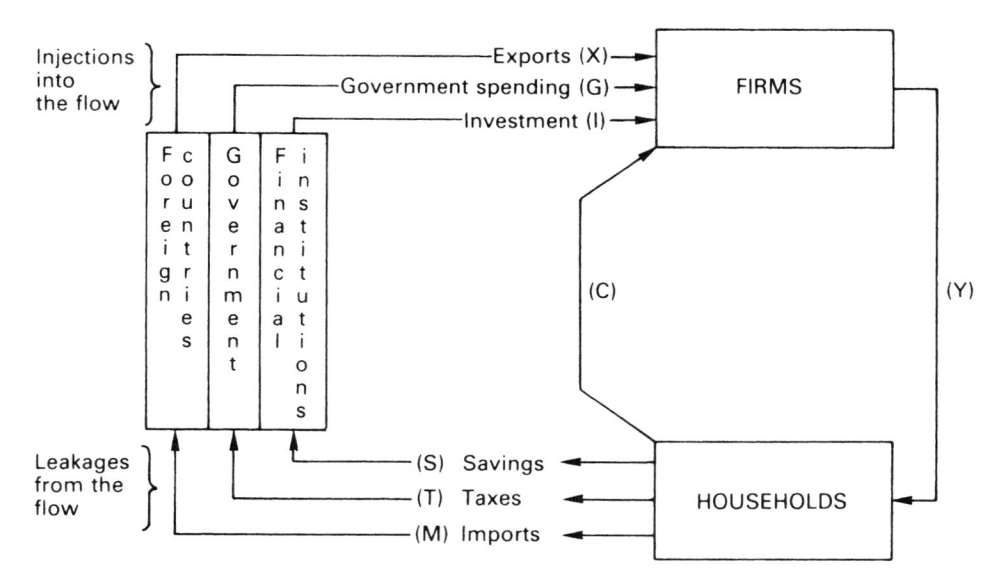

Figure 7.4 The full-economy model of injections and leakages

To summarize:

- Savings, all taxes and imports are leakages from the flow.
- Investment, government spending and exports are injections.
- The flow is in equilibrium when leakages = injections, i.e. $S + T + M = I + G + X$.
- If injections exceed leakages and there are unemployed resources in the economy then national income, output and expenditure rise.
- If leakages exceed injections, national income falls.
- *Aggregate demand* is the sum of:
  Consumption + Investment + Government + Exports − Imports
  (i.e. $C + I + G + X - M$)

This is the *pressure of demand on domestic businesses* to produce goods and services and is of critical importance in determining levels of activity and employment.

ACTIVITY 7.1

Draw a diagram linking the income and expenditure flows between households, firms, government and overseas and trace the effects of the following:

- An increase in domestic consumption even though total spending on consumption remains unchanged.
- The government agrees to fund a high-speed rail link.

Use newspaper or bank review reports to calculate the pressure of demand in your economy relative to capacity. Is it rising or falling? What is the leading aggregate in the total? (**See** Activity debrief at the end of this unit.)

Deflationary and inflationary gaps

If there is insufficient aggregate demand to enable businesses to operate profitably utilizing all available resources in an economy, a *deflationary gap* exists. This means the flow will be in equilibrium at less than full employment. Alternatively, if aggregate demand exceeds the amount necessary to secure employment of all available resources, an *inflationary gap* would exist. General prices would rise to ration out the available supply of goods.

An economy like Britain, still with relatively high unemployment and low inflation, is a current example of the former gap (though it is narrowing fast), while Hong Kong, with the opposite conditions, is an example of the latter. Since neither situation is desirable you may conclude that the solution is to remove the gaps. This would involve injecting extra purchasing power for the former and withdrawing the excess demand for the latter. This would have to involve government action and such policies will be discussed later in this unit.

QUESTION 7.3

If your economy, along with other trading partners, is stuck in a deep recession with activity levels falling and unemployment climbing to disturbingly high rates:

- Which of the aggregate demand components would you expect to rise, fall or stay unchanged, and why?
- Which component(s) could be altered?
- Would falling interest rates, exchange rates and wage rates:
  Increase activity levels in the short run?
  Increase activity rates in the long term?

(**See** Activity debrief at the end of this unit.)

The multiplier and accelerator

An extra injection of government or investment spending actually increases the level of income in the flow by more than the initial expenditure. This *multiplier effect* arises due to the circular nature of the flow. The injection creates demand for extra output which requires businesses to employ more resources, thus generating new incomes which are paid to households. Households receiving this income pay taxes, buy imports and save but the rest is spent on domestic consumer goods and services at the second round of the process.

The businesses produce more output to meet this demand, more resources are brought into employment and incomes are paid out to households and the process repeats. Leakages determine the ultimate size of the multiplier. The higher these are as a proportion of the circular flow, the lower the multiplier value and vice versa.

Employment is affected in a similar way in that construction jobs are created directly by, say, a Channel Tunnel type project. As these workers receive incomes they spend them in the local economy on goods and services, creating further jobs in these sectors. Do note, however, that the multiplier also works in reverse, as falling injections (e.g. on a contracting road spending programme) cause a cumulative fall in income, output and jobs.

QUESTION 7.4

The multiplier may be defined as:

$$\frac{\text{Change in national income}}{\text{Change in injection}}$$

It may also be expressed as:

$$\frac{1}{\text{Leakage ratios}}$$

If an industrial economy has the following leakage ratios calculate the value of the *realistic multiplier* for a $5 billion project:

Taxes 0.4 ; imports 0.2 ; savings 0.1

If your government decided to cut the tax bill by $5 billion would the size of the tax multiplier effect be smaller or larger than the investment multiplier?

(**See** Activity debrief at the end of this unit.)

The *accelerator* reinforces the effect of the multiplier. It arises from the fact that the value of capital equipment required to produce a given annual volume of output is four or five times as great. For example, if capital has a useful life of ten years and total car production of 2 million units is supplied by ten similar-sized plants then average replacement investment, equivalent to one plant, is required each year. Suppose that household demand rises 10 per cent to 2.2 million units. By how much will investment rise?

You may well be surprised at the answer, since a 100 per cent rise in investment spending is substantial and will trigger further multiplier expansions in income. In practice, of course, the effect is not usually this dramatic. The car firms will wish to be sure that the increase in demand will be sustained before expanding capacity. They may also utilize existing plants more intensively or repair plant rather than scrap it. In any case, the capital goods sector will find it difficult to cope with a doubling of demand.

> **QUESTION 7.5**
>
> What would happen if investment doubled but sales then stabilized at 2.2 million in the following year? What would happen if sales then fell back to 2 million units?
>
> Given that multipler–accelerator effects do operate in an economy, what kind of economic activity pattern would you expect over time?
> (**See** Activity debrief at the end of this unit.)

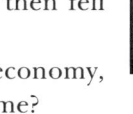

The measurement and meaning of national income

The circular flow represents the value of goods and services produced in an economy. This can be measured in three ways:

- *National income*   the incomes created from producing the output
- *National output*   sum of the value added by each domestic firm
- *National Expenditure*   aggregate spending on national output

Annual gross domestic product or GDP is what is being measured and is the terminology used in government reports and the quality press. It differs from gross national product (GNP) in that this includes 'net income from abroad', although in Britain's case this only represents about 1 per cent of GDP.

GDP, as the term implies, is not adjusted for capital used up in the process of producing annual wealth due to difficulties in agreeing its value. Great care is taken, however, to avoid double-counting output or incomes. Only final output is accounted and transfer incomes such as pensions and student grants are ignored. The three measures are so defined as to be equal to each other, although in practice a balancing item is required to ensure equality. Errors and omissions in the collection of the data on income, output and spending make this necessary.

> **EXAM TIP**
>
> Many economic concepts are of value in revision and examination technique. Your time is the scarce resource and you must allocate it efficiently. You may be taking more than one examination, so you must allocate your revision time between each. Opportunity cost means that additional hours spent on one subject equals fewer hours on the others.
>
> In the exam itself you must allocate time between questions effectively and this means the equi-marginal principle. You should aim to achieve a position where you could not have improved on your overall mark by trading more time on one question for less on another.
>
> For example, do you spend more time on the first question you answer or on questions you like or know more about? Do you write just a few lines on the last question? Do you answer a three-part question even though you can address only one part convincingly? If the answer is yes to any of these you are under-performing in exam situations!
>
> **Note:** The Chief Examiner highlighted these very points in his report of both the December 1995 and 1996 series.

The uses of national accounting data

In Britain the Office for National Statistics collects this data and publishes it in the so-called *Blue Book*. The information provides the basis for forecasts and analysis of the health of an economy. The Treasury has developed a sophisticated computer-based model to predict the future path of the economy and upon which the government will partly base its policy judgments. The financial markets, on the other hand, will respond immediately to any unexpected deviation.

The marketer must therefore understand the significance and potential weaknesses of these figures if decisions affecting the business environment are to be anticipated.

GDP figures can provide a measure of the following:

- Gross physical output of goods and services of domestic firms
- Annual percentage increase or growth in the economy
- Productivity or GDP per head/capita by dividing GDP by working population
- Average standard of living by dividing GDP by the general population.

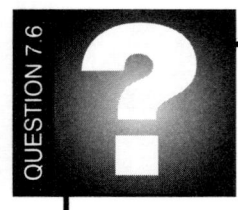

QUESTION 7.6

If Britain's GDP is growing by 3 per cent per annum, and its population is growing by 0.5 per cent while Malaysia is growing by 9 per cent and its population by 1.5 per cent, which country is better off?

- What is the GDP of your economy in local currency terms?
- Does an increase in GDP automatically mean that you are better off?
- How has your country's GDP fared over time?

(**See** Activity debrief at the end of this unit.)

- Comparison of performance between different economies.

Care must be taken by the marketer when assessing the potential of overseas markets using national income data. Different countries have different values, tastes and needs and the proportions spent on armed forces will affect the amount of available disposable income. Asian economies tend to have higher savings ratios than Europeans, while America's high energy-consuming life style is more than double that of other countries.

The efficiency of governmental statistical agencies also varies widely and currency comparisons are very difficult to make. Some economies may even understate their GDP to attract aid from international agencies while others have very wide disparities in income, making figures on average living standards very misleading. Less-developed economies also tend to have large barter economies, making many transactions difficult to record.

ACTIVITY 7.2

Select an overseas country which may represent a possible market for your company's product. Use sources like the OECD, IMF, WTO and World Bank to gather national income data. Critically appraise its likely degree of accuracy in the light of the points made above and report on your assessment of prospects.

Limitations of the data

We have already seen that there are a number of reasons for caution over the accuracy of the statistics. One other vital factor to note is that GDP data are normally expressed in nominal or current prices terms. If inflation in Malaysia was 8 per cent while only 2 per cent in Britain then the overall position is 0.5 per cent *real* growth for the latter and −0.5 per cent *real* decline in the former!

Always check if the figures are expressed in nominal or real terms to avoid being misled, i.e. GDP at constant prices adjusts for inflation by expressing GDP in terms of prices prevailing in a base year (e.g. at 1992 prices).

Even if all the calculations and estimates were entirely accurate, some problems of interpretation would still remain:

- An increase in exports or investment will not increase *current* living standards.
- An increase in GDP may be due to either the workforce working much longer hours or increased female participation rates. This might involve unaccounted costs in terms of stress or reduced health.
- No account is taken of *externalities* associated with growth such as emissions, effluents and waste. Economic activity to remedy environmental damage is actually counted as part of GDP. Measurement of *sustainable* income would also have to take resource depletion into account.
- GDP increases when people pay to have services undertaken they would have previously performed themselves. Child-minding, garden maintenance, laundry and so forth are all examples. If someone married a person they previously employed to provide services, GDP would actually fall (this is known as the Pigou effect)!
- No attempt is made to value leisure time or unrecorded activities occurring in the informal economy (see Unit 1).

> **EXAM TIP**
>
> The sales and marketing environment provides a number of opportunities where the examination candidate can illustrate an understanding of the subject by using diagrams or charts to represent a framework of ideas. While these can be extremely useful, you should only use them if:
>
> - They can be drawn correctly
> - Both axes and the relationships shown are labelled
> - They are relevant to the question.
>
> Nothing exposes ignorance of the macro-economic and competitive environments so obviously as an incorrectly drawn relationship!

The business cycle

This refers to the periodic fluctuations in economic activity that occur in industrialized economies. Left to themselves economies tend to oscillate between periods of high activity, growth in employment and booming confidence, and opposite conditions of falling output, unemployment and despondency.

The underlying trend of real GDP growth has been firmly upward since the Second World War, particularly in Japan and subsequently in other parts of East Asia. However, even these strongly export-orientated economies have had irregular oscillations superimposed due to their interdependence with the main markets they supply. High specialization and focus on a narrow band of products and market segments exposes countries to risks identical to those confronting companies. A downturn in European markets or new US trade rules might severely affect Singapore electronic exports or Hong Kong textiles.

The business cycle represents the *average* of a multitude of individual industry cycles. Any one business may therefore be in advance or lag the main cycle. The marketer must locate their relative position since published data always refer to the average. The duration of the cycle up to World War I was 8–9 years while a 4–5 year pattern prevailed from 1945 to 1979 in Britain. Since then, the two deepest and longest recessionary shocks since the great depression of the 1930s has produced a 9–10-year cycle. Figure 7.5 shows the typical stages of the cycle.

> **ACTIVITY 7.3**
>
> A useful activity for any salesperson or marketer is to track the business cycle. Statistics are published monthly showing trends of output and expenditure.
>
> You can also track your own industry cycle by plotting orders received. You may wish to smooth this information by using a 12-month moving average. This involves dropping the order value of 12 months ago, adding the current one and dividing by 12.

Businesses in the capital good sector will exhibit much greater fluctuation and follow (lag) the business cycle. Can you think why?

(**See** Activity debrief at the end of this unit.)

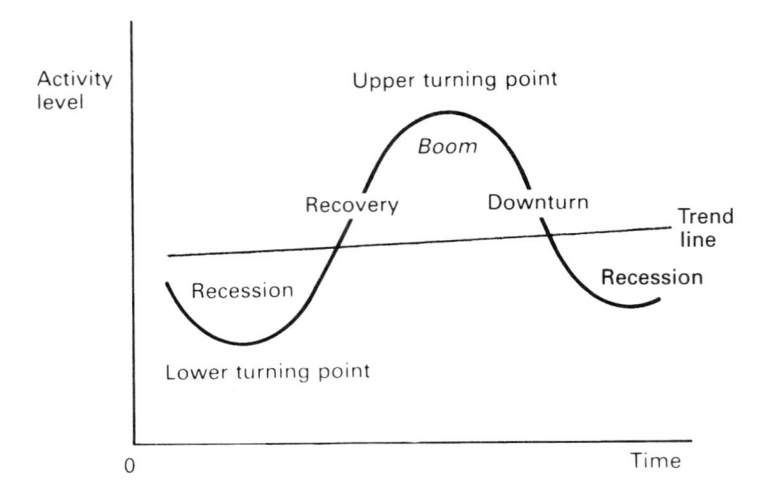

Figure 7.5 The stages of the business cycle

Recession is defined as at least two successive quarters of *falling* GDP. Unemployment will be rising alongside considerable spare capacity. Wage and price rises will be difficult to achieve, so inflation will moderate, as will labour militancy. These are difficult times for the marketer since competitive forces will mount while budgets come under increasing pressure. Profitability will be declining, business confidence will be low and investment spending depressed.

QUESTION 7.7

Now identify the key features of the following phases:

- Recovery
- Boom
- Downturn

(**See** Activity debrief at the end of this unit.)

The severity and duration of these phases vary from cycle to cycle. The 4–5-year cycle, which characterized Britain up to the mid-1970s, had short phases and limited amplitude. It was known as *stop-go* since business experienced fast growth, often as elections approached, followed by no growth at all as the economic brakes were applied. The long-term trend growth was just over 2 per cent per annum.

In contrast, Britain has experienced two serious and long-lasting recessions in 1979–1982 and 1990–1992 interspersed with a boom between 1986 and 1989 when 3 million new jobs were created and the economy grew by 15 per cent in real terms. However, as is often the case, the bigger the boom, the bigger the bust, and much of the benefit was reversed as GDP fell for more than two years and unemployment climbed to over 3 million. These patterns may be seen in Figure 7.6.

The marketer must clearly seek to anticipate fluctuating economic conditions of this nature. The upper and lower turning points are the key moments in time to identify since they signal a significant change in economic conditions to which the business must actively respond. Once the turning point is passed, the multiplier-accelerator mechanism should progressively move the economy to boom or recession conditions.

> **ACTIVITY 7.4**
>
> The previous activity asked you to plot the cycle for your firm or industry using order data and a moving average. Using historical data, you will be able to plot the course of the cycle and divide it into phases. The point of doing this, however, is to provide a framework within which the cycle can be *managed*.
>
> For each phase of the cycle, set out the kind of policies the business should be pursuing. For example, in the *boom* phase, the rate of growth of sales level out as demand bumps along a peak. The firm must remain in stock but all expansion plans should be frozen. Any surplus plant should be sold at this time to realize top prices. New markets may be explored but emphasis should be on controlling costs to meet the gloomier times just around the corner.
>
> (**See** Activity debrief at the end of this unit.)

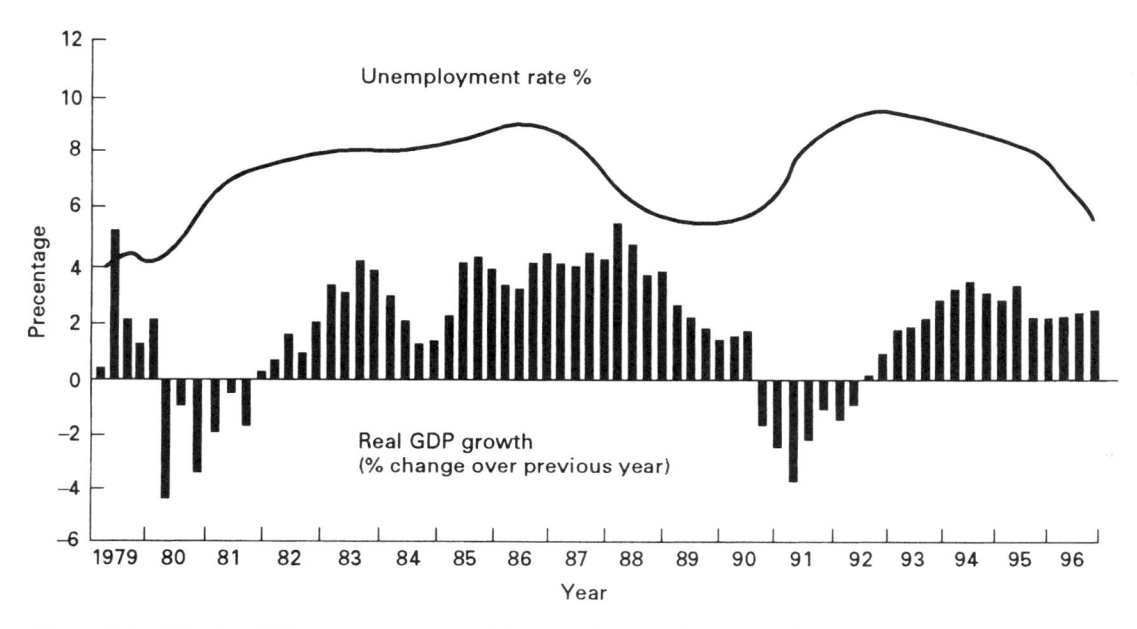

Figure 7.6 The British business cycle – real GDP and unemployment 1979–1995

If the marketer expects cycles they will not come as a surprise. Look at them as positive opportunities which can assist new product launch and market penetration if introduced at the right time. The key to success is in timing and the rule of thumb is that the higher and longer the period above the growth trend line, the lower and the longer the subsequent period below.

Forecasting the turning points is not easy as seen in the failure of highly respected forecasting groups, including the UK Treasury, to predict the 1990 recession, then failed to predict its length and finally overestimated the speed of recovery! Businesses may, however, be able to judge developments more effectively using two monitoring techniques:

- *Leading indicators* These foreshadow change in the pace of the economy by identifying indicators that consistently give advance warning of upward or downward movement. A composite index is used, including the FT 100 share index, total dwellings started, the rate of interest and the aggregate financial surplus or deficit of all companies. In early 1997 housing starts were up 30 per cent, the stock market was exceeding all time highs and the corporate surplus was rising sharply. Can you predict real GDP growth in 1997–8?
- *Confederation of British Industry Trends survey* A large representative cross-section of domestic companies is surveyed in depth to measure changes in *business confidence*. Psychology is important and the famous British economist John Maynard Keynes suggested that the *animal spirits* of capitalism produced alternating phases of optimism and pessimism, both of which tend to feed on themselves! The marketer must always

beware of being carried away by such 'herd instincts' which may cause capital spending to fluctuate from over to under-investment.

Investment takes time and is an act of faith in the future. The penalties of a wrong decision are considerable since if the firm commits resources and the market then fails to materialize, or if it does not but demand booms, then market share will be lost to competitors. Environmental changes will often influence expectations and competitive decisions which may be *self-fulfilling* in the short term. If a critical mass of households and businesses *believe* things will improve, and invest and spend on that assumption, then things will, in general, improve, *feeding back* into even more positive expectations. The process can also work in reverse as the gyrations on the Japanese stock markets have emphasized. A 'feel good factor' is the current expression of such considerations, easy to visualize but economically less easy to achieve.

> **QUESTION 7.8**
>
> Review your grasp of this important aspect of the macro-economic environment by working through the effects of the following on the business cycle:
>
> 1. Multipler – accelerator
> 2. Adjustment in stock levels
> 3. Business confidence
> 4. Openness of the economy
> 5. Elections
> 6. A shift towards services
> 7. Random and erratic shocks (e.g. trade war)
>
> (**See** Activity debrief at the end of this unit.)

Government economic objectives and priorities

Governments, like businesses, have a number of objectives. They range from social concerns to national security and political aims. In the economic realm it has been traditional to identify four main objectives together with a variety of subsidiary goals:

- Faster and more sustainable economic growth
- Maintaining higher levels of employment or 'real' jobs
- Controlling inflation at very low levels
- A favourable balance of payments averaged over a period.

Subsidiary goals might include:

- A balanced regional development
- Resource conservation and concern for the environment
- Distribution of income reflecting equity, economic contribution, etc.

> **EXAM TIP**
>
> To help focus your mind on the syllabus and the pattern of questions posed, it is always helpful to draw up a matrix of syllabus elements against which you place a tick or number if a question was included. This is done for each occasion there is an available and relevant examination set. The resulting grid enables you to identify patterns, trends and possible bankers at a glance. Remember that your examiner will be using one to ensure coverage of the syllabus content over a run of papers. Refer to Unit 11 and study the patterns in the current grid.

Economic growth

This is the fundamental objective, since a growing economy allows a government to achieve other goals requiring resources, to resolve allocational conflicts and, most importantly, to win re-election. An electorate that experiences real improvements in purchasing power, job opportunities and increased spending on health, education, defence and pensions is more likely to vote for the return of the party in office. They say that oppositions do not win elections, governments lose them, and failing to deliver improvements in living standards is often the main cause.

Growth does not always mean rising consumption, of course, even though this accounts for two-thirds of aggregate demand. An export or investment-led rise in output will be much healthier for the longer-run competitiveness of the economy but does nothing to raise domestic consumption in the short term. A distinction has also to be drawn between an increase in GDP, which is achieved by employing spare or unemployed resources and *real* growth, sustained by rising productivity in resource use through investment in skills, infrastructure, capital and new technology or products.

The *production possibility curve* (Figure 7.7) illustrates these ideas and is drawn on the assumption that scarce resources can be used to produce just two types of good. If available resources are fully and efficiently used they could produce 0X of consumption goods *or* 0Y of investment goods or a combination of both at any point along the curve. If the economy is operating at 0P then it is below capacity and inefficient. It could produce more of both goods, shown by the shaded area, if resources are better utilized. Point 0Q is currently unattainable and real economic growth would be required to push the curve out. This could take the form of either new or more productive resources through investment in skills, for example, or improved methods and technology making existing resources more productive. Investment in research and technology would be required in this case. None of this is costless, and more investment today, to increase production possibilities tomorrow, will require resources to be diverted from current consumption.

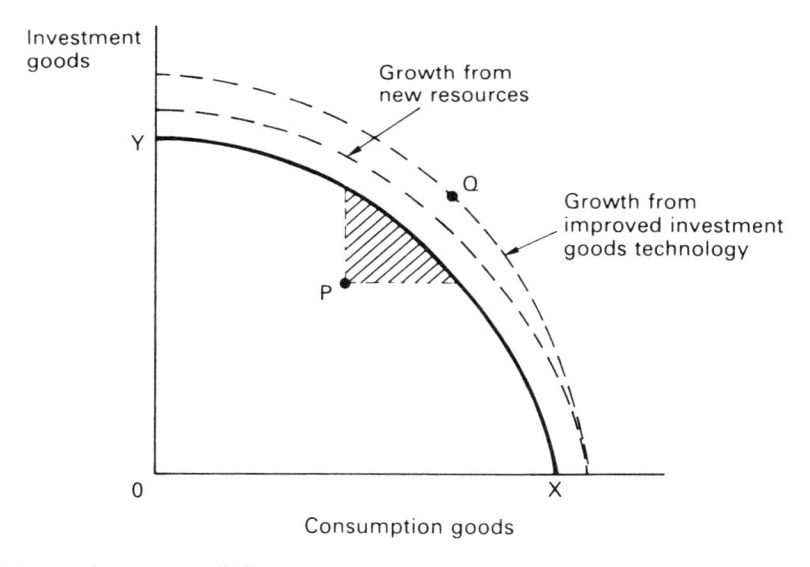

Figure 7.7 The production possibility curve

> **ACTIVITY 7.5**
>
> Use the above framework to list the factors you consider account for the different rates of economic growth between your own country and another that you know is significantly more or less successful in this respect (e.g. a European and Asian economy).
>
> Once you have identified economic explanations, brainstorm other dynamic contributing factors from the macro-environment.
>
> (**See** Activity debrief at the end of this unit.)

Economic growth as an objective has attracted growing criticism because of externalities associated with it. Concern has focused on non-renewable resource depletion and greenhouse effects arising from the combustion of carbon fuels in power stations and vehicles. Projected growth, particularly in developing countries, is expected to expand greenhouse gases and raise the temperature of the planet. Melting polar icecaps will raise sea levels and disrupt climatic conditions with potentially damaging side effects on living standards. Acid rain, ozone depletion, oil and chemical spillages, industrial pollution and rising congestion are just some of the other 'bads' associated with economic growth.

> **QUESTION 7.9**
>
> Is there a solution to the quandary outlined above? If so, what are the marketing implications?
> (**See** Activity debrief at the end of this unit.)

Higher employment

Full employment was the primary goal of post-war governments up to the mid-1970s. The existence of 22 million unemployed in the European Union in 1997 suggests that it no longer has priority. Even at the height of the Lawson boom (1989–90) in Britain, unemployment failed to fall below 1.5 million and within three years had doubled. Even in recovery unemployment has only recently fallen below 2 million or 7 per cent and large-scale redundancies continue to be announced, not only in traditional sectors like coal and steel but also in banking, retailing and utilities. Even German unemployment rose by half a million to 4.5 million in early 1997.

Unemployment is often referred to as a social and economic evil which can and does impact negatively on businesses:

Economic evil	*Social evil*
Scarce resources not utilized	Loss of income
Tax burden of benefits reduces incentives to work/invest	Relative poverty compared to those in work with affluent life styles
Reduces mobility of labour	Alienation from society leading to crime, vandalism and other social ills
Reduces purchasing power	
Depresses confidence	Dual society of haves/have-nots
Discourages risk taking	Young entrants to labour market particularly hit

Unemployment is a personal tragedy since work binds us to society and gives meaning to our lives. Not only is our income lost, but also our status, esteem and self-respect. Long-term unemployment affects specific groups such as the young, as employers cease recruitment; the unskilled; ethnic groups and the over-50s; the disabled and those living in inner cities or areas of structural decline (e.g. mining communities). The young are forced to move away from such areas, condemning the latter to a downward spiral of decay and producing a marketer's nightmare.

> **QUESTION 7.10**
>
> Is unemployment an 'evil' as far as business managers are concerned? Think carefully about this question from the view of your own company. Think about wage levels, recruitment, discipline and ease of achieving change.
> (**See** Activity debrief at the end of this unit.)

The seeming inability of many governments to achieve permanently lower unemployment and their 'acceptance' of a certain rate as unavoidable is a reflection of a number of factors:

- A more rapid rate of technological change
- Customer orientation, changing tastes and shortening life cycles
- Inflow onto the job market exceeding outflow as married women's participation rises

- The idea of a 'natural' unemployment rate that is compatible with low and stable inflation
- A more turbulent environment making business focus on job flexibility rather than long-term security and commitment.

These factors can be best understood in the context of different types of unemployment arising from the three main causes:

1. *Insufficient aggregate demand* This gives rise to *cyclical* unemployment due to a deflationary gap. The downturn and recession phases of the cycle imply activity rates well below capacity. Businesses will respond to a downturn in orders by cutting overtime, halting recruitment and curtailing its use of contractual labour. Only then will they be forced into redundancies and these will be voluntary where possible. Unfortunately, as an economy begins to recover there is normally a lag before employment responds. Employers who have suffered the costs of redundancy and restructuring will seek to avoid new full-time recruits until they are reassured that the recovery is firmly based and all flexible alternatives are exhausted (i.e. the existing workforce will be used more intensively and part-timers employed where possible).

> **ACTIVITY 7.6**
>
> For each of the types of unemployment being considered, brainstorm possible policies to minimize its occurrence. Once you have generated a list of possibilities go through each one and ensure that they meet the following requirements:
>
> - The policy *will not* lead to increased inflation.
> - The policy *will not* lead to inefficiency/uncompetitiveness.
> - The policy is consistent with people's needs and wants.
>
> (**See** Activity debrief at the end of this unit.)

2. *Imperfect market forces* These prevent labour markets clearing at wage levels where no *involuntary* unemployment exists. Many factors prevent a matching of the supply and demand for different types of labour skill such as lack of knowledge, immobility, discrimination, employment legislation and poor management. *Frictional* unemployment arises due to a mismatch between the end of one job and the start of the next for many of the millions of job changers each year. Its duration is short and reflects the mobility of labour in response to vacancies in expanding sectors of the economy. *Structural* is the longer-term variety of resource reallocation. It is caused by shifting tastes, technologies and competition, and is reflected in changing patterns of consumption and production. Certain industries and employments contract while others expand. Skills are often so specialized and industry-specific that redeployment is only possible if completely new ones are acquired. If job opportunities also involve moving, then housing cost and availability may preclude this.

3. *Relative wages are too high* If the wage is set too high to clear the market due to minimum wage levels or union bargaining power then unemployment will result. The productivity associated with the wage paid is also part of this equation. If European wage-for-productivity levels are too high then business will respond by:

   Moving operations to lower-wage countries
   Investing in technology as a substitute for relatively expensive labour.

> **QUESTION 7.11**
>
> From the point of view of the 'lower-wage economy' assess the positive and negative business impacts of a multinational company transferring its operations there.
>
> (**See** Activity debrief at the end of this unit.)

Technological unemployment arises from *new process innovations* which have typically displaced the tasks performed by semi- and unskilled manual and clerical workers. The increasing sophistication of computers and information systems, however, is now threatening the jobs of middle managers (known as downsizing) and other knowledge worker groups. Employment in the British manufacturing sector has already shrunk rapidly for over three decades, with a contraction of more than 15 per cent since 1990 reducing numbers to below 4 million.

This type of unemployment tends to emerge in the following downturn as obsolete factories and technology are closed. Ever since the Luddites in the early nineteenth century, technology has been viewed by workers as an enemy in the short term even though over time it has created clusters of *new product innovations* which until recently have allowed jobs to grow in line with the working population. This is not surprising, since whenever wants exceed our ability to satisfy them, human resources along with capital and land will be scarce. Machines will specialize in doing what they do best, as will humans.

There is now a clear mismatch between those with unwanted skills and abilities in declining industries, or where machines have a comparative cost advantage, and skill shortages in high-technology and creative knowledge-based employments. Considerable investment in education and flexible skills will be required if a permanent 'underclass' of the hard-to-employ is not to emerge. Little wonder that education policy was a key issue in the election campaign and the top priority of the Labour government. The alternative of large falls in the relative wages of unskilled may well be resisted by unions or through pressure for minimum wage legislation as enshrined in the European Union's social chapter.

> **EXTENDING ACTIVITY 7.1**
>
> Research the meaning of the term 'de-industrialization' and examine its implications for the supply and demand for marketing services.

Control of inflation

Inflation is a general increase in the average price level that is sustained over a period of time and is usually calculated by changes in the retail price index (RPI). This is measured by a 'basket' of around 600 goods and services typically consumed by the average household and weighted by their importance in total spending. You should distinguish between the so-called 'headline rate' and the 'underlying rate'. The latter excludes mortgage interest which tends to inflate the index in times of rising rates.

Inflation has been a persistent problem in many countries for most of the post-war period. Governments were happy to trade off a little more inflation for a little less unemployment. However, from the late 1970s both tended to rise together to politically and societally unacceptable levels. Known as *stagflation*, this is the worst of both possible economic worlds!

Conservative governments under Margaret Thatcher pledged themselves to control inflation as the central priority even at the expense of sharply rising unemployment. The battle to conquer inflation became a constraint on the government's ability to achieve both growth and jobs, and politically acceptable unemployment became the level that was sustainable without inflation increasing, or rising significantly above levels in the major economies with whom we compete internationally. The policy was a 'success' with inflation falling to 30-year lows by early 1997, although still above major competitors like Japan, France and Germany.

> **ACTIVITY 7.7**
>
> The retail price index (RPI) or your national equivalent is normally published monthly. Watch the quality press for the publication date and analyse the news report. Identify which categories in the index are rising more than the average and which are rising less.
>
> Can you explain the price trends you observe? Are they supply or demand driven? Are they the result of government policies? What is the effect on prices of imported goods and services?

Is inflation a problem from the marketer's point of view?
The answer to this question depends on the rate of inflation involved. If this is slow and predictable then it can be a good thing. *Creeping inflation*, when associated with buoyant high demand, can generate buyer confidence and business investment. Since borrowings are repaid in gently depreciating currency and the value of stocks appreciate, it tends to enhance profitability. Households experience 'money illusion', whereby they feel better off than they really are as nominal incomes rise. They fail to notice or account the real value eroding through cost of living rises. This eases the process of change and is preferable to the depressed economic conditions that may be necessary to keep prices from rising at all.

However, once inflation exceeds a critical rate the costs outweigh any possible benefits as:

- A rapid fall in the value of money hits confidence.
- Uncertainty over future price levels deters firms from entering long-term contractual commitments and makes future planning very difficult.
- Arbitrary and unintended redistribution of income occurs:
  Debtors gain and creditors/savers lose;
  Fixed income groups like pensioners suffer;
  Weak bargaining groups are unable to keep pace.
- Taxation rises as allowances are eroded and rising nominal income moves consumers into higher tax brackets.
- Domestic marketers suffer competition from more competitive imports while rising export prices hits overseas sales.
- Frequent price changes means continuous adjustment to lists, packaging, etc. which upsets customers.
- Prices no longer accurately reflect 'relative' values, confusing the consumer but making them more price-sensitive and less responsive to other marketing-mix elements.
- Investment funds move into unproductive inflationary hedges such as antiques and property.
- Wage groups fight for income shares, disrupting business activity with strikes.
- It may trigger price wars in oligopoly situations due to misinterpretation of rival intentions.

Finally, the marketer must remember that what goes up must come down! As inflation accelerates so governments will be forced to drastically reduce demand pressures to restore stability. Curing inflation, with the attendant squeeze on spending, is often worse in its effects than the disease itself!

> **EXAM TIP**
> Remember that examination questions on the macro-economic environment will frequently revolve around your knowledge and understanding of current economic conditions. You must therefore have a good grasp of growth, employment, inflation and the balance of payments and the *effects* of each on business and the marketer. This applies whether they are improving or deteriorating!

The causes of inflation
The marketer needs to understand the causes of inflation so that an assessment may be made as to the likely future path of general prices and to avoid being damagingly surprised by sharp changes in their pace or direction. The sources of inflationary pressure originate on both the supply and demand side of an economy:

- *Demand-pull inflation* As we have seen above, too much spending relative to productive capacity results in an inflationary gap which bids up prices of both inputs and outputs. As wage costs rise these feed into higher prices, prompting further wage demands and creating a wage–price spiral. A. W. Phillips showed (Figure 7.8) that as the pressure of demand increased, the rate of change of wages rises more than proportionately, accelerating this process.

- *Monetarist inflation* Money is the fuel that sustains inflation. If the money supply is not expanded to justify higher wages and prices, then real aggregate demand in the circular flow declines, goods are left unsold and businesses reduce their employment of factors. Inflation is then only possible at the expense of rising unemployment.
- *Cost-push inflation* This occurs when a cost element causes prices to rise but in the absence of any excess demand to justify it. Stakeholders such as employees may push up wages through militant action to increase their real income at the expense of profits. If businesses then raise prices to restore profit margins this reduces the purchasing power of wages and the process repeats, producing a wage–price spiral. Competition between different wage groups to maintain *wage differentials* can also lead to a *wage–wage spiral.*

Figure 7.8 The Phillips curve

QUESTION 7.12

- Cost-push inflation can only continue if the government accommodates the higher prices and wages by raising aggregate demand and money supply. Why should it do this?
- Think about what makes up the total cost of a good or service and list the other types of cost-push inflation possible.
- Which type is the biggest threat in your own economy at the present time? Why are the others lesser threats?

(**See** Activity debrief at the end of this unit.)

We have seen that when inflation becomes rapid and uncertain it creates net costs for business and society. It poses difficult marketing-mix problems for the marketer, especially those serving segments most seriously affected. In the extreme, *hyper-inflation*, defined as price rises in excess of 50 per cent per month, causes all confidence to be lost in paper money and barter re-emerges.

Consider the recent situation in Russia or the customer service problems of German café-owners in 1923, forced to raise coffee prices while customers sat waiting for their bills. At one stage during the German hyper-inflation prices were rising by 5 per cent per hour!

Governments have also learnt that *expectations* adjust as actual inflation is experienced. Any attempt to run an economy at less than the natural or non-accelerating inflation rate of unemployment would cause prices to rise more than expected and compensating wage demands to occur. No permanent trade-off of a little less unemployment for a little more inflation is possible. Inflation would accelerate instead.

Balance of payments

This is a constraint on the achievement of the other objectives rather than an objective in its own right. It can critically limit the rate of growth and level of employment that is achievable. As will be explored in more detail in Unit 10, all countries rely to some degree on international trade. The benefits of specialization and trade have made most economies dependent on the import of certain materials, fuels, manufactures or services. Japan and East Asia, for example, have few indigenous resources other than their skills, but have succeeded in creating large payment surpluses with the rest of the world.

The balance of payments is the record of all transactions between a country and the rest of the world. The current account comprises trade and payments in visible goods combined with invisible services. Britain's manufacturing account went into deficit for the first time in 1983, worsening significantly up to the 1990 recession, when a slow improvement began. Still in deficit in 1997 it is projected to deteriorate sharply due to faster growth and a stronger pound.

Since the balance of payments of all countries must logically sum to zero, some countries cannot avoid being in deficit at times. What is more important is the cause, whether it is manageable through overseas borrowing or reserves, and the direction of change. If a developing country, such as Nigeria, incurs a deficit in order to import investment goods to develop its oil and gas deposits, this will increase productive potential (and exports) in the future, a very different case from one importing conspicuous consumption goods and living beyond its means.

ACTIVITY 7.8

You must familiarize yourself with the trade and payments position of your economy, the direction of change and the possible implications of policy changes: Obtain an annual or monthly copy of your government's *Annual Abstract* or *Digest of Statistics*. On graph paper plot the following, against time, over a ten-year period. You will need positive and negative values graduated on the vertical axis.

- Visible trade balance (food, materials, fuels, semi-manufactured and manufactured goods)
- Invisible trade balance (services)
- Current balance (visible + invisible)
- Volume of exports (in real terms – exclude price changes)
- Volume of imports (use the same base year for both).

Assess the balance of payments position in the light of the above.

Economic indicators and economic policies

Governments use economic indicators to decide on policy changes and monitor their effectiveness. The newly empowered Bank of England will consider a wide variety of indices before deciding interest rate policy. Stock markets may react quite strongly to publication of such figures when they diverge from expectations and cause a fundamental reassessment of the underlying health of the economy. Such indicators are equally important for businesses in determining their future marketing plans and policies. We have seen that governments have a number of objectives and may be faced with the problem that achievement of one goal may conflict with realizing the others. It is therefore necessary to have as many policies as objectives if they are to be mutually accomplished.

EXAM TIP

Make sure that you know and memorize the current values of the main economic indicators in your own country.

The key indicators that you should monitor are as follows:

Activity and growth rates
- Volume of retail sales
- Volume of output
- Output and income per head
- Industry surveys (e.g. CBI) of investment intentions/confidence
- The rate relative to main competitors (gaps may prompt action!)
- The public sector borrowing requirement (see below)

Inflation rates
- Cost of living index (e.g. RPI)
- Rate of change in earnings
- The growth in the money supply (e.g. £M0 – basically notes/coins)
- Underlying rate of inflation
- Tax changes in the pipeline
- Rates of main competitors (implication for balance of payments)

Unemployment rates
- The rate of change is more important than the level
- Vacancies partially reflect strength of demand
- Unemployment rates elsewhere (beware comparability problems)
- Regional spread of unemployment
- Rates among key groups: skilled, young, male, female

Trade figures
- A potent symbol of international 'competitiveness' and success
- Relate to phase of cycle: should improve in recession
- Figures are often unreliable and subject to revision
- Share of world trade in manufactures reflects longer term performance

Exchange rates
- Rate at which one currency exchanges for another
- May be fixed by government or be free to reflect supply and demand
- Rise reflects strengthening in future prospects and vice versa
- Terms of trade reflects relative movement of import/export prices
- Exchange rates tend to fall if deficit on trade payments occurs

Interest rates
- The price of borrowed money
- A fall encourages consumer spending and investment, reduces costs but discourages savings and overseas funds inflow
- A rise reflects the need to choke off demand or attract overseas funds to finance a balance of payments deficit.

EXTENDING ACTIVITY 7.2

Using the material in this unit so far and the results of the various activities, undertake a SWOT analysis of your economy.

Draw up a balance sheet of it strengths and weaknesses and then identify opportunities and threats. Such an approach could easily form the basis of a question in the exam since it would summarize your overall appreciation of your country's macro-economy.

(**See** Question 1 at the end of this unit.)

Economic policies

The main types of policy available for use by a government are:

- Fiscal and budgetary
- Money and credit control
- Physical policies – wage and price controls
- Supply side

Space allows for only an outline consideration of these and you should consult the recommended text for greater depth. Our concern will be with the impact of such policies on the business.

> **EXAM TIP**
>
> At this stage of the workbook you will be giving serious thought to revision for the forthcoming examination. One important key to planning a revision schedule is to try to determine possible topics. Bear in mind that your paper will have been set up to a year previously due to the administration required in approving it and ensuring efficient distribution to centres around the world.
>
> What questions would you choose if you were setting an exam paper based on the syllabus and relating it to a dynamic environment? Why don't you brainstorm some possibilities with your tutor? Look at previous papers and think about 'topical' issues at the time the paper was prepared, which would still be relevant 9 months or so later.

Fiscal and budgetary

Taxation is the main source of revenue for government to finance its expenditures. Both are also instruments of economic policy as we saw when we considered the circular flow. Revenue and expenditure are now decided together in the unified annual budget in late autumn. The budget balance will determine if there is a net injection or leakage in the flow and the direction of any multiplier effects.

Britain, faced with close to a £50 billion *public sector borrowing requirement* (i.e. net injection) in 1994, was forced to raise taxes and curtail government spending with the intention of eliminating it by the end of the decade. For marketers and sales forces this meant the prospect of reduced consumer spending at a time when recovery from recession was fragile. By the end of 1996 GDP growth was picking up to 2.5 per cent and consumer spending was rising above 3 per cent per annum. A shortfall in expected tax revenues kept PSBR in excess of £30 billion in 1996. The budget projection for tax and expenditure may be seen in Figure 7.9. Government spending represents just over 40 per cent of national income.

Indirect taxes like Value Added Tax have been widened to include fuels, causing inflation to be affected. Taxes also affect incentives to work, to start new businesses and to save. A change in the overall tax burden may therefore have adverse or beneficial consequences on activity levels.

Government spending is, however, a very quick and effective means of expanding economic activity with little initial import content. The Japanese government has recently used massive *budget deficits* to try to stimulate their stagnant economy.

Money and credit

This involves control of the supply of money and the credit-creating power of the retail banks. In a process similar to the circular flow, banks are able to lend and re-lend cash, multiplying the original deposit. In Britain over £90 billion of bank deposits are built on a cash base of only 4–5 billion in what is, in effect, a gigantic confidence trick. The central bank will, however, seek to control this capability if it fears that inflation will result by:

- Controlling the supply of new money
- Open-market operations which remove cash from the banks
- Cash/liquidity ratio requirements limiting the multiplier
- Quantitative controls rationing credit to certain groups
- Interest rates and the lender of the last resort.

Such measures can expand or contract credit as required, but frequently impact on businesses in a discriminatory way.

(£ billion)

where it comes from		where it goes	
Income tax	72	22	Defence
		38	Education
Social security contributions	49	53	Health and personal social services
Corporation tax	27	15	Housing, heritage and environment
Value Added Tax	51	17	Law and order
Excise duties	34	100	Social security
Council tax	11		
Business rates	15	13	Industry, agriculture and employment
Other taxes	24	9	Transport
Other financing	13	23	Other spending
Borrowing	19	25	Debt interest
Total	315	315	Total

Figure 7.9 Public money 1997–8: where it comes from and where it goes (*Source:* HM Treasury)

QUESTION 7.13

Which type of firms are most affected by a credit squeeze?
(**See** Activity debrief at the end of this unit.)

Removing these limits on credit creation, as occurred in Britain in the mid-1980s with the Competition and Credit Control Act, caused the opposite problem of inflation and instability as both the property and stock markets boomed and overheated before collapsing. The effect was to depress confidence and consumer markets for nearly three years! The marketer must therefore carefully monitor any measure that might affect the stability of money. As Milton Friedman observed, 'inflation is always and everywhere a monetary phenomenon'.

Prices and incomes policy

Such policies were much used in the UK during the 1960s and 1970s in an attempt to achieve lower unemployment without incurring higher inflation and consequent balance of payments problems. If wage groups could be forced or persuaded to moderate their pay settlements and firms their price increases, despite demand pressure to justify them, then employment and output would rise.

In practice, such policies proved short-lived due to widespread evasion and an eventual pay and price explosion. The appropriate analogy was with a boiling pot with the heat (demand pressure) turned up and the lid tightly on.

The Conservative government introduced a 1.5 per cent public sector pay restraint in the mid 1990s as a means of controlling public spending and as a demonstration effect to the private sector. Set in the context of nearly 3 million unemployed and significant job insecurity, this policy proved initially successful. However, with the salaries of executives rising at over 5 per cent (following rises for top directors of over 30 per cent!) and an election looming, the policy softened in the 1996/97 pay round.

> **QUESTION 7.14**
> - Why is inflation so difficult to cure?
> - Why is unemployment so difficult to cure?
> - Assess the consequences of a determined effort to eliminate both.

Supply side policies

These grew out of disillusion with UK government policies to manage aggregate demand to achieve the four objectives. The standard response to low growth and rising unemployment had been to stimulate consumer, government and investment spending on the assumption that domestic firms would raise production and resource use. Multiplier and accelerator reactions would then stimulate businesses to invest in extra capacity and productivity improvements. The business response in practice was:

- To improve margins and profits instead of raising output
- A reluctance to invest due to stop-go patterns of demand
- An inability to respond quickly enough led to import penetration
- Inflation and payments deficits quickly forced policy reversal.

Supply side policies aimed to promote higher growth and employment without triggering inflation by relaxing constraints on productive capacity and efficiency. The policies involved:

- Reform of trade unions to ensure that their reduced power was used responsibly and democratically
- Removal of tax distortions and disincentives to work and invest
- Measures to improve the quality, quantity and relevance of training
- Improved job, career and training information
- Measures to encourage mobility and flexibility
- Encouraging employee share-ownership and self-employment
- Reducing red tape and regulations inhibiting business
- Greater competition and removal of minimum wages
- Privatization and the opening up of state services to private competition or internal markets, as in the National Health Service.

> **ACTIVITY 7.9**
> Supply side policies such as deregulation, tax reform and privatization, are being taken up by governments around the world. Others, like Hong Kong and Singapore, have always encouraged enterprise through free-port status, etc.
>
> By scanning newspapers and databases, approaching government departments and

so on, summarize the specific supply side policies currently applying in your own country and any new ones in the pipeline.

Think carefully how these developments affect sales/marketers in various businesses.

We may conclude that governments are continuing to grapple with the problems of achieving its objectives simultaneously. Supply side policies are directed towards making markets work more effectively and altering the structure of incentives. However, unemployment of 1.8 million and high general taxation makes this appear to be a long-term solution, and experience has already shown that when demand rises strongly, inflationary forces tend to reassert themselves.

It is hard to escape the conclusion that any sustained improvement in economic conditions will quickly produce profit and wage-push forces. Marketers must make their own assessment based on circumstances in their own country and act accordingly.

One basis for assessing the possible course of future government policy is to consider the recommendations of an Institute of Public Policy Research report published in January 1997. As Figure 7.10 indicates, there are four problems to be overcome if future prosperity is to be promoted.

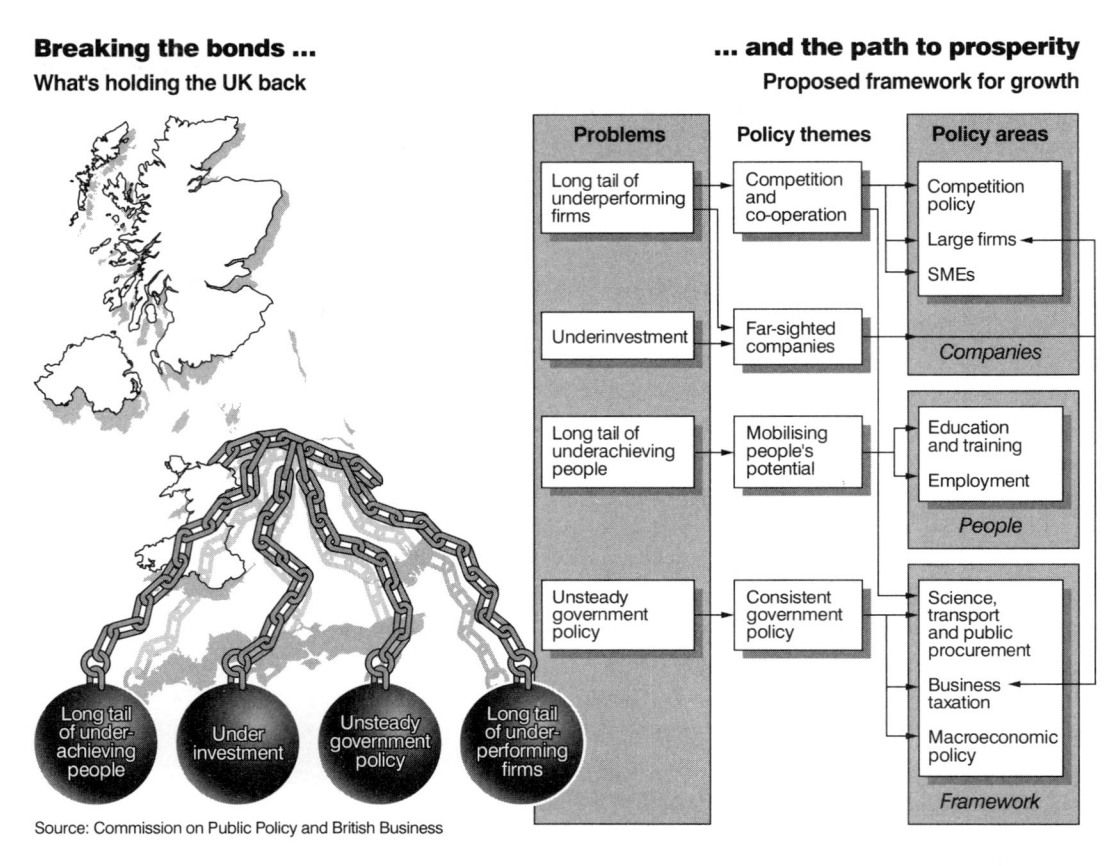

Figure 7.10 Breaking the bonds... (*Source: Financial Times*)

The main recommendations include:

- Competition Policy
  - replace current feeble controls over anti-competitive practices with a tough legalized approach on the EU model
  - enhance investigative powers of OFT: right to raid offices for evidence.
  - OFT redefined to focus on investigation, MMC on adjudication and Secretary of State must give reasons if intervenes.
- Corporate Governance
  - widen reporting to other stakeholders and longer term view of relationships.

- Macro-economic Policy – promote stability through an independent Bank of England operating within a government set target for nominal GDP growth (immediately implemented by incoming Labour government). Entry to the EMU is advocated if a substantial number of countries join in the first wave (see Unit 10).

Summary

In this important unit we have analysed important aspects of the macro-economic environment and focused on the need for marketers to appreciate the meaning of economic indicators. A grasp of future economic conditions will provide an important edge over rivals. To achieve this we have:

- Investigated the workings of the circular flow to understand how changes in income, output and expenditure occur.
- Examined the workings of the multiplier–accelerator mechanism.
- Looked at the meaning and measurement of GDP.
- Identified the phases of the business cycle and considered how it might be managed to advantage.
- Assessed each of the main macro-economic objectives.
- Focused on the key indicators for sales/marketers to monitor.
- Outlined the impact of the main policy weapons on businesses.

Activity debrief

Question 7.1

- They will save more as a precaution (currently over half the work force feel insecure in their jobs, which adversely affects the 'feel good' factor and willingness to spend).
- We are taught that thrift is a good thing and happiness cannot be achieved by spending more than income. Yet saving without corresponding investment leads to lower income and employment and therefore unhappiness.

Question 7.2

- The rate of interest. As the rate of interest falls, less is saved and more is invested and vice versa. It will not work quickly because other factors also affect the decision to save (e.g. income, expectations and preferences) and invest (e.g. expected returns, competitive pressures).
- Where injections = leakages.

Question 7.3

- *Consumption* will remain unchanged due to uncertainty and savings as a precaution against unemployment. *Investment* will be unchanged or falling due to idle capacity and 'wait and see' attitudes. *Exports* will be unchanged or falling due to depression in overseas markets. Only *government* can be increased to stimulate activity. This was Keynes' main policy recommendation.
- No significant effects in the short run due to stickiness in the response. In the longer run costs would fall and business would become more competitive leading to higher activity rates. However, Keynes observed that 'in the long run we are dead' and people want jobs and incomes today.

Question 7.4

- Multiplier $= \dfrac{1}{t(=0.4)+m(=0.2)+s(=0.1)} = \dfrac{1}{0.7} = 1.43$

- The tax multiplier is smaller because households who receive £5 billion of new disposable income save 0.1 before any spending occurs.

Question 7.5

- One plant if stabilized and no investment at all if demand falls back to 2 million.
- A cyclical pattern between ceilings and floors.

Question 7.6

- Malaysia 7.5 per cent to Britain 2.5 per cent.
- No, not automatically – see 'limitations of the data'.

A century of relative decline

- GDP per capita, 1995 (UK=100; at purchasing power parities)

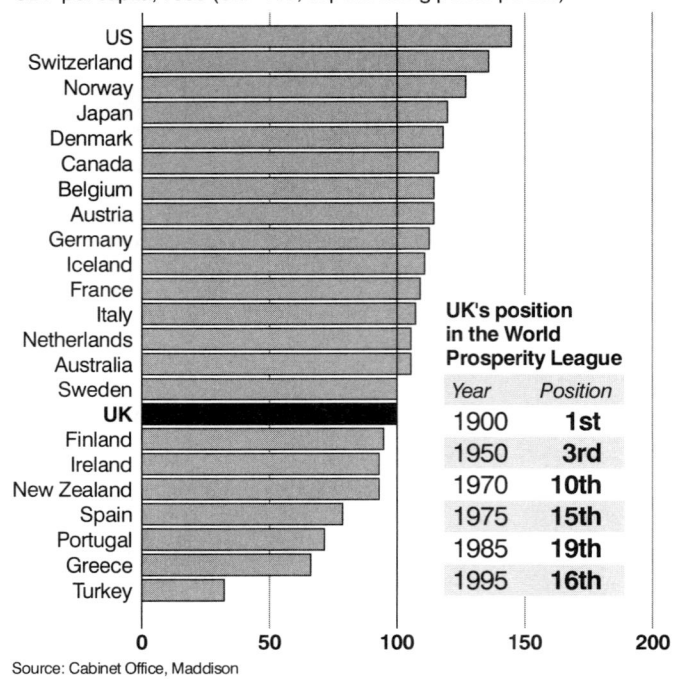

UK's position in the World Prosperity League	
Year	Position
1900	1st
1950	3rd
1970	10th
1975	15th
1985	19th
1995	16th

Source: Cabinet Office, Maddison

Question 7.7
- *Recovery* starts from lower turning point; income, output and expenditure rise at an increasing rate; unemployment levels off; caution at employing full-timers; new investment planned; inflation remains low as increased utilization occurs.
- *Boom* bottlenecks in faster growth sectors; resource prices bid up; passed on in higher prices; fully utilized resources; productivity is the only source of higher output; investment and confidence high; interest rates rising sharply, imports sucked in.
- *Downturn* starts from upper turning point; momentum through multipler–accelerator; confidence and spending falls; precautionary savings rise; investment becomes unprofitable; business failures rise and cut-backs multiply.

Question 7.8
1. Cumulative expansion/contraction.
2. As 1, since retailers faced with unsold stock will cut back orders and sell from stock. This forces a bigger cut in output by the manufacturer. However, once desired stock level reached, reorder occurs providing stimulus.
3. As 1.
4. More vulnerable to imported fluctuations.
5. Cycle tied to duration of elections.
6. Services are less sensitive to income changes than manufactures.
7. May trigger turning point.

Question 7.9 The only viable solution to this conflict between growth and a pollution-free environment is to pursue *sustainable growth*. Zero growth is not a real option due to concern over rising unemployment in industrial economies and rising populations in less-developed ones. Continued progress towards industrialization is required but using cleaner technologies, renewable energy and recyclable products.

Question 7.10 High and rising unemployment means downward pressure on wages. Businesses can recruit without raising wages to attract labour. With many people chasing each vacancy in Britain managers can pick from the top of the barrel. Workers are likely to work harder to preserve their jobs and also accept technical and other change.

Question 7.11 Think in terms of technology transfer, value added (wages + demand for local components + local taxes), balance of payments (initial investment + exports), demonstration effect for positives. Competition, remitted profits, power (e.g. avoid taxes) for negatives.

Question 7.12
- If the government puts a higher priority on growth and high employment or if an election was close and it feared the effects of cutting spending on voting decisions.

- *Profit-push inflation* may occur in the recovery phase of the cycle as firms widen margins to restore profitability.
- *Import-push inflation* is often important in open economies when primary product prices rise sharply in a boom or a depreciating currency value raises import prices.
- *Tax-push inflation* occurs when wage groups seek to compensate for tax erosion of their real earnings. The steep rise in British taxes after April 1994 might have triggered such a reaction, for example, but failed to.

Question 7.13
- Small firms who tend to rely on bank credit for cash flow
- Small firms who suffer when large customers delay payment
- Fast-growing firms
- Manufacturing firms with higher working capital requirements
- Such firms suffer in three ways – higher interest costs, limited credit and reduced consumer spending power (e.g. small builders).

Activity 7.1
- Increased domestic consumption means less is spent on imports. Leakages fall and demand for domestic output rises.
- Increased government spending is an injection of aggregate demand and income, output and expenditure rises.

Activity 7.3 This is the accelerator effect and consumer demand has to increase in other sectors before investment orders pickup.

Activity 7.4
- *Downturn* = control stock in line with order slowdown. The psychology is still one of growth with orders up on a year ago. This is the right time to conduct a Pareto analysis to weed out weak products and channel outlets. Recruitment should be halted and no further long-term commitments taken on.
- *Recession* = sit tight and wait for upturn. Be aware of brighter times ahead so retain skilled core and upgrade. Order capital equipment for installation 18 months hence since prices are at the lowest for all resource contracts.
- *Recovery* = Talk is still of recession but the rate of change in orders is upward. Start building stock and encourage distributors to do likewise. Start hiring and prepare new products for launch.

Activity 7.5 Economic growth is primarily determined by the quantity, quality and distribution of resources; the proportion of resources invested; growth in the workforce; efficiency in resource use, and ability to shift resources from low to high-productivity sectors. Non-economic factors are known as the 'substantial residual' since they often account for much of the differences in growth rates: flexibility and mobility of resources, incentive structures, quality of management, power of trade unions, deficiencies in education, regulations and so on.

Activity 7.6 Policies fall into six groups:
- *Stimulate demand for labour directly* (e.g. government spending)
- *Reduce the number of job seekers* (e.g. more in higher education)
- *Improve the matching of unemployed to vacancies* (e.g. job centres)
- *Reduce the real wage* (e.g. pay restraint)
- *Share out the available work* (e.g. part-time, early retirement)
- *Increase domestic at expense of overseas* (e.g. tariff barriers)

For jobs to be *sustainable* they must not be subsidized. Unemployment can only fall if the growth of GDP exceeds the net growth of the working population and its productivity.

Examination hints and specimen question

The economy is always going to be an important part of the macro-environment and the origin of major impacts on the business. It is the aspect that the marketer is primarily concerned with on a day-to-day basis and it would therefore be surprising if there was not at least one question based on the content of this unit.

As we saw in the specimen question at the end of Unit 6, a sound knowledge of your own economic environment is very important. The economic situation in your own country might be summarized under headings such as: inflation, unemployment, balance of payments, economic growth, phase of the cycle, investment activity and the economic policy stance, in brief. The use of a variety of *broad* statistics drawn from some of the mentioned sources would be expected by the examiner.

The specimen compulsory question in Unit 4 also had questions relating to the meaning of the business cycle.

1. (a) Your government has approached an independent group of economic forecasters to undertake a SWOT analysis of the national economy.
   Prepare a short series of relevant slides to support the forthcoming presentation of this analysis. (20 marks)
   (CIM Marketing Environment paper, June 1995)

2. (a) Demonstrate your understanding of the business cycle. (6 marks)
   (b) Compare the ability of large and small business to
      (i) weather recessions
      (ii) benefit from booms. (10 marks)
   (c) Comment briefly on the significance of the 'feel good factor' to the marketer. (4 marks)

Hints: Indicative content and approach

Question 1
- Adopt a slide format for presenting the material.
- You have time to prepare five or six slides.
- Don't crowd the slides and do use bullet points.
- Relate to your own economy.
- No set format, but an introductory slide might define SWOT analysis with examples of economic indicators which forecasters would use.
- Use a slide each to summarize the *main* strengths and weaknesses of your own country in macro economic terms.
- Use a slide each to indicate current opportunities and threats.
- Use your final slide for main conclusions and recommendations.

Question 2
- Provide a diagram and specify the stages and turning points involved.
- Briefly refer to the characteristics of each stage.
- Define the concept and refer to current cycle.
- Focus on the key word 'ability'.
- Compare in terms of capital, reserves, cash flow, management resources, flexibility and so on.
- Define the feel good factor and relate to consumer confidence, credit sales, luxury goods etc.

UNIT 8

The demographic and social environment

OBJECTIVES

In this important and challenging unit you will:

- Appreciate the fundamental importance of population trends to market analysis.
- Consider the implications of change in the structure of the population.
- Review the shifting patterns of employment and identify those with particular significance for sales and marketing.
- Briefly examine the emerging role of women in work.
- Assess the cause and effects of social changes.
- Relate specific social influences to segmentation.

By the end of this unit you will:

- Have acquired an insight into important demographic changes.
- Recognized the interrelatedness of the social environment.
- Examined the meaning and importance of cultural change.

STUDY GUIDE

A knowledge and understanding of demography and socio-cultural change is vital if the marketer is to truly appreciate the origins of buyer behaviour. Both evolve very slowly but their cumulative impact over time on market realities is considerable. Real living standards are more likely to be determined by population changes, for example, than the economic policy making of governments.

Change in this environment is the most difficult to assess, yet the opportunities presented must be grasped and exploited by the marketer. The relevant variables are interrelated, thereby making it difficult to understand the contribution of any one element. As we will see, much that is important in this environment is often unspoken and unwritten, making it one of the greatest challenges to the marketing practitioner.

As a member of society you will be able to identify with much of the content of this unit. It is shorter than the economic unit but no less important as far as examination content is concerned. Accounting for just under 10 per cent of the total syllabus, this should normally be a reliable source of a part or whole examination question.

Spend 2–3 hours studying this unit and 3–4 hours addressing the various questions and activities. You should subsection your file into demographic, social and cultural segments. There is less continuous coverage of this environment than the economic but what there is tends to be very business related. Just as *The Economist* is a useful weekly periodical for the economic, so *New Society* is the equivalent for the social. The Office of National Statistics (ONS) also publishes useful articles on current population trends and the census is available on CD-ROM.

Trends in population

Demography is important to the marketer because of its concern with the size, structure and characteristics of the population. Segmentation and the assessment of market potential is clearly related to the analysis of such factors but for a specific target population. The ONS publishes detailed population statistics deriving from full censuses every ten years and updating sample surveys every five years. The last full census was in 1991 and businesses may supplement the data obtained with targeted surveys of their own.

The important trends to appreciate include changes in:

- The context of world population
- Developed as against less-developed country growth rates
- The future size of a population
- The age and gender structure of a population
- Its distribution by region and locality
- Migration within and between national borders

ACTIVITY 8.1

You must become familiar with both the structure of, and the change in, your national population. Use the resources of your local or college library to prepare a revision brief on the following:

- Total population, current and trend rate of change
- Comparison with neighbouring, import origin and export destination countries
- Age, gender, marital status and location of population
- Occupational structure and ethnic mix
- Significant trends in structure (e.g. ageing, urbanization, etc.)

The implications of population trends to the marketer are felt:

- On the demand side, in the size of different market segments
- On the supply side, in the availability of labour
- On the mix of public services required
- On the taxation impact of the dependent population
- On aggregate spending and its distribution.

One of the most significant trends in mature industrial economies, for example, is the ageing of the population structure. Japan, Europe and, to a lesser extent, the USA are facing a sharp increase in the proportion of pensioners as the new millennium approaches. Falling birth rates, greater longevity and the ageing of earlier baby booms are combining to 'grey' the population and shift the centre of gravity of spending power in the economies affected.

Old, but still fit, healthy and *affluent* pensioners will become the norm in future rather than the old-age pensioner (OAP) image still prevalent today. Better educated, better off and better informed than their forebears, they will command considerable purchasing power. By 2050 there will be some 70 million West Europeans aged 65+, representing over 20 per cent of the population. In Britain there are forecast to be more over 65s than under 16s by the year 2016.

QUESTION 8.1

Taking a local company such as Saga Holidays in Britain (specializing in holidays for the over-60s) or McCarthy & Stone (building retirement complexes), suggest how and why their marketing mix may have to be modified to meet the needs of those retiring at the beginning of the next century.

(**See** Activity debrief at the end of this unit.)

The dependency ratio

This is the ratio of the number of dependents in the population relative to the working population. Figure 8.1 shows an improvement in the ratio until around 2010, when lower birth rates will combine with retirement of the post-war baby boomers.

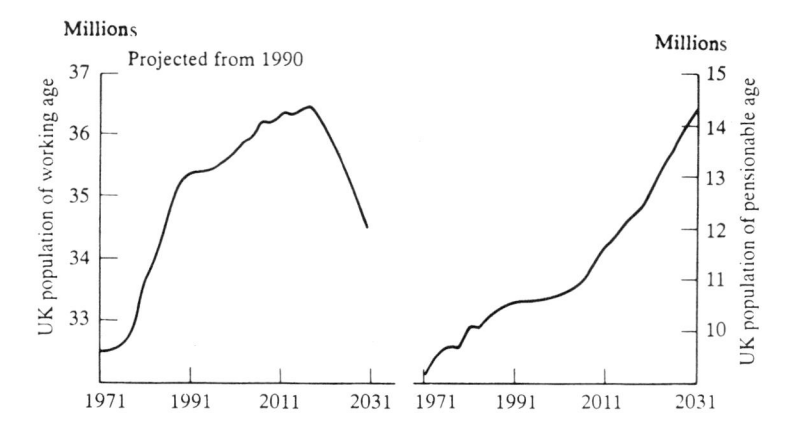

Figure 8.1 UK population of working age and pensionable age in millions (projected from 1990). (*Source*: OPCS)

This will be good news on the unemployment and career advancement fronts with opportunities for promotion, but bad news on the taxation front since real resources will need to be diverted to support those no longer contributing productively to society (Labour government entrants face the prospect of personal pension and higher education payments). Health services will need to expand continuously in real terms especially as life expectancies keep on rising. Health expenditure for the over-65s is already 4 times the average for the under-65s, while for the over-75s it is 8 times. Life expectancy has risen to over 75 for men and 79 for women, but the 'healthy life expectancy', before a limiting long-term illness is suffered, is stable at 59 and 62 respectively.

QUESTION 8.2

What is the dependency ratio in your economy? In Singapore, for example, how is it affected by the ethnic mix? What was the effect of the boat people on this ratio?

What are the implications of dependency ratios for

- Your own sales/marketing career?
- Sectors offering the greatest sales/marketing opportunities?
- Your company?
- Recruiting sales and marketing personnel?

Before moving on to consider other demographic aspects you must note that the age, gender and location of a target population is only one of the factors relevant to marketers. The fall in the number of births would seem to be a serious development for manufacturers dependent on this segment. Silver Cross, for example, makers of quality prams, might have been expected to lose sales volume. In practice, however, married couples who were now delaying births were more likely to spend more on their fewer offspring, and with established careers, could afford to do so. On the other hand, rising car ownership was shifting preferences towards a dual-purpose carrycot/pram. The marketer must therefore take nothing for granted in this complex area.

World population

Global population has grown exponentially over the last two or three centuries, as Figure 8.2 shows. Stability up to around AD 1000 was replaced with progressively rising rates, especially with industrialization and advances in health care and hygiene.

As industrial economies matured, however, they enjoyed a *demographic transition* whereby customarily high birth rates fell to levels closer to already-reduced death rates. This process has yet to be completed in many less-developed countries, especially in Africa, meaning that world population will continue to rise, at a reducing rate, at least until the middle of the next century.

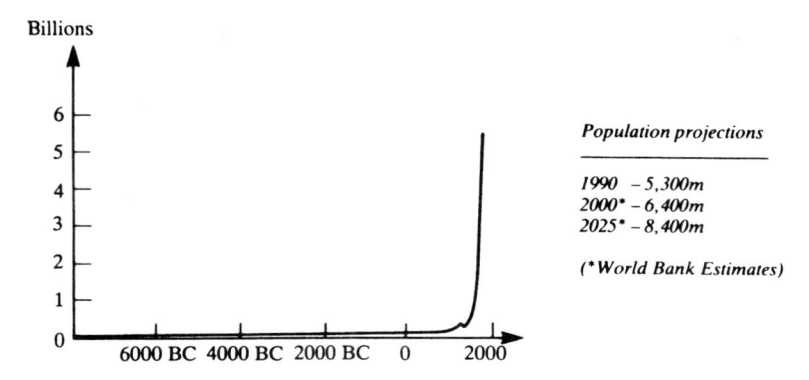

Figure 8.2 World population growth

Population projections

1990 – 5,300m
2000* – 6,400m
2025* – 8,400m

(*World Bank Estimates)

Less-developed countries therefore account for a steadily increasing proportion of total population while the already industrialized will shrink from 25 per cent to 17 per cent by 2025. Such trends have raised the spectre of T. R. Malthus, who predicted a 'dismal' outcome some 200 years ago. He suggested that if food production grows arithmetically (i.e. 1–2–3–4) while population grows geometrically (i.e. 2–4–8–16) then crisis was inevitable. In the absence of voluntary preventative measures to restrict population (e.g. China's one child policy) then equilibrium could only be restored by positive checks such as war, disease, pestilence and famine.

> **QUESTION 8.3**
>
> How did developed economies avoid Malthus's dismal predictions? Think about factors that shift out the production possibility curve when trying to answer this.
> Do the same arguments apply to less-developed economies today and what are the implications for the international marketer?
> Is there such a thing as an optimum level of population?
> (**See** Activity debrief at the end of this unit.)

Aggregate population

The record in population forecasting has been remarkably inaccurate, especially as regards births which tend to fluctuate quite considerably. As can be seen in Figure 8.3, the old OPCS published three variants based on different assumptions about births.

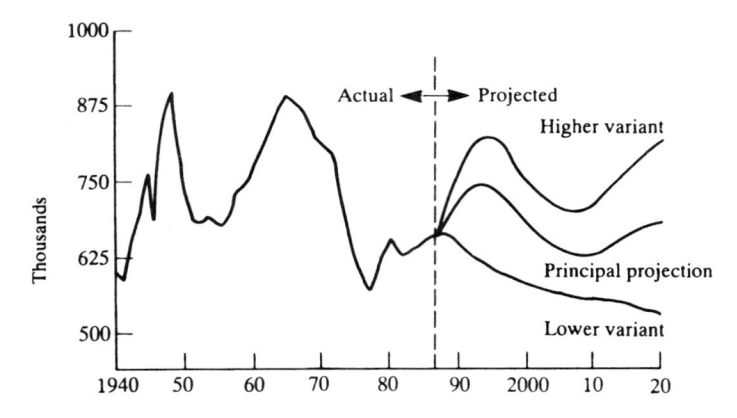

Figure 8.3 Actual and various projecions of live births, 1940–2027. (*Source: Office of Population Census and Survey*)

The projected rise is based on a peak occurring about 27 years previously. This means more women of childbearing age since the average age when giving birth to a first child in Britain is currently 27 and rising. On this basis, the steady rise in births from 1997 is set to fall back from around 2000 onwards.

Population growth = birth rate – death rate + net migration

Total population is currently around 58.5 million but with a rate of increase of only 1 per cent per decade this is unlikely to be much higher by the end of the century. Indeed, with the average European woman of childbearing age producing only 1.7 children, while 2.1 is required to replace the population, the long-run trend is downward.

> *Did you know?*
> If the German fertility rate remained at its recent level of only 1.3, its native population would actually become extinct by around 2300. Italy's fertility rate has been even lower!
>
> **EXAM TIP**

Net migration is now negative due to tightened inward restrictions and a continuous trickle outwards to Commonwealth countries and Europe. Known as the 'brain drain', the latter have tended to be young, enterprising and often disillusioned but highly skilled workers. Births per 1000 of the population have recovered from the low in 1977 and exceed deaths by a small margin.

While the crude death rate has been relatively predictable, the age-specific death rate, defined as the number of people (per 1000) of a particular age cohort that die in a year, is falling, especially for women. The life insurance industry is built on this reliability with actuaries establishing probabilities to determine risk premiums for various customer age groups. The marketer must, however, always be alert to the possibility of unexpected rises in the death rate, whether due to new contagious illnesses, environmental deterioration (e.g. skin and other carcinogens from ozone depletion and pollution) or higher fuel prices.

> Account for demographic transition to lower fertility rates (defined as the total births per 1000 women aged 15–44 years).
> You should consider a PEST framework for explaining this and relate it to the experience in your own country. Undertaking this activity will also give you an insight into the importance of socio-cultural factors which are considered later in the unit.
> (**See** Activity debrief at the end of this unit.)
>
> **EXTENDING ACTIVITY 8.1**

A couple's decision to have one more or less child to complete the family is a marginal one for them but will have compounded effects if repeated across the age group. Medical and genetic breakthroughs which may provide the ability to both determine sex at conception and eradicate defects may, if legalized, have far-reaching implications for future births.

Population structure

While aggregate population may be stable this can seldom be said for the various segments that can be identified. The dimensions of a population structure include:

- Age
- Gender
- Marital status
- Region
- Ethnic group
- Occupation

The age and gender distribution in Britain may be seen in Figure 8.4. The indentations are significant, as we have seen already, for the economy in general and specific markets in particular. Change the base line to 10 and it indicates the numbers in each cohort as of 1998.

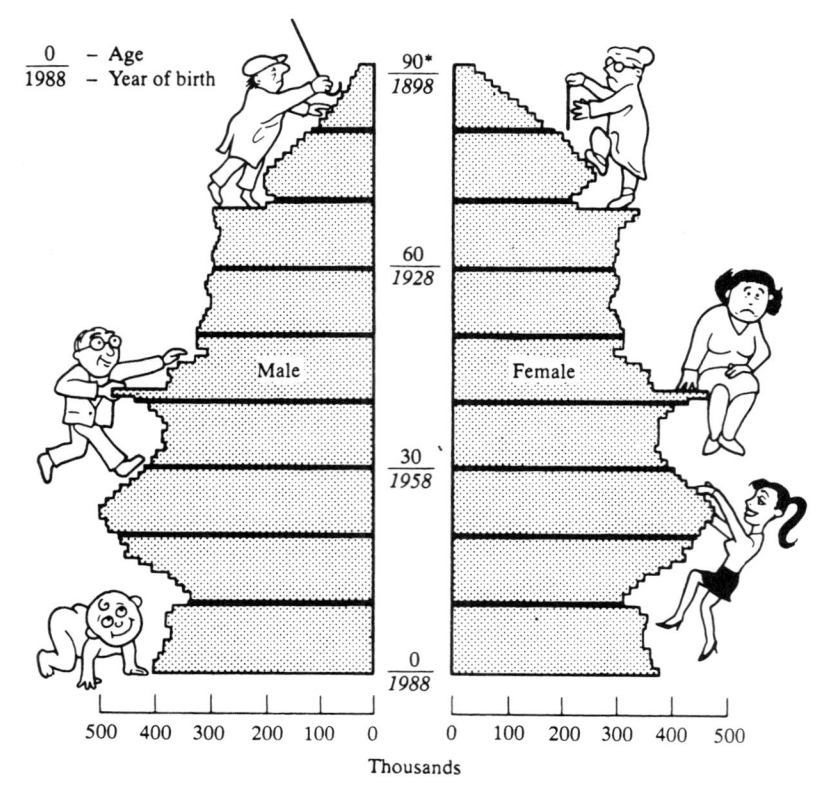

Figure 8.4 Britain's population structure, 1988 estimate. (*Sources:* OPCS, *The Economist*)

> **ACTIVITY 8.2**
>
> Study the histogram in Figure 8.4 or derive one for your own economy. Note that a developing economy will tend to have a broader base, due to higher birth rates, and a narrower neck, due to lower life expectancy arising from less mature health and welfare systems.
>
> What sales/marketing opportunities or threats will be faced by the following:
>
> - A recording company?
> - A university?
> - A firm of undertakers?
> - A cosmetic surgeon?
> - Private health insurers?

One implication of Britain's ageing population is the corresponding shrinkage in the number of school-leavers by nearly a quarter to 1995. The impact of this so-called 'demographic timebomb' has been much reduced in Britain by the effects of deep recession, investment in technology and contraction in the armed forces. However, many businesses responded positively to the prospect of future labour shortages. Buoyant East Asian economies have also had to deal with tightening labour markets by:

- Greater marketing of the business and its prospects to potential recruits
- Building closer links with local educational establishments
- Tapping alternative workgroups using flexible employment patterns
- Internal marketing for retention, retraining and promotion
- Improving pay and incentives especially for flexibility
- Considering offshore production.
- Selective immigration, e.g. Malaysia.

> **EXAM TIP**
>
> This environment of social and demographic change offers the examiner a fertile area of trends and changes upon which to build compulsory questions. An example has therefore been provided in the examination section at the end of the unit. So make sure you are aware of the key changes.

Figure 8.5 shows clearly how employers have compensated for contraction in the under-25s by increased employment of married women and older age groups. Women will account for 46 per cent of the workforce by 2006, according to the latest edition of *Social Trends*. Many school-leavers have opted to enter higher education in recent years as a result of planned expansion and the absence of attactive job opportunities elsewhere. This near-doubling, to almost a third, implies a much better qualified and well-informed consumer group in future. It may also lead other European Union countries, affected by falling births, to recruit qualified staff from Britain as their economies recover.

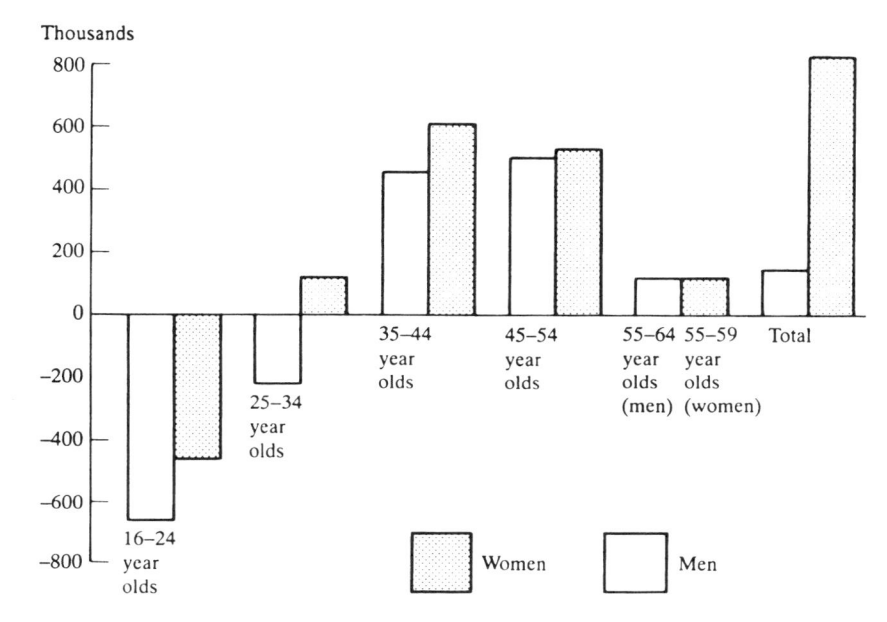

Figure 8.5 Projected change in the UK civilian labour force of working age, 1989–2027.
(*Source:* Department of Employment)

The youth-orientated society of Britain in the 1960s is giving way to a more conservative middle-aged culture in the late 1990s. With an average age around 40 and rising and the number of retired about to boom worldwide to an estimated 600 million, the face of marketing is bound to be affected.

> **QUESTION 8.4**
>
> What product values and characteristics will be central to an effective sales and marketing strategy focused on the over-45s?
> (**See** Activity debrief at the end of this unit.)

As the old become more numerous, better educated and live longer, so their political and economic power will increase. Financially well endowed and with a greater propensity to vote, they will exert more pressure on decision makers as well as constituting an important but discerning market segment. The marketer must also recognize, however, that the retired at present also include among the poorest in society, with nearly 2 million qualifying for supplementary benefits and a further 1 million qualifying but not taking it up.

Marital status and household structure

This is undergoing considerable change in Britain due to later marriage, rising divorce rates and remarriages. As we have seen, the fertility rate has fallen below the replacement ratio of 2:1, causing the traditional marketer's assumption of 2 adults + 2 children to become the exception rather than the norm.

Divorce rates at 40 per cent in Britain are the highest in Western Europe especially among those marrying young. Earlier marriages have, however, fallen sharply in recent years but cohabitation has increased as have illegitimate births. Remarriages already account for a third of the annual total and may produce 'composite' family groups, combining different ages from previous unions. The rise in single households is accounted for by the rising number of elderly, greater independence among the young, people staying single for longer, and rising divorce rates. This clearly forms a complicated tapestry for marketing analysis, but also a rich seam of potential segmentation.

ACTIVITY 8.3

Analyse Table 8.1 and suggest sales and marketing implications that may arise.

Table 8.1 Percentages of people living in different households (UK)

Households, %

	Married *couple	Cohabiting *couple	Lone parent	Other multiperson	One person	All*** households
Estimates						
1971	71	1	2	7	18	15,942
1981	64	3	4	7	23	17,306
1991	55	6	5	7	27	19,215
Projections**						
1996	51	7	6	7	29	20,177
2001	49	7	6	8	31	21,046
2006	46	7	6	8	33	21,897
2011	44	7	6	9	35	22,769
2016	42	7	5	9	36	23,598

*With or without children. **1992 based projections. ***Thousands
Sources: ONS, *General Household Survey.*

Regional distribution

The marketer must be aware of the shifting distribution of population across regions and localities arising from both natural increase and net migration. The broad movement affecting all industrialized societies has been the steady drift from rural to urban living. Economic decline and depopulation has left a relatively old and poor residue in many parts of the North, Wales and Scotland.

There has also been reverse flow from the inner cities to suburbia and, more recently, the ribbons of development along the motorway and rail routes radiating away from city centres. As young couples move into these dormitory urban fringes to escape either inner-city decay or rural remoteness, so births increase to reinforce the process. East Anglia in particular has registered an annual growth of over 1 per cent while the major conurbations, including London, have lost 0.5 per cent per annum for two decades now.

Despite a near-static population overall, redistribution will continue along similar lines. The marketer must also identify where target populations reside, especially the retired, with localities on the South and South-west coasts benefiting significantly. The rise in single households is also putting pressure on rural land with 4.5 million new homes projected to be required by 2010. A new town is already being planned in Hampshire, for example.

> **QUESTION 8.5**
>
> In Britain, one-third of the population live in the South-east while only one-sixth inhabit the much larger areas of Wales, Scotland and Northern Ireland combined. In the light of this or similar disparities in your own country, assess the implications for sales forces and marketers seeking to serve these populations.
> (**See** Activity debrief at the end of this unit.)

Ethnic groups

Many populations are diverse in their origins and therefore their buying patterns. Countries like Malaysia and Singapore will have a strong mix of Malay and Chinese, while Britain reflects its European and Commonwealth heritage. Ethnic minorities account for around 5 per cent of the total with Indians, West Indians and Pakistanis comprising the largest groups but with Chinese, Africans, Bangladeshis and Arabs well represented.

These groups tend to be younger than the indigenous white population with only 4 per cent over 60 (compared to 21 per cent). This produces a very different pattern of needs which must be accounted for by marketers and local authorities alike. Where ethnic concentrations occur the number of births have therefore been more buoyant than elsewhere, although West Indian experience, the oldest New Commonwealth immigrant group, exhibits rates little different to overall average.

> **QUESTION 8.6**
>
> Why have ethnic minority-owned businesses been able to exploit profitable niche markets among these populations without attracting substantial competition from established businesses?
> (**See** Activity debrief at the end of this unit.)

Occupational structure

At the outset of the Industrial Revolution 60 per cent of the employed workforce were engaged in the *primary sectors* of agriculture, forestry, fishing, mining and quarrying. A century of industrialization saw 60 per cent in the *secondary sector* of manufacturing, construction and utilities such as electricity. By 1980 a further transformation had occurred, with over 60 per cent employed in the *tertiary sector*, including transport, financial, retail and personal services.

The current position is shown in Table 8.2 with a significant contraction in both primary and manufacturing industries. Indeed, Professor Stonier, in his book *The Wealth of Information*, predicted continuing contraction in manufacturing to half the 1992 total by the year 2000.

Table 8.2 Employment status by industry group

						Britain (%)
Industry group	Self-employed			Employees		
	Men	Women	All	Men	Women	All
Primary, energy and extractive	11	7	10	10	3	6
Manufacturing	11	9	10	26	12	19
Construction	27	2	21	7	2	5
Services	51	81	59	57	83	69
All industries (thousands = 100%)	2 321	770	3 091	11 182	10 171	21 353

Source: Labour Force Survey, Autumn 1992.

The workforce in employment

This has been relatively stable over the three decades to 1996 but with deep depressions in 1980–1983, and 1990–1993, when it fell to 23 and 24.25, million respectively. Between 1983 and mid-1991, however, over 3 million net new jobs were created, contributing to an overall rise of 6 per cent over the last decade. By late 1995 it stood at 25.5 million, and is projected to increase by 1.5 million up to the year 2006. Two-thirds will be part-time women.

Manufacturing employment in the latest recession contracted by 1 million to just under 4 million. Service employment fell back slightly but since mid-1993 has been creating net new jobs as recovery strengthened. The armed forces continue to contract with an 11 per cent fall over the decade so far.

There are now 11.1 million women (46 per cent of the total) in the workforce and increasing while male employment continues to fall. This reflects the decline in full-time industrial employment where men predominate and the rise of services and part-time work, where women are mainly found. Forty-eight per cent of women as against just 12 per cent of men work part-time. The latter percentage is, however, rising quickly as male employment attitudes alter.

The increase in jobs as Britain recovered from recession has been in part-time employment. Over the last decade, part-time employment has risen by a dramatic 43 per cent while full-time has contracted by 4 per cent, little wonder that male part-timers have nearly doubled while female part-timers rose by a third.

QUESTION 8.7

Normally as an economy emerges from a deep recession there is a long lag before unemployment falls. Employers are cautious about the outlook and prefer to use existing resources more intensively.

In the light of the recent rises in part-time employment, what are the attractions of this mode of work to:

- The business?
- The employee?
- The government?

How might recent legal developments affect this assessment?
What are the implications for sales and marketing of these work patterns?
(**See** Activity debrief at the end of this unit.)

Some important employment trends

We have already identified a number of important developments:

- *The decline in full-time employment*   The 'norm' of a 9a.m.–5p.m. 40-hour week may cease to be normal by the next century.
- *The corresponding rise of part-time employment*   This has risen from just under 5 per cent to nearly 30 per cent of all employment in just 25 years.
- *Hours are lengthening for those working full-time*   A quarter of all males work over 50 hours, against just 5 per cent of females.
- *Self-employment is rising sharply*   The percentage had doubled by 1993 to 12.7 per cent compared to 15 years earlier and are projected to rise by a quarter in the next decade. The incidence varies widely between industries, being especially high in building and construction. Hotels and catering are understandably above average while manufacturing records only half the overall rate. Table 8.2 reflects this distribution as well as the predominance of services for women.

ACTIVITY 8.4

Conduct a survey of men and women who are self-employed to ascertain the following:

- What are the main reasons for being self-employed?
- Are there any differences in the reasons given by those recently becoming self-employed?
- Are there differences between reasons given by men and women?

- *A rise in contractual and temporary employment* As many businesses have faced an increasingly competitive environment in recent years they have been forced to concentrate on core activities. Unless specialized resources can be fully utilized it has become more efficient to contract-out services or contract-in labour as and when required. The convenience of a large directly employed labour force has become a luxury not even the public sector can afford. Transport and distribution may be contracted-out to third-party operators while specialized marketing skills are hired or 'outsourced' through agencies as and when required.
- *The emergence of flexible organizations* Charles Handy in his book *The Age of Unreason* suggests that more and more organizations employ *a core* of full-time scientific, technical, marketing and managerial employees with company-specific skills and proprietary knowledge to coordinate and direct the fundamental activities of the business. A flexible workforce is utilized to achieve this, composed of readily adjustable groups including:

    High turnover semi-skilled full-timers
    Part-timers
    Temporary workers
    Job sharers
    Staff on short or temporary contracts
    Student industrial placements
    Government trainees
    Homeworkers
    Subcontractors
- *The rise of the knowledge worker* Under 45 per cent of the total employed are now officially classified as manual. Since only a third of those employed in manufacturing are likely to be on the shopfloor, well over half of the workforce may now be designated as knowledge workers. This includes those occupations that produce, process, use and distribute knowledge as well as maintain the infrastructure for its transmission. Since most jobs will require brains rather than brawn in the next century, the government is belatedly expanding vocational and higher education in an effort to avert critical skill shortages from inhibiting high-technology growth opportunities. With the Japanese pattern of educating virtually all its highly motivated 18-year-olds being emulated by the other emerging dragons of East Asia, they appear much better equipped to effect the transition to post-industrial society than is the case in Britain. Malaysia, for example, aims to triple its students on scientific and technical courses by the year 2000.

ACTIVITY 8.5

Classify all of the people working in your organization into manual or knowledge workers using the criteria given above.

You will find that it is not so easy in practice since most jobs have some knowledge components involved in them.

- *Flexible work lives* The need for flexibility in business today is producing a kaleidoscope of working patterns for the marketer to observe:

    Flexitime   enabling employees to plan their own time allocation
    Staggered hours   lengthening but spreading the 'rush hours'
    Flexible work years   to match seasonal patterns of activity
    Flexible shifts and rosters   to effectively cover customer service requirements
    Longer days but shorter weeks   to maximize actual working time
    2 × 12-hour weekend shifts   to maximize utilization of plant
    Planned reduction in hours towards retirement
    Working from home   telecommuting through office computer intranet links.

This flexibility is in both employee and business interests. It is underpinning much less standardized life styles and demanding a marketing response to cater for three day weekends, all-night and even all-day entertainment as well as the late-night banking and retailing we increasingly take for granted.

- *The self-service economy* Non-standard work patterns imply non-standard leisure patterns and more of this leisure time is being absorbed doing tasks which were previously undertaken by business. Self-service is already well established on much of the high street while home-shopping cable and video systems take the process one step further. Interactive computer systems linked to databases offer dramatic potential to transform the way in which many services are currently marketed, sold and performed. Home banking, direct insurance and distance learning are just a sample of leading-edge applications.

> **EXAM TIP**
>
> Remember that any question posed on the environment must be answered in context. The regurgitation of academic content alone is insufficient. It must be shaped to fit the question context.
>
> This is why it is inadvisable to prepare model answers to questions you think might be set in the exam. It is highly unlikely that the way the question is posed will match your preparation. Unless you are very careful you will be tempted to make the question fit your prepared answer rather than the other way round! Better to be flexible, read the question precisely, and determine exactly what the examiner requires.

The changing role of women in work and society

The situation of men and women at work in Britain during the early 1990s still remains very much one where the different genders are employed in different sectors, different industries, different occupations and different levels in the hierarchy. Women usually have family responsibilities yet nearly half now go out to work, at least part-time. Domestic duties combine to ensure that they often work harder (an estimated 10 hours a week on average) but they are promoted less often and are generally less well paid than male counterparts. Despite a four-point improvement since 1987, women in Britain earn, on average, only 77 per cent of men's wages. This is up to 10 percentage points less than in most other European countries. The gap is even greater in terms of weekly pay because men generally work longer hours, attracting overtime rates.

Women are under-represented in manufacturing but dominate in many service industries. Caring occupations such as health and primary education register a ratio of 80:20 in favour of women overall but, interestingly, men still dominate the top positions.

The rising proportion of women in higher education, to nearly half by the 1990s, has contributed to an improvement in their representation in managerial and professional occupations. This is now over 25 per cent but is not reflected in senior management, where they form just 2–3 per cent of the membership of large company boards. This is highlighted in Figures 8.6 and 8.7, which also show women predominating in people- or service-centred staff functions rather than line positions, contributing directly to profitability.

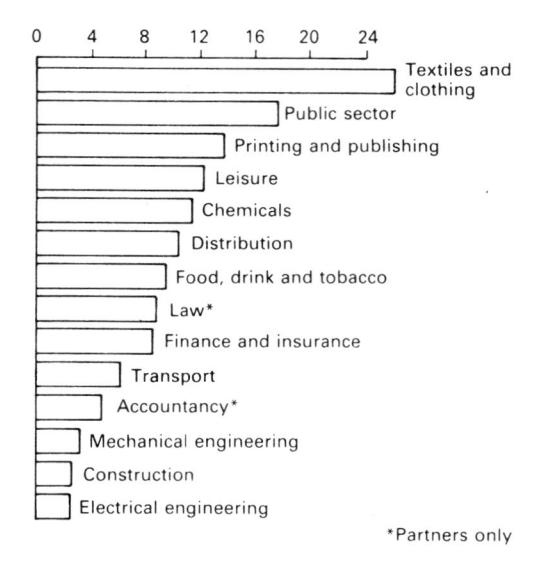

Figure 8.6 Percentage of British managers who are women (by industry). (*Sources:* British Institute of Management; *Remuneration Economics*)

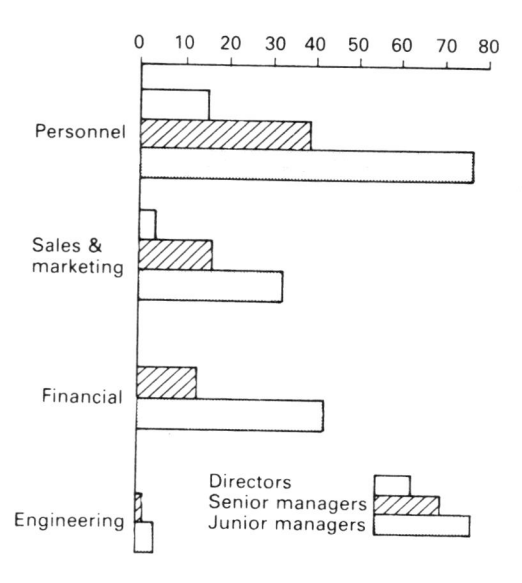

Figure 8.7 Percentage of British managers who are women (by function and status). (*Sources:* British Institute of Management; *Remuneration Economics*)

> - Identify the areas, in an organization of your choice, in which women appear to be under-represented.
> - Investigate the causes of this situation.
> - Consider the ingredients of a 'positive action plan' to improve the utilization of women in the organization.
>
> ACTIVITY 8.6

Since women already account for half of the educated workforce and given the decline in births, the only source of untapped labour potential, how should business respond? Recession and high unemployment may have relieved the pressure until now, but sustained growth will quickly expose critical shortages. The British government has also shown its concern by launching Opportunity 2000, an initiative encouraging major organizations to set targets for employing more women in senior positions by the end of the decade. This includes the NHS, largely run by men but with women comprising 80 per cent of its 1 million workers. The Labour Party's attempt to introduce 'all women' lists for selecting Parliamentary candidates, however, fell foul of sexual discrimination legislation although over 100 female MPs were returned at the 1997 election. The policy responses have included:

- Career break keep-in-touch schemes
- Flexible working patterns
- Women-friendly recruitment, selection, appraisal and promotion procedures
- Attitude retraining and training in 'core' activities
- Common pay and conditions – equal reward for work of equal value.

It must be recognized, however, that the Civil Service adopted similar policies some years ago to allow women to mix family and career. The result has been an actual decline in those prepared to dedicate themselves to get to the top. One of the main comparative advantages of the male executive is that they have the support of a wife, a luxury denied to the latter!

The actions women require organizations to undertake, to allow them to fulfil the demands of higher positions, would include:

- Positive retraining after career breaks
- Flexible work hours
- Workplace nurseries or
- Financial support for private child care

Unfortunately, only 23 per cent of companies in a recent survey provided career breaks, and only a small percentage provided workplace nurseries. State nursery provision has until recently been limited and private childcare is very expensive, however the Labour government's replacement of vouchers with guaranteed places for 4 year olds should improve matters.

One other problem is the tendency, identified by Kantor, for those in large organizations to hire and promote those who resemble themselves. Women who are promoted may be only token gestures for public relations purposes and not treated seriously. Such feelings will tend to make women less forceful.

An Institute of Directors study in 1992 found that three-quarters of female directors believed that they were discriminated against in the workplace while an Institute of Management study in the same year found men's club networks, prejudice and harassment to be three of the top four barriers women encountered. Most respondents opposed positive discrimination as a solution however, with selection on merit the preferred option.

Recognition of so-called 'glass ceilings', preventing women's advancement, has begun to stiffen government resolve for more positive action. Pressure groups are also becoming more active and even shareholders are asking questions at AGMs. However, the most effective catalyst for fundamental change remains a diminishing labour supply which confronts businesses with the choice between hiring more women or lower-quality men.

> **EXAM TIP**
>
> The Marketing Environment is a challenging syllabus. It is therefore doubly important that you practise using your understanding of the subject knowledge. As you are now three-quarters of the way through this workbook have you:
>
> - Developed answer plans to each of the past examination questions set?
> - Practised writing a complete answer to at least one of these?
> - Obtained feedback on your answer from a tutor or practitioner? and ... will you be making the time to undertake the complete paper provided at the end of the workbook *under timed examination conditions* and *before* studying the model answers?
>
> Do not make the mistake of making the actual examination the first opportunity to practise your answering technique. The outcome is likely to be an expensive, time-consuming and confidence-sapping resit. As in other skill areas, practice makes perfect, so do not be tempted to skip answering the specimen questions.

The social and cultural environment

The difficulties experienced by women in employment relative to men outlined above are largely a reflection of societal attitudes in general and male-dominated corporate cultures in particular. The marketer and sales executive can exert little influence on this aspect of the environment but understanding is vital, if the buying behaviour that results from it is to be fully understood.

Our culture moulds and regulates daily behaviour through constant conditioning and reinforcement. We learn what is and what is not appropriate behaviour in different social situations. Our attitudes, beliefs, values and language derive from such cultural influences as the family, community, religion and education.

Our culture, then, is reflected in what we eat, how and where we live, our life styles and buying preferences, not to mention our humour, art and music. The international marketer, especially, must become aware of the social mores of any country in which they seek sales. When in Rome, do as the Romans do is apt advice since the accepted norms of business behaviour in, say, Japan are very different compared to those in Europe. Business and general societal customs must also be observed if offence is to be avoided.

> **ACTIVITY 8.7**
>
> The social mores or norms of accepted behaviour in Islamic or East Asian countries are radically different in many ways from those of Europe. Under the various headings mentioned in the paragraphs above, research all the main differences you can identify.

> Prepare a short report comparing and contrasting the two cultures and provide behavioural guidelines for an international marketer trading between the two.

The marketer must recognize that while many social mores and customs are deeply rooted, others are in the process of change:

- *Role of women* The primacy of the domestic role has declined with developing opportunities for work and career. Smaller families and enhanced parental aspirations have freed resources for girls to pursue higher education. Changing female stereotypes are reflected in advertisements where the subjects are less likely to enthuse about the relative merits of detergents and more prone to be confident and assertive. However, there has been some reaction to the behavioural changes involved, not least in respect to the degree of 'political correctness' now required in this area. For the marketer and salesperson, the full- or part-time working woman has provided extra discretionary purchasing power to the household and over which disposal she has had increasing influence. Demand for property, consumer durables and holidays have been sustained by these incomes. Work and domestic pressures have also put a premium on time and its effective management. Convenience foods, time-saving appliances and the combined versatility of the freezer and the microwave have transformed food preparation. Central heating and instant warmth at the flick of a switch have extracted the drudgery from another basic household function. Life style and mail order catalogues and one-stop shopping are other necessary innovations to enable the management of enlarging household consumption within the declining non-work time available. The need to be satisfied here is to enable the household to maximize work and leisure by economizing on the non-productive time required to service them.

> **EXAM TIP**
>
> A high proportion of CIM candidates are women, so on the premise that the examiner will wish to appeal to all constituencies of the target candidate market, from time to time, expect an occasional question in this area.

- *Religious values and Sunday observance* Church attendance has fallen sharply in the last twenty-five years partly reflecting declining religious values among post-war age groups and secularization. The latter supposes continuing belief, but the absence of its formal expression in places of worship. The increasing mobility of households and an array of possible family activities on Sundays have provided alternatives and the means to satisfy them. The rising ownership of cars and television and a parallel decline in the cohesion of many local communities have also contributed to the erosion. Eventual success in the Sunday Opening campaign in late 1993 was the culmination of these forces for change, opening a vast new market for large retailers and do-it-yourself stores. On the other hand, fast-growing membership of new 'religions' may reflect a trend of individualism and diversity in cultural terms.
- *Healthy living and fitness trends* Concern for health and natural foods was mainly the realm of eccentric hippies up to twenty years ago. Smoking was also the norm and thought to symbolize maturity and sophistication. Attitudes are markedly different today with widespread concern over heart disease, cancer, obesity and lack of exercise. Significant sales and marketing opportunities have developed as a result not least in the markets for low-fat foods, trainers, leisure clothing and fitness clinics. Although jogging as an activity may have waned, the pseudo-image provided by designer sports wear is a symbolic substitute. 'Appearances' are increasingly important to all generations and offer complex but profitable marketing opportunities.

QUESTION 8.8

What other examples of socio-cultural change over the last twenty years can you think of? List them and brainstorm their implications for marketers and sales managers: e.g. animal rights and vegatarianism.
(**See** Activity debrief at the end of this unit.)

Social class

One way of classifying groups within society is according to their class. A class comprises individuals who share common characteristics including occupation, level of income, educational background and various aspects of life style. For the marketer it is not always the actual social class an individual belongs to that is significant but rather the class they identify with or to which they aspire.

The young in particular may adopt life styles that differ from those of their parents. Open educational access and rising incomes for all classes has facilitated this class movement.

Class and class aspirations are important since they will be reflected in purchasing preferences and form one of the most widely used methods of segmenting product markets. Examples of widely used categorizations based on class include:

Social class category	Occupation
A	Professional, administrative, top management
B	Intermediate professional, etc.
C1	Supervisory, clerical and lower management
C2	Skilled manual
D	Semi- and unskilled manual
E	State pensioners, long-term unemployed, etc.

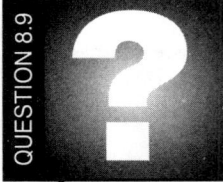

QUESTION 8.9

- Critically appraise the usefulness of the above classification system.
- Can you think of an alternative approach to segmenting socio-economic groups that would be more appropriate?
- Is your buying behaviour more related to your income or the social class to which you aspire?

(**See** Activity debrief at the end of this unit.)

In mass urban centres where people are unable to get to know one another with the closer intimacy possible in small communities it is perhaps unsurprising that symbols are adopted to signal who we are and where we stand in society's pecking order. We classify those we meet on the type and quality of clothes they wear, the cars they drive, their sports and social activities, the houses and localities they live in as well as their manner, speech and the type of job they do. These are, in effect, badges of class membership and therefore vital pattern indicators for the salesperson to recognize and the marketer to mobilize in focused promotional campaigns.

ACTIVITY 8.8

Select one of the following sectors and research how spending patterns vary by class (look for Mintel market research reports or the most recent copy of ONS's *Social Trends* to assist you in this):

- Eating out
- Holidays and weekend breaks
- Arts and entertainment

Reference groups

Related to class is the concept of the reference group whose actions and behaviour influence the attitudes and values of large numbers of others who seek to imitate them. Reference groups may be large or small and include:

- The family
- Student peer group
- Work colleagues
- Clubs

Since most individuals wish to 'belong' to certain preferred groups they will tend to conform to the norms of dress and behaviour laid down by them. Those within the group whose influence over what is and is not acceptable is substantial are known as opinion formers or leaders. Their influence may be based on expertise, knowledge or perhaps a charismatic personality. If a business can persuade such leaders to adopt their product then 'opinion followers' will also tend to purchase. Little wonder that sports equipment manufacturers secure endorsements from top players; use their product and you can be a winner too! Movie makers are also getting in on the act, although Reebok's legal action arising from an altered film ending suggests potential conflicts between art and commercialism.

Marketers must therefore identify the relevant reference groups in the segments they have targeted, especially where expensive purchases (relative to the group's income) involving conspicuous consumption are concerned. The need to 'keep up with the Jones' or emulate members of a reference group to whom the consumer aspires is a powerful basis upon which to charge premium prices, not least to reinforce the implicit snob appeal involved.

The family

The family is a close and influential reference group. It conditions behaviour and values from birth and continues to influence buying decisions throughout the individual's life. This has led to the identification of a *family life cycle* made up of different stages or phases in family life with significant implications for buying behaviour as follows:

> **EXAM TIP**
> Are you still keeping those files on Units 1–7 up to date? Revision is so much easier if you do this as you proceed through the course.

- *Young unmarried* Young and footloose with relatively high disposable income due to limited commitments. Fashion and entertainment orientated.
- *Newly married/no children* Dual income with expenditure focused on home building, consumer durables and holidays.
- *Young married/children* Home and family expenditure orientated. Limited scope for entertainment/luxury items
- *Middle-aged married/teenage children* Approaching maximum dual earnings, high replacement expenditure on quality durables
- *Older married/children left home* Disposable income at a peak and focused on retirement planning and luxuries. Well-established tastes and preferences in many cases
- *Older retired/single* Reduced disposable income but increasingly numerous and affluent. Conservative tastes and less susceptible to marketing campaigns. Important purchasers of one-off items like cars, holiday homes and expensive garden equipment.

> **ACTIVITY 8.9**
> Scan the advertisements in newspapers and magazines and classify their appeal according to (a) reference groups and/or (b) family stages.

In understanding the family and its spending decisions salespeople and marketers must seek to identify not only who makes the final purchasing decision but also the influence exerted by other family members. Only in this way can they be sure as to whom they should direct their promotional messages. Who is it that decides the type and location of this year's family holiday? Do parents decide on style of dress or their teenage children? Are changes taking place in the distribution of this decision-making power as more married women work and men share more of the domestic responsibilities?

Stereotyped notions of the male deciding the type of car and home improvements while the female decides the food and furnishings may be increasingly suspect and the business must keep a finger on the changing social pulse if the marketing mix is to remain relevant and effective. That said, the most recent edition of *Social Trends* saw little evidence of 'New Man' emerging among younger age groups. The division of roles in households persists, with mothers spending six times as long cooking and cleaning and twice as long shopping.

Life style
Life styles are defined as the patterns in which people live, spend time and money. They are a function of the individual's motivation and prior learning as well as class, personality and other variables. They are measured by analysts using *attitude, interests and opinions scales (AIO)* alongside demographic factors to establish market segments with clusters of common characteristics.

The central idea is to build a picture of how individuals interact with the environment around them by identifying their behavioural patterns. This will then allow marketers to more effectively segment the market and tailor campaigns designed to appeal to particular life-style types. The presumption is that these groups will respond to different marketing mixes which can then be exploited to advantage.

Companies such as Laura Ashley, Next and Habitat have used such analysis to drive their marketing communications and encourage readers of their catalogues to identify with a particular cluster and therefore focus their purchasing behaviour on the products offered.

The marketer must, however, avoid oversimplified categorization. Individuals may exhibit multiple life style characteristics or evolve from one type to another as time and circumstances alter.

> **ACTIVITY 8.10**
>
> Consider the realism of the following life style trends and their implications for niche furniture manufacturers and retailers:
>
> - *Instant gratification*   Live now pay later
> - *Easy credit attitudes*   to finance the good life
> - *Time conservation*   critical resource constraint on consumption
> - *New work ethic*   working to live, not living to work
> - *Consumerism*   concern for price/quality/service/environment
> - *Personal creativity*   desire for self-expression/improvement
> - *Naturalism*   return to nature but retaining material comforts.
>
> What other life style trends can you currently identify in society?
> (**See** Activity debrief at the end of this unit.)

A summary of segmentation bases in consumer markets
The main types of segmentation considered so far have been:

- Geographic
- Life style
- Demographic:
  Age, sex, nationality and education
  Income
  Family size and life cycle
  Occupation and social class

The final aspect to consider is segmentation based on *neighbourhood and type of dwelling*. As a composite index of factors relevant to buying behaviour this is thought to represent a more accurate assessment than those based solely on one factor such as class or income. A well-used example of this approach is the ACORN system (i.e. A Classification of Residential Neighbourhoods), which classifies households into one of eleven major groups and thirty-six specific neighbourhood types:

- A Modern family housing for manual
  - A1 local authority and new-town housing: high wage
  - A2 mixed housing, young families
  - A3 recent council housing
  - A4 modern low cost private
- B Modern family housing, higher incomes
- C Older housing of intermediate status
- D Very poor quality, older terraced
- E Rural areas
  - E13 Villages with some non-farm employment
  - E14 Rural areas with large farms
  - E15 Rural areas with own account farmers
- F Urban local authority housing
- G Housing with most overcrowding
- H Low-income areas with immigrants
- I Student and high-status non-family areas
- J Traditional high-status non-suburbia
- K Areas of elderly people
- U Unclassified (e.g. hospitals and prisons)

> **QUESTION 8.10**
>
> Some of the specific neighbourhood types (A1–A4, E13–15) have been included in the table above. How would you subdivide the other groups in a meaningful way?
>
> Which of the above groups would you estimate contains the highest proportion of British households? Which has the lowest?
>
> To what extent do you feel ACORN will be a good indicator of purchasing behaviour? (**See** Activity debrief at the end of this unit.)

Final thoughts on culture
- As we have seen above, culture is a complex blend of acquired values, beliefs, attitudes and customs which provide context and behavioural guidelines for life within a given society.
- A national culture is usually composed of subcultures based on such considerations as origins, religion or some basis of shared outlook and values.
- Subcultures form important bases for segmentation whether on a regional (e.g. Welsh), urban (e.g. Bradford, Pakistani) or locality (e.g. Jewish community, North London) grounds.
- Individuals from different cultures are likely to respond to different imperatives in terms of what, where, when and how they buy goods and services.
- Ample data exist for analysis of purchasing variations related to regional cultural differences. *Regional Trends* is compiled by the ONS and may be supplemented by market research often derived from the regional television companies.
- While the South-east with its concentration of higher-income households may provide useful insight into future buying trends in other less prosperous regions the marketer must also recognize the degree to which purchasing behaviour is culturally driven.

Summary

In this unit we have seen:

- The importance to the marketer of monitoring and understanding the implications of demographic changes. These change slowly over time but their cumulative impact over a period can have immense consequences for buying patterns.
- The relevant factors in population structure and their effects on both the supply and demand sides of the market.
- Some of the important employment trends, with particular emphasis on the drive for greater flexibility by businesses.
- The changing role of women in work and society and the ongoing impacts of this transformation.
- The meaning of the term 'culture' and its relevance to successful international and regional marketing.
- Some of the more important social trends and the marketing lessons to be learnt from them.
- The significance of social influences such as class, occupation and life style as bases for segmentation, with particular attention to reference groups such as the family.

Activity debrief

Question 8.1 Those retiring will have state pensions supplemented by private pensions. They will have planned financially for retirement and may have inherited valuable properties in recent years. They will form a market segment with clear ideas regarding their requirements. They will still be fit and active. The mix must reflect this, especially in terms of the product and the financing arrangements. Promotion must address their wants.

Question 8.3

- New technology improved agricultural productivity; industrialization; opened up the lands of the New World; emigration; refrigeration; demographic transition, etc.
- No unexploited continents; global competition; immigration laws; pollution consequences of modern agriculture. A lot therefore rests on development of sustainable technologies and overseas aid. Population growth does not necessarily mean market opportunities because it tends to correlate with very low or falling income per head.
- An optimum population allows full advantage to be taken of resources. A growing population can revitalize and bring larger markets and more mobility. Excessive population as seen in parts of Africa and Latin America can unbalance the ecology through overgrazing and deforestation.

Question 8.4 Quality, service, value for money and greater durability. Over-45s will be renewing household effects after child-rearing and will look for design, not functionality.

Question 8.5 Apart from logistical considerations, life styles will be different. Outlying areas poorly served by public transport will have higher car ownership and infrequent, high-spending trips to retailers.

Question 8.6 The culture, attitudes and buying habits of these groups differ significantly from the indigenous population. The entrepreneurial abilities of some of these minorities are also outstanding: 17 per cent of the Indian community are self-employed against 11 per cent for all groups.

Question 8.7

- For business the main attraction is flexibility to employ when the labour is required (e.g. retail shopping peaks). Wages tend to be lower and other wage costs are avoided. Exemption from employment legislation and National Insurance also contribute.
- For employees, especially married women, it may fit well with other responsibilities and needs. It also suits the semi-retired.
- For government it reduces the overall unemployment rate.
- Recent legislation has put part-time workers on equal employment status to full-time.
- A change in work patterns implies changes in buying and shopping patterns. One-stop shopping and convenience purchases are reflections of this trend. It is also more likely that the male is more involved in routine shopping decisions.

Question 8.8 Examples may include changing attitudes to:
- *Credit* previously disapproved of but now an accepted part of marketing activity.
- *Single-parent families* even the term 'illegitimate' is losing social stigma.

- *Virtue of hard work* unemployment experience may be causing a swing back in this direction not least as companies downsize their management numbers, putting pressures on those that remain.
- *Concern for quality of life* green products, outdoor life styles, demand for the 'good' things of life.
- *Less formality* reflected in dress and decor.

Question 8.9
- The classification is based solely on occupation and ignores the fact that changing wage relativities have altered comparative purchasing power. Some C2s are better off than many C1s and Bs, for example, and this is reflected in purchases. Others are not easy to fit into the classification (e.g. those living on inherited wealth).
- An alternative classification would be to select specific classes (e.g. upper middle, lower lower, etc.) and define the households concerned in terms of source and size of income, place of residence, type of work, core attitudes and so forth.
- Social classes tend to have distinct and recognizable product and brand preferences which symbolize their position.

Question 8.10
- J includes modern private housing/high income; medium status inter-war private; established suburbs of high status and very high status areas.
- J and F both account for around 20 per cent each while G is less than 2.5 per cent.

Activity 8.4 Factors might include independence, lack of paid employment, redundancy payments provided, opportunity, encouragement through tax measures, lack of promotion or recognition in paid employment, etc.

Extending activity 8.1 The factors you may have identified are:

Political	Economic
Provision of welfare services	Rising real incomes
State pensions	Cost of housing
Equal-opportunity legislation	Rising opportunity cost of children
Erosion of family allowances	Recession/poor employment outlook
Social	*Technical*
Children no longer an insurance for secure old age	Decline in child mortality via medical advance removes need for more
Changing religious attitudes	birth control advances
Cultural norms changing on women's role in society	Media influences
	Marketing influence – nuclear family
Concern for health/figure	and promotion of consumer durables
Decline in marriage and rise in illegitimacy rate (28 per cent!)	

Activity 8.10 Other trends might include health and fitness; novelty and change; energy and environmental friendliness; value for money; supranational or global orientation.

Examination hints and specimen questions

We have already seen in Unit 6 that a question may be posed on the environmental set of a business organization. This provides ample scope for the examiner to select at least one factor or trend from the social, demographic and cultural environment.

Clearly, any of the aspects discussed above could form the basis of a question and you should prepare accordingly. Note that a question may test not only your understanding of the trend but also its impact on, or implication for, the business concerned.

Optional question – illustration only

(a) What is the significance of the social environment for the marketer. (6 marks)
(b) Select two significant social trends and discuss their marketing implications for either a grocery retailer or a bank. (10 marks)
(c) Provide a bibliography of relevant sources on social trends. (4 marks)

(CIM Marketing Environment paper, June 1996)

Specific questions may also be posed, as the following shows:

PART A:
Compulsory question

With a greyer picture of the future in mind

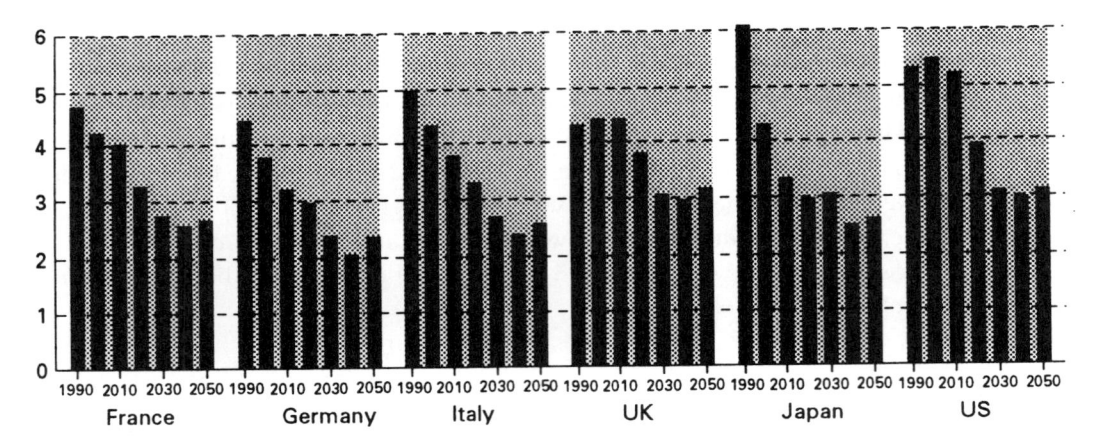

Age structure switches towards the elderly
Ratio of the number of people of working age, 15 years to 64 years, to support each person aged 65 years and over

While there are few trends which can be forecast with confidence over decades, there is one prediction that can safely be made about the industrialized countries – their populations will grow older over the next 40 years.

In the 18 western European member states of the OECD, the number of people aged 65 and over will rise from 50 million to more than 70 million between 1990 and 2030. During the same period, the number of people of working age will fall. The result is that, by 2030, there will be fewer than three people of working age in these countries for each person over 65, compared with five now.

Similar trends can be seen in other leading world economies such as the US and Japan. The populations of the tigers of the Pacific rim, such as Singapore and Taiwan are also ageing fast. In contrast, developing countries such as China, India and Brazil, will have a much lower share of elderly people.

Economists predict that ageing will have an enormous impact on economies and their international competitiveness, but there is little agreement over the precise nature of the change. Dr Paul Johnson states that 'demographic restructuring could alter patterns of consumption, employment, saving, investment and innovation, but because of the interactions between these separate elements, it is impossible to be sure of either the scale or, in some cases, the direction of the economic impact. Our understanding of the processes of economic growth and of innovation are too primitive to make long-term predictions.'

This uncertainty extends even to the question of whether an ageing population will save more (to provide for old age) or save less as nest-eggs are cashed in for retirement. Lower savings rates could threaten economic growth, although the evidence so far from all over Europe is that ageing populations save more.

The economic consequences of a changing demogrphic structure will be felt unevenly, as some countries face more radical demographic change than others. The greatest impact in the EU will be felt in Germany where the population will decline by 15 million between now and 2030. Today a fifth of the population is aged 20 or younger; by 2030 only 16 per cent will be. Ageing will be less in the UK and US but globally it would be the NICs, such as China and Brazil, which would gain the greatest competitive advantage by virtue of their much younger populations.

(Source: *Financial Times*, John Williams, 8 March 1994)

1 (a) Write short notes on two of the following terms used in the article briefly summarizing their economic significance to the marketer:
- The OECD
- The Pacific rim
- NICs
- Demographic structure

(6 marks each)
(Total 12 marks)

Either
- (b) Discuss the likely impact of ageing on the labour market. What recommendations would you make to a business currently reliant on recruiting large numbers of school-leavers to meet its labour needs? (16 marks)

Or
- (c) 'Businesses will have to cope with changes in demand patterns as older consumers become more significant in their markets and younger people less so.'
  Explain, with examples, some of the opportunities provided by these changing demand patterns and how the marketer should address this buyer segment. (16 marks)
- (d) 'Ageing is one of the few trends that can be forecast with confidence.'
  Briefly explain why this is so, and suggest **two** forecasting approaches, showing how they might enable the marketer to forecast the future with greater confidence. (12 marks)

(CIM Marketing Environment paper, June 1995)

Hints: Indicative content and approach

Question 1(a)
- Attempt the first three options after you have completed Unit 10.
- Note the tendency for compulsory questions to take terms from the text and require you to explain their meaning and significance (see sample compulsory question in the Guidance on revision and examination unit at the end of the workbook for another example).
- Follow the rubric instruction and only answer two terms.
- When short notes are asked for, produce notes and keep them short! (i.e. 6 marks each warrants only 10 minutes per term).
- Divide the bullet points into notes on meaning and significance.
- Demographic structure relates to age, sex, distribution, etc., not patterns.

Question 1(b)
- Choose carefully between the optional parts to make the best use of your demographic knowledge.
- Relate the impact of ageing to the mobility, fluidity and efficiency of the labour market – new blood and ideas.
- Concentrate on recommendations and use a good example such as the National Health Service or the armed forces who recruit large numbers.
- Adopt a broad approach, e.g. recruitment policies; alternative labour forces; substitute technology; relocation; retention strategies, etc.
- The alternative is a more marketing oriented question combined with economic analysis of changing demand patterns.
- Provide examples of expanding older segments and shrinking younger segments.
- Remember that purchasing power depends on discretionary income as well as numbers.

Question 1(c)
- This question was poorly answered because candidates failed to understand it was about forecasting methods rather that research methods.
- The first part of the question is not about why people are living longer but why it is predictable. Given that births and life expectancies are known, then only a serious discontinuity could undermine the confidence.
- Forecasting approaches could be quantitative (e.g. moving average) or qualitative (e.g. Delphi or Scenario).

UNIT 9

The technical and natural environments

OBJECTIVES

In this unit, which examines the all-embracing effects of technological change with particular reference to its impacts on the natural environment, you will:

- Investigate the nature and characteristics of technology.
- Understand some of the mechanisms responsible for producing change in this environment.
- Assess its impact on the sales executive and marketer, in different types of business.
- Recognize some constraints and limitations on the pace and quality of change in this important environment.

By the end of this unit you will:

- Have understood the role of business as the main medium for the development and diffusion of new technology.
- Appreciate the factors driving change.
- Recognize the importance of technical monitoring and forecasting.
- Have assessed the significance of the absorptive capabilities of the natural environment, as limits to the nature and direction of future change.

STUDY GUIDE

We live in a technological society whose effects impact on all aspects of our life. Our work is particularly subject to such influences and major transformations have occurred in recent years in the majority of industries and occupations. Other aspects of our life have also been increasingly affected; our means of transport, how we shop, the ways we spend our leisure time, how we learn, the houses we live in and the way our health is monitored. Only our sleeping habits seem relatively unaffected, although even here new drugs, insulation, bed designs and environment control are affecting the lives of many.

The technological environment is an area which can generate a diversity of examples as context for examining its impacts. This unit will therefore concentrate on general themes and leave you the responsibility of finding relevant applications from your own experience and reading.

As you will see from the past examination question at the end of this unit, the examiner may require you to select technologies of your own choosing and discuss their effects or define the general meaning and implications of terms such as 'software' or 'multi media'. You do not necessarily have to select typical areas such as information technology, cars or drugs. Relevant applications from your own industry are more likely to interest and impress the examiner, since it shows you are seeking to relate your studies to your work situation. Do make sure, however, that you have a working knowledge of technical terms affecting the work of marketers (see the Glossary for some of these).

> A very useful supplement to this unit is Chapter 11 in *The Business and Marketing Environment* (second edition) by Palmer and Hartley, which deals in detail with specific applications of information technology to the marketing context.
>
> This unit again accounts for around 10 per cent of the total syllabus, inferring that a question might be expected in alternative exams. Do not bank on a full question, however, and remember that the compulsory question may provide scope for part-questions. To expedite your studies in this area you will require a file sectioned into at least five parts:
>
> - The technological environment
> - Technology and change in your own industry
> - Sales and marketing impacts: (a) general, (b) own industry
> - Resistances to change
> - The natural environment

Definition of terms

The successful development of new technology comprises a number of distinct stages:

KNOWLEDGE – RESEARCH – INVENTION – DEVELOPMENT – INNOVATION – DIFFUSION

New technology represents the means of satisfying consumer needs and wants, more efficiently and effectively. It allows more and better value-for-money goods to be produced with given resources. It is one of the primary means of shifting out the *production possibility curve* (PPC), as seen in Figure 9.1. If the change only affects, say, the production of investment goods then the PPC will pivot outwards since no impact will be felt on consumer goods.

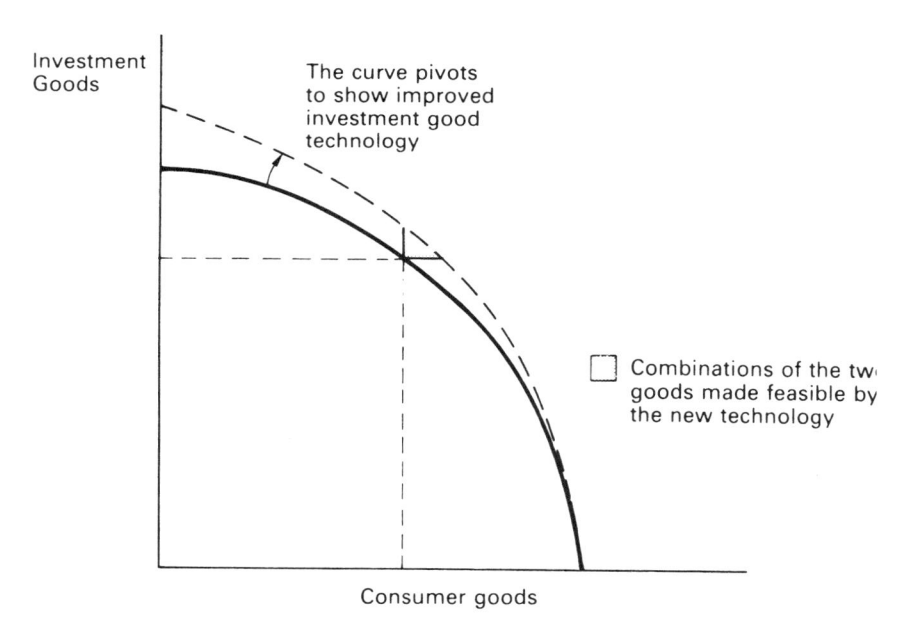

Figure 9.1 The production possibility curve revisited

The state of technology is a function of resources and the knowledge and skills to use them while technical change is the result of changing resources, increased product and process knowledge and the accumulation of applications experience. Knowledge of the current state of technology is the base upon which research takes place. New ideas and developments in sciences often form the basis of advance and synthesis in others. Research and invention is the generation of new ideas, or improvement of existing ones, while development is their useful application to specific products or processes.

Innovation relates to the actual commercial exploitation of a development while diffusion refers to the rate of its adoption through the potential target population concerned.

Characteristics of technology

This environment is not just about hi-tech and computers but it is all-pervasive. Change is affecting virtually all industries and sectors e.g. Courtauld's new fibre, Tencel. Some advances are relatively simple, such as adhesive message pads, while others are more complex, as in new packaging technologies.

> **QUESTION 9.1**
> - Think of at least six examples of industries that have had significant cost-saving innovations over the last five years.
> - Can you think of at least three examples of industries that have *not* had significant cost saving innovations over the last 10 years?
>
> (**See** Activity debrief at the end of this unit.)

As one of the major macro-environment variables it has a breadth of impact that affects all the other elements. The stock market crash of 1987, for example, was triggered by automatic computer sell signals. Increased employment of married women has been facilitated by the development of labour-saving, controllable and convenience technologies in the home. The political complexion of Eastern Europe and China has altered beyond recognition, with exposure of their material expectations to the telecommunication broadcasts of Western democracies.

According to Alvin Toffler in his book *Future Shock*, technology involves not only change but accelerating or exponential change. He illustrates this in a number of ways, including the 800th lifetime:

- The first 650 were spent in caves
- Effective communication in the last seventy
- Printed word to the masses in the last six
- Measured time in the last four
- Electric motor in the last two
- Mass material affluence in the last one

Technology progressed in phases until industrialization, when a marked acceleration occurred. Technology has always extended human capabilities and industrialization massively extended human musculature. Just three lifetimes have seen transformation from agricultural through industry to service economy and the pace is not slackening as developed countries enter a post-industrial 'information/communication' society. This is based on:

- Technology as the primary driving force for social change
- Convergence of computer and telecommunications media technologies
- A high and rising proportion of communications technology ownership
- Extension of the powers of the human nervous systems of sight and sound via TV, telephone, fax and other information systems such as the Internet
- Development of digital super-highways unifying communications technologies
- Credit transfer rather than cash-based society e.g. Switch cards
- A high percentage of knowledge workers
- A diverse, decentralized and differentiated society.

> **QUESTION 9.2**
> What was the typical life style twenty-five years ago? What products and services that are taken for granted today did not exist then?
> (**See** Activity debrief at the end of this unit.)

The role of business

Business is the main conduit by which science and technology impacts on society. Most change is incremental and progressive in nature but breakthroughs can and do bring sudden and dramatic change. Organizations must therefore give as much, if not more, attention to monitoring their technological as other macro-environments. If a rival succeeds in achieving a technological advantage it is a much more significant competitive edge than any other, due to the time, difficulty and resource commitments required to counter it. You may recall the damage inflicted on the Swiss watch industry by Japanese microprocessor-controlled timepieces, or more recently the impact on Apple of the Microsoft Windows '95 launch.

Most businesses are in a position to partly shape the threats and opportunities of their own technological environment by inventing and developing new ideas. Some industries compete on the state of their technology whereas others exhibit little innovation. This disparity is related to a number of factors:

> **EXAM TIP**
>
> Have a look at the compulsory question posed at the end of this unit. Plan out an answer as you work through the remainder of this section.

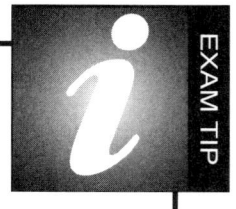

1. *Stage of the product or technology life cycle*   The introduction and growth stages of any new invention will be characterized by creative product innovation which will continue until the technology matures.
2. *Size of the firm*   Studies suggest that small firms provide a more productive climate for invention but lack the resources and organization to diffuse it quickly and effectively. Small firms tend to specialize and the risk of failure is high. Even large firms must beware of overcommitment (e.g. Rolls-Royce RB211 engine).
3. *Nature of competition in the market*   Considerable debate surrounds the best market structure for encouraging innovation. The drive is powerful in competitive markets but the resources and size to exploit them successfully is often lacking. Financial resources and control of the market exist in monopoly but innovation would make obsolete previous investments. The ideal combination is oligopoly, where size and market share is combined with considerable rewards if innovation can undermine rival product offerings. Interdependence, therefore, ensures that each company will maintain considerable research and development capability as a precaution against rivals obtaining such an edge.

> **ACTIVITY 9.1**
>
> Scan advertisements in magazines and the trade press for products or services which are being marketed on the basis of their technical sophistication or innovativeness (e.g. Dyson's Vacuums).
>
> - Examine how they are promoted.
> - What are the advantages for customers or unique selling propositions that are stressed?
> - Does the appeal vary between (a) consumers, (b) industrial users?

4. *The pace of change in consumer tastes*   If the existing market is static then new products supplied to new consumers in new ways may be the only strategy for growth.

What are the technical imperatives?

We live in a technological era where such knowledge and expertise confers status and societal approval. The Japanese and other Asian economies are admired for their ability to emulate and improve on Western technology. In their turn, European and American companies such as General Motors (Saturn project – robotized production), Fiat and Volkswagen have invested staggering sums in an effort to counter the lower wage costs and team-based productivity of Asian competitors. *Global competition* is clearly one of the imperatives forcing technological change.

Technology can also be viewed as a Pandora's box which, once opened, can never again be closed. Advances in one sphere of science provides the catalyst for a dozen others in adjacent fields where time, money and human expertise provide the only limits to the expanding frontiers of knowledge.

The development of global information networks such as Internet, for example, eliminates the constraints of national boundaries and allows small companies, students and researchers to access vast international databases. So-called web sites offer a value added means of providing further information to existing and potential clients. However, a survey of web site operators in 1996 suggested less than 60 per cent were happy with the business they had won and one in five had had security breaches. As communications companies invest to widen and commercialize these networks into 'information super-highways' so they will be capable of delivering not just research capability but a myriad other services. Similarly, organizations are linking subsidiaries and micro-environment stakeholders in so-called 'intranets'.

QUESTION 9.3

- What do you understand by an information super-highway and do you know of any under development?
- What services of relevance to the sales executive and marketer will they provide?

(**See** Activity debrief at the end of this unit.)

Fifty-year innovation cycle

Another technology imperative may be provided by this long-wave cycle. It has been observed that economic development since the Industrial Revolution has progressed in fifty-year cycles based on successive clusters of critical innovations.

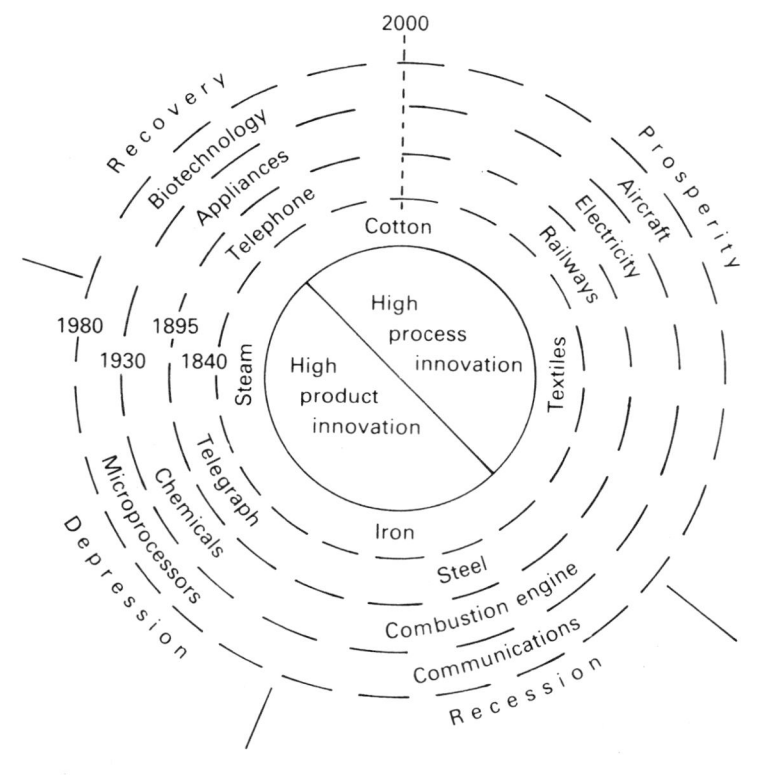

Figure 9.2 The long-wave cycle

As can be seen in Figure 9.2, steam power and textiles formed the basis of the first wave, railways and steel the second and so on. As each product or technology innovation cluster matured so their ability to generate further growth and jobs declined. Economies then tended to suffer an unusually severe depression as occurred in the 1880s and 1930s.

Businesses initially respond by cost cutting and retrenchment but as depression continued were forced to consider more radical solutions to declining sales and profitability. A new wave of innovations therefore occurred, as businesses became prepared to risk resources on new and existing inventions.

Considerable debate exists as to whether a long-wave depression was experienced in the decade following the oil crisis in the 1970s. Certainly, a cluster of technologies underpin current growth and development based on, among others:

- Microprocessors
- Satellites
- Biogenetic technology
- Materials
- Fibre-optics
- Lasers

> Taking the above state-of-the-art technologies, brainstorm as many product innovations based on them as possible. Can you think of any product or process innovations that represent fusions of these separate technologies?
>
> **ACTIVITY 9.2**

Creative destruction

Schumpeter, as we saw in Unit 2, viewed innovation as the source of creative destruction whereby dominant established firms and industries based on mature technology are challenged by new firms, using substitute products or processes, often from a different industry. Such entrepreneurial initiatives constantly threaten to shake up monopoly and oligopoly market situations, keeping them on their toes (e.g. IBM and Compaq in PCs). The joint venture between Mercedes-Benz and Swatch may provide an interesting example of this in the urban electric car market.

Technological change is part of the *dynamic of capitalism*. The expectation of new and improved products is part of our culture and businesses are rewarded when these needs are satisfied. Businesses are motivated by the need to survive and make profits, governments to promote growth and people to improve and change. This produces a drive for technology which feeds on itself, rippling through society as one advance triggers other applications in a technological *multiplier–accelerator effect*.

New generations of products are introduced with progressively reducing lead times, stimulating the planned obsolescence of current offerings. The power of snob appeal conferred on pioneer consumers and the requirement for followers to 'keep up with the Jones' reinforces the treadmill of constant novelty and change.

> What are the opportunities and threats of technological change as far as the business organization is concerned? What steps can the business take to minimize the threats and maximize the opportunities?
> (**See** Activity debrief at the end of this unit.)
>
> **QUESTION 9.4**

Microprocessors: a metatechnology with universal applications

This has become the most important technology of the late twentieth century. Despite a progression from valves and transistors, it represents a 'technological leap' innovation. This has allowed the enhancement of design and performance in a wide diversity of products and services.

The technology has also significantly contributed to the efficiency and effectiveness of communication systems, information services and other infrastructures (e.g. computerized traffic signals and electronic-based road-pricing systems to relieve congestion).

Microprocessors both extend and increasingly displace a wide range of intellectual and intuitive skills. In effect it constitutes the most rapid and dramatic industrial change in history and is still proceeding rapidly with the latest Pentium chips manufactured by Intel.

> **QUESTION 9.5**
>
> Suppose that an unusual electrical storm unaccountably disrupted the workings of all microprocessors that have ever been produced. What would be the immediate effects on the following:
>
> - The motorist?
> - The household?
> - The shopper?
> - The marketing department?
> - The individual?
>
> (**See** Activity debrief at the end of this unit.)

A number of characteristics have accounted for the cost and technical effectiveness of microprocessor-based technology as seen in Figure 9.3. When applied to manufacturing processes these characteristics have led rapidly towards the development of computer-integrated semi-automated plants. These are self-organizing systems that learn from their environments as well as from their experience. It may be noted, however, that the limits of power and performance that can be packed on a chip are being approached. Alternatives currently being considered include DNA-based 'living' computers.

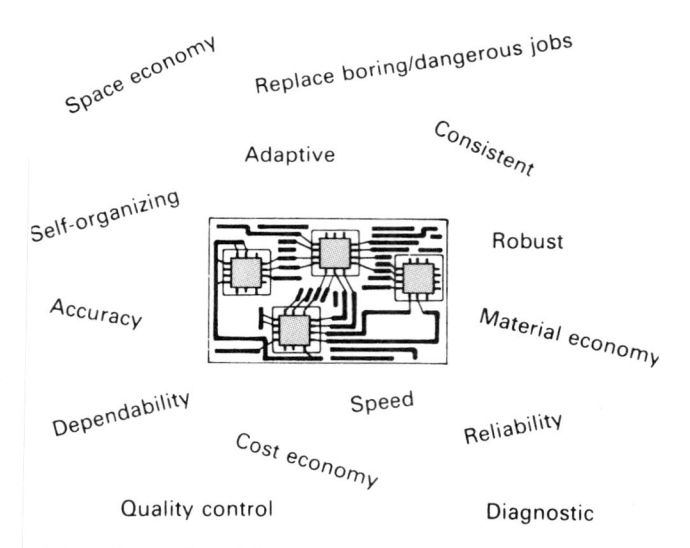

Figure 9.3 Characteristics of the microchip

The technological diffusion process

Adoption of new technology by businesses involves both cost and risk as well as the prospect of return. The rate at which firms adopt innovations, appropriate to their industry and market, is known as the rate of diffusion.

The process

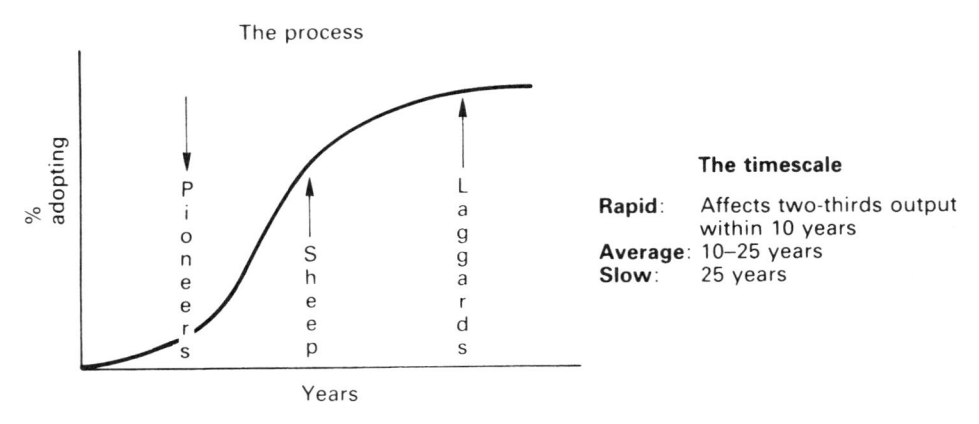

%adopting

Pioneers → Sheep ↑ Laggards ↑

Years

The timescale

Rapid: Affects two-thirds output within 10 years
Average: 10–25 years
Slow: 25 years

Figure 9.4 The diffusion process

As can be seen in Figure 9.4, the process is similar to the product life cycle. Factors which determine whether the rate is rapid or slow include:

- *Profitability* The rate of return will depend on a number of cost and revenue factors. The larger the impact on these of the new technology, relative to what is currently in use, the more rapid the diffusion.
- *Deterrence* This measures the consequences of *not adopting* the new technology. If a serious loss of sales is likely due to the superiority of the new technology then diffusion will be rapid as producers are forced to jump on the bandwagon or go out of business.
- *Scale of investment* Hi-tech generally means large financial outlays on both hardware and software aspects of operations. Businesses have limited internal resources and access to external risk capital, causing diffusion to be slower in such cases.
- *Market structure* It has been argued that oligopoly is the the most effective structure for rapid diffusion. Multinationals in particular have the organizational ability and resources to effect this globally.
- *Characteristics of the new product or process*
- *Potential range of applications* Clearly the greater the number under both of these headings, the greater the profitability and sales potential of the technology.
- *Environmental acceptability* as we will discuss later in this unit, the actual and perceived impacts of a new technology on the natural environment will affect diffusion due to legislation and liabilities that may arise. The cost of verifying drugs, for example, is said to account for the halving of R&D expenditure growth in 1993 compared to the 1980s.
- *Change agents* For a new idea to succeed in a business it needs a champion to challenge the status quo and persuade decision makers of the need for change. Much is invested in the current way of doing things and resistance to change occurs among management, customers and the workforce. The government is often a change agent through initiatives to support innovation or willingness to place orders.

ACTIVITY 9.3

Using the above diffusion factors, conduct a comparative analysis of some of the following technologies:

- Information technology
- Biotechnology
- Nuclear technology
- Satellite technology
- Synthetic materials technology
- Supersonic transport technology
- Automated surveillance (CCTV)

Do your conclusions bear out the actual rate of diffusion of these technologies? (**See** Activity debrief at the end of this unit.)

Technological transfer

Another aspect of diffusion is the transfer of technology from:

- Basic research to practical applications
- Military/aerospace applications to industrial products
- Hi-tech to consumer goods and services
- Developed to less developed countries

Fundamental new technologies originate from a number of sources, including universities and research institutes, military establishments, government agencies as well as businesses. Despite its record of Nobel Prizes, however, Britain has only a third to a half the number of scientists and engineers as a percentage of its population as the USA and Japan. Future trends bode no improvement as declining numbers opt for science and technology subjects at 'A' level and university.

An alternative is to license technology from the inventor, or encourage leading-edge multi-nationals to locate high-technology subsidiaries and transfer expertise into the economy. American and Japanese computer companies have been attracted to locate plants in Central Scotland, for example, providing opportunities for third generation indigenous companies to prosper.

> **QUESTION 9.6**
>
> If your firm has invested large sums in developing a revolutionary new product or service idea, what actions would you advise it to take in order to generate maximum returns?
> (**See** Activity debrief at the end of this unit.)

Technological forecasting

This idea is not new since good managements have always intuitively kept a cautious eye on the pace of change in both their own and adjacent industries. However, this has tended to be a 'defensive' eye to the danger of being overtaken by substitute technology rather than with a proactive intention to achieve competitive advantage.

A shifting balance of trade has meant that Britain, in particular, has had to learn to cope with rigorous competition from advanced, high-technology high-wage, capital-intensive economies first in Europe and latterly in East Asia. Insufficient resources force Britain to specialize in areas of greatest expertise and comparative advantage: chemicals, aerospace, pharmaceuticals, oil and financial services. Research and development spending as a percentage of sales is high by international standards in pharmaceuticals, for example (20–30 per cent, nearly double the average), but is static and low in manufacturing as a whole. British Telecom spends only 2 per cent of sales while oil companies spend even less.

The government is partly the cause since it decided, in the late 1980s, to progressively reduce subsidies, tax concessions and direct spending on civil R&D, forcing companies to assume more responsibility for product and process development. Short-termism (demands for profits today) among City analysts might also have worked against it.

A technological forecast should be the foundation block of long-term plans, based on effective collusion between the technologist, designer and marketer. This is necessary to achieve the essential balance between creating and satisfying the needs of the customer.

> **EXAM TIP**
>
> The technological environment is one area where you must keep up to date in the examples you provide to illustrate your answers. A useful strategy would be to list and summarize those changes which are currently impacting on the marketer's role.
>
> Break this down into the various aspects of the marketing mix in your file and make short notes on current developments in each:

> *Product* e.g. CAD/CAM and design cycles
> *Place* EDI with intermediaries, satellite tracking of vehicles
> *Promotion* interactive TV, computer-designed samples, database marketing
> *Price* barcode scanning

A basic forecasting approach for a business is shown in Figure 9.5. Forecasts of technologies are the product of two types of analysis:

1. Evolution of the current technology must first be ascertained. Many such forecasts are made for key technologies often using extrapolation of trends. Figure 9.6 from a *Financial Times* industry survey is such an example.
2. Alternative or substitute product or process technology is more difficult to forecast and requires a more qualitative analysis. Morphological analysis explores technological opportunities by systematically defining the basic features of current technology, identifying the known alternatives to each and then looking for feasible alternative combinations.

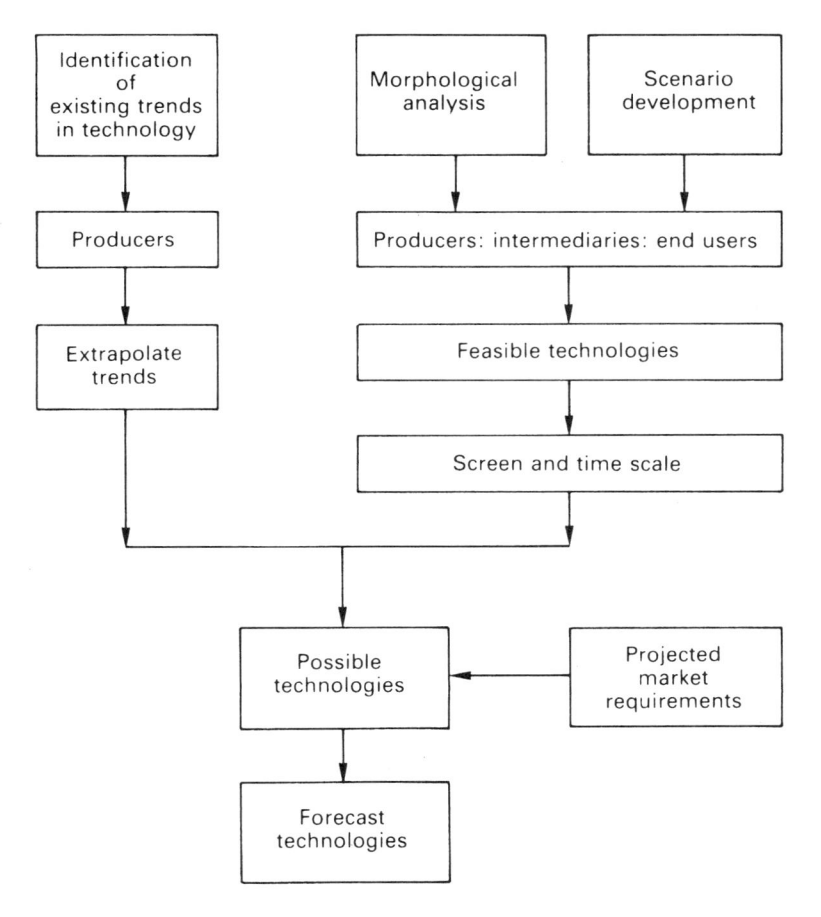

Figure 9.5 A framework for technological forecasting

A car, for example, can have alternative fuels: petrol, diesel, battery, gas, solar; alternative body materials: steel, plastic, aluminium, fibre-glass, etc.; alternative braking systems: friction disk, air, cable, etc. These can then be combined in different formulas to produce alternative-concept cars (hybrids are also possible, e.g. diesel/battery). This provides a fresh perspective on customary technologies and a fruitful basis for brainstorming feasible product alternatives.

Scenarios provide broader views of the future and insight into more diverse developments. Alternative personal transportation systems, for example, might include microlight aircraft systems but equally, developments in interactive video, teleworking and virtual reality might make many such journeys unnecessary in future.

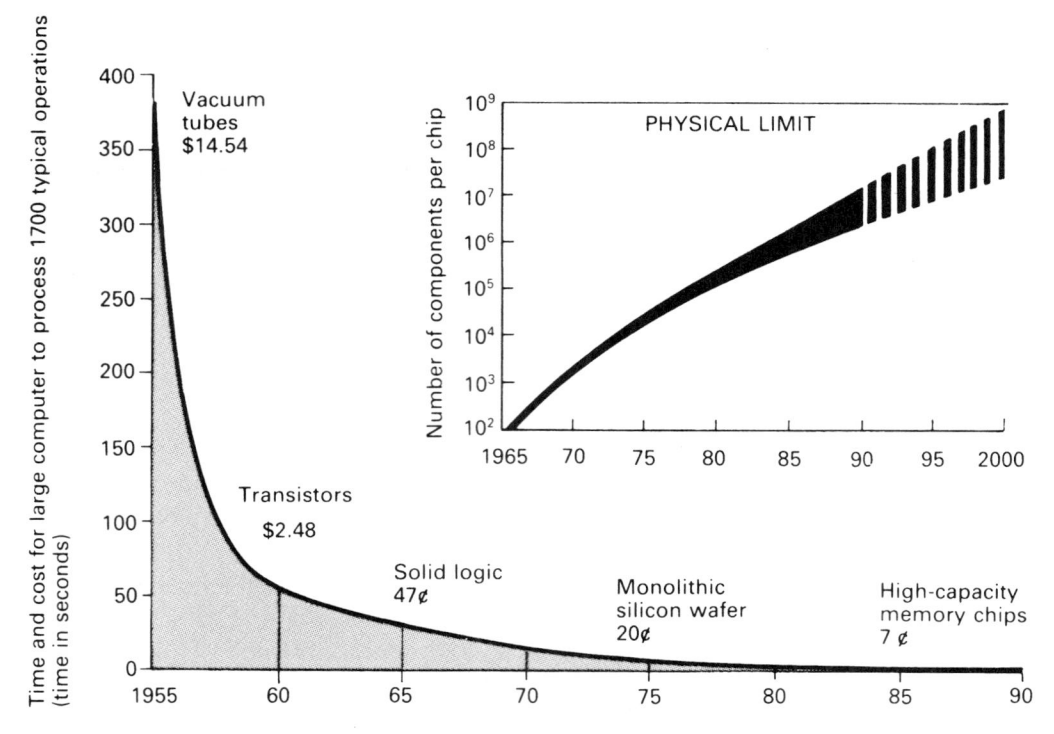

Figure 9.6 Advances in computer technology

ACTIVITY 9.4

Taking either the industry in which you work, or one of your choice for which information can be accessed (see below), undertake an outline technological forecast.

You might find it useful to consider the prevalent technology in various time periods: short term (say, up to 2 years), medium term (5 years), long term (10 years) and very long term (10+).

Information sources

Forecasts of technical possibilities may be drawn from a variety of sources:

- Research journals and conference papers
- Trade press reports
- Channel intermediaries and ultimate customer-need surveys
- Technical abstracts and databases
- Professional associations and industry networks.

Potential impacts must be identified, not only for the industry itself but also for channel intermediaries and end users. Feasible technologies are then screened to remove improbable options due to considerations of cost, environmental safety and so forth and a time scale determined for the remainder. This might be done by the use of Delphi techniques, drawing on the expertise of practitioners in the field.

Possible technologies must, however, be set against marketing forecasts of what the demand will be. Timing is also critical in achieving innovative success and avoiding technological failure. An innovation which is right for its time must have not only all the requisite technical building blocks in place but also receptive users, with the need, income and strength of preference to demand it in profitable volumes.

QUESTION 9.7

Can you put a time scale on the following applications?

- A chequeless society
- Virtual reality holidays

- Five per cent of residences with interactive access to databases
- Videophones in normal business use
- Drive-by-wire electronic systems for congestion-free motorways
- Speech-responsive computers
- Windscreen maps in cars

Technology and sales/marketing applications

In this section we will briefly summarize the main applications for marketers arising out of information technology. More detailed coverage may be found in the text mentioned in the study guide. As already indicated, you should keep abreast of all developments that potentially facilitate the effective execution of the sales/marketer's task.

The logical order to consider this is from product conception through to after-sales service and eventual disposal. German companies like Mercedes, for example, must now maintain computerized records of all vehicles sold so they may be tracked and accounted for in compliance with recycling legislation.

- *Product development* This is based on forecasting and the use of various databases to assess customer requirements and tastes. Marketing research is facilitated through the use of computerized analysis packages such as SPSS.
- *Product design* Product development times are falling sharply through the flexibility, versatility and time saving involved in CAD/CAM/CAE. New cars which once took seven years from drawing board to production line now take less than four with computer-aided technology. The main implication is a shrinking maturity and decline stage for many products combined with a geometric expansion in models and parts numbers.

Match up the following acronyms with their definitions:

- CAD/CAM/CAE
- FMS
- CIM
- JIT
- EPOS
- EFTPOS
- EDI

1 A just-in-time system of stock control which involves delivery of parts directly onto the shop/sales floor when required.
2 Computer-aided design, manufacture and engineering of products.
3 Electronic cash registers at the point of sale to the customer.
4 Systems to link up the computers of different businesses allowing the interchange of electronic data between them.
5 A flexible manufacturing system that allows small batches or units to be produced as efficiently as large runs.
6 A point-of-sale register which also allows for the electronic transfer of funds from the customer's to the retailer's account, e.g. Switch.
7 Computer-integrated manufacture automates all aspects of customer order, purchase, supply, manufacture and distribution.

(**See** Activity debrief at the end of this unit.)

DEFINITION 9.1

- *Manufacturing operations* Integrated computer control has enabled production to become increasingly flexible and versatile. Whereas cost efficiency used to demand large production runs, due to long set-up times, these can now be altered in seconds.

Waiting time is eliminated and small batches produced at near-equivalent speed and cost. This is of great significance to the marketer in terms of product availability and the ability to respond to increased demand arising from promotional initiatives. The spread of the JIT stock control concept from Toyota has also transformed volume production and distribution systems. Responsibility for delivery of parts onto the shopfloor, as they are required for assembly or processing, is transferred to suppliers. Work in progress is therefore minimized. Similar systems have been adopted by retailers in order to maximize selling areas and sales per square metre. Range can be extended by minimizing the stock that has to be carried.

- *Warehousing and logistics* Service levels for fast-moving consumer goods are improving progressively through the automation of storage and handling facilities. Maximum availability and rapid response to changing tastes and preferences now require a system which can instantly capture changing sales trends and translate them into the necessary supply and stock adjustments. EPOS systems using product barcodes and increasingly sensitive laser readers provide the sales data for stock control, sales analysis, automatic replenishment or new-order placement. More and more businesses are linked through EDI systems to facilitate such automatic computer linkage. Linked systems allow interrogation of stock and order status together with the transmission of marketing mix-details. Delivery now often takes place around the clock to avoid traffic congestion and conform to JIT requirements. Computerized transportation programmes plan optimal routes while satellite beacon systems and radio links allow flexible redeployment.
- *Point of sale* EFTPOS has transformed the potential of retail outlets in terms of not only additional sales area and frequently replenished demand related stock ranges but also speedier and more accurate customer transactions, shorter queues, improved cash flow and enhanced security. Some supermarkets have introduced trolleys with mini-scanners, enabling customers to process their own transactions as they shop and avoiding the need for checkouts.

Future applications of technology

Although it is difficult to be specific about the timing of particular developments it is clear that there is still considerable scope for new applications of relevance to the salesperson and the marketer.

ACTIVITY 9.5

Conduct a Delphi study of relevant internal and external stakeholders on their views and predictions regarding innovations thought likely to affect relationships between themselves and your organization.

Do not restrict this to stakeholders in different functional areas of the business. Contact suppliers, distributors, third-party contractors, banks, local authorities and so forth where possible.

Teleworking

Alternatively known as telecommuting or the electronic cottage, this involves working from home using telecommunications and computing equipment. A 1993 Department of Employment study on teleworking in Britain concluded that over 5 per cent of employers employed such workers. The most frequently cited occupations expected to figure in future plans were data entry, sales or marketing work and computer-based activities.

The main benefits of teleworking include:

- Flexibility
- Reduced cost
- Solution to travel problems
- Employ staff with care responsibilities
- Convenience
- Space saving
- Retain skilled staff

Other benefits include savings in travel time and stress; greater productivity due to fewer distractions and ability to work in preferred locations. The falling cost of technology and increasingly versatile equipment that is available makes this option attractive as office and non-labour costs soar in urban centres. Global telecommunications will also allow teleworkers from less developed countries to compete with high-wage equivalents in affluent nations. Telework may be processed in India or Pakistan at one-tenth the cost of London.

There are, however, a number of drawbacks to teleworking:

- Management and communication difficulties
- Social isolation
- Losing touch with the organization
- Unavailability for meetings

Technical and security problems may also arise as well as difficulties in ensuring quality control. Many workers find work discipline a difficulty and miss the creative spark provided by fellow-workers. Employers have therefore often taken steps to increase social integration by providing more communication with colleagues, managers and customers.

> **QUESTION 9.8**
>
> Technology now allows a vehicle to be fitted with the equivalent of the electronic office (i.e. portable computer, fax, carphone, etc.). With regard to sales and marketing, do you think the future lies with mobile or residential teleworkers?
> (**See** Activity debrief at the end of this unit.)

Electronic meetings

Meetings can take up to two-thirds of a manager's time. It is therefore essential that such time is used productively, especially where clients are involved. If, say, ten people meet for an hour then the average contribution of each is just 6 minutes. Since 20 per cent of those present tend to speak 80 per cent of the time the contributions of the majority are actually restricted much further.

Technology can not substitute for brain power and human interaction but it can vastly increase contributions. Given appropriate technology, participants can type their ideas and contributions onto a network of screens and react to those provided by the others. Brainstorming and evaluation can take place quickly and anonymously if necessary.

Remote metering

New electronic meters and remote-sensing devices now allow a competitive transformation in UK utility markets such as gas and electricity. After 1998 it will be possible for consumers to buy power from competing companies by virtue of these devices. The system will still be operated by British Gas, for example, but rival marketing companies will be responsible for supplying sufficient gas through it to meet customer demand. A highly competitive pilot scheme in the South West has resulted in fierce and sometimes questionable competitive practices.

Database marketing

The ability of the computer to capture, store, communicate and process vast amounts of data opens up massive opportunities for the far-sighted marketer. Database marketing involves the fusion of information gathered on actual and potential customers; actual and potential competitors; as well as internal cost and sales data. This can be used to screen then select target customers and fine-tune the marketing mix offered, in order to achieve maximum profit contribution in the light of operational and financial constraints.

ACTIVITY 9.6

> Refer to the company reports you were asked to obtain in Unit 1 and study them for references to the technological environment.
> Companies often take the opportunity presented in reviewing the past years performance and future plans to outline new technology initiatives and achievements. This provides a very useful insight into their research, development and capital expenditure.

Resistance to change

Technology has been the major engine in the development of mass affluence yet it has always been resisted. From the Luddites, who smashed the knitting frames that threatened their livelihoods at the outset of the Industrial Revolution, to print workers displaced by computer typesetting and more recently miners made redundant by cheaper alternate fuels, the outcome has always been the same: beneficial advance may have been delayed but never prevented.

The short-term impact of technologically induced unemployment has frequently been considerable, not least on communities dependent on the industry in structural decline. In the long run, however, there has been a growth in demand for labour that has broadly paralleled the growth in the labour force.

Process technology has substituted machines for labour to minimize costs but new product technology has created employment opportunities in so-called sunrise industries. Adaption has been difficult, however, because the new jobs have generally required higher-order skills than the ones they replaced.

It is not only employees who resist change, but also consumers, distributors and managers themselves. Changes in method and organization are as readily resisted as in technical processes, although change in one normally requires change in the others.

QUESTION 9.9

> Management is about the efficient allocation of resources to match changing consumer needs and wants, yet British management has frequently been criticized for its reluctance or inability to bring about change. Identify factors, the lack of which, may account for this weakness. Identify conditions which enable management in your own country to become effective change agents.
> (**See** Activity debrief at the end of this unit.)

Customers may resist product changes out of force of habit, prejudice or conservatism born of age. Product revivals may succeed on similar grounds as adults relive their youth or bring their children up consuming equivalent goods and services. Market understandings may also make the business reconsider introducing changes that disrupt competitive relationships.

Change might also be resisted by external forces such as pressure groups, concerned with the impact on the environment. Laws and regulations also constrain what is possible. The Data Protection Act, for example, required that mailing list organizations register and abide with its provisions, thereby limiting their scope for use by direct marketing businesses. Provisional EU legislation will forbid unsolicited fax transmissions unless prior permission is obtained. This will inhibit the activities of many direct marketers and provide resistance to the growth in corporate junk mail.

The symptoms of resistance to change

The marketer should be aware of why people resist change and take steps to minimize it. This applies as much to marketing staff as to affected stakeholders in the micro-environment. An important first step is in the identification of resistance to change as evidenced by:

- Increased turnover rates
- Illness and absenteeism rises
- Reduced productivity or operational effectiveness
- Failure to cooperate or communicate
- Head-in-the-sand attitudes
- General loss of morale
- Increased membership of unions or staff associations
- Action up to and including actual sabotage of operations.

> **QUESTION 9.10**
>
> What would be the symptoms to look for among the customer base as evidence of an adverse reaction to a change in order-processing procedures initiated by your organization? What steps might you have taken to reduce this resistance?
> (**See** Activity debrief at the end of this unit.)

'All the forces which contribute to stability in personality or in social systems can be perceived as resisting change' (Goodwin Watson). Such forces work to the advantage of established brands, for example, since consumer behaviour is also governed by:

- *Habit* In purchasing patterns.
- *Primacy* The first successful means we find of solving a problem or meeting a need is used again in future. Hence a firm keeps using the same advertising agency.
- *Selective perception* Evidence that conflicts with preconceptions is ignored (e.g. Buy British despite the fact that some foreign alternatives are now superior in quality).
- *Dependence* This relates to buying patterns to maintain our sense of belonging to a group or a class (e.g. keep up with the Jones).

Change is also resisted if it is against our better interests. Indeed, it is not the change itself but the results and consequences of it that are often the cause of the problem. We have also seen that the interests of both individuals and stakeholders do not always coincide with those of the organization. The individual will therefore be concerned not only with economic and security needs but also social and status considerations when technological change takes place. Other factors increasing resistance to change might include:

- *The nature of past experience of change* If this has been negative and prejudicial then resistance will be stronger.
- *If apprehensions are unanswered* If people mistakenly fear that they will not be able to cope with change then misapprehensions arise, producing unnecessary resistance.
- *The manner of the change* Resented if autocratic.
- *Lack of consultation or participation.*
- *Where change is infrequent* Experience and confidence are therefore lacking.

> **EXTENDING ACTIVITY 9.1**
>
> Identifying the symptoms and causes of resistance to change is one thing, but managing change to prevent them arising in the first place is a more effective strategy. Undertake research into how either Japanese management or excellent Western companies have succeeded in accommodating turbulent environmental change. Indicate how their approach addresses each of the sources of resistance outlined above.

Conclusions

Technological change is very much a double-edged phenomenon. It has so far prevented the dismal predictions of both Malthus and Marx by enabling rising productivity and real living standards but at the cost of high transitional unemployment. Its accelerating pace has enabled a sharply rising population to be accommodated but has produced 'future shock' among many seeking to cope with the myriad changes involved. It has provided convenience through increasingly intelligent products and services but also unforeseen consequences as the effects have rippled through society. Genetic technology, for example, may cure inherited diseases but might equally release uncontrollable mutations.

> **QUESTION 9.11**
>
> Identify some unintended consequences of the following product developments:
>
> - The car, e.g. the RAC claims that the average motorist spends five days per annum stuck in traffic – this could rise to 14 days by 2005!
> - The telephone
> - The television
>
> How have they changed the nature of marketing?

In the final section of this unit we will briefly consider what is perhaps the central aspect of this tension between technology as a force for good or a force for evil. That is, its impact on the natural environment and the limits this may impose on continued economic development.

The impact of technology on the natural environment

We looked at the relationship between the business and environmentalists in Unit 4. In this section we will consider the impact of technology and business activity on the environment in more general terms. Three fundamental constraints limit the pace and nature of technological change:

- *Social and institutional* Reflected in customs and legislation intended to curb the appliance of science in ways felt to be undesirable to society (e.g. a moratorium on nuclear programmes after Chernobyl).
- *Depletion of non-renewable resources* This includes fuels, minerals, fertile lands through overgrazing, tropical rain forests and biological diversity in terms of animal and plant species extinction.
- *Pollution of the ecosystem* Ecology is the study of plants and animals and their interaction with each other and the environment as a whole. Ecosystems include biodegradation processes which decompose wastes to provide nutrients for renewed growth. Problems arise only when their absorptive capabilities are overloaded due to the volume and/or nature of the wastes concerned:

  Industrial Effluents, emissions, solid wastes
  Toxic and chemically complicated wastes
  Plastics and non-degradable materials
  E.g. *Sea Empress* spillage, Milford Haven, 1996

  Consumer Vehicle emissions
  Disposable packaging
  Human wastes

> **DEFINITION 9.2**
>
> Many terms are used frequently in discussion of the environment. Can you match up the following terms to the brief descriptions below?
>
> - Effluent
> - Emissions
> - Acid rain
> - Ozone-layer depletion
> - Greenhouse effect

> 1 Carbon dioxide absorbs and radiates back heat which would otherwise escape into space, causing temperature rises.
> 2 Liquid wastes discharged into seas or watercourses.
> 3 Discharges of sulphur dioxide from power stations or vehicle exhaust gases combine with water vapour in the atmosphere.
> 4 Release of gases into the atmosphere.
> 5 Caused by the discharge of CFCs in aerosols, solvents, foam plastics and fridges allowing through dangerous ultraviolet rays.
>
> (**See** Activity debrief at the end of this unit.)

The source of the overload

The natural environment has found no difficulty in coping with the wastes created by our economic development, at least until recently. Natural disasters have also been easily accommodated, be they bush-fire, volcano or hurricane, because their impacts have been both localized and reversible. However, the cumulative effects of the nineteenth century's industrial development has involved a different order of 'impact magnitude and irreversibility' in many of the effects created. Figure 9.7 shows the main factors responsible.

```
              Industrialization
                    ↑
                    |
Mass affluence ←————+————→ Population explosion
                    |
                    ↓
           Environmental consequences
```

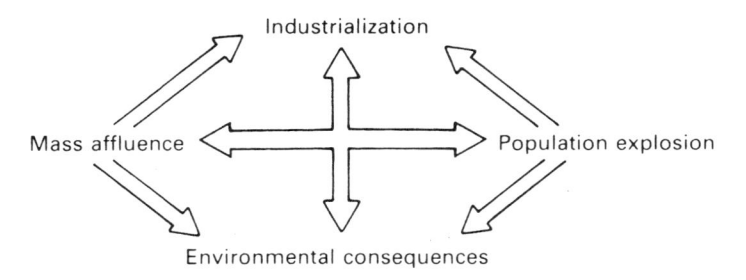

Figure 9.7 Key factors in environmental degradation

While any one of the three factors identified will cause environmental problems, their combined and interdependent effects are much more serious. Three-quarters of the world's population still live in less-developed countries and should they wish to emulate the high resource-consuming life styles of already industrialized countries, the environmental consequences are likely to be unsustainable. If every Chinese household merely aspires to own a fridge, for example, then the impact on the ozone layer would easily offset current international attempts to reduce CFC emissions.

The effects of the above are compounded by the pressure of competition and the pursuit of economic gain. Many natural resources are neither privately nor corporately owned but are subject to common exploitation with little regard to environmental costs and benefits. We have also recognized the political imperative of economic growth in all countries.

Belated recognition of these consequences has mobilized both government and business interests to seek solutions. The immediate reaction of halting or even reversing economic growth has, however, quickly given way to a more pragmatic concern for achieving *sustainable* development.

> **EXAM TIP**
>
> This is only a very short section, but still a very important aspect of the syllabus. The natural environment is one of the main business issues of the 1990s and will therefore recur as a question theme.
>
> Have you attempted the specimen question at the end of Unit 4 as well as question 2? As with many questions, the latter gives you the choice of context or examples.

This involves meeting the needs of the present generations without compromising the needs and requirements of future generations. In effect, the objective is to achieve the relationship between GDP and pollution shown in Figure 9.8.

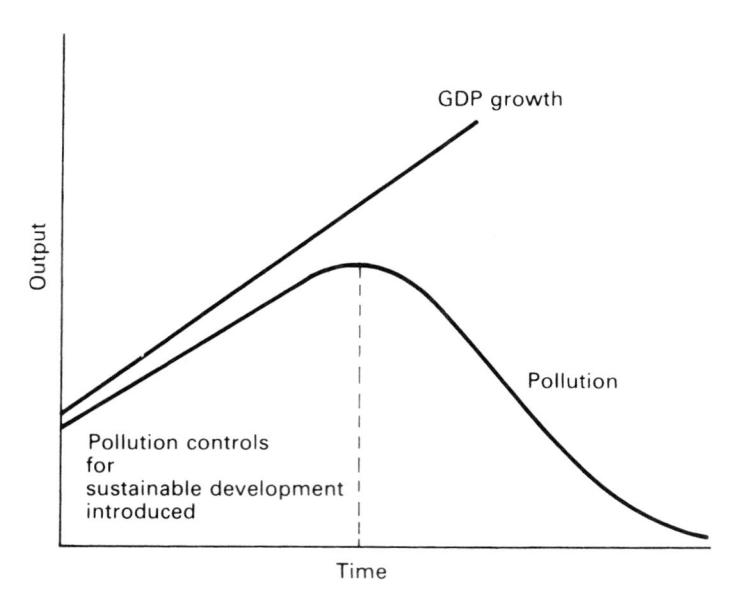

Figure 9.8 Desired relationship between GDP and pollution

Since pollution and resource depletion do not observe boundaries, they are global problems which can only be solved by global initiatives. The Montreal Protocol, for example, agreed to cap CFC production but with reduced targets applying to less-developed countries.

> **ACTIVITY 9.7**
>
> This is an appropriate point at which to review the strategies available to the environmentally conscious company and the benefits that might be exploited by the marketer in order to achieve a competitive edge.
>
> Consider two or three of the following strategies and think through how they might be marketed successfully in an industry of your choice. Try to find case studies (e.g. McDonald's packaging):
>
> - Clean technologies
> - Recycling
> - Waste minimization
> - Conservation
> - Biodegradable packaging
> - Renewable energy use.
>
> What are the main government policies forcing firms into such strategies in any case? (**See** Activity debrief at the end of this unit.)

Conclusions

It is clear that a heightening concern for society and the natural environment will require that new technology is only introduced with care and foresight as to its likely impacts. Society still divides into technical optimists who see salvation and sustainable development through accelerated research and development and pessimists who view unforeseen threats to the ecosystem as unavoidable, no matter how enlightened the technological intent. It is therefore an area which society already views as too important to leave to business decisions alone and is likely to become increasingly regulated as a result.

From the sales and marketing point of view the environmental market in the UK alone will be worth an estimated £140 million by the year 2000. This is not a very consistent market, however, as action–awareness gaps arise between what green consumers profess to want and what they actually buy. Awareness also cuts across segments, with children and women being more environmentally aware than men.

Another important point to be noted by companies is that up to 30 per cent of graduates and managers view this aspect as very important.

Finally, it should not be assumed that environmental impacts are primarily the concern of large firms. A recent OECD study concluded that it was small and medium enterprises (SMEs), accounting for less than 10 per cent of GDP, that were responsible for 70 per cent of pollution. A strategic response is clearly required from such firms with the addition of *packaging* and *people* to the marketing mix as a useful first step!

Summary

In this unit concerning the technological environment we have:

- Identified some of the main characteristics of technology and its main phases, culminating in the information or communications era which developed economies are currently entering.
- The critical role of business was examined and the factors that caused some firms to be more innovative than others.
- Technical imperatives driving the pace and diversity of technological change were identified and explained. The capitalist dynamic and the source of fifty-year long-wave cycles were studied in some detail.
- The microprocessor, as the key enabling technology in the information revolution, was described in terms which accounted for the all-inclusive impact it has had an all aspects of contemporary society.
- The diffusion process was explained and the need for technological forecasting emphasized. Sources of information by which a business can keep track of potential developments were outlined.
- Various applications to sales and marketing were discussed with reference to the supply chain. Some future applications were assessed including telecommuting and marketing databases.
- The symptoms and sources of resistance to change of the customer and employee were explored.
- The impact of technology on the natural environment was considered. The fundamental restraints of non renewable resources and the absorptive capacity of the ecosystem were recognised. The marketer must increasingly focus on sustainable development or be forced to do so by society through government control and regulation.

Activity debrief

Definition 9.1   2, 5, 7, 1, 3, 6, 4.
Definition 9.2   2, 4, 3, 5, 1.
Question 9.1
- Industries affected by innovations are numerous, especially where information technology has been applied. Others include pharmaceuticals, chemicals, car design, financial services, etc.
- Unaffected sectors are difficult to find since most have been affected by IT systems. Craft goods and personal services of various types provide possibilities.

Question 9.2   None of the information technology-based consumer products and services were available – colour TV, video, calculators, cash dispensers, microwaves, camcorders, computer games etc.

Question 9.3
- A super-highway involves the laying of fibre optic cable which allows high-speed transmission of a variety of information services. BT is laying a domestic system while Cable and Wireless is providing transPacific services.
- Interactive TV, on-line shopping, video-conferencing, database access.

Question 9.4   The main threats involve the loss of market share/profitability as a result of technological surprises; when to invest since rapid technological change will make premature investments obsolete; hi-tech may involve highly specialized plant and inflexibility in the face of changing consumer tastes; high cost of investment (e.g. microchip plants currently cost $1billion); risk and loss of failure (e.g. Sinclair C5 car, Phillips videodisc). The main opportunities involve excess profit, competitive advantage, lower costs, faster growth, greater flexibility. See also the benefits of microprocessors.

Question 9.5 Example: the *motorist* would be stranded since microprocessors control ignition, steering, braking and in-board control systems on modern cars. Traffic lights would cease to function as would petrol pumps. *The sales and marketing department* relies on 'information systems' defined as the products, services, methods and people used to collect, store, process, transmit and display information. It also relies on the telephone now controlled through digital exchanges not to mention televisions that receive advertisements. Product information derived from bar code scanners would be lost and banking and credit systems would fail.

Question 9.6 Clearly, an array of marketing strategies are relevant here including price skimming and penetration. Licensing and franchising are other possibilities to consider in achieving rapid coverage of the national/international markets.

Question 9.8 Portable computers are already transforming the capability of the sales force, giving them the opportunity to access the corporate database to answer customer queries regarding product availability, order status, promotions, etc. They could also enter orders immediately ensuring that stock is allocated. Intelligence regarding competitors could be input into the system. These combine through the power of the computer to offer massive potential to the sales force of the future. Legislation may limit mobile phone use.

Question 9.9 Factors include lack of: competitive pressure, incentive, finance, support from the board, champions, a risk-taking culture, long-term horizons, skills and experience of change, awareness of potential.

Question 9.10 Resistance may lead to loss of orders in the extreme, increased returns, more queries and complaints, a rise in errors, etc.

- You may have suggested such things as joint consultation over the proposed changes or, more importantly, involving customers in formulating them in the first place. Communications and incentives also have a role to play.

Activity 9.3 Information technology rates highly on nearly all counts. The scale of investment is high, however. Supersonic transport rated highly on change agents due to the impetus provided by government defence spending and subsidies but low on environment, safety and scale of investment. Nuclear has a similar pattern. Biotechnology has intermediate scores.

Activity 9.7 Policies include environmental incentives (e.g. subsidies, tax breaks); environmental standards; environmental charges for pollution caused; tradable permits.

Extending activity 9.1 Such companies achieve a culture favourable to change; single status; suggestions welcomed/acted upon; atmosphere of trust; involvement; security needs recognized; retraining and support; support from the top.

Examination hints and specimen questions

Technology, as we have seen in this unit, is an all-pervasive aspect of the business environment. It also knows no boundaries and companies of every nationality will be seeking to exploit its potential for competitive advantage. It is therefore likely to be a popular aspect of the macro environment for examination questions, given its general applicability to all CIM international centres. Refer to the compulsory question in the Guidance on revision and examination unit at the end of the workbook for a further example of examination topics from this area.

1 (a) What is the significance of technical change to the marketer? (8 marks)
   (b) Comment on the impact of technical change on the natural environment and suggest what direct action marketing activity must take if future growth is to become sustainable. (12 marks)

   (CIM Marketing Environment paper, June 1995)

Hints: Indicative content and approach

Question 1(a)
- This is a relatively straightforward question.
- Deal with both opportunities and threats arising.
- Product and process innovation impacting on costs, design and development.
- Refer to creative destruction, diffusion, substitution and potential competition.
- Examples to illustrate significance, e.g. intelligent products.

Question 1(b)
- Impacts would include emissions, effluents, solid wastes and resource depletion.
- Identify particular issues arising out of industrialization and mass consumption, e.g. the greenhouse effect, ozone depletion, acid rain, etc.
- Comment on the double-edged nature of change with examples, e.g. nuclear power releases no greenhouse gases but involves toxic waste.
- Define sustainability.
- Provides an opportunity to develop green marketing strategies based on cradle-to-grave approaches to product design and development.

Compulsory Marketing Environment question – illustration only

On-line for speedy sale

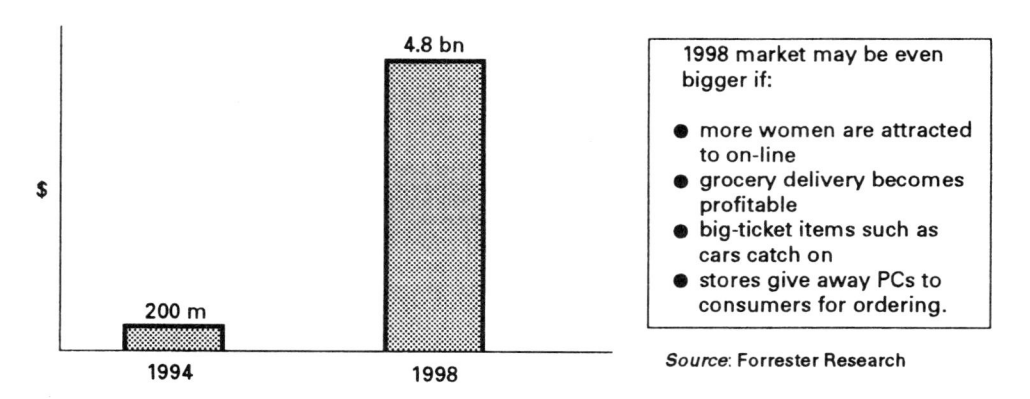

[Bar chart: $ values — 1994: 200m; 1998: 4.8bn]

1998 market may be even bigger if:
- more women are attracted to on-line
- grocery delivery becomes profitable
- big-ticket items such as cars catch on
- stores give away PCs to consumers for ordering.

Source: Forrester Research

Do you want to send roses to your sweetheart, buy a new car, choose a cookbook for your mother's birthday or purchase computer software? One of the quickest, if not the cheapest, ways to make these purchases in the US and increasingly Europe and East Asia is via on-line computer information and communications services.

On-line computer shopping has been around for several years, but until recently most of the products available were aimed at computer hobbyists. Now the proliferation of home computers, with about one third of US households equipped with a personal computer, is attracting the attention of a broad variety of retailers to on-line shopping as a potentially important new sales channel.

An on-line service jointly owned by Sears Roebuck, the US retailer and IBM offers products from 150 merchants while America On-line allows subscribers to offer their homes for sale. Shopping centres are also being built on the internet, a global network that links an estimated 20m computer users offering software, hardware and related products.

While no-one is predicting that computer retailing will replace every trip to the local shopping centre, on-line merchandising is expected to grow rapidly over the next few years as the installation of communication 'superhighways' makes multimedia technology both cheaper and more accessible to consumers. To date this technology has generated only modest sales of less than $200m in the US compared with total retail sales of $1500bn. Of this, mail order accounted for $53bn and home shopping channels, placing orders by phone, a further $2.5bn. However as the chart shows, some market researchers are predicting dramatic increases driven by a swelling potential customer base, improved product presentation and the low comparative costs of selling on-line.

In San Francisco, consumers with the necessary software can shop at their local Safeway supermarket without leaving home. On-line shoppers can either wander through the 'virtual reality' supermarket aisle by aisle or go to specific locations. Personal shopping lists carrying regular items can be created and special offers highlighted. The grocery order is then delivered at the customer's convenience.

Currently prices are no lower and the transmission of pictures to the home computers is slow but multimedia PCs are transforming this. One company has launched a CD-Rom catalogue to supplement its on-line shopping service with pictures and videos of available products. Even this combination is primitive compared to the 'interactive' shopping planned by US cable television companies. These services will require substantial investment but would supply full video and sound and may even provide customers with 'assistants' to help armchair shoppers with their fashion choices.

(Adapted from Louise Kehoe article in FT 23/6/94)

1 (a) Write short notes **two** of the following technical terms used in the article and briefly comment on their wider significance for the marketer:

  (i) Multimedia technology
  (ii) Virtual reality
  (iii) CD-Rom
  (iv) Interactive television shopping
  (v) Communications superhighway
  (vi) Computer software   (6 marks each Total 12 marks)

(b) Draw on your understanding of the marketing environment to explain why no one is predicting that computer retailing will replace every journey to the shopping centre. (7 marks)

(c) Suggest further reasons why growth in on-line retailing may expand more rapidly than predicted. (7 marks)

(d) Provide an outline structural analysis of your grocery retailing market. What recommendations would you make to a traditional retailer like Safeway?

                      (14 marks)
                (Total 40 marks for question)
          (CIM Marketing Environment paper, December 1995)

UNIT 10

The global environment

OBJECTIVES

In this, the final unit of the workbook, you will:

- Investigate the basis for international trade.
- Assess the advantages and drawbacks to direct investment by multinationals.
- Identify the differences involved in international marketing and recognize the entry and marketing-mix strategies required to bridge the gap between national and overseas markets.
- Recognize government trade and payments policy options and the conditions which trigger their adoption.

By the end of this concluding unit you will be able to:

- Understand the role and importance of various international institutions and trade blocs which impact on trade performance and conduct.
- Recognize and account the impact of political and legal constraints on national and global trade relationships.
- Access relevant sources of information on international markets.

STUDY GUIDE

Civilizations throughout the mists of time have grown and prospered as a result of trade. Recognition of the gains to be made from exchanging surpluses, with a relatively low value in the domestic market, for scarce and desirable products from far-off lands, led in the seventeenth century to the development of international trading companies and then colonial empires. International trading networks now form a tightening web of linkages between virtually all corners of the globe with multinational subsidiaries the nearest modern equivalent of a colonial outpost.

Trade in the late 1990s is therefore more complex with multilateral exchanges facilitated by international finance. It is also the case that participating nations and businesses are increasingly vulnerable to global political and economic influences.

The international environment therefore presents the marketer not only with considerable opportunities but also with greater challenges than the domestic market. The sales and marketing principles to be applied may remain constant but the context for their application is much less familiar. Potential rewards are considerable but so too is the care and effort required to reap them and avoid the many extra risks and pitfalls involved.

This unit accounts for 10 per cent of the syllabus, which qualifies it for a full or part question, on average, in each paper. To this you should add the fact that CIM is a qualification undertaken by students from at least thirty-six countries from around the world. The global environment forms a context common to all and may provide more than its fair share of questions as a result.

As with your own economy, it is therefore vital that you have a clear appreciation of your country's international trade position. Is its balance of payments in surplus or deficit? What is its pattern of trade with other countries and the composition of its imports and exports? Does it belong to a trading bloc and, if so, what regulations govern its internal and external relationships?

This workbook can provide only an outline of such factors and you must take steps to fill in the gaps by monitoring press reports and referencing texts such as *International Marketing* by S. Paliwoda (published by Butterworth-Heinemann). Further extensive treatment may be found in section 8 of *Economic Theory and Marketing Practice* by Hatton and Oldroyd.

Despite providing only an outline of the global environment, this is a substantial unit which may take you longer to complete than any of the preceding ones. You should open a final file on this global environment and divide it into sections concerned with:

- The benefits of trade and constraints upon it
- The impact of trade blocs and international institutions
- The national trade position and policy implications
- Micro aspects of trade for the business, sales manager and marketer
- The multinationals.

The basis for international trade: at the macro level
A number of benefits arise from international trade and exchange:

- *Choice and diversity of products*   Trade allows countries to obtain a variety of goods and services which would be otherwise unobtainable. Temperate lands could not enjoy the bounty of tropical fruits, East Asian island economies would have no oil and European jewellers would have no pearls or diamonds.
- *Advantages of specialization*   Trade provides a country with the opportunity to concentrate its available resources on producing what it is best at, while importing those items in which it has an absolute or comparative disadvantage. This enables an outward shift of its production possibility curve without the need for extra resources. Total output rises by transferring resources to produce where comparative advantage is greatest compared to other countries, and exporting the surplus to provide for its other requirements.

Even if a country is less efficient at producing all products, trade is still advantageous despite this absolute disadvantage. Assume that two countries and only two traded products rice and fish. If by dividing its given resources:

- Country A can produce 30 units of rice and 30 of fish while
- Country B can produce 10 units of rice and 20 of fish

Country A has an absolute advantage in both, but still benefits from concentrating most of its resources on rice production, while B specializes where its comparative disadvantage is least and supplies most of the fish. Trade and exchange benefits both countries.

> **QUESTION 10.1**
>
> Using the above information, complete the following table:
>
> | | \multicolumn{2}{c}{Country A} | \multicolumn{2}{c}{Country B} | Total |
> |---|---|---|---|---|---|
> | | *Before specialization* | | | | |
> | | Country A | | Country B | | Total |
> | Product | Units | Resources | Units | Resources | |
> | Rice | 30 | 15 | 10 | 15 | 40 units |
> | Fish | 30 | 15 | 20 | 15 | 50 units |
> | | *After specialization* | | | | |
> | Rice | 50 | 25 | 0 | 0 | ? units |
> | Fish | ? | ? | ? | ? | ? units |
>
> What is the gain from trade?
>
> (**See** Activity debrief at the end of this unit.)

The basis for trade then is specialization and mutually beneficial exchange. National differences in respect of materials, human skills and ingenuity, capital availability and technology, lead to differences in costs of production and final prices. Countries supply the world economy with the goods and services they can produce most competitively and buy from others on the same basis. This is not always apparent to the ordinary person who might:

- Instinctively buy home-produced goods rather than imports
- Believe that national prosperity and jobs depends on this
- Naturally fear the consequences of becoming overdependent on imports
- Consider that you receive more after-sales service with domestically produced products

1. *Consumer prices* When confronted by a choice of goods of identical quality, but with the foreign one much cheaper, the consumer often opts for the latter, overriding the above reactions. A country can therefore obtain not only goods and services it is unable to produce itself, but also those it could only produce at a much higher cost if it did not import them. This is clearly of benefit to consumers and can be a major factor in improving living standards. The recently concluded GATT agreement, which has reduced subsidies and protectionism in agricultural trade, should benefit European and Japanese taxpayers as well as free trade producers, particularly among the Cairns Group (e.g. Australia).
2. *Lower costs of production* International trade creates worldwide sales opportunities, increases the size of markets and makes extensive specialization possible. Each person, firm, locality, region and country can focus on their relative strengths, and benefit from exchange. Businesses can operate on a larger volume enabling economies of scale to be realized as in Figure 10.1. If Switzerland only produced watches for the domestic market, its costs of production would be much higher than when it supplies the rest of the world.
3. *Shortage and surpluses may be ironed out* Localized shortages arising out of a natural disaster may be offset by obtaining supplies from elsewhere.
4. *Curbs monopoly power* Actual or even potential competition will tend to cause powerful domestic businesses to moderate their prices and profitability. They come under pressure to become more innovative and dynamic, bringing long term benefit to the society in question.
5. *Rapid diffusion of ideas and inventions* This speeds up innovation, stimulating economic growth and technological development. Further job and wealth creation is the result.
6. *International cooperation* Trade brings contact, mutual interest, cultural interaction and dependence, fostering peace and cooperation. The fact there is Coca Cola in Beijing and a McDonald's in Moscow helps to make the world a more secure place.

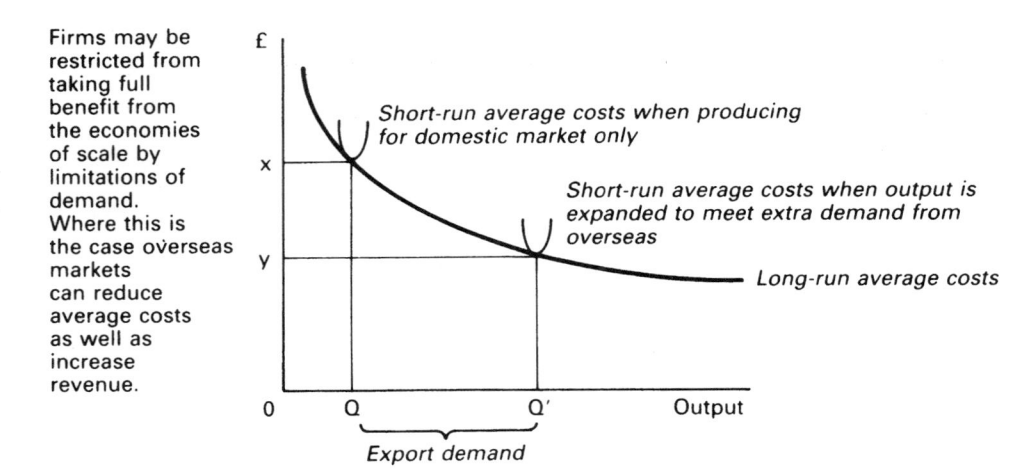

Firms may be restricted from taking full benefit from the economies of scale by limitations of demand. Where this is the case overseas markets can reduce average costs as well as increase revenue.

Figure 10.1 The impact of overseas trade on long-run average costs

ACTIVITY 10.1

Examine government statistics on international trade and the balance of payments to determine in what goods and services your country has a comparative advantage. What are the factors that account for the comparative advantage? Are there any factors that appear to be eroding this advantage (especially if trade is deteriorating)?

The basis for trade: at the micro level

Although the principle of comparative advantage holds across a range of commodities, in practice, equivalent consumer and industrial goods are imported and exported by many countries. Trade in such goods as cars and computers is partially explained by the fact these are differentiated products and the consumer desires a wide choice. Households do not want identical telephones or saloon cars and, in addition, each manufacturer gains economies by producing one main brand for an international market rather than lots of brands in low volumes for a purely domestic one. Gains from trade in this case do not necessarily derive from relative cost differences but rather from brand diversity and effective marketing.

Although large numbers of small and medium companies either do not participate in international trade or engage in only a peripheral way, the advantages for them can be substantial:

1. Providing a wider market for specialist niche producers
2. Additional volume to reduce the cost base and secure economies
3. Escape from a saturated or threatened domestic market
4. One possible means of extending the product life cycle
5. As a source of volume growth to support expensive R&D
6. To counter a depressed home market and maintain capacity
7. As a competitive strategy to counter and deter foreign rival entry into the home market
8. As a means of spreading risks.

If a business is to become an international marketing company then it must make a serious commitment to enter foreign markets. It is a long-term strategic decision, and not be taken lightly, since the implications of subsequent withdrawal due to lack of preparation would be substantial and expensive in terms of finance, image and credibility.

QUESTION 10.2

'Successful entry into foreign markets requires adaption and attitude change within the organisation concerned.' In the light of your studies in previous units (especially Unit 7) of this workbook, what are the factors that make marketing in international markets qualitatively more difficult than in domestic ones?

(**See** Activity debrief at the end of this unit.)

Growth in international trade

The rapid post-war growth in world merchandise trade can be seen in Figure 10.2. This was in marked contrast to the sharp declines in trade (from a 1929 peak) during the early 1930s triggered by American tariff rises and the competitive devaluations of currencies in response to depression. Beggar-my-neighbour protectionist retaliation and world war combined to ensure that full recovery did not occur until 1950.

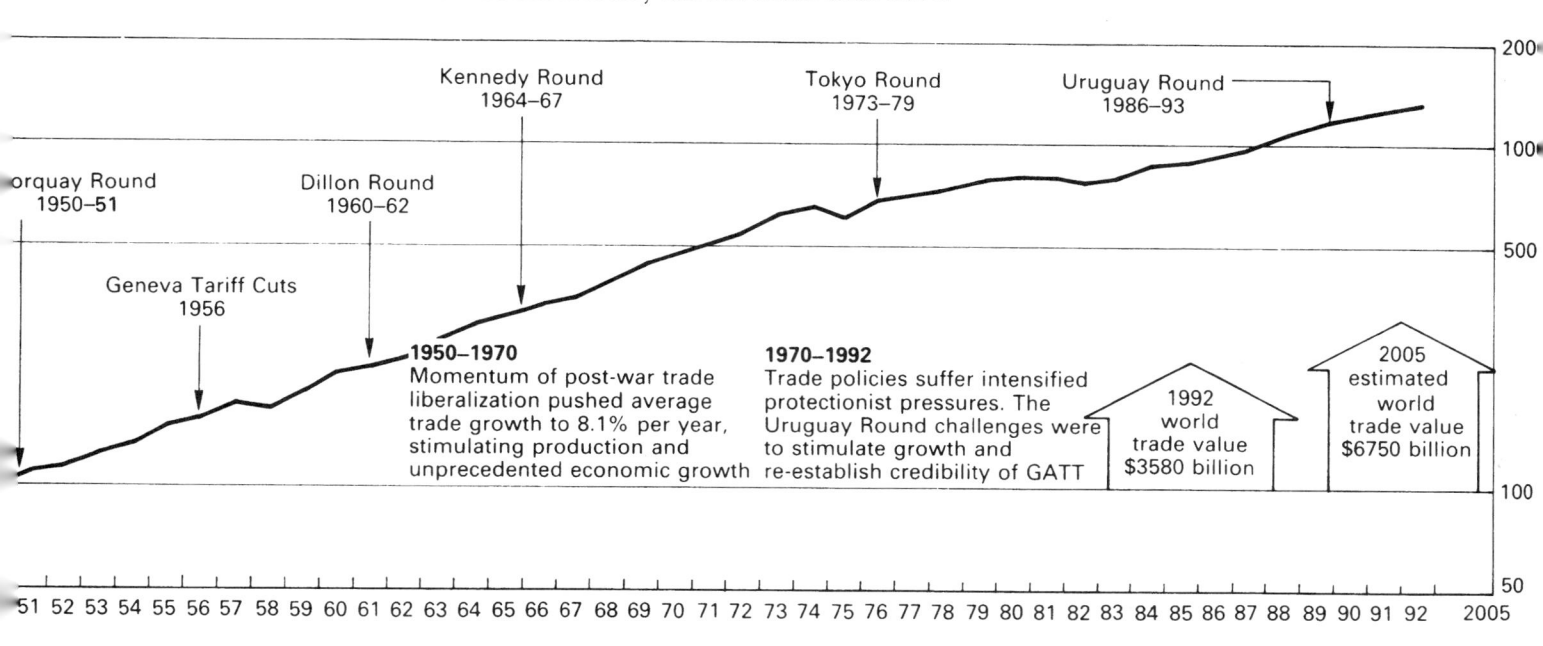

Figure 10.2 The growth in merchandise trade, 1950–2005. (*Source: Financial Times*)

> **QUESTION 10.3**
>
> Can you account for this unprecedented expansion in international trade? A number of different factors account for this and you should think in terms of institutional, technological, political, social, economic as well as business explanations.
> (**See** Activity debrief at the end of this unit.)

Except for a sharp setback caused by the 1973 oil price crisis, the growth since 1950 has been near-continuous. Whether this trend continues into the next century is of considerable concern and interest to the international marketer. Factors affecting this include:

- Successful trade liberalization agreements such as the recent GATT deal and formation of the World Trade Organization (WTO) to oversee implementation
- Continued progress towards economic reform and integration with the world economy by the former planned economies of Eastern Europe and Asia
- Buoyancy in the global economy as a whole and the ability of the larger countries to manage their economies in a mutually beneficial manner
- Unimpeded development of international communication, travel and trade links producing movement towards a global culture
- Uninterrupted spread and development of multinationals.

Limitations to the growth of international trade

Before accepting the idea that, because of the comparative advantage principle, gain will always result from extra specialization and trade, you should recognize that it requires certain conditions:

1. Resources are mobile between different uses.
2. No resources are left unemployed or underutilized as a result of the increased specialization.
3. There is a demand for any increased production made possible.
4. There is no movement of productive factors between countries.

In a modern high-technology society these are not easy conditions to sustain. Geographical and occupational mobility are difficult and often unwelcome where labour is concerned. Specialized machines are usually built for one purpose and workers may take years to retrain. Older people displaced from one activity may be unable to learn new skills producing high unemployment in this area and shortages in another.

Transport costs may offset any gain from trade. Bulky items such as building materials are seldom traded internationally and many personal and convenience services, which must be produced at the time and place of their consumption, are similarly precluded.

Unexpected shifts in currency values may also inhibit trade since a risk is always present that the rate at which one currency exchanges for another will move unfavourably before the transaction is completed (see the last section of this unit). This is not a problem in domestic markets.

ACTIVITY 10.2

It is important that you not only recognize the basis for international trade and factors encouraging and inhibiting its growth, but also that you are aware of the *sources of turbulence*. Even though the trend in recent years has been upward a number of developments could: (a) Cause the trend to reverse or (b) cause fluctuation about the trend.

Sources of turbulence in the global economy is a section of the CIM syllabus and you should be able to think through the possible explanations by reflecting on the content of this unit and previous ones in the macro-environment.

Prepare a report for your college tutor or work superior summarizing these sources. (**See** Activity debrief at the end of this unit.)

Barriers to trade

There is always a tension between the advantages to be gained from free trade by the world as a whole, and the specific self-interest of any one country. For the benefits of trade to flow, it must be open and fair, yet one country can always gain by introducing import controls so long as the others continue to trade freely.

The main reason preventing countries from adopting protectionism is therefore more likely to be the fear of international retaliation rather than continued faith in the benefits arising. Experience of the 1930s showed the consequences for production, trade and unemployment when protectionism was widely adopted. If, however, a country does decide that the benefits of trade controls do outweigh the dangers of retaliation, a number of arguments can be advanced in its support.

Protection for infant industries or restructuring mature ones

Infants need protection until they can stand on their own feet. Newly established firms will be at a size and cost disadvantage compared to existing international concerns with internal and external scale economy advantages. Japanese companies grew in this way, building competitive advantage in the protected domestic market before going international. Similar arguments have been applied to mature industries in Europe where equivalent protection has been negotiated to give them a breathing space in which to re-equip to meet competition from the Pacific Rim economies.

QUESTION 10.4

- Which are the Pacific Rim economies?
- What is the case against this specific protectionist argument?

(**See** Activity debrief at the end of this unit.)

Protection against dumping

Dumping involves goods sold in foreign markets at prices lower than at home. This may be done to avoid swamping the domestic market, which would cause prices to fall (e.g. the disposal of Common Agricultural Policy crop surpluses). Alternatively, it might reflect the dumping of excess supply arising from operating at the capacity which minimizes costs or an overt intention to kill off domestic producers by undercutting them. Japanese companies were frequently accused of such tactics in Western markets.

Dumping is viewed as an unfair trading practice by the international community and for that reason industries suspecting competition from dumped goods can ask for protection under WTO rules. On the other hand, the number of dumping actions has increased sharply and interpretation is difficult. The lower prices might actually mean comparative advantage and superior efficiency. America, in particular, had been taking increasing unilateral action against those it suspected of dumping.

DEFINITION 10.1

Match the following terms with the appropriate definition:

- Tariff
- Quota
- Embargo
- Non-tariff barrier
- Terms of Trade
- Customs duty

1. Taxes imposed on imported goods with the intention of reducing their competitiveness with domestic equivalents.
2. Various standards and regulations to which imports must conform.
3. A tax imposed on imports in order to raise revenue.
4. The index of average export prices compared to average import prices.
5. A quantitative limit on the volume of imports per time period.
6. A prohibition on the export of a particular good or classes of goods to certain countries, usually for political reasons.

(**See** Activity debrief at the end of this unit.)

Increase in employment and improved balance of payments

The threat of imports to domestic jobs is one of the most important pressures on governments to introduce protection. Japanese rice farmers, European steelmakers and American car workers have all benefited in this way. Tariffs and quotas divert spending towards domestic products and beneficially impact on the circular flow. This argument is also used against 'cheap foreign labour', justifying protection as a means of equalizing costs of production so that foreign and home producers can *compete on equal terms*.

An adverse balance of payments may be temporarily alleviated by tariff protection, but the cooperation of trading partners would be required if retaliation was to be avoided. Import controls can be applied specifically to industries where home firms are under greatest competitive pressure.

QUESTION 10.5

- Do you accept the 'cheap labour argument' for protection?
- If a balance of payments deficit cannot be solved by protection, because of international trade agreements, how can it be rectified?

Which policy does the least harm to: (a) the domestic economy or (b) the international economy?

(**See** Activity debrief at the end of this unit.)

National security and independence
Certain industries may be viewed as of strategic importance and therefore vital to protect (e.g. defence, agriculture) so the nation is not vulnerable in times of global instability. Avoidance of overspecialization through encouragement of a balanced industrial structure may also be a factor.

To raise revenue at the expense of foreigners
The revenue raised provides finance for government spending. If foreigners need to supply the market more than the domestic buyers need to buy then the tax incidence will fall on the former. In effect, the price rises by less than the duty imposed.

International sales and marketing challenges and the means of protectionism
The international marketer faces a number of challenges which makes trading overseas more difficult than at home. Some arise out of the distances involved which makes face-to-face contact with customers and the export sales team more difficult. Distance is compounded by the complexities of culture both between and within countries.

Since much of what is culturally significant is unspoken, unwritten and learned from life experience in the society in question, the mere acquisition of language is insufficient to appreciate the subtleties of social mores and etiquette. Yet, as the marketer is only too aware, the marketing mix must conform to and reflect these if it is to be completely successful.

> **ACTIVITY 10.3**
>
> Conduct an investigation into the culture of a target market for a meat-based convenience party food. Design a promotional campaign for the product which would be a marketing disaster!
>
> If you live in a multi-cultural society you may wish to interview members of another culture to identify relevant etiquette, taboos, religious beliefs, superstitions and so forth that might affect this promotion.
>
> What steps would you take to ensure that the promotional campaign did not fall into any of these cultural pitfalls?

Another challenge for the international marketer is to ensure that laws and regulations are complied with and documentation relating to exports and imports are in order. This is an expensive process when a number of overseas markets are being served. Many companies therefore make it a practice to label product contents and instructions in major languages.

Governments, often under pressure from domestic producers, use such requirements to restrict trade. Major trading nations, reluctant to openly breach trade agreements, may opt to make life hard and more costly for the foreign marketer by introducing *non-tariff barriers*. For example, imports may be required to conform to specific national environmental, quality or safety standards which necessitate expensive modification. Customs officials may then employ cumbersome and complicated import procedures which delay, hinder and increase the cost of imports.

The marketer may also find a far from level playing field as home producers receive a variety of preferential assistance:

- Tax advantages or hidden subsidies
- Government procurement contracts unavailable to foreign bidders
- Exchange controls regulate the inflow and outflow of payments
- Prompting or rewarding 'buy home goods or parts' patriotic attitudes among consumers and firms.

Japan has been particularly criticized on these grounds due to its low import-to-export ratios. However, despite a number of relaxations arising from Western government pressure, domestic consumers remain culturally resistant to many of these imports.

> **EXAM TIP**
>
> As mentioned in the 'Study guide', the international environment has global candidate appeal. Since the papers are set with at least a one-year lead time it always pays to see if anything significant was happening at exam time minus 12/18 months. Remember, the examiner will be influenced by current events as well as syllabus content and its coverage over a run of papers.
>
> So check it out: was anything of major global importance happening then? If so it *could* be the basis of a question in *your* examination.

The marketer must also recognize the effect of various other controls on international trade:

- *Embargoes* These are unusual but when applied make legal trade impossible with the country concerned. They are often applied on high-technology and defence goods to suspect regimes e.g. Iraq or North Vietnam.
- *Quotas* These limit the quantity that can be supplied into a market in a given period, providing absolute protection beyond it. The Multi-Fibres Agreement (MFA) between the EU and textile producers in many Asian countries allows quotas, as do the *voluntary export restraints* (VERs) with Japan on cars. Quotas are administratively simple and can be readily altered. VERs are planned to end in 1999 but could easily be extended, confounding sales and marketing plans. On the other hand, Japanese companies were able to charge higher prices due to the restricted supply, and plough back the profits into locating plants in Europe. They also supplied higher value-added, up-market cars as the quota.
- *Tariffs/duties* These are the most common form of control and may be *specific* (lump sum per unit) or *ad valorem* (percentage of price). They reduce imports, generate revenue, raise consumer prices and reduce welfare by inhibiting choice. Home firms supply more of the market at a higher price. As taxes, they are subject to Parliamentary control and any change may be contested. This takes time making them more predictable for the marketer. Also as efficiency improves it becomes profitable for importers to supply more to the market.

> **ACTIVITY 10.4**
>
> Research suggests that the costs of protectionism outweighs the benefits in the long run. You should now be in a position *to draw up a balance sheet* to demonstrate this finding.
>
> Despite the logic of such analysis, explain why protectionism still occurs and why international institutions and agreements, as discussed in the next section, are therefore still required.
>
> (**See** Activity debrief at the end of this unit.)

The role of international institutions and trade blocs

Most institutions were set up after the Second World War to facilitate greater economic cooperation and establish a framework within which international trade and payments could be sustained and grow. The marketer needs to be aware of their role and importance since they impact both on the stability of the global economy as a whole and on the capability of specific countries to finance trade. They also collect a wealth of information on the state of the world economy and its constituent nations, providing a database for marketing research on trade potential.

The Organization for Economic Cooperation and Development (OECD)

Comprising twenty-one of the most industrialized and powerful economies of the world, this is sometimes known as the 'rich country club'. Its main role is the coordination of national economic policies to avert the possibility of a mutually reinforcing downward spiral of activity and international trade. Meetings and declarations by the G7 group of major governments are particularly important since they often signal shifts in economic policy which will impact on both sales and the marketer. Russia may soon join to make G7 into G8.

> **ACTIVITY 10.5**
>
> Reference to international institutions such as the OECD does not strike too many candidates as interesting or relevant to sales and marketing. However, you may be surprised if you take the trouble to analyse the summary content of an OECD annual report in a quality newspaper. Do the same with a G7 communiqué, making brief notes on any implications for national or international marketing.
>
> This activity may be repeated with the other institutions outlined below since their annual reports and important policy statements are always reported in the press.

The International Monetary Fund (IMF)

The IMF's original membership of thirty-eight has now grown to 168 and it deals primarily with member governments and their central banks. Membership grew rapidly in the late 1980s and early 1990s with the entry of African and former socialist bloc nations. Its main role has been to supervise and maintain the stability of globalized world financial system by providing temporary lending to members suffering balance of payments deficits. The IMF would then agree a programme to address the problems without the need for crisis measures which threatened national or even world prosperity.

The IMF was also responsible for promoting currency stability and providing a mechanism for orderly exchange rate changes when these became unavoidable. It deserves much of the credit for the avoidance of a return to beggar-my-neighbour policies and promoting credible adjustment to turbulent change.

More recently its emphasis has shifted towards resisting strong protectionist trends in many debt-affected developing countries. It provides support and advice as well as funds and seeks to encourage responsible economic management and greater reliance on markets. In the absence of private sector lenders it provided support to East European and former Soviet Union economies during the critical early stages of economic reform. With lending programmes totalling over $23 billion in place in over fifty countries it has considerable leverage over world economic policies. A fund programme is often seen as the only means for a developing country to achieve sustainable growth and internationally it gives a 'seal of approval' which opens the way to commercial lending and trading activity. However, as the IMF has moved to making longer-term 'structural adjustment' loans it overlaps with World Bank territory.

Consulting its *World Economic Outlook* publication may be a vital first step for the marketer seeking expanding economies with whom confidently to do business.

> **EXAM TIP**
>
> Have a look at the logo from a recent CIM marketing conference shown in Figure 10.3. It should sum up your approach to the marketing environment!

The World Bank (IBRD)

The current role of the World Bank is to provide long-term capital for development purposes. The International Bank for Reconstruction and Development lends to better-off developing countries at market rates of interest, while its International Development Association (IDA) lends at highly concessional rates to poorer nations.

Its priority is the eradication of world poverty by promoting sustainable growth through investment in labour and skills with due consideration for environmental factors. With repayments to multilateral creditors such as the IMF and World Bank rising from 20 to 50 per cent between 1980 and 1994 it has proposed a threshold for debt sustainability at 20–25 per cent for the debt service to exports ratio. If debtors demonstrate a thorough track record of reform and sound policies they will receive relief to achieve this within a reasonable time period.

The Bank only invests in specific projects which will contribute to the earning capacity of the borrowing country. Marketers of capital projects will therefore have the assurance of repayment of the foreign exchange component.

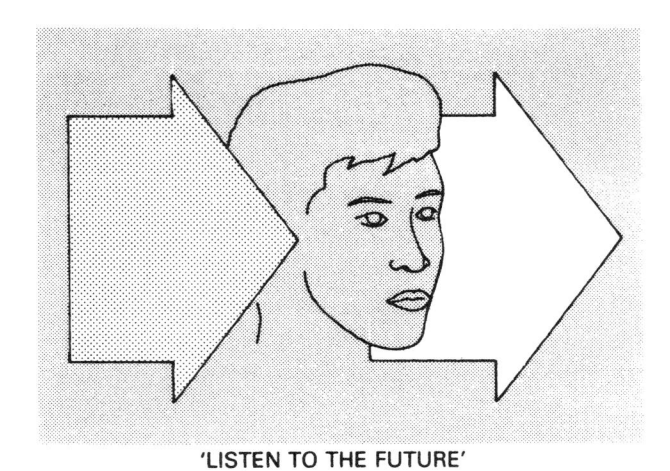

'LISTEN TO THE FUTURE'

Figure 10.3 A marketing logo

General Agreement on Tariffs and Trade (GATT) and the World Trade Organization (WTO)

GATT focused on international initiatives to reduce or eliminate multilateral tariffs and quotas. Its membership rose to 124 in parallel with its success in liberalizing world trade through the negotiated removal of mutually restrictive barriers and represented in excess of 90 per cent of world trade. All these GATT members will belong to the WTO once they have ratified the Uruguay Round. Twenty others, including China, Russia, Taiwan, Ukraine and Vietnam, wish to join.

GATT was best known for its *trade rounds* (see Figure 10.2) of which there were nine from its formation 1947 culminating in the Uruguay round 1986–93. Its guiding principles included:

- Multinational rather than bilateral negotiations
- Non-discriminatory reductions using 'the most favoured nation principle'
- Eliminating existing trade barriers, including non-tariff constraints, and deterring the formation of new ones.

> **QUESTION 10.6**
>
> What do you understand by 'the most favoured nation principle'?
> (**See** Activity debrief at the end of this unit.)

The WTO was created to strengthen management of the world trade system and global economic integration. It will have bigger powers and a wider remit than GATT in overseeing multilateral trade in goods, services and intellectual property. Trade disputes will be referred to a disputes panel and offending countries will be required to put things right, pay compensation to trading partners or face authorized trade reprisals. It can't compel acceptance of rulings and much will depend on it establishing confidence in its even-handedness.

The main outcomes of the Uruguay round included reductions of around a third on agricultural and developed country manufactures tariffs; an increase in the scope of 'bound' tariffs (which cannot be raised later) from 78 per cent to 97 per cent in developed and 21 per cent to 65 per cent in developing countries; a doubling to over 40 per cent in the proportion of duty-free merchandise entering developed countries; a commitment to abolish the Multi-Fibre Agreement over the next decade and offers to liberalize services from many countries.

Three official studies (GATT, OECD and World Bank) have estimated the rise in global economic welfare likely to result from the round as between $213 and 274 billion by 2002 in 1992 US dollars. However, these predated the actual agreement and are thought to underestimate the likely outturn. Figure 10.4 shows the current flows of trade within and between the major areas and the projected impact on annual growth of output and exports.

The benefits will be more substantial because:

- No account is taken of services – already 21 per cent of world trade – WTO will continue to negotiate liberalization
- No account is taken of the effect of strengthened rules and procedures in deterring unfair trade
- No account of the dynamic benefits of a more competitive and integrated world economy:
    - Growth in exports leads growth in output – see Figure 10.5
    - East Asian experience supports this
    - Largest impacts in clothing, textiles and agriculture – also the most protected.

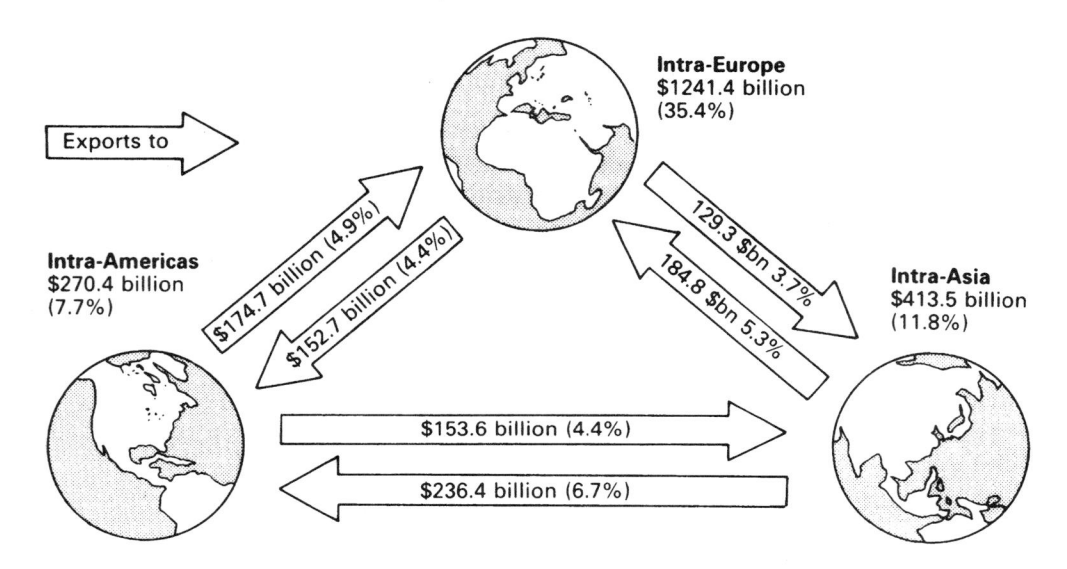

Figure 10.4 How the trade winds will blow. Merchandise trade in US$ billions and as a percentage of world trade. (*Source: Financial Times*)

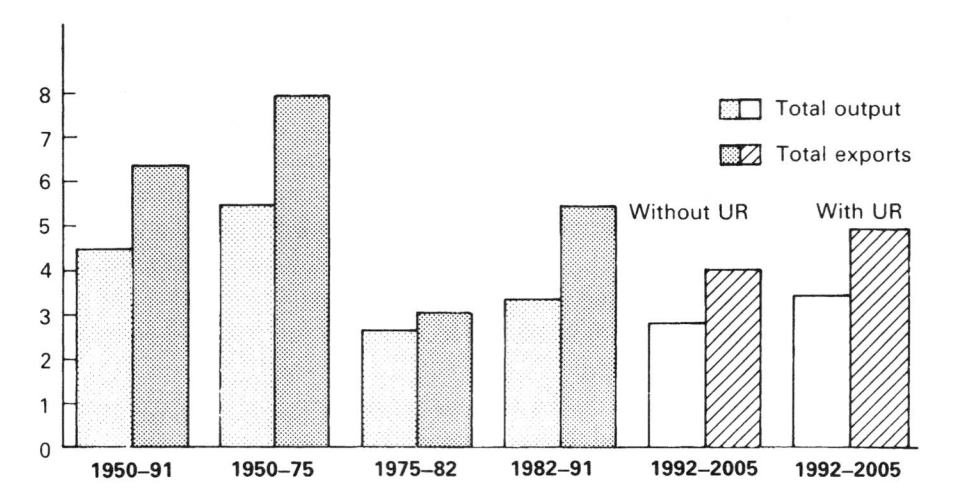

Figure 10.5 Annual average growth of world output and world exports (%). (*Source:* GATT Secretariat)

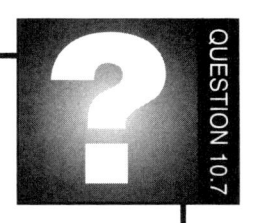

> **QUESTION 10.7**
>
> Who will be the main gainers and losers as a result of GATT? How will your own country in particular be affected?
> (**See** Activity debrief at the end of this unit.)

The agenda for the future does not include further 'rounds' but the possibility should not be ruled out. Meanwhile the WTO will focus on issues such as:

- The interaction of trade and environmental policies and how to promote sustainability and ecological well-being without resort to protection.
- Regulating private barriers to trade to ensure a level playing field. This might include access to foreign direct investment, competition policy and possibly labour standards.

If WTO procedures for regulating unfair trading practices do operate more effectively they may well herald a reversal of recent worrying trends towards increased non-tariff barriers and unilateral action to resolve trade disputes. America and the EU have reserved the right unilaterally to seek concessions from non-WTO members or where rules are unclear. The marketer must therefore take nothing for granted, but with world exports rising in 1994–5 at 8–9 per cent per annum, and 5 per cent in 1996, the stage could be set for renewed expansion in global trade.

Trade blocs

Trade blocs have become much more important in recent years. They represent attempts by countries with similar interests to obtain the benefits of free trade, on the one hand, while retaining the advantage of some protection against the outside world, on the other. They also provide smaller countries with a much more powerful collective voice on global issues and negotiations such as GATT. A number of regional trade blocs can be identified in Figure 10.6 below:

The main regional trade groups

Efta	EU	Afta	Nafta	Andean Pact
European Free Trade Association	European Union	Asean Free Trade Area	North American Free Trade Agreement	Venezuela, Colombia, Ecuador, Peru, Bolivia
Norway, Switzerland, Iceland, Liechtenstein	Belgium, France, Italy, Luxembourg, Germany, Netherlands, UK, Denmark, Greece, Ireland, Spain, Portugal, Austria, Finland, Sweden	Brunei, Indonesia, Malaysia, Philippines, Singapore, Thailand, Vietnam *(limited member)*	United States, Canada, Mexico *(Chile next in line to join)*	

UEMOA	SADC	SAARC	Apec	Mercosur
Ivory Coast, Niger, Burkina Faso, Togo, Senegal, Benin, Mali	Angola, Botswana, Lesotho, Malawi, Mozambique, Mauritius, Namibia, South Africa, Swaziland, Tanzania, Zimbabwe	India, Pakistan, Sri Lanka, Bangladesh, Maldives, Bhutan, Nepal	Australia, Brunei, Malaysia, Singapore, Thailand, New Zealand, Papua New Guinea, Indonesia, Philippines, Taiwan, Hong Kong, Japan, South Korea, China, Canada, US, Mexico, Chile	Brazil, Argentina, Paraguay, Uruguay
West African Economic & Monetary Union	South African Development Committee	S. Asian Association for Regional Co-operation	Asia-Pacific Economic Co-operation	

Figure 10.6 The main regional trade groups (*Source: Financial Times*)

More than 100 such arrangements have been formed, 29 since 1992. Supporters see them as promoting free trade by acting as building blocks which can eventually be cemented into multinational agreements. Sceptics fear fragmentation of the global economy into mutually exclusive or even warring blocs. The latter seems less likely, although regionalism is posing another challenge to the world trading system through proliferating rules and regulations and a formal WTO committee has been set up to examine them.

DEFINITION 10.2

Match up the following terms with their definitions:

- Free trade area
- Customs union
- Common market
- Trade creation
- Trade diversion

1. Goods and services now imported in preference to domestic production.
2. A customs union with a common system of commercial law which permits the free movement of goods, services, capital and labour.
3. A grouping with no internal tariffs but its members are free to set their own tariffs with the rest of the world.
4. Involves discrimination in favour of member imports even though non-member costs, prior to imposition of the common external tariff, were lower.
5. Sets a common external tariff but no internal customs.

- Can you identify the membership of the trade blocs identified above and the category into which they fall?

(**See** Activity debrief at the end of this unit.)

The European Union (EU) and the Single European Market (SEM)

The EU is the most integrated and economically powerful bloc of countries in the world. Its twelve members, currently set to expand to sixteen with the entry of a number of EFTA countries, represent a combined market of 345 million affluent consumers. As such, it is a magnet for salespeople and marketers from around the world.

The SEM initiative originated over concern with Europe's declining competitiveness relative to America and the emerging nations of the Pacific Rim. Despite the Common Market, Europe remained fragmented into culturally differentiated markets protected by an array of non-tariff barriers to trade. A common desire for increased competitiveness and employment opportunities was the driving force behind the idea of a truly free market, which, it was hoped, would release a dynamic and revived spirit of enterprise within European businesses.

In marketing terms, much of European industry appeared to be in the late maturity stage of both product and industry life cycles. Unless a new innovativeness emerged, or the life cycle was extended, it would enter the decline stage as the centre of gravity of world economic power shifted permanently from the Atlantic to the Pacific. Deregulation was seen as the means of releasing competitive forces which would revitalize its mature industrial base.

ACTIVITY 10.6

Use CD-ROM databases or newspaper summaries to locate any surveys assessing progress to date in implementation of the SEM.

Identify any evidence either for or against the hypothesis that European industry is becoming more competitive as a result.

Progress so far

Implemented at the beginning of 1993, the SEM involved the removal of physical, technical, administrative and fiscal barriers to the creation of an integrated market. These prevented cost economies from being realized in production, research and development as well as in sales and marketing. The main changes were:

- *The removal of frontier controls* reducing delays, journey times, customs resources deployed and costs. Cross-border distribution and JIT is facilitated
- *Public procurement opened up to non-national companies*
- *Financial services deregulated*
- *Supply side changes* to create European product standards and regulations.

The aim of all the above measures was to expose protected and inefficient sectors to greater competition, encourage restructuring and secure greater cost economies. These would help to make European companies a more formidable global competitive force. This was, of course, on the assumption that the timetable of directives and measures (279 in all) were in place on schedule. Slippage has already meant that the full effects will not be felt until the end of the decade.

Impacts on Europe, sales and the marketer

The 1988 Cecchini Report attempted to estimate the impact of the SEM. In total these represented just 4.5 per cent of GDP with half of this arising from longer-term benefits. Many observers now believe that the impacts will be substantially greater as investment increases and becomes more productive, raising the European growth rate. However, with much of Europe in recession and unemployment still rising, many of the benefits have yet to appear.

From the point of view of the international marketer, the SEM represents a considerable opportunity. As far as the purely domestic marketer is concerned, it is a threat that must be strategically addressed. Firms that do currently serve profitable domestic niche markets must now recognize that they have the opportunity to exploit their advantage across an enlarging Community.

Entry strategies into these markets represent a spectrum of not only increasing commitment, but also control and include:

- *Licensing agreements* with European companies giving them rights to produce a product for a fee
- *Sales agents (capital goods)/distributors(fmcgs)*
- *Franchise arrangements*
- *Joint ventures and other collaboration*
- *Acquisition of a foreign concern*
- *Direct investment in own facilities*

ACTIVITY 10.7

Refer back to Activity 10.3 relating to the particular problems confronting companies seeking to expand internationally. Rate each of the above entry strategies in terms of their ability to overcome the problems of distance, culture, etc.

What advice would you give to a niche producer in making its decision on whether to go 'European' or not?
(**See** Activity debrief at the end of this unit.)

Summary

Very few industries will escape the structural changes implied by the SEM and businesses should be restructuring their operations, taking the EU rather than, say, Britain as the relevant market. This may necessitate considerable relocation of production and distribution facilities if benefits are to be fully realized. Avoiding being competitively disadvantaged will require taking full and early advantage of opportunities, but European standards and simplified procedures should allow reduced research and development costs, more innovation, rapid diffusion of new products and accelerated life cycles.

European Monetary Union, Euro 2002 and future uncertainty

Progress towards ever-closer political and economic integration is embraced by the Maastricht Agreement, ratified in late 1993, which paves the way towards full European monetary union timetabled for 1999. This involves the establishment of a single European currency with monetary policy controlled by a European Monetary Institute located (and mainly staffed) in Germany. Introduced in 1999 the Euro will displace participating currencies in 2002.

Under the agreement, the European Commission will have increased legislative and executive powers in the areas of health, education, culture, environment, transport and distribution, consumer protection, enterprise and innovation. Most decisions will be by qualified majority voting and will become law throughout the Union.

Uncertainty arises over a number of recent developments which pose question marks over the timing or even ultimate achievement of these moves towards a European federation, with its division of power between the Brussels Commission in certain areas and member governments in others:

- The collapse of the Exchange Rate Mechanism in August 1993: this fixed exchange rate system of Community currencies was intended to be an important step towards final monetary union (a new transitionary ERM was proposed in early 1996).
- British resistance to changes in voting rights with the proposed enlargement of the Union to include Norway, Finland, Sweden and Austria reflects wider concern over centralized power. Further enlargement to include East European and some Mediterranean states looks uncertain.
- Support for the principle of subsidiarity, i.e. devolving power to the lowest appropriate decision-making level, reflects this desire for a looser form of union, with the Commission as a regulator rather than an initiator of directives. These have fallen, in any case, but some fear they would increase again as the union took hold.
- Achievement of the strict Maastricht guidelines has forced France and Germany to pursue tight economic policies resulting in over 12 per cent unemployment. Political pledges to create jobs while cutting government borrowing have proved to be optimistic and doubts are growing whether even Germany will meet the convergence criteria in 1997 without some 'fudging' (e.g. German proposal to revalue its gold reserves).
- Those countries entering the EMU in the first wave will be decided in 1998. Britain has an opt-out but also the strongest job creation record due to its labour market reforms.

QUESTION 10.8

What evidence is there to suggest that it is Japanese and American multinational companies who have responded most positively to the opportunities presented by the SEM and why?
(**See** Activity debrief at the end of this unit.)

Sources of information

As we have seen, it is even more important that the global marketer has access to detailed and reliable information in order that market opportunities can be assessed and future threats identified in time for appropriate action to be taken. Much of the data may be country-specific and assistance will be required from local market research organizations. However, much can be achieved through secondary sources before field research need be considered. The following provide either assistance or the basic building blocks to a marketing information system for a British-based company:

- Government foreign trade and payments statistics
- British Overseas Trade Board (BOTB)
- Department of Trade and Industry (DTI)

- Special country reports – *Financial Times*, *The Economist* and business magazines
- Newspapers and trade press
- International trade directories (e.g. *Kompass*)
- European Commission Reports and statistics
- UN, IMF, OECD, GATT reports and papers
- International banks and other financial institutions
- On-line databases
- London Chamber of Commerce and Industry
- British embassies and consulates also provide advice/assistance
- Foreign embassies and consulates
- Customs and Excise
- Export Credit Guarantee Department – insurance against non-payment
- Market Entry Guarantee Scheme – up to 50 per cent of costs for SMEs.

> **ACTIVITY 10.8**
>
> - It is important that you familiarize yourself with the quality and nature of the information the above sources can provide. Select a foreign market in which you are interested and then access as many of the above sources as possible to build up a profile of characteristics. Do not forget the embassies, who often provide free business guides to trade and investment opportunities in their country. You will find, however, that the less developed the economy, the less the reliability and quantity of information available.
> - Use the above information to assess the relative attractiveness of your own or another country to direct investment by multinationals. (See 'Activity debrief' for UK example at the end of this Unit.)

The multinationals

Multinationals now account for a staggering one-third of total global trade. Their rate of growth has outpaced that of international trade in general and many have become global enterprises with sales revenues that exceed the GDP of all but the largest countries. A multinational is a company that owns and controls operations in different countries. Its investment is 'direct' and any profits or dividends earned will be remitted to the parent country.

Many multinationals are American, with many of the rest owned by Britain and other European countries. However, in recent years, Japan and, latterly, other East Asian companies have moved from direct exporting to joint ventures and then transnational production. A third wave of component manufacturers have begun to follow the initial vehicle and electronic good makers.

Reasons for this surge of multinational activity are many:

- Rapid improvements in transport and business communication systems allow the central control of global operations
- Efficient international capital markets provide the finance
- Avoidance of transport costs
- Advantage taken of lower operational costs for re-export back to the home market
- Tariff barriers avoided and advantage taken of various locational incentives on offer. Local-content requirements may, however, apply for output to be considered national (e.g. cars 70–80 per cent)
- More effective access to and knowledge of the local market
- Developing countries in Africa, Asia and Latin America offer market growth. Such countries have recently, become more open to the entry of foreign companies, viewing them as means of speeding up national development and a source of much-needed foreign currency earnings. Restrictions on ownership and profit repatriation may, however, be applied.
- Avoidance of restrictions and resistance to technical change and working methods.

QUESTION 10.9

Think of what the term 'multinational' means to you and then suggest appropriate adjectives to express your feelings – e.g. gigantic or even tentacular!

List as many US, European and Japanese multinationals as you can think of in the following industries:

- Vehicles
- Consumer electronics
- Banking

Consequences of multinationals

To home country	To host country
Loss of investment to host	Gains investment/jobs
Loss of low-skilled jobs	Balance of payments gains
Visible exports fall	Transfer of skill/technology
Visible re-imports rise	Cost of incentives necessary
Invisible earnings rise	Risk of dependence

The gains to the host nation must not be overstated. It is notable, for example, that newly industrializing countries such as South Korea, Greece, Hong Kong, Mexico and others, in spite of gaining a substantial share of world production in industries like textiles, shoes and electronic equipment manufacture, still have a balance of payments deficit with advanced industrial countries. This derives largely from heavy payments for technical and managerial services as well as remitted profits.

The power and scale of multinationals make them controversial. On the one hand, they have been powerful engines for global economic development and greater integration between nations. Direct investment in developing and newly developed economies has contributed significantly to faster growth. On the other hand, they have sufficient economic leverage to play off one country against another to gain maximum concessions. Both Toyota and Unilever have suggested they would reconsider future investments if Britain stayed out of the Euro.

They also have the power, through transfer pricing, to avoid tax payments in high-rate countries. Finally, they have been criticized for undermining national identity and culture through global product marketing.

QUESTION 10.10

- What is transfer pricing?
- Can multinationals be controlled without the risk of losing their investment in your country?

(**See** Activity debrief at the end of this unit.)

Government policies and the global environment

To appreciate the global environment fully the marketer must be able to analyse and understand the balance of payments position of those countries with which trade takes place. This is important because one of the main sources of uncertainty and often abrupt changes is government policy to correct a payments imbalance. A balance of payments deficit is also a major constraint on economic growth.

The fact that Britain, for example, has a deficit which is beginning to worsen as the economy recovers suggests that future expansion and national income growth will be limited. It also suggests that the problem will have to be addressed in policy terms, implying possible exchange rate depreciation or interest rate rises. Such an analysis would be an important input in future business planning in this market.

> **EXAM TIP**
>
> By now you should know the meaning of the many acronyms used in this subject. These might arise in the examination paper, so make sure you revise the meaning of IMF, WTO, SWOT and SLEPT.

The balance of payments

This is a systematic annual account of all the exchange transactions between the residents of one country and the rest of the world. Credit items yield a positive inflow of foreign currency and vice versa. In a fundamental sense, the payments always balance since the value of purchases of foreign currencies must equal the value of sales by foreigners. However, particular parts of the overall accounts may be in a state of imbalance.

The components of the accounts include:

- The *visible balance of trade* = foods, fuels, materials, semi-manufactured and finished goods
- The *invisible balance of trade* = services: financial, travel, government transfers, overseas earnings
- The *current balance* = visible + invisible balances
- The *capital account balance* = short- and long-term capital movements
- The *balancing item* = adjustment for errors and inaccuracies
- The *balance for official financing* = the 'balance' necessary to/from reserves or borrowing.

The current account is the best indicator of the health of an economy, since it reflects whether a country is trading successfully. No country can run a continuous deficit since its reserves would run out and its ability to borrow from overseas would diminish. Action must be taken well before this point to deal with a persistent deficit.

> **EXTENDING ACTIVITY 10.1**
>
> Space does not allow a comprehensive analysis of a series of balance of payments figures. As suggested in the study guide, it is much more valuable for the marketer to get first-hand experience of analysing such figures.
>
> Obtain an up-to-date edition of a government digest covering trade statistics for your country and research the following:
>
> - Changes in the direction of trade over the last twenty years
> - Changes in the composition of trade over the last twenty years
> - The trade and invisible balances over the past decade
> - The current account balance over the past decade
> - The capital inflow or outflow over the past decade
> - The size of the balancing item
>
> Can you account for the changes that you have found?

Sources of a persistent deficit

A short-term deficit need not necessarily give rise to concern. It may reflect capital imports to promote economic development which subsequently generate extra export revenues. Loans are often forthcoming from the IMF or World Bank to support such a rise in productive potential. If, however, the deficit derives from excess consumption it is a different matter. Sources include:

1. *Excess demand*   Imports are sucked in to reduce inflationary pressures
2. *Import prices rise faster than export prices*   An adverse movement in the terms of trade

3   *Economic weakness*   This may arise for many reasons, such as:
- World demand is declining for the country's main exports
- A failure in supply (e.g. internal conflict)
- Tastes develop for imported goods
- Business structure favours declining industries
- Business culture, regulations or vested interests are preventing improvement.

How can a persistent deficit be remedied?

In the short term the deficit can be financed from foreign currency reserves or by raising interest rates in order to attract foreign capital flows. The latter will only succeed if creditors believe a fall in the exchange rate is not imminent, which would offset the interest gains. Higher rates will also depress consumer and investment spending, reducing aggregate demand and therefore sales.

Expenditure reduction versus expenditure switching

A persistent deficit will require a fundamental and lasting policy response if the progressive drain on reserves and economic confidence in the economy is to be reversed. This normally implies that correction of the problem will be painful.

Expenditure reduction involves policies to reduce the level of aggregate demand. Tax increases on income and consumption combined with government spending cuts will ensure that expenditure on imports will fall. As businesses experience falling domestic sales they will be encouraged to promote extra exports to maintain capacity. The fall in aggregate spending will also tend to moderate wage claims and demand-pull inflation. This will progressively increase relative competitiveness, depressing imports still further and enhancing the competitive advantage enjoyed by exports.

QUESTION 10.11

Expenditure reduction policies appear to be an effective solution for a persistent deficit. Referring back to Unit 7 on the economic environment can you explain why:

- This might not be a wholly effective solution?
- Why governments are reluctant to use them?

(**See** Activity debrief at the end of this unit.)

Expenditure switching involves policies which transfer resources and expenditure from the purchase of imports to domestically produced goods and services. It may still be necessary to reduce expenditure in order to free resources for transfer into exports or import substitution. Policies could include:

- All forms of trade protection
- Incentives for exporters
- Exchange rate adjustment – devaluation

The first two approaches have already been discussed and are designed to deal with the symptoms of a deficit, at the expense of trading partners, rather than with the basic cause. International agreements, however, limit their scope especially now that non-tariff barriers are also being removed (e.g. SEM).

All countries seek to promote exports and we have seen that information, assistance, insurance and advice are services normally provided. Aggressive use of hidden subsidies to obtain an unfair trade advantage, however, are not internationally acceptable. The Japanese Ministry of International Trade and Industry (MITI) was frequently accused of orchestrating the focused export strategies of its major companies, while the French government has been forced to withdraw subsidies to car and aerospace industries following protests.

Exchange rate adjustment

If a business wished to increase its overseas sales or increase its domestic market share at the expense of overseas competitors what could it do? The professional marketer's approach would be to work on the marketing-mix variables to develop a unique selling proposition that delivers more value for money to target customers than rival offerings. A government, however, while not in a position to influence the marketing-mix of domestic companies directly, is able to manipulate the *price* of domestic offerings relative to foreigners by adjusting the exchange rate.

QUESTION 10.12

Which is which?

- Devaluation
- Depreciation

1. A fall in the value of currency as a result of market forces.
2. A downward adjustment to a fixed exchange rate value by a government.

(**See** Activity debrief at the end of this unit.)

When an exchange rate is devalued it will buy less foreign currency than previously, meaning, in effect, that domestic goods and exports now become cheaper in foreign currency terms. The effect should be to increase exports and reduce imports, on the assumption that other things remain the same. However, the marketer should recognize certain qualifications:

- *The J-curve effect* The full effects of a devaluation take time to work through and initially the deficit will worsen before it improves. This can be seen in Figure 10.7, where more expensive imported materials and semi-manufactures are incurred before extra exports can be produced and shipped. As plans and trading patterns adjust, thus shrinking demand for other imports and increasing foreign demand for exports, so the balance should improve.

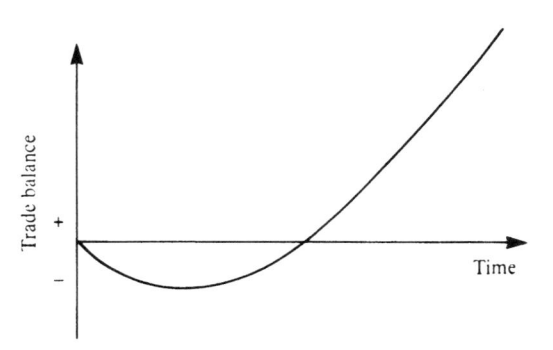

Figure 10.7 The J-curve effect

- *The importance of demand elasticities* The strength of the reaction to the devaluation determines whether the deficit will be eliminated. Success requires that the combined price elasticities of demand for exports and imports sum to more than unity (known as the Marshall–Lerner rule). The rise in export volume must more than compensate for the devalued price, especially if the import bill has risen in foreign currency terms.

> **QUESTION 10.13**
>
> What are the likely elasticities of demand for the goods and services your economy imports and exports? Check back to Unit 3 to remind yourself as to the factors that determine price elasticity. Apply the same analysis to the country you chose to investigate in Activity 10.8.
>
> Any beneficial effects of a devaluation appear to wear off over a period of time. Can you explain why?

Implications for business, sales and marketing

Exchange rate changes are beyond the control of individual businesses but must be accounted for and responded to if international marketing is to be successful and profitable. When a currency depreciates, a company is faced with the choice of leaving domestic currency price unchanged, thereby stimulating extra sales volume, or raising price and profitability to match the devaluation. The decision will depend partly on the elasticity of supply (i.e. can extra volume be produced?) and partly on elasticity of demand (i.e. is it sufficiently responsive to make supplying extra volume a more profitable option?).

Price is only one part of the overall mix and the marketer must coordinate the response to the opportunity provided by the currency depreciation. This is particularly important in the case of currency appreciation where the firm must meet the threat to its sales by either cutting prices in foreign currency terms or reinforcing product and promotional policies to reduce the sensitivity to price.

Minimizing the impact of exchange rate changes

Sound foreign exchange management is of crucial importance to exporters if currency risks are to be minimized. These risks are:

- *Transactions risk*   exposure to currency value changes
- *Translation risk*   arising from ownership of foreign assets
- *Economic exposure*   to changes in relative competitive advantage arising from exchange rates changes.

Minimizing impacts involves hedging these risks but this is seldom straightforward and costs are involved. If, for example, a currency is bought forward to hedge commodity purchases, the company then becomes locked into that exchange rate and the cost structure implied. If a domestic rival delays purchase and the exchange rate appreciates, it will gain a competitive advantage.

From this example it should be obvious that the marketer needs all the knowledge of the global environment that can be mustered to ensure that such decisions turn out right for most of the time!

Once hedging is decided upon, a number of alternative methods offering varying degrees of protection and cost exist:

- Natural hedges – match assets and liabilities in currencies
- Forward contracts – guarantees future price, but locked into the agreed exchange rate
- Option forward contracts – range of alternative settlement dates
- Currency options – confer a right to buy or not at the agreed time.

The potential costs and risks involved in unexpected exchange rate changes underpinned the attractions of fixed exchange rate systems such as the ERM. To be effective, however, such systems require that member governments comply with the disciplines required to maintain exchange rate parities. A degree of flexibility is also necessary to accommodate short-term pressures and the need for longer-term fundamental adjustment to reflect changes in the underlying relative strength of the participants.

> **EXTENDING ACTIVITY 10.2**
>
> As a final but important activity use the references given in the 'Study guide' to undertake the following:
>
> - List the attractions and drawbacks to the marketer of international trade with a country:
>   1. With a fixed exchange rate system
>   2. With a free floating or flexible system
>   3. Who is a member of a trading bloc with a single currency.

Summary

In this the final unit we have been concerned with important issues concerned with the global environment:

- The positive benefits that flow from trade and the work of various international institutions in promoting its development.
- The factors underpinning the growth in world trade and indications supporting its continuance.
- The forces of protectionism and the possibilities offered by the GATT agreement.
- The difficulties confronting companies wishing to trade internationally and the strategies and information sources available to them.
- Reasons for the growth of the multinationals.
- Government policy prescriptions to deal with balance of payments disequilibrium and the marketing implications.

Activity debrief

Definition 10.1 1, 5, 6, 2, 4, 3.
Definition 10.2 5, 3, 2, 1, 4.
Question 10.1 50, 10, 5, 40, 30, 50.
Pre-specialization/trade output is 40 + 50 = 90
Post-specialization/trade output is 50 + 50 =100
There would be a net gain of 10.
Question 10.2 Culture, laws, distance, language, documentation, management and other resources required.
Question 10.3 Institutions such as GATT, IMF and the World Bank have greatly facilitated the freeing and encouragement of trade; the breakdown of political barriers, especially East–West; economic policies to pursue growth and trade (e.g. East Asian island economies built on freeports/entrepot trade; technology has improved communications/logistics; societies have travelled more and become more cosmopolitan; multinationals have expanded rapidly.
Question 10.4 Vested interests (the firms, trade unions, component suppliers, local communities, etc.) will oppose removal of the protection and the infant never grows up to stand on its own feet. If you believe that competition is the main incentive to business efficiency then protecting even mature industries may make them less able to compete. The longer the controls lasted, the more they would be needed. Also, a loss of choice and higher prices.
Question 10.5
- The argument is nonsense. International trade takes place *because* of comparative cost differences. If all countries imposed this condition trade would disappear. Also, what matters is the wage relative to productivity.
- Deflation and devaluation.
- Deflation badly affects the domestic economy and has the same negative effect on international trade as the other two. The answer depends on which policy will encourage greater competitiveness in the long run: devaluation benefits may disappear with inflation.

Question 10.6 Equality of treatment, in that a tariff reduced/raised against one member must be reduced equally against all. Governments can use this to resist vested interest pressure.

Question 10.7 Developed countries due to farm reforms (farm sectors will lose, consumers/tax-payers gain) and they account for two-thirds of goods and all services. Poor food-importing developing countries worst affected (loss of subsidized food/or preferences) (e.g. Africa and Caribbean. EU the biggest gainer, also China and South-east Asia due to textile liberalization.

Question 10.8 Direct investment in Europe has been substantial since the late 1980s, much of it in Britain. Mergers and acquisitions have also risen, even by the Japanese, who do not normally favour this entry methods: ICL computers, Dunlop tyres.

Question 10.10
- Multinationals transfer parts and components between different plants. The transfer price is the internal price charged to another subsidiary. If it is set high little profit will be made and vice versa.
- Possibilities include codes of practice, exchange of information between countries, trade bloc regulations.

Question 10.11 What happens as the expenditure rises again? Will not wage and price inflation resume? What if other economies are in recession? Will this mean that the economy will have to be kept in a state of low demand for a long period? What of the cost in terms of unemployment and lost economic growth?

Question 10.12 2, 1.

Activity 10.2 Sources include *political*: war, terrorism, breakdown in relationships, even elections in a major trade economy; *economic*: coordinated recessions, multiplier – accelerator effects, major trade disputes, movement toward protectionism, failure to coordinate economic policies; *confidence*, and *technical* factors also figure. Turbulence will vary in different parts of the world and affect different industries to different degrees. Natural factors can also disrupt trade.

Activity 10.4 Protectionism occurs because:
- Jobs are *obviously* saved in the threatened sector.
- Jobs are highly visible and protected by powerful lobbies.
- Export sector jobs lost due to the adverse chain reaction via the international circular flow will be spread and difficult to link to the protectionism.
- The consumer loses via higher prices/less choice but is a diffused pressure group.

Countries are more likely to trade responsibly and therefore secure the benefits if they believe all are bound by agreements that prevent cheating. The same applies to mutual tariff cuts.

Activity 10.7 Your advice would probably include: a strategic review/SWOT analysis to be undertaken; market and competitor research in selected market(s); establish a network of contacts; investment in training for skills and changing the culture of the business; evaluation of entry strategies re cost, investment, control, risk and return; adopt European standard; rethink the marketing mix for European context.

Activity 10.8 Membership of EU, position on trade routes, regional status for EU grants, active efforts of local authorities and Invest in Britain Bureau, political stability, 58 million affluent population, consumer good orientated, demonstration effect of existing multinationals, liberal policies, relatively low wages and tax rates, just legal system, compact, good infrastructure, skilled workforce, efficient distribution, supplier network, buoyant economy, weakened unions, enterprise policies, ease of remitting profits, limited domestic competition, the world's business and computer language, EuroTunnel, etc.

Examination hints and specimen question

The global environment offers a diversity of possible questions. These might focus on the macro-environment for example, the gains from trade or protection or on the micro aspects (for example, the opportunities and threats confronting the individual marketer). Part-questions in the compulsory section are equally likely (see Unit 8, sample question 1(a)). As such, the fact that it is a broad area is likely to be rewarded in most examinations with at least a question.

1 Your consultancy firm has decided to produce a brief booklet, in bullet point format, to provide advice to marketing clients who are considering establishing overseas operations.

(8 marks)

Using relevant headings and points, produce an outline draft for this booklet including a bibliography of useful sources of further information. (20 marks)

(CIM Marketing Environment paper, June 1995)

2. A Japanese vehicle manufacturer is considering your country as the manufacturing base for its overseas operations. As a research consultant, you have been asked to provide a résumé of your findings on the following:
   (a) The information needs of the manufacturer to enable it to evaluate the relative merits of locating in your country. (10 marks)
   (b) The key information sources the manufacturer should monitor in order to assess the market and its participants. (10 marks)

(CIM Marketing Environment paper, December 1995)

3. You have been asked to write a short article, suitable for inclusion in a marketing newsletter, on the issue of: 'Potential turbulence arising from the balance of payments'. The text should address the potential impact of government corrective actions on the marketing environment and not exceed 700 words. (20 marks)

(CIM Marketing Environment paper, June 1996)

Hints: Indicative content and approach

Question 1

- This is a complicated format. Be sure to:
  - (i) Provide a booklet heading and signify your consultancy as the author
  - (ii) keep it brief
  - (iii) make the headings relevant so as to structure the booklet
  - (iv) use bullet points throughout
  - (v) outline key aspects only
  - (vi) append a bibliography with titles, authors and dates if known.
- Clients considering establishing overseas operations suggests direct investment, but advice may cover alternative entry strategies.
- Content relatively straightforward, covering society, culture, market size, segmentation, competition, cost factors, government support, etc.
- Include recognized sources on the industry, market, companies – government, banks, chambers of commerce, etc.

Question 2

- This is a very similar question but in a different guise.
- It explicitly refers to relative merits – compared to probable alternatives.
- It relates to your own country.
- Its format is different but still requires only summary points.
- Be sure to include information sources on the market and its participants.

Question 3

- The emphasis on short article and space limits is not window dressing.
- Target audience is marketers so focus accordingly.
- Explain the nature of the turbulence.
- Focus on expenditure switching and reducing policies.
- Specify the potential impacts on sales volumes and margins.

UNIT 11

Guidance on revision and examination

Study guide

As you will be aware, throughout the workbook, examination tips and specimen questions have been provided to help you relate the course content to the examination requirements. In this short unit a brief summary of the *key elements in learning and examination success* will be outlined. These should be studied well in advance of the date of your examination to obtain maximum benefit from them.

You will then find a full *examination* paper which you are advised to attempt under controlled examination conditions. An alternative compulsory question has also been included for your perusal.

It would be a great advantage if you could find someone appropriate to provide feedback on your attempt since only the exceptional candidate can perform excellently on the first try. A tutor, your marketing manager or a previously successful candidate may be able to give you invaluable pointers in improving your focus and technique in subsequent attempts.

To help you further, a set of *model answers and commentaries* have been provided. *It is important that you do not consult these until you have attempted the question paper.* The commentaries concentrate more on structure and approach to the questions while the model answers provide detailed substantive content which you may readily supplement from the various units. Remember that *practice makes perfect* and the more practice you can have at actual past questions, the better.

As further examination papers become available it is essential that you obtain copies not only of the papers themselves but also the senior examiner's report on how candidates had fared (a summary of recent examiner's reports is provided below and you should study it carefully) and perhaps copies of the specimen answers, obtainable from CIM Direct. Attempt these questions before you read the report and model answers and compare how well you did. Then analyse why you did not do better!

- Had you revised enough?
- Did you choose to do the right questions?
- Did you focus on what the question asked for?
- Did you run out of time? and so on.

Perhaps you should consider doing a SWOT analysis on yourself and the examination based on where you went right and where you went wrong in attempting the paper. Recognize your strengths and exploit them fully. Acknowledge your weaknesses and work to improve them. Consider the shape of the paper, what the examiner was looking for and the opportunities this presents for the next paper you sit. Look for the threats in terms of failure to adopt the right format, failure to revise sufficient topics, failure to keep up to date with environmental developments and even failure to answer the required number of question.

The subject knowledge contained in this workbook is a necessary but not a sufficient basis for passing the examination. You must also supply the following:

- A high proportion of the activities and further reading completed
- The necessary effort put into revision of the material
- Effective communication of your knowledge to the examiner
- Efficient management of your examination time.

A businesslike approach

Approaching a CIM Sales or Marketing Environment examination is like confronting a business problem. Your *primary objective* is to *pass first time*, in the shortest study time duration and with an A or B credit or distinction standard. Your *strategy* involves revising in good time, allocating your time between different syllabus areas, deciding which topics to concentrate on and, in the exam, which of the optional questions to actually answer.

Market research involves study of the course material, the activities, awareness of developments in the sales and marketing environment and comments in examiner's reports. *Planning* will require a revision schedule and a framework of understanding about the marketing environment and appropriate concepts to apply in solving examination problems.

Implementation will necessitate effective use and distribution of your time between and within questions, set in a constrained examination situation, where the emphasis must be on supplying well, structured and professionally presented answers.

Key elements in learning

There are three elements involved here:

1. *Learning* Many students do not know *how to learn*! You should not fall into this category if you have used this workbook correctly. You learn very little if all you do is passively read the course material, memorize some and then try to regurgitate it in the exam. Our minds do not react well to such a passive approach, we are easily distracted and nothing much sinks in. We can waste many hours in this way, pretending to study!

    For learning to be truly effective it must be active and applied. You must involve yourself in the learning process by thinking about it, testing it against your experience, making links with your existing knowledge and developing it further. There is an old adage that suggests we 'learn by doing' so do not be tempted into passive learning but instead apply active learning techniques such as:
    - Make your own set of notes, in words you understand, combining all sources of information and activities.
    - Whenever an example is provided, always stop to think of one of your own, preferably from work/company experience.
    - Try to develop an environmental way of thinking about business sales and marketing and relate concepts to your own experience.
    - Make sure you can define *all key terms* concisely.
    - Make revision notes using headings/bullet points possibly on 'prompt cards' since these will provide the framework for answers in the exam.
    - Do not try to memorize ideas but work on understanding and applying them. This way you will remember them automatically.
    - The exam is about the environment, so make sure that you are *well briefed* on current developments *in your own economy*.
    - Think about relevant and topical questions that might be set
    - *Do* attempt all the sample questions provided in the workbook since these are vital tests of your active learning and understanding. Don't treat them as a chore, but as a cement that will fix knowledge securely in your mind and strengthen your confidence for the 'real thing'.

2. *Memory* Active learning will fix knowledge, understanding and application in your 'long-term memory'. Passive learning will, at best, fix it in your 'short-term memory'. Memorizing parrot-fashion is also unlikely to be effective because examiners are experienced at recognizing such a tactic. Such a technique is, in any case, unlikely to match the exact question posed since a tailored response to the 'slant' of the question is necessary and this means real understanding is required, not an 'off the memory shelf' answer. It is, however, useful to use memory aids such as SLEPT and SWOT to ensure that you recall all key points when under the considerable pressure of exams.

3. *Revision* This should be an ongoing process rather than a panic measure implemented just before the exam itself. You should be blending a set of notes that are comprehensive and easy to revise from as you proceed through the syllabus. For each

concept you should generate two or three examples and link ideas as you go along. Knowledge is a building process and you must lay solid foundations upon which to construct your understanding and application of the material.

Key revision skills include such things as:

- Keeping your file well organized, easy to reference and updated.
- Practise defining key terms from memory. These are an essential ingredient of exam question introductions.
- Progressively refine and condense your revision notes into key word clusters.
- Prepare topic outlines and essay answer plans, then prepare some more. Get them checked out to make sure you are on target.
- Read your concentrated notes the night before the exam and immediately before going to sleep. This should help to fix the notes in your short-term memory throughout the following day. Do not overdo it and get a reasonably early night so that your mind will be fresh and alert for the exam itself!

Key elements in examination success

There are five main elements involved here.

Spotting topics

Any good salesperson or marketer will want to forecast the future and the examination questions are no exception! However, as you will already have learnt, it is one thing to forecast accurately in a stable, predictable and known environment, but quite another where new product development is involved.

With a relatively new syllabus and a subject area which is substantially different from what most candidates have experienced before, it is vital that you must absorb *all* the examination hints and tips provided in this workbook.

You already have a good idea of the likely distribution of questions across the syllabus and a set of past examination questions set by the senior examiner. Study these carefully in terms of form and style of presentation.

As past papers become available, the task of forecasting becomes a little easier. You can construct a grid relating the syllabus areas to questions arising in successive exams to get a feel of patterns and topic areas with a higher probability of occurrence. The examiner will be setting questions to cover the whole syllabus area over a run of years, so be prepared for a topic that has not come up for a while.

Remember the lead time in preparing exam papers and do some market research on current events a year before yours is due. It is *not advisable*, though, to try to spot specific questions and prepare for these in detail. Your chances of predicting the precise question format is remote, but having invested considerable effort in 'preparing' a model answer you may be tempted to show the examiner what you know under the pretext of answering the actual question that has been set. Do not be tempted to do this since *you must answer the question set*, not the one you hoped for, otherwise all you might get is a red line through your work.

Examiners – the nature of the beast!

It is often quite a revelation for students to learn that examiners are on their side. They would like you to pass and derive no satisfaction or benefit from failing candidates. Indeed, it is psychologically much more difficult for them to fail you than to pass you. The CIM also guarantees that fairness prevails by ensuring that marginal fail marks are personally second marked by the senior examiner. However, one of the primary responsibilities of the examining team is the maintenance of standards and to ensure that those who gain the CIM certificate are worthy of the qualification in the eyes of both actual and potential employers.

Why not take a leaf out of the marketer's handbook of success and:

- *Be examiner-friendly* and orientate your answers to what *they* need. With a lot of other scripts to mark as well as your own, make life easy for them!
- Provide them with *value for money* by understanding and answering precisely what the question requires. Read their needs (i.e. the question) very carefully and don't provide unwanted frills (i.e. waffle).

- Make the job of marking your script straightforward by answering the right number of questions, clearly and concisely in well-laid-out report-type style with white space separating the points made.
- Deliver the answer in the format requested in the question.
- Give the examiner something to mark. If you do not attempt a question or write very little then the examiner is in a fix in terms of awarding any marks. Even if you have not prepared the topic use your common sense, define the terms, provide a couple of examples, etc. The extra mark or two this generates may make all the difference!
- The examiner is your ultimate consumer so use your 'marketing mix' to meet his or her needs. Provide a strong sense of enthusiasm and professionalism in your answers supported by relevant examples and applications where appropriate. Try to 'differentiate' your product from run-of-the-mill scripts, consider critical success factors and make it a pleasure to mark. Your reward will be substantial.

Examination practice

This has already been heavily emphasized as the means of getting it *right first time*!. Make the effort to practise papers under exam conditions and sketch out outline plans to as many questions as possible. Time is a scarce resource and you must use and distribute it between questions effectively. Writing at length on three questions and then penning a note of apology to the examiner that your time has run out for the fourth will cut no ice at all. If, however, you have badly mistimed the previous question then provide the examiner with your outline answer plan in note form with a list a bullet point conclusions.

Examination technique – planning the answer

Planning is the keystone of success in examinations. You must:

- *Plan* to cover the majority of what is a big syllabus.
- *Plan* to prepare more topics than you will need.
- *Plan* an orderly revision schedule with time built in for unforeseen pressures on your time.
- *Plan* for emergencies which might disrupt your schedule.
- *Plan* your sample questions and learn from your mistakes.
- *Plan* to be fully informed on the time and venue of the exam.
- *Plan* to be fully prepared, fresh and relaxed for the exam.
- *Plan* to avoid nervous colleagues prior to entering the exam.
- *Plan* to channel natural examination nerves into alert awareness.
- *Plan* out which three questions to answer from the six options.
- *Plan* all your answers at the outset since one might trigger ideas for the others. Do not be rushed into writing because others around you are. Your plans are the key to a good pass! Make simple single trigger word plans, not detailed ones. Each word represents an idea, then number the order you are going to develop them.
- *Plan* to allocate time equally between questions.
- *Plan* to allocate time within questions according to the marks.
- *Plan* to relate what you say to the question posed. Do not insult the examiner (who set it!) by not specifically addressing it.
- *Plan* to read the questions *very* carefully. Underline key words, identify the context, the marks allocated, the number of parts and the problem being posed.
- *Plan* the structure of your answer – provide an introduction, define the terms, signpost your approach, adopt the required format, supply reasoned arguments, draw conclusions.
- *Plan* to label diagrams correctly if you use them, and only use them if you can!
- *Plan* to focus *only* on what the question asks and not to waffle.

Examination technique – presentational effectiveness

This is an often overlooked but critical aspect of examination success. How do you judge people or companies you have dealings with? First impressions often condition our reactions, and so it is with examiners. If they pick up a scruffy, near-illegible script which is poorly structured and presented they will immediately develop negative feelings whatever the actual content. Examiners do recognize, however, that for many candidates English is their second language and will make some allowance for this. There is no excuse, though, for an unprofessional script!

If you do not appear to care, then neither will the examiner! Sales and marketing students should in any case be adept at presentation and persuasion and you should seek to demonstrate these skills. The key requirements here are:

- *Compliance*   answer the exact question set and
- *Clarity*   in layout, legibility and presentation

Practise laying out answers in a semi-report rather than essay style since this is what is adopted in business. Headings, a list of bullet points and a paragraph of explanation and discussion is far easier for the examiner to absorb than big blocks of solid text.

> **ACTIVITY**
>
> As a final activity take the past paper on page 233 and, once you have answered it under examination conditions, go through the following checklist of points. Better still, ask a friend or your tutor to do so on your behalf. If any are answered in the negative then work out an action plan that will guarantee a positive outcome in the actual examination itself.
>
> | | | *Yes* | *No* |
> |----|--|-------|------|
> | 1 | Is your layout professional? | | |
> | 2 | Is it clearly legible? | | |
> | 3 | Have you used semi-report-style format? | | |
> | 4 | Is there white space between points? | | |
> | 5 | Have you numbered the questions clearly? | | |
> | 6 | Have you saved time by *not* writing out questions? | | |
> | 7 | Have you used black ink/biro? | | |
> | 8 | Have you avoided/deleted crossings out? | | |
> | 9 | Are diagrams relevant, clear, labelled and explained? | | |
> | 10 | Did you answer the questions posed exactly? | | |
> | 11 | Did you define all relevant terms in the question? | | |
> | 12 | Did the amount written reflect the marks allocated? | | |
> | 13 | Did you answer the compulsory question? | | |
> | 14 | Did you finish in time? | | |
> | 15 | Would you have given it a pass mark? | | |
> | 16 | Was it really up to the standard required by CIM? | | |

Examinations in practice

In the section above on 'Spotting topics' it was suggested that you construct a grid relating syllabus areas to questions arising in successive examinations. With five series of examinations now complete and one in progress it is helpful to examine such a grid. The table that follows summarizes the syllabus areas and highlights the proportions allocated to the main sections. Ticks represent the location of optional questions and stars compulsory parts from (a) to (d). The letter P designates part questions. A word of warning, however – some questions draw from across the syllabus so the location of the tick or star only represents the primary focus.

The grid provides a useful overview of the question pattern within and across the examination series. Empty columns have been left for you to extend the grid as papers become available. You might also wish to indulge in some predictions of your own. Such a process should carry candidate health warnings since the risks of depending on 'bankers' have been mentioned and *all* sections of the syllabus appear to be examined regularly.

Syllabus reference	Syllabus area	Dec 1994 (10 questions)	June 1995 (10 questions)	Dec 1995 (10 questions)	June 1996 (7 questions)	Dec 1996 (7 questions)	June 1997 (7 questions)	Dec 1997 (7 questions)	%
3.1.1	Legal forms of organization	✓		✓					The organization
3.1.2	Objectives, social responsibility, stakeholders	✓	✓P	✓	*b	✓P			
3.1.3	Organizational size, structure		✓	✓P	*c	✓P			15%
3.1.4	Development of structures, marketing role			✓P		✓P			
3.2.1	Appreciation of micro-environment	✓P			✓P				The micro environment
3.2.2	Role and function of intermediaries and suppliers, relationship marketing		✓		✓				
3.2.3	How size and industrial structure influence competitive activity – models to predict	✓✓				*b,d			30%
3.2.4	Structural analysis		✓	*d		✓P			
3.2.5	Publics and impacts Marketing role Consumerists and environmentalists	*d		✓	*d	✓P			
3.2.6	Legal relationships and obligations	✓	✓	✓	*a,d	✓			
3.3.1	Monitoring environment Environmental set Scenarios, threats and opportunities	✓P ✓	*d ✓P *c		✓P ✓	*a ✓P			The macro environment
3.3.2	Social environment Regulatory environment Economic environment Political environment Natural environment Technical environment	✓P	*b ✓ ✓ ✓	*a,b,c	✓ ✓	✓			45%
3.3.3	Sources of information, how to monitor and interpret	✓		✓		✓P			
3.4.1	International trade, multinationals Sources of turbulence	*b,c		✓P	✓	*c ✓			Global
3.4.2	Trade blocs, institutions	*a	*a						10%
3.4.3	Information sources and limits to global operations		✓	✓P					

Figure 11.1 Marketing Environment Examination grid

A useful supplement to the above exercise is to construct an equivalent grid for format requirements specified in questions. As you know, marks are allocated for providing answers within the context of these and might represent up to 10 per cent of the total marks in some cases. Such a grid not only allows you to review the patterns across papers but also the variety used. Make sure you are familiar with all these format types and note recent developments such as space-limited responses where you must restrict your answer to, say, one page or 700 words. You will lose marks if you ignore this requirement, which in effect means the examiner wishes you to be concise and to the point.

Specified format	Dec 1994	June 1995	Dec 1995	June 1996	Dec 1996	June 1997	Dec 1997
Appendix		✓					
Appropriate/Own format					✓		
Bibliography		✓		✓			
Brief/Outline [O]	✓		✓	✓	✓O		
Bullet points		✓		✓			
Checklist/list	✓	✓	✓				
Cite industry example	✓	✓		✓	✓		
Commentary					✓		
Debate							
Memorandum					✓		
Notes	✓	✓	✓✓	✓			
Other, e.g. Article [A], Booklet [B], Draft [D], Resume [R]	✓R	✓D✓B	✓R	✓A	✓A		
Report/Submission [S]	✓				✓✓S		
Slides/Presentation	✓	✓	✓	✓	✓		
Space-limited response				✓1 page ✓700 words	✓2 page		
Summary		✓			✓		

Figure 11.2 Business format requirement grid

Finally, you may wish to survey the types of articles used in past papers. They cannot be predicted in advance but do give you a feel for the nature and spread of topics covered and underline the importance of practising evaluating similar articles in the context of your studies.

Month/Year	Title
December 1994	GATT to boost world income by $213 billion – effects of Uruguay trade liberalization
June 1995	With a greyer picture of the future in mind – implications of ageing
December 1995	On line for a speedy sale – technological potential and the marketer
June 1996	New line of attack in Great Soap War – non-price competition and regulation
December 1996	US ranked as most competitive nation – sources of competitiveness and consequences
June 1997	
December 1997	

Figure 11.3 Cases or articles used in past examinations

Key point summary from the senior examiner's reports

December 1994 series

- Only relatively small numbers entered this first examination of a brand new subject, reflecting the limited time available to centres and candidates to adjust to its requirements.
- A breadth of choice in optional questions was provided but success often hinged on dealing effectively with the broadly based compulsory question.
- Results proved disappointing and clear lessons had to be learnt for standards to improve.
- This subject is not a 'soft option' but a demanding and important area of knowledge for the marketing practitioner. Centres must ensure candidates are aware of this, have access to the appropriate texts and cover the whole syllabus at least in broad terms.
- Candidates from the same centre tended to answer the same questions suggesting a tendency to only cover parts of the syllabus. Low marks resulted if the compulsory questions had been missed.
- Many scripts produced only brief answers with little evidence of necessary reading.
- Business communication formats were often overlooked and essay style answers were given to report style questions with marks being needlessly lost.
- Overseas candidates frequently ignored the requirement to provide an industry context or examples. This might have been due to failure to read the question carefully enough. It might also suggest the need for greater effort to relate their understanding to business and marketing applications.
- Distinctions were achieved by candidates who focused on the question posed in a well balanced manner, adopted the required business formats and effectively demonstrated their knowledge and understanding of the marketing environment by convincingly relating it to marketing practice.

June 1995 series

- A learning curve from the first paper and availability of customized texts resulted in some overall improvement.
- Improvement was most noticeable in home centres while overseas performance was rather patchy.
- The use of a text and workbook are highly recommended to cope successfully with this holistic subject.
- A notable feature was the tendency to misinterpret instructions leading candidates to ignore parts of questions or include both a. and b. into one long essay.
- Candidates are advised to read the whole paper very carefully and make clear precisely which question they are answering. It is not necessary, however, to write out the question in full causing valuable writing time to be lost.
- Candidates should avoid the folly of writing up to two sides of notes before commencing the actual answer. Notes and plans that do not form part of the answer should be crossed out.
- A small number of candidates adopted a very 'economic' approach to their answers whereas an 'environmental' approach is necessary. Candidates should also beware of adopting a wholly 'marketing' perspective without explaining the environmental aspects first.
- Formats were adopted in the main but candidates must take care not to provide all report format without the necessary content to answer the question. Only a framework format is required.
- Plan all questions before writing to provide structure and avoid unnecessary repetition of points in different questions.

December 1995 series

Home centres

- A significant improvement in standards and pass rate performance was recorded in most centres. Distinction grade papers also saw a pleasing rise.

- Evidence now clearly suggests that the majority of centres fully understand the detail of the syllabus requirements.
- Candidates and centres appear to have taken on-board the senior examiner's advice to practice previous examination questions and base their studies around recommended texts and workbooks.
- A steady, consistent standard across *all four* answers in the examination was the surest route to a pass.
- Avoid the temptation of writing *too much* on the first question/part question. Relate the amount you write to the marks available. A compulsory question worth only 6 or 8 marks should not have more written than for a whole optional question worth 20 marks! The rule of thumb is 17/18 minutes for each 10 marks.
- *Optional questions will fall from **nine to six** in the June 1996 series.* This makes it all the more vital that centres fully cover the whole syllabus.
- Much less care was taken in adopting the appropriate and required business formats this series. Requests for appendices, résumés, note or presentational form should not be ignored Candidates *must* aim to answer the question within the spirit of the spirit of the required format (*see* Model answers following this section).

Overseas centres

- Pass rates improved once again but not as sharply as in home centres and continue to lag significantly in overall standard.
- Some excellent scripts were received, particularly in some African centres.
- There is disturbing evidence that some centres/candidates are still not using the recommended texts and workbooks.
- Candidates can not afford to miss out parts of the compulsory or optional questions. If you can't answer all parts of an optional question, attempt one that you can.
- Running out of time or writing *too little* to achieve a pass remains a problem. Proposals at the CIM to provide overseas candidates with up to *15 minutes reading time* will help compensate in this area.
- Evidence of only partial coverage of the syllabus.
- Evidence of some difficulty in understanding terms and relating material to the candidates' own experience.
- Some centres still seem to assume that this is an easy subject which can be passed with marketing knowledge alone supplemented by a grasp of current affairs.

June 1996 series

Home centres

- The choice of optional questions fell from 9 to 6.
- A disappointing slippage in progress to a higher pass rate occurred, although it was comparable with other Certificate subjects.
- Consistency across all answers remains the key. Weak performance in just one or two parts may produce an overall marginal fail.
- One or two questions were surprisingly unpopular, suggesting some centres were omitting significant sections of the syllabus, e.g. the political environment.
- Some candidates were relying too much on 'breadth' and 'appreciation' and too little on real depth and understanding. Centres must work hard to get the balance right.

Overseas centres

- Marred by an inability to conform to the required format:
  - Overhead projector slide format was poorly attempted in question 1(d).
  - The requirement for a one-page brief in question 2 was largely ignored.
  - A number selected one from each of the four pairs of terms rather than two pairs as directed.
- Even after allowance is made, communication skills sometimes fall below the standard that would be acceptable in business.

December 1996 series

Home centres
- The need is to improve the tail of weaker candidates up to the standards of the better ones in some centres.
- The pass rate slipped in the face of a challenging paper.
- Some candidates continue to rely on their marketing knowledge when attempting marketing environment questions.
- The main source of weakness is the failure to address the precise question posed. One question clearly asked for an evaluation of opportunities or threats, yet many candidates addressed strengths and weaknesses, or policy recommendations rather than what was required.
- Use of required format improved but should not be provided if not asked for.

Overseas centres
- Despite a fair paper relating to candidates' own experience and country a degree of needless misinterpretation occurred.
- Reading time allowance did not prevent a number of candidates answering less than the required four questions – two candidates scored over 40 per cent from just two questions but only answered two questions and so failed.
- One candidate wrote eight pages of essay plan notes but only ten pages of answer.
- Many continue to write far too much on the first question attempted or those where only a few marks are allocated.
- Format requirements continue to be either ignored *or* provided to the exclusion of actual answer content.
- There is insufficient evidence of reading recommended texts or workbooks such as this.

Specimen exam paper   December 1996

The Marketing Enviroment
This examination is in two sections.
Part A is compulsory and worth 40 per cent of total marks.
Part B has six questions, select three. Each answer will be worth 20 per cent of the total marks.
DO NOT repeat the question in your answer but show clearly the number of the question attempted on appropriate pages of the answer book.
Rough workings should be included in the answer book and ruled through after use.

Part A: Compulsory question

Marketing Environment

US Ranked As 'Most Competitive' Nation
The US and Singapore have further consolidated their lead in the past year as the world's two most competitive economies, while Japan has continued to lose ground, according to The World Competitiveness Report published by the World Economic Forum based in Geneva. IMD, a leading Swiss business school, produces the report by ranking 48 leading economies on the basis of a weighted index of 380 economic, social and political criteria, and an opinion poll of international executives.

World Competitiveness Scoreboard*
Top twenty, 1995   1994

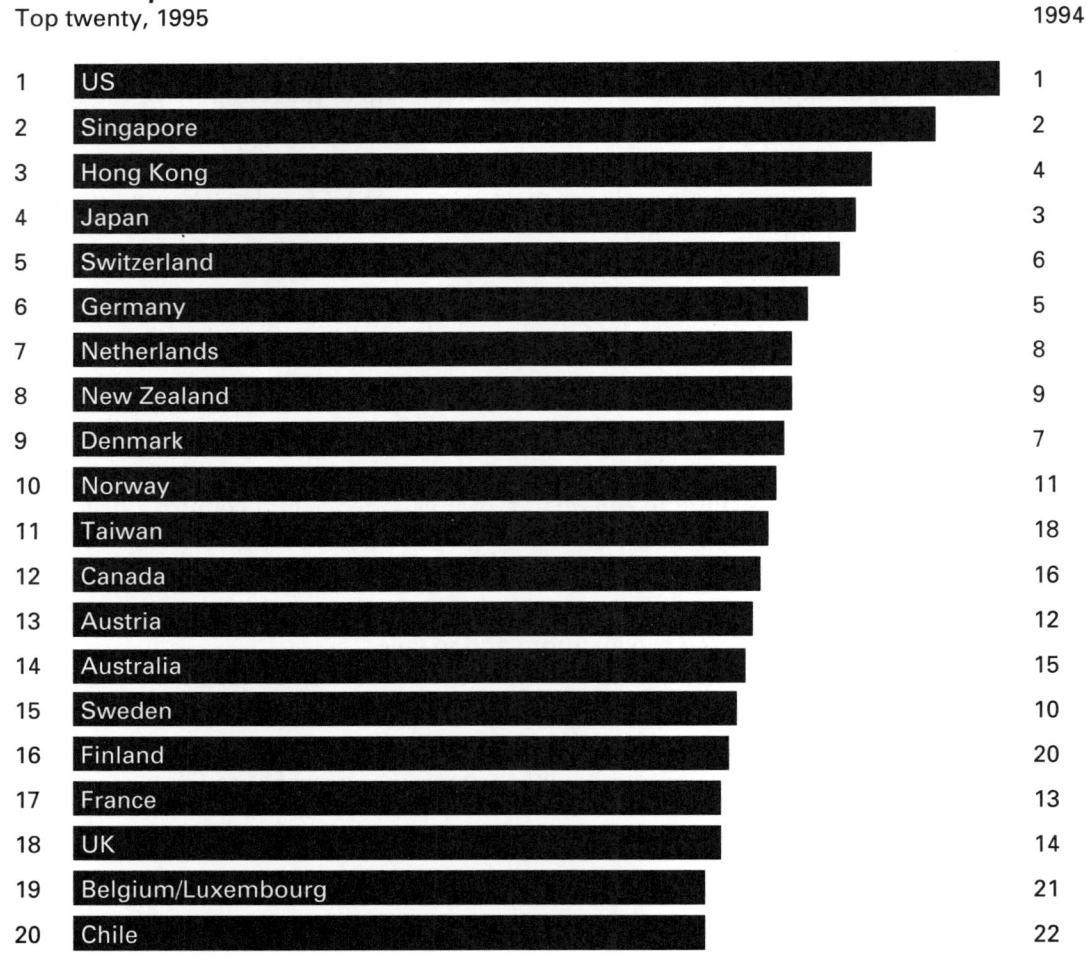

Rank 1995	Country	Rank 1994
1	US	1
2	Singapore	2
3	Hong Kong	4
4	Japan	3
5	Switzerland	6
6	Germany	5
7	Netherlands	8
8	New Zealand	9
9	Denmark	7
10	Norway	11
11	Taiwan	18
12	Canada	16
13	Austria	12
14	Australia	15
15	Sweden	10
16	Finland	20
17	France	13
18	UK	14
19	Belgium/Luxembourg	21
20	Chile	22

*Weighted index based on statistical data and an opinion survey of international executives

The gap in performance between the strongest and weakest performers in Western Europe has also widened – a trend which looks bad for efforts to promote greater economic convergence in the European Union. 'The name of the game in Europe now is how to manage diversity, not convergence', suggested the report's director.

The most striking advance was achieved by Taiwan, which had moved from 18th to 11th place ahead of countries like Canada and Australia, while Malaysia had slipped from 16th to 21st. Britain too had fallen back from 14th to 18th place, while Russia was the worst performer.

The US owed its position chiefly to aggressive deregulation, strength in innovative technologies, adoption of new management techniques and tight control over labour costs. The report conceded that the improved competitiveness had involved great social costs which could create problems in future and would prevent the US becoming a model for countries that prized social stability highly.

Japan, which headed the rankings till 1993, appeared to be suffering from multiple economic, political and social crises which had shaken faith in its national values. Japanese confidence, measured by the executive poll, was at an all-time low. Other Asian economies scored particularly highly for their economic dynamism.

One contradiction which the report found hard to explain was the relatively low ranking of Britain despite its exceptional attractiveness to inward investors.

(*Adapted from a Financial Times article by Guy de Jonquieres*)

Part A

Question 1
(a) Select **one** of the following terms used in the article and provide a short definition, an example and a brief commentary on each:

i) A Weighted Index.
ii) Economic Convergence.
iii) Social Costs.
iv) Innovative Technologies (10 marks)

(b) Assess the potential implications of a policy of aggressive deregulation for:

either
i) Consumers.
or
ii) Marketers In The Sector Concerned. (10 marks)

(c) Prepare a short article for inclusion in an international publication explaining why Britain is exceptionally attractive to inward investment despite poor relative competitiveness. (10 marks)

(d) Asian economies scored highly in the report due to their economic dynamism. With reference to a country or company of your choice explain what this term involves and comment on the marketers contribution to its achievement. (10 marks)

(40 marks total)

Part B – Answer THREE Questions Only

Question 2
'The idea of business development implies both growth and change'.

(a) Prepare a brief report explaining the likely organisational changes that must occur if a small business is to develop and grow. (12 marks)

(b) Summarise current trends in the organisation of a large business and suggest the most appropriate structure for a marketing department operation of your own choosing.
(8 marks)
(20 marks total)

Question 3
A second rank Japanese vehicle manufacturer is actively considering your country as a marketing base for its products. As a research analyst you have been commissioned to provide the following:

(a) An outline of the key information sources the firm should monitor in order to assess the market and its participants. (8 marks)

(b) In an appropriate format, summarise your assessment of the market structure, including an evaluation of the threats and opportunities, currently facing existing vehicle distribution business. (12 marks)
(20 marks total)

Question 4
Produce a memorandum to your managing director citing:

(a) Three marketing related examples of the continuing legal trend conferring increasing rights for the consumer on the one hand and additional duties for the seller on the other.

(b) The practical implications of these trends for a business. (20 marks)

Question 5
Produce a series of slides for a Trade Association presentation, describing the current effects of **four** of the following macro-environment influences on the transport and distribution industry:

i) Social And Demographic Changes
ii) Environmental Pressures.
iii) New Technology.
iv) Market Forces.
v) Political And Legislative Trends.   (20 marks)

Question 6

It has been argued that changes in business values are one of the keys to future success for companies.

(a) Distinguish between Ethics, Values and Responsibilities.   (6 marks)

(b) What values are the key to future marketing success?   (6 marks)

(c) Critically discuss the concept of **either** ethical behaviour **or** social responsibility in respect to levels of top executive pay or an 'issue' of your own choosing.   (8 marks)
                                                                (20 marks total)

Question 7

(a) Precisely define the meaning of **three** of the following terms:

   i) Gross Domestic Product.
   ii) Current Account Balance Of Trade.
   iii) The J Curve Effect.
   iv) Non Traiff Barriers.   (6 marks)

(b) A balance of payments crisis in your country has made policy action inevitable. You have been delegated the task of preparing a two page submission to the responsible government minister on the case for and against expenditure switching, and expenditure reducing policies, making clear the impacts of each for domestic and international marketers.   (14 marks)
                                                                (20 marks total)

Specimen answers   December 1996

In what follows you will be provided with four sections:

1 A brief rationale of what the intention was in the mind of the senior examiner when the question was set.
2 An answer which would have earned the candidate a very good A/B grade pass.
3 Some further points that might have been introduced which would probably result in a distinction grade.
4 A summary from the senior examiner's report indicating the main areas of weakness in candidate scripts.

Answer – Question 1

Rationale

The intention of Question 1 was broadly to test the Candidate's grasp of an article which could have appeared in the quality press of any country where CIM have an examining Centre.

(1a) Offered considerable choice for candidates to demonstrate their understanding of various key terms used within the article. All these terms were related to different aspects of the syllabus and candidates should have been capable of providing a brief definition and example as directed in the question. The commentary aspect provided a degree of freedom to discuss effects, impacts or implications of the terms.

(1b) Focussed on a trend which is literally sweeping the world as countries strive to make their economies more competitive and productive. Candidates were expected to briefly explain the meaning of the policy and then assess potential implications from the viewpoint of consumers **or marketers**. These alternative perspectives should have provided sufficient scope to develop both short and longer-term repercussions of the policy.

(1c)   Appeared to be specific to Britain but the majority of the arguments relating to inward investment apply no matter what the country concerned. The short article format should have been familiar to candidates who have presumably read many such items in the course of their CIM studies. In an increasingly global economy the marketer should be keenly aware of the risk, revenue and resource factors that help determine international investment flows.

(1d)   Provided something of a counterbalance to 1c. given its concern with economic dynamism. This is often exemplified by the rapid growth of newly industrialising economies. The same concept can be equally applied to particular companies and even more mature economies who have sought to liberalise and revitalise their resources. The question clearly required an explanation of the term as well as commentary on the specific contribution made by marketers to its achievement.

Overall this made for a challenging compulsory question which drew from various parts of the syllabus. The case content provided a limited context and it was expected that candidates would draw on taught course material for the majority of their points.

1a.

i)   *A Weighted Index*
Definition
An index may be briefly defined as an effective numerical means of measuring the changing values of a set of related factors during the period between a given base year and the current time. The weighted aspect refers to the relative value or importance of the various items comprising the index. In this case there are 380 separate variables or criteria and each will be given a weight. Thus political stability might be thought to warrant double the weight of say social mobility.

Example
The retail (RPI) or wholesale price indexes are probably the best known examples of weighted index. The RPI tracks the price movements of over 600 items purchased by the 'average' family in Britain. Weights are then assigned to each item to reflect their relative importance in overall spending. Rent is weighted heavily compared to soft drinks but the latter are likely to have their weight revised upwards over time as tastes move in their favour.

Commentary
The index in the article is a very complex one. Its weakness is its potential subjectivity regarding the weights accorded to different 'growth' factors. There is no agreement on what are the precise determinants of competitiveness, let alone what their specific contribution to the outcome are. Similarly the criteria used in such an index are not price based, and therefore readily measurable, as in the RPI, nor are they volume or physically based. How is the degree of 'openness' or political 'stability' measured? Clearly per capita expenditures may be used but these say nothing about effectiveness.

A virtue of the IMD report is that it compares countries on the same relative criteria over time. Even if one disagrees with the weights, at least the direction of change is indicated.

ii)   *Economic Convergence*
Definition
This term concerns the progressive convergence or coming together of different economies at varying states of economic development. It implies that the countries con-

cerned are in the process of achieving a similar economic structure, commercial and legal framework which enables the development of common policies and objectives such as the free movement of goods, services, capital and labour.

Example

The European Union provides the best example of such convergence having been initiated to meet the challenges primarily from the Pacific rim. Having introduced the common external tariff and single European market the member countries are currently moving towards monetary union and a common currency, the Euro in 2002. Countries wishing to join the monetary union must comply with criteria laid down at Maastricht. These included requirements such that interest and exchange rates were close to the average and public borrowing at less than 3% of GDP. The union of East and West Germany provides another example of accelerated convergence.

Commentary

There are considerable attractions for business in a single currency and convergent economies. The market of 380m becomes a less differentiated one which promises greater economies and competitiveness. Considerable savings will be made by international businesses who no longer require to hedge their currency requirements. Monetary management, coordinated by a European Central bank, may bring greater stability over time. On the other hand national sovereignty is being lost to Brussels. With only limited control over fiscal policy remaining, a country may find itself confronted with long-term structural problems but no suitable adjustment mechanism. Adjustment of the exchange rate and interest rates will no longer be possible and national marketers may suffer the consequences of long-term recession. As countries prepare to meet the convergence criteria so unemployment rates have risen and popular support has waned. If, as the report suggests, there are considerable areas of diversity between the economies concerned then the outcome remains uncertain.

iii) *Social Costs*

Definition

These are the costs of an action by an individual or firm that are borne not by them (i.e. private costs) but by society as a whole. They are therefore often termed externalities since the impact falls on the environment beyond the business that caused them. The private costs of the lorry include fuel, capital wages and taxes, the social costs include those involved in remedying the effects of emissions, noise, dirt, congestion and damage. The costs are borne by the taxpayer, the individual, the government and environment which is polluted.

Example

The examples implied in the case would include:

- Rural shops or city centres displaced by more competitive out-of-town superstores.
- Redundancies/increased unemployment arising from downsizing.
- Increased stress, workloads, job insecurity.
- Loss of status, esteem, amenity etc. as a result of change.

Commentary

The government may internalise social costs by the use of taxation or regulation. These are applied on the principle that the polluter pays or must clean up the mess. Pressure groups have grown rapidly to lobby legislators for such changes and also to monitor corporate compliance. Businesses deplete society's resources so it could be argued that they have a duty or social responsibility to minimise such costs. Competitive pressure and the effects of deregulation may, however, tend to produce the opposite outcome as companies struggle to cut private costs and survive.

iv) *Innovative Technologies*

Definition

Technology is the apparatus or equipment used in production, or the process/methodology itself. Innovation is the translation of a radical new invention or developments into commercial use. The term is therefore applied to operational techniques but would also underpin the introduction of original products at the innovation stage of the product life-cycle. The technology will normally be state of the art and provide a cutting edge for the achievement of competitive advantage.

Example

Innovative technologies abound across all sectors due to the acceleration in the pace of technical change. They range from the power of the Pentium processor through the versatility of Microsoft Windows to the transforming impact of laser scanners, bar-codes and electronic point of sale systems. The latter provides the retailer, for example, with computerised stock control, re-order and cash flow management. Virtual reality offers the prospect of interactive armchair shopping and a further transformation in our leisure activities and life-style.

Commentary

Innovative technologies and their effective diffusion are critical to increasing the productive potential of the global economy. High cost and considerable lead times are involved in the process making larger firms, often operating within oligopolistic market structures, the main vehicle for such change. Continuous innovation is one means of earning long run profitability although the risks of being first mover must be borne in mind. An innovation is not one for long and a business must aim to be a 'moving target' by financing the underlying research and development from which the new technologies derive. Innovation is part of Schumpeter's creative destruction process and can generate new jobs as well as displace them as suggested by the article. They will certainly work to the interests of consumers by reducing costs and improving design as well as quality.

1b.

i) *Consumer*

Deregulation involves the removal or relaxation of restrictions on the production, distribution or sale of goods and services. It embraces privatisation, trade liberalisation and removal of red tape and entry barriers. For companies it brings greater freedom in the market-place as outdated or unnecessary rules are removed. An aggressive policy would be applied across the economy with deep cuts in the degree to which laws and regulations applied in strategic aspects of the economy.

The implications of such a policy are not clear cut and may for example be more positive in the short-term. The probable consequences would include:

- Wider range of choice of products and services.
- Tendency to price competition and possible price wars.
- A focus on improved customer service.
- Increased consumer power as companies are more accountable.

In the longer-term, however, the implications may change:

- Tendency to over capacity causes a shake-out and take-overs.
- Pressure to cut costs to compete may jeopardise standards.
- Product quality and safety may be prejudiced among less than scrupulous operators.
- The inefficient will be driven out of the market but price competition will decline – tend towards oligopoly.
- Innovation in new product developments yields benefits.

Rail deregulation is a case in point where service improvements, greater choice and price cuts have been enjoyed on high population density routes but reduced cross subsidisation has cut services and investment to rural areas.

ii) *Marketers In The Sector Concerned*

Deregulation involves the removal or relaxation of restrictions on the production, distribution or sale of goods and services. It embraces privatisation, trade liberalisation and removal of red tape and entry barriers. For companies it brings greater freedom in the market-place as outdated or unnecessary rules are removed. An aggressive policy would be applied across the economy with deep cuts in the degree to which laws and regulations applied in strategic aspects of the economy.

The potential implications for marketers are significant due to the changed competitive situation. Using Porters analysis, deregulation increases the threat of entry and from substitutes. The bargaining power of suppliers and distributors will also be increased in the new situation. Equilibrium will have been disturbed within the industry and the marketers must be prepared to deploy all their ingenuity to counter threats and exploit emerging opportunities. Implications include:

- Less time need be devoted to form filling.
- Competitor analysis is crucial – watch them carefully.
- Greater emphasis required on differentiation of the product offering in the context of increasing choice.
- Invest in product development to secure edge over rivals.
- Continuous innovation and improvement in value for money as the route to a competitive edge.
- Exploit new opportunities e.g. removal of regulations preventing advertisement of sanitary products.
- Beware unfair competition, predatory pricing.

Organisations must become much more entrepreneurial following aggressive deregulation. As strictly regulated sectors, such as the professions are deregulated, so they must refocus their activities towards a marketing orientation. Market research will be required to establish the real needs of consumers and a service tailored accordingly.

1c.

The Undoubted Attractions Of An Uncompetitive Britain
...Article Submitted To The Economist Magazine
...By C I Marketer, 6th December 1996

Britain ranks as the most attractive base for inward investment into the EU partly because of its disappointing overall economic performance. With 40 per cent of total EU direct investment and a string of recent high profile investments by the likes of BMW, LG, Nissan and Ford it must be doing something right and, more importantly, doing it better than its continental rivals.

Even a cursory glance at the list of Britain's comparative advantages, when it comes to investment attractiveness, quickly resolves the paradox:

- Dense population (58m) with high income per capita and a willingness to spend rather than to save.
- A compact economy with extensive infrastructure and efficient distribution systems.
- A member of the EU (380m) with regional status for Economic and Social funds and an opt out on the Social Chapter (up to May 1997).
- A government and local authorities who are very eager to welcome incoming companies and provide attractive incentive packages.
- Low barriers to entry and plenty of suppliers.
- A skilled, available and relatively cheap labour force.
- Trade Unions in decline and a high degree of stability.
- Relatively low corporate taxes and freely repatriated profits.
- Demonstration effect of other investors e.g. Nissan's productivity.

- English as the world's business and computer language.
- Liberalised economy and well located on trade routes.

If incoming firms can combine their leading edge technologies and managerial skills with the generous grants and relatively low wages, then they should have little difficulty in turning in a No. 1 performance in European if not global terms. The very weakness of the rest of the economy merely enhances their prospects of success. Only the recent rise in Sterling threatens this rosy prospect!

1d.

Dynamism suggests a rapid pace of development and change within an environment that creates few frictions. Economic dynamism equates with driving forces producing growth, technological adaption and rapid structural change in line with emerging market needs and wants.

Singapore and Hong Kong provide excellent examples of what the term involves. As so-called Asian tigers, they have driven their rapid growth and development by virtue of an interaction of complementary factors such as:

- Emphasis on education and training.
- A large skilled workforce and flexible work practices.
- A liberalised economic system based on free trade.
- A multi-cultural society encouraging entrepreneurship.
- An ability to learn from older developed economies.
- Entrepôt ports and strategic locations.
- Attractive to inward investment.
- High investment and R/D spend compensating for lack of natural resources.
- Influx of risk taking entrepreneurs with low tax regime.

British Telecom transformed from a sleepy nationalised industry into a dynamic privatised business in one of the most exciting sectors of technological change. As computers and digital telecommunications converged, so BT had to re-invent itself not least in the face of progressive deregulation and increased competition. Freed from the shackles of government control and able to make its own decisions on the volume and distribution of investment its management were able to release dynamic potential from its resources by reallocating them to more effective uses. It has dramatically diversified its product portfolio, forged partnerships, taken over MCI and established pre-eminent positions in video conferencing and multimedia applications.

Comment On Marketers Contribution

With marketers responsible for the identification and anticipation of consumer needs they are clearly instrumental in focusing the energies generated through economic dynamism. Market research deriving from a strong marketing orientation is essential to ensure the dynamic is effectively and profitably deployed. Since a competitive market is a condition for producing dynamism so the marketer must continuously apply competitor analysis to ensure an edge is achieved and maintained. The marketer must beware the risks of success and develop new products and services before the competition make existing stars decline. Some dynamic companies apply a policy of 65% of sales originating from products under 3 years old.

Whether it be new methods of distribution, improved products or innovative promotions, the marketer must be proactive and the opportunities seized if the dynamic is ever to realise its full potential.

Answer – Question 2

Rationale

This question combines aspects of all four sections of the Marketing Environment syllabus on Organisations. Part a. of the question is focussed on the subject of change in size with reference to the small firm in general and the implications for organisation in particular. Any candidate who had covered this important section of the syllabus should have had little difficulty with this question so long as they concentrated on relating their knowledge of organisational change to the growth stages of a small business. A lot of material could reasonably be introduced into this answer, hence the rubric requirement for a brief report.

Part b. shifted the focus to larger businesses, but with only 8 marks available only a short summary of current trends was required as stated in the first part of the question. The wording of the question suggested **general** rather than company specific trends and they needed to be recent to earn full marks. The second part of b. required an **appropriate** structure for a specific marketing operation. Any organisational form provided required at least brief justification perhaps linked to responding to the trends identified in the first part of the question.

Overall a challenging question but one that many candidates might reasonably expect to relate to.

2a.

Report

To: **Executive of the Small Business Club**
From: **CIM Consultancy Ltd.**

Business Development And Organisational Change Within Small Firms

1.1 Introduction

Small businesses, by virtue of their initial size, expand rapidly and quickly when they do grow. Development must therefore take place apace if they are not quickly to outgrow their strength and effectiveness. It has been suggested by Gremer that as a young firm grows larger it must weather a series of potential crises in its adaption to the changes involved. An outline of these may be seen in the chart below:

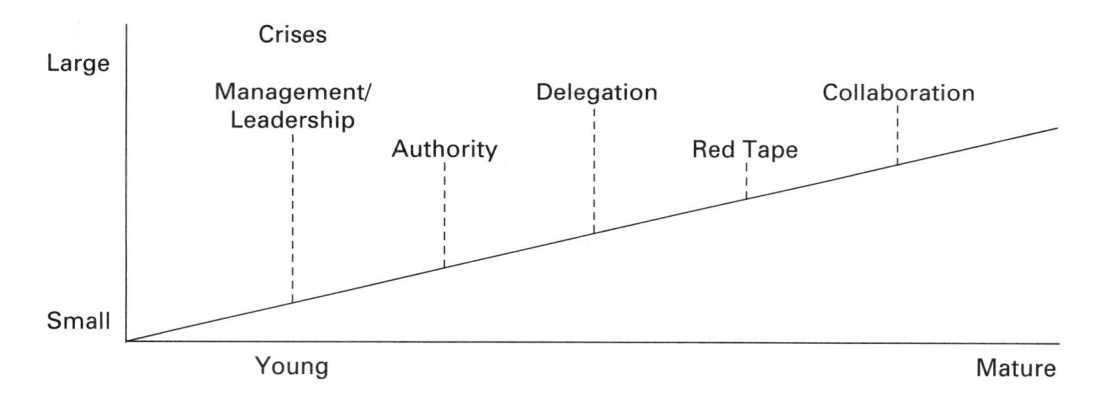

```
Large |         Crises
      |
      |    Management/        Delegation         Collaboration
      |    Leadership                                         ___
      |                Authority         Red Tape        ___--
      |                                            ___---
      |                                       ___--
      |                                  ___--
      |                             ___--
      |                        ___--
      |                   ___--
Small |              ___--
      |_____
         Young                                         Mature
```

Clearly the small business must be alert to the internal strains imposed by rapid growth while adapting to the changes occurring in the external environment.

2.1 Change In Legal Organisation

Growth and development requires resources. Sole traders and many partnerships with unlimited liability find it difficult to raise the necessary finance or justify the risks involved. A limited company will not only help resolve such problems but will provide a framework within which additional expertise can be hired and more rigorous financial controls introduced.

2.2 Formalisation

Company structure will change to accommodate development. Initially a spider's web structure would emphasise the central importance of the founder. As growth occurs and the limits of time and capacity are reached, the founder must delegate, securing the advantages of specialisation and division of labour. Operations and Finance directors may be appointed, followed quickly by a Sales director as the business pushes more aggressively for turnover growth. The founder will retain control of strategic direction but rely increasingly on the counsel of his/her management team. As a marketing orientation emerges so the functional structure might look as follows:

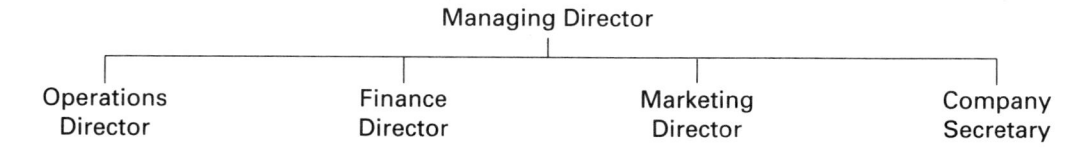

```
                        Managing Director
          ┌─────────────────┼─────────────────┬─────────────┐
     Operations          Finance          Marketing       Company
      Director          Director          Director       Secretary
```

2.3 Organisational Style

Other organisational changes to be considered include:

- Employment of an experienced management team.
- Increased emphasis on control systems e.g. cash management.
- Development and implementation of a business plan.
- A progressive shift from producer to consumer focus.
- Emphasis on innovation to sustain growth.
- Formalisation of training and the personnel function.
- Movement into larger and more appropriate premises.
- MD to develop outward looking role – networks/grants.

3.1 Conclusion

As the report makes clear, small firms must continuously evolve if they are to develop successfully to maturity. Their objectives, organisation, orientation and even culture must be adapted in the on-going process.

2b.

Current Trends Affecting The Organisation Of Large Businesses

- **Decentralisation** – pushing greater responsibility for decision-making closer to where they should be made. This may involve the creation of cost or profit centres so that parts of the organisation are clearly responsible for their performance.
- **Downsizing** – as competitive pressure increase and technology advances, many organisations are stripping out management personnel from the middle levels but not replacing them. Remaining staff are expected to take on the work of those who have to leave.
- **De-layering** – reduction in the number of levels in the hierarchy thereby reducing the time it takes for information to flow up and decisions to flow down.
- **Out sourcing** –part of the focus on core activities and strengths while contracting out peripheral tasks to third party specialists.

An Appropriate Marketing Department Structure For Virgin Atlantic

If an organisation such as Virgin is to achieve the following:

- A strong marketing orientation.
- Clear organisational focus on identifying/satisfying needs.
- Teamwork and collaboration for the sharing of views/expertise.
- Participative and responsive decision-making.
- Creativity and ideas generation.
- A flat and flexible structure with empowered employees, then a formal hierarchical approach is unlikely to be appropriate.

A flexible matrix structure might provide the basis for flexible task forces drawing on a mix of those responsible for effectively delivering the service involved. These teams would draw on functional expertise not only from within marketing but across the other operational areas. Teams might embrace areas such as marketing information; customer service; business development; promotion; relationship marketing and so forth. The drawbacks would be potential complexity and cost in management time and resource. Authority and loyalties might also be divided in the absence of effective team leaders.

Answer – Question 3

Rationale

Part a. was intended as a relatively straightforward question testing knowledge of relevant information sources to be consulted in a market and competitor analysis. Other than indicating what the source provided the question did not require a discussion of what to collect or why.

Part b. required the candidate to select an appropriate format. As a commissioned analyst this was likely to be a report format. There were two parts to the report. The assessment of the likely market structure depends on the country selected and the state of its market development. An oligopoly was the most likely form but the examiner would accept any, given appropriate justification. The evaluation of threats and opportunities clearly focussed on the external environment and an analysis of internal strengths or weaknesses would have been inappropriate.

3a.

Key Information Sources – Re Proposed Entry To British Market

Preamble

The UK vehicle market is at the maturity stage of the product life-cycle and is largely dominated in the mass segments by European, American and front rank Japanese multinationals. It is therefore critical that you identify a target market and position yourselves accordingly, assuming that the segment is not already approaching saturation. Key information to determine these matters is widespread in secondary source terms and a careful scrutiny of the following is respectfully recommended:

The Market

- New vehicle registration data (DVLC) for data on the size, composition and growth trends of the vehicle park.
- Trade association (SMMT) research reports will provide further analysis and development of such data e.g. regional patterns.
- Demographic data (Census) summarises age and gender structure as well as distribution of population and employment patterns. This will assist in the identification of possible segments.
- Government data in the form of Social trends and National income statistics to track trends in income per capita and how discretionary income is spent.
- The government also publishes information on tax rates applying to classes of vehicle and various fuels.
- Market research reports on the industry as produced by Mintel, EIU etc.

The Participants

- Company Directories such as Kompass will provide information of companies, products, locations etc.
- Company accounts and reports to assess strengths and weaknesses.
- Databases such as McCarthy summarising recent press coverage of different companies i.e. competitors, suppliers and distributors.
- Trade press and Consumer publications for new models, quality and customer service.
- SMMT for sales shares and trends.

Conclusion

Sources of information are legion in this industry and while data is required on both the macro and micro environment the danger of overload must be borne in mind. If however, you are considering developing a novel vehicle concept then you may consider commissioning primary research into customer tastes and preferences.

3b.

To: S. Sumitomo, Marketing Director, KOI MOTORS
From: CIM Research Analysis Ltd
Subject: Market Structure of the Vehicle Distribution Sector – A Study Of Threats And Opportunities
Date: 6th December 1996

Further to our recent meeting when you commissioned me to provide an analysis of the existing vehicle distribution businesses in Britain I would make the following points:

Market Structure
- The market is in effect an overlapping oligopoly with each area of population density having a number of relatively large and well resourced distributors, each normally representing a given marque such as Ford, Rover or Nissan.
- The market is mature although a number of multi-dealerships are springing up and one Japanese manufacturer, Daewoo, is selling vehicles without a formal distributor.
- Consumers are mature and distribution channels well defined. A high proportion of new sales are to companies.
- Interdependence is characteristic of the structure with emphasis placed on non-price competition.
- Distributors are faced with a kinked demand curve and know that rivals would follow suit with any serious price discounting.
- Occasional price wars can occur particularly in times of manufacturing over capacity and where new entrants disrupt the accepted patterns of competitive behaviour.
- Firms invest a lot of effort into building long-term relationships with customers in order to tie them to the marque.

You would therefore need to identify a market niche, although existing suppliers purposely seek to saturate the market space in order to deter entrants. Most quality distributors will already be tied in long-term relationships. You may have to consider a Daewoo like alternative if you are to achieve rapid penetration of the market.

Threats And Opportunities Facing Distributors
These may originate anywhere in the external environment. Social, legal, economic, political and technical change in the macro environment may be the source, or they may originate in the micro environment embracing customers and their changing tastes, suppliers, distributors, creditors or competitors.

Threats
- Political and economic uncertainty associated with an impending election may adversely affect buying decisions.
- Rising interest rates to head off inflation will impact significantly on short-term vehicle sales due to reliance on credit finance.
- Environmental concerns have caused Governments to raise fuel duties as well as progressively reduce company car allowances.
- Reduced spending on road programmes and limited private finance initiatives are contributing to congestion and deterring buyers.
- Rail privatisation may raise the quality of rail travel.
- Information technology such as internet/video conferencing is reducing the need for executive travel and encouraging car pools.

Opportunities
- The economy is growing in a sustainable way and vehicles continue to enjoy a positive income elasticity of demand.
- Electric cars are becoming more cost-effective and offer a solution to city centre pollution concerns.
- Lighter engines and fuel efficiency help to offset the impact of rising taxes.

- Information technology offers the means of maintaining a long-term relationship with customers.
- The Internet offers a low cost promotional medium.
- Rising vehicle reliability and no quibble assurances may tap into a vein of greater consumer willingness to buy direct.
- Computer integrated manufacturing allows the customer to customise their vehicle when ordering thereby reinforcing the move away from mass consumption patterns.

Answer – Question 4

Rationale

This question provides the candidate with a large degree of choice with respect to examples of the legal trend conferring additional rights for the consumer. The Examiner was prepared to adopt a broad definition of legal trends to include codes, regulations and the like. Including the practical implications, each example was worth just under a third of the total marks with the balance available for a memorandum format.

4a.

Memorandum

To: **C. I. Emms, Managing Director**
c.c.: **L. Eagles, Marketing Manager**
From: **U. P. Sales, Marketing Assistant**
Re: **Legal trends increasing consumer rights**
Date: **6th December 1996**

As early as 1962, President Kennedy formulated the key elements of Consumerism. These embraced four basic rights, to be enshrined in legislation, which would ensure the individual was not disadvantaged against the collective power of the organisation.

- **The right to be heard** – e.g. Trading standards, Which reports.
- **The right to safety** – e.g. Food Safety Act 1990, secure packaging.
- **The right to be informed** – e.g. ingredients, labelling.
- **The right to choose** – e.g. restrictive trade practices, books.

New legislation continues to be enacted placing extra duties on the seller. It is considered necessary because the knowledge and relative negotiating power of the two sides is still considered unequal. The increasing size and sophistication of business aided by more powerful information technology ensures this.

Example 1

Proposed European Union legislation will forbid the transmission of unsolicited facsimile communications. This would appear to breach the right to choose when unsolicited newsletters or promotional materials monopolise the equipment. Equivalent to junk mail for the private individual, the sender would have to obtain the permission of the recipient before material could be sent. Businesses currently using this medium will therefore have to either make contact and secure agreement or find alternatives.

Example 2

Food must now have metric weight or measures formally labelled. Loosely packaged foods are no longer exempt. The Food Safety Act formalises requirements for ingredients and sell by dates. However recent food scares over BSE and E-coli bacteria show the gaps in the public's right to be informed. Some retailers have gone further than the minimum legal requirement in voluntary labelling e.g. alcoholic content (CRS) and comparative unit values.

Example 3

Tickets purchased from a theatre ticket agency or coach company for any theatre or concert venue, such as the National Exhibition Centre, must now by law inform the customer of the location of the seat i.e. stalls, balcony etc. This again advances the customer's right to be specifically informed rather than fobbed off with vague generalities.

These and many other improvements in consumer rights are often the result of pressure from consumerists who lobby legislators and raise the public profile through media programmes such as 'Watchdog'. They target organisational practices which seek to deliberately misguide, misinform or put consumer safety at risk. Access for redress in the Small Claims Court has also been recently extended by raising the claim limit to £3000 for those without legal representation.

Practical Implications

As more and more consumer rights are legislated so an organisation such as ours must be aware of the implications:

- Compliance costs of meeting the legislation e.g. alter packaging and product instructions, install expensive safety equipment.
- A 7 day 'cooling' period for phoned orders, for example, would cause considerable problems for perishable good suppliers since backword produce could not be resold.
- Need to keep abreast of legal changes and bring to attention of relevant management and personnel.
- Costs involved in record keeping.
- Extra personnel will need to be recruited to administer policy.
- Increased costs put pressure on margins and may require price increases – consumers might turn to cheaper imports not necessarily subject to all the extra costs.
- Increased awareness of legal rights may cause a change in attitude amongst customers and a greater willingness to resort to law with all the expenses that involves.
- Opportunities are also present since strictly applied regulations will deter cowboy operators and raise the overall standards and reputation of the industry.
- Fairer trading favours the reputable firm.
- Costly safety standards are a barrier to entry.

New consumer rights may therefore have practical benefits as well as possible costs for the business.

Answer – Question 5

Rationale

This was intended as a test of candidate conciseness and focus within a very specific slide presentation context. The choice of specific examples within the broad macro-environment categories was left to the candidate but the key to high marks was to concentrate on current effects within a clear but content orientated slide format. The question related closely to 3.3.2 of the syllabus and the choice of transport and distribution was one that all had experience of.

Slide One

> Presentation
> To The
> Trade Association
> Of The
> Transport & Distribution Industry
>
> **MACRO-ENVIRONMENT INFLUENCES**

Slide Two

i)	*Social And Demographic Changes*	
	• Ageing population	– more older drivers on the roads.
		– pressure for safety regulations.
		– market for automatics/luxury travel.
	• Working women	– increased demand for town cars.
		– rise in two worker family expenditure e.g. package holiday demand.
	• Flexible working hours	– demand for improved scheduling of public transport.
		– staggered rush hours reduces congestion.
	• Move from cities	– increased traffic along motorway ribbons.
		– rise in commuter service demand.
	• Rise in leisure	– increased demand for overseas flights.
		– demand for leisure vehicle.

Slide Three

ii)	*Environmental Pressures*	
	• Increasing congestion	– rising costs and delivery times.
		– night-time services.
		– city centre pedestrianisation.
	• Rising concerns: noise	– local authority limit night flights.
		– resistance to airport expansion.
	• Rise in pressure group membership	– increased profile/public awareness.
		– loss of non-renewable resources.
	• Ozone/greenhouse gases emissions	– international pressure to limit.
		– media attention to climate changes.
	• Questioning of roads expansion	– traffic expands to fill the capacity.
		– demands for bus/bike lane.

Slide Four

iii)	*New Technology*	
	• Video surveillance	– curtails practical speeds due to automatic fines.
	• Lighter engine/bodies	– greater payloads and fuel efficiency.
	• Computerised mapping	– satellite locators for route planning.
		– minimise journey time by avoiding probs.
	• Information technology e.g. PC/internet	– home shopping requires home delivery.
		– home working reduces demands.
	• E-mail	– reduced demand for couriers.
	• Automatic tolls	– allows discriminatory road pricing.

Slide Five

iv)	*Market Forces*	
	• Rail privatisation	– increased competition for roads.
		– improved quality and service.
	• Free skies policy	– reduced prices/improved services.
	• Just in time	– pressure on suppliers is raising frequency of journeys.
		– pressure to locate closer to customers.
	• Merger activity	– rationalisation of bus services.
		– predatory pricing practices arising.
	• Government taxation	– altering the relative attractiveness of different fuels.
		– reluctance to apply to aviation fuel due to feared loss of airport business.

Slide Six

v)	*Political And Legislative Trends*	
	• Impending Election	– shift of emphasis to public transport.
		– greater stress on green issues.
	• Restrictions on deliveries to town centres	– scheduling problems.
		– unsocial hours payments required.
	• Opt out for Social Chapter	– flexibility in working rotas.
		– greater freedom of operation.
	• Opt out from EMU	– could reduce trade with EU.
		– multinationals may move operations.

Answer – Question 6

Rationale

This type of question had not been posed before but was intended to test the candidates broader perception of these terms and ability to relate their knowledge of ethics or social responsibility in practical terms. It related specifically to 3.1.2 but candidates might also usefully draw on elements from 3.2.5/6. No format was required in part c., but it was expected that both sides of the argument would be outlined in an objective manner. The onus was again on the candidate to select a context issue as an alternative to executive pay.

6a.

Ethics are moral principles which govern the behaviour of individuals and organisations and their decision choices. They reflect beliefs as to what is right and wrong and may become enshrined in a formalised code to guide the actions of organisational members. Professional bodies often have such codes and the CIM itself is currently formulating one for marketers.

Values are a reflection of our ethical position since they indicate the importance we attach to various behaviours and concerns. They are often deeply rooted and strongly held, springing as they do from upbringing, conditioning and formative experiences. They might include values such as punctuality and loyalty.

Responsibilities arise where an organisation or individual is held accountable for the maintenance of certain standards. The standards or objectives set will reflect their underlying values and/or ethical stance. These responsibilities may involve legal obligations e.g. in health and safety, or extend to a variety of stakeholders. As a corporate citizen the organisation may shoulder social responsibilities beyond the legal minimum.

6b.

Values that provide the key to future marketing success may differ according to the target market and customer needs concerned. However, in a world of increasing education and media intrusion perhaps a mix of traditional and future orientated values might be considered. These include:

- Cleanliness – where food/drink is involved.
- Honesty, integrity, trust and reliability in relationships.
- Openness – fully informing customers/other stakeholders.
- Fair play with competitors.
- Care of the environment and pursuit of sustainability.
- Value for money.
- Continuous improvement in product quality and design.
- Decency and moral values in advertising/promotion.

6c.

Concept Of Ethical Behaviour

Ethics are the standards of behaviour and conduct applied by managers in carrying out the business. Examples of business ethics would include:

- **Obey the law**
- **Tell the truth**
- **Respect for individuals**
- **Above all do no harm**

With respect to top executive pay, the issue appears to be one of equity i.e. is it fair that the pay of top executives is increasing relative to that of others in the organisation. Added to this is the point that any improvement in organisational profitability, which may be used to justify this relative increase, is arguably the product of all employee efforts. If so this appears to undermine the ethic of mutual respect.

There is no law which currently prevents such increases but one could suggest there is a question of natural justice involved. On the other hand there is the question of efficiency and responsibility. Directors have a duty to the company and also the shareholders. If they do not attract top managers with the necessary skills, knowledge and experience then profits will suffer. Top management provide key strategic direction and it is a scarce skill. Such people also work long hours and face considerable stress.

There still remains, however, a concern that a perfect market does not exist in which 'fair' executive salaries are set. If instead they are set behind closed doors with no clear accountability for subsequent performance then perhaps the full truth is not being told.

Concept Of Social Responsibility
Social responsibility is acceptance by business of obligations to protect the welfare of society as well as its own interests. It goes beyond the minimum requirement of law, to account a variety of stakeholder concerns. Action is voluntary and net cost is often involved.

If we take the case of an oil storage platform intended to operate in difficult weather conditions then a number of social responsibility issues arise:

- Health and safety of employees both in situ and transit must be best available: includes technology and management procedure.
- Maintenance standards should guarantee against any toxic leaks.
- No flaring of gas residues – i.e. capture and utilise.
- Design of the rig-life cycle orientated, allowing safe dismantling and maximum recycling when useful life ended.
- Construct rig in high unemployment shipyard area.
- Retraining scheme for redundant miners to become rig workers.
- Percentage contribution to wildlife conservancy projects.
- Openness to media and various publics.

As the case of Brent Spar recently showed, even a company with a good overall record on social responsibility can encounter costly pressure group resistance to its plans. The fact that these were agreed with the government was not sufficient and inspection of the rig prior to its intended sinking would have been advisable.

Answer – Question 7

Rationale

This question clearly focussed on the global environment of the syllabus. It sought to test the candidate's grasp of some key terms, three of which were mainstream concepts. The main part of the question called for attention and conciseness since there was a substantial question to address but only two pages were allowed.

A balance of payments crisis is a significant source of turbulence and the marketer should appreciate the implications of policies to deal with it, on their own operations.

7a.
i) **Gross Domestic Product** or GDP is the sum of market values of all final goods and services that are produced during one year in a country by domestically and foreign owned firms. It does not include net income from the activities of nationals abroad.

ii) **The Current Account Balance Of Trade** is that part of the overall balance of payments which records both visible trade in goods and invisible trade in services. It does not include capital or foreign exchange transactions and is the key indicator of the trading health of an economy.

iii) **The J Curve Effect** is the short-term reaction of the balance of payments to a depreciation or devaluation of the exchange rate. The resultant higher price of imports worsens the balance of payments initially before the positive effects of more competitively priced exports eventually improve it.

iv) **Non Tariff Barriers** are obstacles to imports other than tariffs and quotas. They include all types of standards and regulations to which imports must conform e.g. product safety. As such they add cost to imports and provide advantage to domestically produced good and services.

7b.

Submission To:	Overseas Trade Minister
From:	Marketing Impacts Advisor
Re:	The Case For/Against Expenditure Reducing/Switching Policies
Date:	6th December 1996

Introduction – the balance of payments crisis means fundamental action is required to correct the underlying disequilibrium. Either exports must rise or imports fall or a combination of the two.

Expenditure Switching Policies – these involve policies that cause domestic spending to switch away from imports to home produced goods. They also may cause foreigners to switch their spending from other consumption to our exports. Policies include export promotion, increased tariffs and quotas, stricter non tariff barriers and devaluation.

The Case For – electorally unpopular measures affecting the domestic economy may be avoided although resources need to be released to allow extra export production. If unemployment exists then they can be recruited into export industries to beneficial effect. Extra revenue is earned from tariffs, and subsidies for promotion will be popular with exporters.

The Case Against – most of these policies deal with the symptom rather than the cause of the disequilibrium. This is suppressed and may require progressive rises in say tariffs and therefore costs and prices. Trading partners will not readily agree to protectionist measures and will eventually retaliate neutralising any benefit. Membership of WTO will be prejudiced. Devaluation will be unpopular and may cause inflationary forces unless demand is checked.

Expenditure Reducing Policies – these involve reducing aggregate demand through higher taxes/reduced state spending. Reduced discretionary income will force households to spend less on all goods including imports.

The Case Against – such policies are unpopular with everyone and large cuts in income may be needed to secure the required fall in imports. A depressed economy will result with rising unemployment and falling living standards.

The Case For – this forces fundamental adjustments since the depressed economy slows the rate of inflation, forces businesses to cut costs and raise productivity as well as turn their attention to export markets. It is not as painful if trading partners are booming.

Impacts – Domestic Marketers – badly affected by expenditure reducing policy. Volumes fall and margins will come under pressure as competition intensifies. Consumers will reduce sharply their demand for high income elasticity products, such as cars. If expenditure switching is used then the position reverses since barriers to entry of foreign goods are raised facilitating the capture of higher market share and improved margins.

Impacts – International Markets – the export promotion initiatives will assist the international marketer as will the exchange rate devaluation. This will either improve profitability in domestic currency terms or allow scope for reducing prices in foreign currency terms so increasing volume sales. However, the retaliation likely to follow higher tariffs will not be helpful. As regards expenditure reduction, the impacts will be slower in coming. There will be pressure from the Board of Directors to increase export efforts and progressive cost reduction will improve relative competitiveness over time.

Conclusion – there is no gain without pain and a combination of exchange rate adjustment and indirect tax increases focussed particularly on high import content sectors is recommended.

Alternative compulsory practice question

As a final exercise in your examination preparation, attempt the following compulsory question from the Selling Environment examination for December 1996. You should time yourself strictly for this allowing no more than an hour and a quarter in total. After you have completed it return to the activity at the end of the examination guidance section (page 228) and check through the points listed with a fellow student or tutor.

PART A: Compulsory question

The retail distribution revolution

Retailers have grown into some of the world's largest companies, rivalling or exceeding manufacturers in terms of global stretch. Wal-Mart, a discount chain that has become the world's top retailer (see table below), has bigger sales than its competitors and many of its main suppliers, its turnover of $67 billion in the year to 31st January 1994 was the fourth largest of any American company. It is Procter & Gamble's largest single customer, buying as much as the household-products giant sells to the whole of Japan.

The retail elite				
The world's top retailers, by sales				
	Main type of trade	Home country	Sales 1993 $bn	Number of Stores 1993
Wal-Mart	Discount	United States	68.0	2,540
Metro Int.	Diversified	Germany	48.4	2,750
Kmart	Discount	United States	34.6	4,274
Sears, Roebuck	Department	United States	29.6	1,817
Tengelmann	Supermarket	Germany	29.5	6,796
Rewe Zentrale	Supermarket	Germany	27.2	8,497
Ito-Yokado	Diversified	Japan	26.0	12,462
Source: Management Horizons				

The distribution chain used to be controlled by manufacturers and wholesalers. The retailer's role was to buy goods from a range offered by the wholesale or other intermediaries, and sell them on to the consumer. The main competitive advantage lay in merchandizing – the skill in choosing the assortment of goods for sale in the store. There was a second potential advantage – closeness to the customer – but its only use, if any, was to beat rival retailers. For it was manufacturers who decided what goods were available, and in most countries at what price they could be sold to the public.

Information technology, mainly through the use of computer systems such as EPOS (electronic point-of-sale), EDI (electronic data interchange), smart cards and the internet, has enabled retailers to transform the way they do business.

Is it time that the distribution system be turned upside down? The traditional supply chain, powered by manufacturer 'push', is becoming a demand chain, driven by consumer 'pull'. Could the next big development be the rise of genuine consumer power? We all know that consumers are sovereign, but so far they have operated a peculiar kind of dominion. They've been able to exercise choice – enough to make or break a company's fortunes.

But that choice has been very limited and highly influenced by external forces. If retailer and consumer purchasing habits are shifting, new channels may have to be cut.

Source: *The Economist* – adaptation of a survey (March 1995)

(a) In relation to **two** of the following technological changes:
- EDI
- smart cards
- touchscreen technology
- home shopping

comment on their significance for:
   (i)   a retailer **(10 marks)**
   (ii) a consumer **or** manufacturer (as appropriate) **(10 marks)**

(b) Drawing on your understanding of the retailing environment, suggest reasons why the power is shifting from seller to buyer. **(10 marks)**

(c) What recommendations would you make to a traditional retailer to retain competitive advantage in the future? **(10 marks)**

(40 marks total)

(CIM Selling, Environment paper, December 1996)

Glossary of terms

This glossary includes all the key terms to be found in the syllabus and past examination papers to date. Further definitions are to be found within the body of the units and these should also be carefully studied. They are not included here since they form part of the workbook exercises.

Ageing is the increase in the average age of the population.
Appendix is a supplement containing explanatory or statistical information attached to the end of a report. To append means to attach an appendix covering some topic in more detail than in the report.
Article is a piece of non-fiction text written for inclusion into a journal, newspaper or similar.

Balance of payments is a record of all transactions between domestic residents and the rest of the world.
Barriers to entry are economic or technical factors or costs that make it difficult for new firms to enter a market.
Bibliography a list of references or writings related to a particular topic and referred to by the author.
Booklet is a format that involves a small and concise version of a larger text and may be presented in bound or leaflet form.
Brief is a concise and short statement of points pertinent to the topic in question.
Bullet points are a list of key concise factors relevant to the subject under discussion.
Business cycle is the regular fluctuations of economic activity and income through boom, downturn, recession and upturn.
Business values are the philosophical and ethical standards adhered to by personnel in the pursuit of the organization's purpose.

Caveat emptor let the buyer beware.
Caveat vendictor let the seller beware.
CD-Rom is a compact disc with read-only memory forming a cost effective and secure information storage device with multimedia capabilities.
Change is a process involving movement from one state to another and often requires resistance to be overcome. Different types of change arise, e.g. organizational, structural, technological.
Checklist is a succession of important or relevant points or tasks which when duly completed are noted with a tick or a mark.
Communication superhighway refers to the Internet or global information networks linking personal computer users worldwide.
Competitive activity involves the actions taken by businesses to improve their profitability at the expense of rivals.
Competitive behaviour is the conduct of businesses in market situations involving actions and reactions to achieve advantage over rivals.
Computer software is a term for the programs and application packages that make computer hardware useful by storing, sorting, manipulating and retrieving data.
Consumerists are those groups and organizations who exert legal, moral and economic pressure on business to account the interests of consumers over profit.
Contractual relationship is an agreement between two or more parties which the law will recognize and enforce.
Current account balance is that part of the overall balance which records both visible trade in goods and invisible trade in services.

Demand patterns are the trends and characteristics associated with consumer expenditure on the various goods and services currently marketed.

Demographic environment embraces the size, structure and characteristics of population.
Deregulation is the removal or relaxation of restrictions on the production, distribution or sale of goods and services.
Dominant firm is one that controls a relatively large share of the market and whose actions tend to be followed by smaller competitors.
Draft a preliminary plan or outline of a topic or report.
Duopoly is a market which is supplied by only two firms.

Economic convergence is a process involving a number of different economies at different stages of development aiming to come together into a union with common legislation, monetary base and policies, e.g. European Monetary Union.
Economic dynamism is associated with high energy driving forces producing rapid growth and development and operating in an environment with few frictions.
Economic environment encompasses the conditions which determine aggregates such as national income, output, employment and price levels.
Economic forecast is a prediction of future economic conditions.
Ethics are a set of moral principles which govern the behaviour of the individual or organization.
Environmental change involves alteration to the nature and significance of factors in the organization's environment. The impetus may arise from a variety of sources, e.g. changing attitudes, tastes, technologies, laws or economic circumstance.
Environmental networks are contacts formed and maintained with various individuals, groups and organizations concerned with the environment.
Environmental set is a ranking of the key environmental factors currently impacting on the organization and specific to it.
Environmentalists are individuals, groups and organizations who seek to apply political, economic and moral pressure on business to adopt sustainable operations.
Expenditure reducing policies involve increases in taxation and reduced government spending programmes to bring about a general reduction in imports.
Expenditure switching policies involve actions to improve the attractiveness of domestically produced products at the expense of imports.

Fair trading is the supply of a good or service without restriction of competition or choice and in accordance with prevailing legislation.
Feel bad factor is a term used for describing depressed consumer and business confidence which results in flat or falling spending on products and investment goods.
Feel good factor is a term for describing buoyant consumer and business confidence.
Five forces *see* Structural analysis.
Forecasting approaches include quantitative and qualitative estimates of the future.

Global environment embraces world markets and developments including changes in the distribution of economic activity and spending power.
Goals provide the broad direction to organizational activities and are the driving force behind its strategies and actions, e.g. to achieve No. 1 market position.
Green environment is a term colloquially used to designate the natural environment and implicitly its protection.
Gross domestic product (GDP) is the sum of the market values of all final goods and services that are produced during a year in a country by domestically and foreign owned firms.

Industry structure is the organizational and competitive characteristics of an industry including the number and size distribution of buyers and sellers, the nature of the product and the size of any barriers to entry.
Information needs refer to areas of knowledge required in order to make an informed and effective decision.
Information sources refer to the locations or holders of the knowledge required for a particular purpose. They may be secondary (published) or primary (research) sources.
Information technology is the science applied to the generation, processing and dissemination of data.
Innovative technologies are radically new methodologies, processes or machines which are developed into commercial use.

Interactive television shopping provides the marketer with a two-way cable or computer link with the customer, allowing purchases to be made in the convenience of the home.

Intermediaries include any organization in the supply chain between the business and its final customers.

Internal markets are established by government within public sector organizations to encourage efficient and effective resource management in the absence of external competition.

International institutions are organizations designed to maintain global trade and payments stability and encourage the development of Third World countries, e.g. IMF, IBRD.

International markets include any target customers located outside domestic or trade bloc frontiers. Domestic sellers will seek exchange transactions with these potential buyers.

International trade is the exchange of goods and services between countries and arises out of comparative cost advantages.

Inward investment is direct investment by overseas organizations in premises, plant and equipment in the domestic economy.

J curve is the tendency for the balance of payments to deteriorate immediately after a currency depreciation due to more expensive imports before starting to progressively improve.

Keynote address is one that sets the tone and focuses on the key issues.

Labour markets are where wages, salaries and conditions of work are established by the forces of supply and demand for labour.

Large business normally a company employing over 200 employees and having a significant share of the market.

Legal status is the standing of an organization in the eyes of the law, e.g. a sole trader is unincorporated.

Legislation is the enactment of new laws.

Macro environment includes those forces which impact on the business, creating opportunities and threats, but over which it has no real control or influence.

Managing director is appoined chief executive by the board and is responsible for the day-to-day running of the business.

Market forces refer to supply and demand and embrace all conditions and influences upon price and quantity.

Market power is the ability of the firm to control its competitive environment.

Market size is the total value or volume of turnover/sales for a product.

Market structure classifies the competitive characteristics of a market in terms of the number of firms, the nature of the product and barriers to entry.

Marketing environment embraces not only competitors, customers and supply chain participants over whom the business can exert some influence but also the wider SLEPT factors.

Marketing orientation places servicing of the customers' needs and wants at the centre of the whole organization's attention and activities.

Memorandum is a means of recording and retaining information which is worthy of note. The heading cites the intended recipient, sender, others who have received copies, what it refers to and the date.

Micro environment includes the groups and organizations that have a two-way operational relationship with the business and which are controlled and influenced by it to some degree (see Stakeholders).

MMC is the Monopolies and Mergers Commission set up in 1948 to investigate monopolies and report to the Secretary of State.

Multimedia technology integrates text, sound, animation, music and moving images with a computer providing the user with a variety of communication possibilities for business applications.

Multinationals are enterprises engaged in simultaneous manufacture/operations in a number of countries and which take decisions from a global perspective.

Natural environment embraces natural resources including land, vegetation, wildlife, air and water and the amenity which they confer.
NIC's are newly industrializing countries such as China.
Non-tariff barriers are standards and regulations to which imports must conform.
Note form involves setting out information in brief points, comments or explanations.

Objectives are specific ends or achievements to be realized at a future time to fulfil the goals of the business, e.g. to increase sales by 10 per cent over the next 12 months.
OECD is the Organization for Economic Cooperation and Development and includes as members the affluent industrialized economies.
OFT is the Office of Fair Trading established by the Fair Trading Act to monitor and investigate trading practices and refer any monopoly situations to the Monopolies and Mergers Commission.
Oligopoly is an industry with a small number of relatively large sellers, who have some control over price but recognize that competitor actions will affect profits.
On-line means that a computer is linked to a wider area network and can interact with the real time or updated system.
Opportunities are changes in the external environment which provide the organization with the ability to achieve its goals.
Organization describes the relationships which arise when two or more individuals agree to coordinate their activities to achieve common goals. It is the vehicle for achieving stated goals.
Organization structure represents the distribution of tasks, power and authority within the business and the relationships involved.

Partnership marketing involves close collaboration and mutually advantageous relationships with linked distributors in the supply chain.
Partnership sourcing is the use of a supplier with whom the organization has a long-term relationship including new product development and efficiency improvements.
Political environment embraces the activities of the state in setting national objectives, legislating, policy making and implementation.
Pressure groups are composed of people with common interests or attitudes who seek to influence relevant decision makers to act on their concerns.
Pacific rim includes the countries around the shores of the Pacific ocean including Japan and the western seaboard of the United States and Canada.
Primary/connected stakeholders include customers, employees, suppliers and creditors (see Stakeholders).
Price war is a systematic reduction in the price of a good or service by two or more competing firms, often occurring after the breakdown of an agreement.
Private sector is the part of the economy in which productive activity is carried out by privately owned/run enterprises and includes the household and personal sector as well as businesses.
Product liability refers to the legal obligation on companies to avoid acts or omissions that could have reasonably been expected to cause harm to consumers.
Profitability is the rate of return on capital or the excess of revenue over total cost of production.
Public relations includes all forms of planned communications between an organization and its publics with the aim of establishing mutual understanding.
Public sector includes the activities of central government departments, local authorities, public corporations and nationalized industries.
Publics are the main external constituencies with an interest in the activities and impacts of the organization (see Stakeholders).

Recession is a stage of the business cycle where GDP has fallen for two consecutive quarters.
Red tape is the unnecessarily complex and time-consuming rules and procedures laid down by bureaucracies.
Regulation is the supervision and control by government of the activities of private and public businesses in the interests of societal efficiency and fairness. A regulation is a rule set out to govern the behaviour of those it applies to.

Relationship marketing is the process of getting closer to the customer by developing a long-term relationship through careful attention to service needs and their quality delivery.
Report is a formal business communication presenting a summarized record of investigations into some topic. It will utilize headings to lay out material.
Responsibilities arise out of a duty or an obligation placed on an individual who holds a position of authority and trust or an organization accountable to various stakeholders.
Résumé is a summary of a longer piece of text, e.g. a report.
Restrictive trade practices are agreements between two or more firms designed to control prices, quantities or qualities of products supplied or on the intermediaries used.

Scenarios are alternative views of the future.
Secondary stakeholders include local community, pressure groups, media, analysts, government agencies, other firms, etc. (see Stakeholders).
Size is a concept which relates to the relative scale of turnover of a business. Concentration ratios measure relative size by calculating the number of firms accounting a given proportion of sales.
SLEPT factors include the social, legal, economic, political and technical environments which may impact on the business in the form of threats and opportunities.
Slides are prepared acetates or photographic material used on overhead projectors. They may also be generated directly from computers.
Small businesses are independently owned and operated with only a limited slice of total sales.
Social costs are imposed on the rest of society and equal the difference between the total cost to society of an activity and the private costs of production.
Social-cultural environment embraces changes in the nature, attitudes, behaviour and values of society which affect employment and buying patterns.
Social responsibility is the acceptance by an organization of obligations to protect and improve the welfare of society as well as its own interests.
Stakeholders are any group or individual, other than shareholders, who can affect or are affected by the achievement of organizational goals. Primary stakeholders make a direct and often continuous contribution to core activities of the business. The impact on or by secondary stakeholders is more intermittent and normally of less significance.
Standards are established by government agencies or the firm itself and normally set a weight, design, quality or process specification to which all production must conform.
Statute is a law passed through Parliament by a government as a means of implementing its policy programme.
Structural analysis refers to M. Porter's five forces of industry rivalry, the threat of new entry and substitutes and the bargaining power of suppliers and customers. These combine to determine the long-run profitability of an industry.
Submission means putting forward proposals for consideration by higher authority.
Suppliers are those who provide resource inputs to specification at an agreed price.
Sustainable growth is that which meets the needs of the present generation without compromising the needs and requirements of future generations.
SWOT strengths, weaknesses, opportunities and threats.

Taxation includes payments to the government from the private sector and constitutes the primary source of revenue to finance state expenditure. Levies are made on income, property and expenditures.
Technological environment embraces changes to products, processes and methods of business which impact on the organization.
Threats are changes in the environment whose impact may prevent the achievement of a firm's objectives.
Trade blocs involve groups or countries who coordinate their trading activities. Internal tariffs are removed but external tariffs with the rest of the world may (customs union) or may not (free trade area) be controlled.
Trade descriptions is legislation requiring that products perform to the specification stated or implied, i.e. they are fit for their purpose.
Trends are general tendencies to move or extend in a specific direction.

Values reflect the worth, significance or importance we attach to human actions and behaviour.

Virtual reality recreates a desired environment using a computer and headset allowing sensual experience of simulated situations, e.g. of a retail display or motor vehicle handling capabilities.

Voluntary codes are freely adopted guidelines to encourage desirable modes of behaviour.

Voluntary sector is made up of not-for-profit organizations which promote good causes by raising funds through donations.

Weighted index is a numerical means of measuring a price or volume series by allocating weights or values to the items comprising it and comparing current changes to a base year value equal to 100, e.g. Retail Price Index.

Index

Accelerator, *see* Multiplier–accelerator mechanism
Advertising Standards Authority, 84, 87
Ageing, 104, 154–5, 158–9, 174, 230, 248
Agency, 94, 97
Asian economies, 102, 108, 114, 116, 120, 123, 132–4, 137, 143, 147, 155–8, 161, 163, 166, 174, 179, 184, 193, 197, 200–8, 210, 215–16, 221–2, 234

Balance of trade/payments, 106–8, 136, 143–52, 184, 199–202, 205, 209, 236, 250–1
Board of directors, 3, 27, 30, 72, 106–8, 164, 252
British Board of Film Classification, 84
Broadcasting Standards Council, 84
Business confidence, 109, 134–9, 146, 148,
 cycle, 77–9, 103, 105–8, 111, 116–18, 127–8, 133–6, 139, 144, 149–52, 180, 195, 215–16
 organization, 3, 12, 17, 173, 181

Cartels, 43–4, 49–50, 58, 89, 94
Caveat emptor/vendictor, 67, 81, 83, 204
CBI, 66, 123, 135, 144
CD-ROM, 5, 113–14, 153, 197–8, 212
Champion/change agent, 34, 183, 190, 196–7
Circular flow, 126–31, 145, 149
Code of conduct, 9, 29, 31, 69, 74, 83, 87, 90–7, 122, 222, 246
Competitive activity, 49, 108, 229
 advantage/edge, 15, 22, 25, 30, 51, 57, 62–4, 68, 71–5, 77, 114, 125, 149, 179, 184, 193–5, 200–2, 213, 218, 220, 230, 240, 252–3
 environment, 14, 41–6, 48, 51, 99, 111, 133, 163
 process/pressure, 25, 41, 181, 193, 196, 212
Competitors, 14, 28, 64, 102, 107, 110, 115, 212, 240, 244
Consumer protection/association, 66, 69, 76, 81–92, 94, 95–8, 214
Consumerists, 60–1, 67–8, 76, 229, 247
Cooperatives, 3, 6, 10, 22
Corporate planning/strategy, 27, 100, 110, 123
Creditors, 28–30, 62
Culture, 17, 37, 52, 104, 153, 157–9, 166–75, 180, 195–6, 200–1, 206, 211, 216, 218, 223
Customer orientation, 27–9, 71, 75–6
 requirements, 2, 14, 27, 69, 163
Customs, 16, 82, 166–7, 187

Deflationary/inflationary gap, 129–30, 137
Delphi technique, 105, 141, 175, 186, 188
Demographic environment, 2, 17, 102, 107–9, 153–66, 170–5, 236, 244, 248
Deregulation, 13–16, 83, 102, 147, 212, 235, 239–41
Distributor, 13, 14, 28–9, 41, 47, 51–7, 93, 111, 115, 188–93, 245

Economic environment, 85, 101–2, 110, 123–4, 126–49, 206, 218, 229
 growth/performance, 125, 131–4, 136–42, 146–51, 174, 180, 192–4, 196, 202, 212, 222
 indicators, 16, 102, 111, 125–6, 143–4, 147
 policies, 16, 127, 143–5, 149–51, 208–9, 221–2, 236
Economies of scale, 32, 45–7, 201–4
EDI/EPOS/EFTPOS, 55, 184, 188–9, 252
Elasticity of demand, 54, 55–8, 219–20

Elections/electoral cycle, 11–13, 102–3, 107–8, 116–17, 134–7, 140, 147–50, 214, 222, 249
Entrepreneur/enterprise, 8, 116, 147, 157, 172, 181, 212, 241
Entry barriers, 42–7, 53, 84–5, 97, 240
Environmental change, 31, 34, 37–8, 52, 104, 107–12, 153, 191
 data/forecasting, 100–7, 111–14, 123–4, 135, 155, 175
 monitoring, 36, 57, 100–2, 171, 176
 set, 61, 100, 102, 107–9, 124, 149, 168, 229
Environmentalists, 28–9, 60–2, 69, 71–3, 77, 86, 191, 229, 236–40
Ethics, 21, 29–31, 61, 65, 68, 72–6, 87, 236, 249
European Union, 64, 82, 96, 102, 107–8, 119, 121, 140, 148, 158, 174, 190, 207, 211, 213–14, 222, 234, 240, 246, 249
Examination guidance, 145, 166, 224–53
Exchange rates, 107–8, 126, 130, 144, 213, 218–23, 252

Fair trading, 69, 89–95, 99
Financial analysts, 28–9, 62, 179
Fiscal policy, 127, 144–6
Five force analysis, 51–2
Forecasting, *see* Environmental forecasts
Franchiser, 3, 6, 10, 196, 213
Functional structure, 35–7, 76, 86, 91, 109, 183

GATT, 70, 102, 107–8, 201–3, 209–11, 215, 217–18, 221, 230
Global economy/environment, 12, 16–17, 99, 110, 115, 154, 173, 179, 183, 188, 193, 199–223, 229, 250–1
Government policies, 31, 49–50, 106–12, 115, 119, 121, 129, 138–41, 194, 216
Grapevine/networks, 112–13
Green environment, 3, 78, 103, 108–9, 132, 137, 173, 189
 marketing, 69, 73, 92, 117
Gross domestic product/GDP, 3, 5–6, 102, 111, 131–5, 137, 145–51, 185–6, 213, 215, 236, 250
Growth, *see* Organizational size/growth

IMF, 132, 208–9, 215, 217, 221
Independent Television Commission, 84, 91
Inflation, 102, 118, 131, 136, 139–50, 210, 213
Informal/hidden economy, 6–8, 17, 89, 133
Information systems, *see* MIS
Innovation, 17, 25, 28, 34, 44, 48–51, 95, 138, 177–81, 201, 213–14, 235, 238–9, 241, 243
Interest rates, 107–8, 124, 126, 134, 139, 144–5, 149, 245
Internal marketing, 13, 27, 73, 75–6, 157
International institutions, 16, 21, 131, 199, 207–8, 214, 220
 marketer, 167, 195, 212
 trade, 143, 199–223, 229

Japan/Japanese business, 23, 25, 132–4, 141, 145, 152, 154, 163, 166, 179, 184, 191, 201, 204–7, 216, 218, 222, 234–5
JIT, 55, 187–8, 213

Legal environment, 15–16, 47, 68, 80–98, 229
Legislation/legislative process, 3, 29–30, 61, 64–72, 102, 116–21, 138, 172, 187, 189, 196, 204, 214, 222, 236, 246–7
Life style, 17, 102, 149, 158, 167–75, 178, 193, 214

Lobbying, 29, 66–7, 69, 86, 117–21, 122–3, 222
Local authorities/economy, 11, 28–9, 81, 90, 108–9, 116, 122, 188, 240
Local community, 13, 28–9, 62, 65, 74, 129, 167

Macro-economic environment, *see* Economic environment
Macro-environment, 15–17, 85, 101–3, 116, 124, 137, 151, 178, 229, 235, 244–5, 247–9
Market forces, 11, 94, 133
 niche, 37, 46, 51, 111, 115, 161, 170, 183, 201, 213–14
 power, 26, 33–4, 51, 57, 60
 research, 35, 65, 113, 115, 171, 187, 207, 214, 221–2, 244
 segmentation, 65, 132, 153–62, 166–72, 194, 223, 244
 share, 25, 49, 70, 111, 134, 179, 195, 251
 structure, 41–51, 52, 57, 179, 245
Marketing department, 19, 22, 33, 35, 235
 environment, 2, 18, 43, 63, 71, 80, 100–2, 120, 132, 198, 206, 223
 mix, 15, 23, 25, 45–6, 56–7, 70, 74, 93, 115, 123, 141–2, 153, 170, 172, 184, 189–90, 194, 199, 206, 219–23
 orientation, 11, 14–15, 23, 36–8, 67–9, 121, 179, 240, 242
 role, 36, 60, 73
 strategies, 25, 41–4, 57, 100–2, 109, 115, 143, 159, 196, 201, 225
Media, 28–9, 62, 66, 69, 83, 112–14, 121–2, 173, 250
Micro-environment, 13–14, 17–18, 41, 51, 54, 80, 101, 180, 190, 229, 244
MIS/management information systems, 39, 54, 109–15, 140, 177–8, 195–6, 199, 214–15, 223, 229
Mission statement, 21, 38, 75
Monopolies and mergers, 5, 33, 44, 46–52, 57, 66, 82, 86, 90, 94–8, 148, 176, 194
Monopoly policy, 126, 145, 206
Monopoly power, 42, 44–5, 86
Multinationals, 3, 6, 14, 34, 57, 61, 67, 117, 139, 183–4, 199–200, 215–16, 222, 229
Multiplier–accelerator mechanism, 130–1, 134–5, 145–9, 151, 181, 222

Natural environment, 71–2, 99–100, 136, 172, 176–7, 186, 192–6, 229
Non-tariff barrier, 75, 206, 209–12, 218, 236, 251

Objectives, 10, 13, 20–31, 136, 143, 148, 229, 238, 242
OECD, 132, 174, 195, 207–8, 215
Organization charts/structures, 35–7, 229–31
Organizational size/growth, 20, 22, 24, 26, 31–2, 41, 46, 72, 81, 89, 95, 100, 174, 235, 242–3
 slack, 26–7, 45, 83

Partnership, 3, 6, 8–9, 14, 54–5
PEST, 15–16, 100–3, 107, 112, 155, 157
Plc/public limited company, 6, 9–11, 23, 107
Political environment/framework, 13, 16–17, 66–7, 81, 100–2, 116–22, 135, 202, 236
Population, 17, 78, 108, 111, 117, 131, 139, 153–60, 166, 172–5, 178, 192–3, 239–40
Pressure groups, 60–1, 65–7, 71–83, 93, 117–20, 159, 166, 190, 222, 250

Private sector, 4, 6, 22
Privatization, 4, 5, 103, 109, 116–17, 122, 147, 240, 245, 248
Product life cycle, 43, 57, 104, 174, 182, 187, 202
  differentiation, 43–6, 50, 52, 54, 57, 117
Production orientation, 2, 15–16, 101
Profit maximization, 23–5, 36–8, 44, 46–7, 53, 195
Protectionism, 199, 204, 212, 221
Public opinion/relations, 67, 75–6, 121, 166
Public sector organization, 4, 11, 16, 21, 27, 36, 61, 75, 109, 117–24, 162, 223, 233–5
  relations, 75, 120
Publics, 60–7, 72–5, 229, 250

Quangos, 3, 5, 66, 84, 122

Recession, 108, 111, 129, 133–5, 139, 143, 145, 148, 156, 162–4, 173, 180, 213, 222
Regulation/regulatory environment, 16, 80–98, 105–16, 146, 190, 195, 198, 203, 210, 226, 229, 240–4, 246
Relationship marketing, 41, 54–60, 73, 76, 229, 245
Resistance to change, 190–2, 195–6, 197, 215
Restrictive practices, 45, 86, 89, 94–5, 99

Sale of goods, 86, 91, 98
Sales orientation, 15, 36–7, 181–2
Satisficing, 15, 38
Scenarios, 42, 100, 106–7, 122–5, 175, 185, 229
SEM/Single European Market, 16, 96, 102, 107–8, 212–13, 218

Shareholders, 9, 13–15, 23, 25–6, 30, 38, 65, 69, 74, 99, 145
SLEPT, 15, 217–18, 225, 231
Small businesses, 31–4, 38, 48–51, 61–2, 72, 83–9, 113, 121, 151, 179, 195, 202, 215, 242
Social environment, 13, 86, 92, 100–1, 110, 124, 133, 153, 166–73, 196, 229
  responsibility, 20–1, 30–1, 33, 37, 60, 63, 71–5, 92, 229, 236, 250
Sole trader, 3, 7–8, 23, 31, 57, 85, 89
Sources of data/information, 54, 100–1, 109–15, 121–3, 131, 186, 195, 206, 215, 221, 223
Stakeholders, 12–14, 18–20, 26–31, 38, 54, 57, 61–7, 72–6, 81, 83–6, 97, 101, 105, 111, 116, 122–4, 142, 148, 166, 180, 188, 190, 229, 249
Standard of living, 125, 130–2, 153, 191, 201
Standards, 16, 70–2, 81–6, 93, 107, 116, 121, 136, 196, 203–6, 214, 224, 242
Strengths and weaknesses, 1, 4, 20, 28, 35, 115, 144, 152, 222–3, 233, 244
Structural analysis, 41, 51–7, 229
Substitutes, 41, 44, 110
Suppliers, 13–14, 28–9, 34, 44, 47, 51–7, 62, 90–4, 104, 111, 188, 222, 229, 240, 245
Supply/demand, 43, 51, 122, 138–40, 143, 172, 218
  chain, 54–5, 57, 195
  side policies, 127, 144–8, 151, 213
Sustainability, 31, 73, 139, 148–9, 172, 185–97
SWOT, 107, 144, 152, 217, 222, 224–5

Tariffs/quotas, 85, 148, 203, 205–212, 251–2
Technical:
  change, 34, 46, 111, 138, 187, 196–7, 214
  diffusion, 101, 176–9, 182–3, 195–6, 201, 214–15
  environment, 13, 17, 33, 96, 99–101, 176, 229
  forecasting, 176, 184–6, 189
  transfer, 150, 184–5, 189
Technology, 7, 34, 47–8, 85, 101–3, 110–13, 137, 139–42, 158, 176–200, 236, 241, 245–6, 248
Teleworking, 103, 163, 185, 188–9, 195
Threats and opportunities, 13–15, 18, 28, 34, 39, 61, 70, 73, 100–2, 107–9, 144, 158, 179, 181, 199, 229, 234–5, 240, 245
Trade associations, 29, 54, 62, 64–6, 97, 115, 119, 123–4, 185, 190, 220–1, 235, 244
  barriers, 203–4, 209
  blocs, 199–20, 207, 211, 221–2, 229
  unions, 15, 27, 66, 104, 107, 110, 138–40, 144–8, 190, 240

Unemployment, 102, 108, 118, 130–7, 134–5, 138–47, 151, 155, 164, 168, 172–3, 280–91, 202, 222, 251

Voluntary organizations, 6

Women's role, 7, 61, 63, 86, 97, 102, 132, 138, 153, 159–60, 162–7
World Trade Organization (WTO), 70, 122, 195, 203, 205, 209–12, 217, 251

your chance to bite back

Sales and Marketing Environment 1997–98

Dear Student

Both Butterworth-Heinemann and the CIM would like to hear your comments on this workbook.

If you have some suggestions please fill out the form below and send it to us at:

> College and Open Learning Division
> Butterworth-Heinemann
> FREEPOST
> Oxford OX2 8BR

Name: _____

College/course attended: _____

If you are not attending a college, please state how you are undertaking your study:

_____
_____
_____

How did you hear about the CIM/Butterworth-Heinemann workbook series?
    Word of mouth ❑
    Through my tutor ❑
    CIM mailshot ❑

Advert in _____

Other _____

What do you like about this workbook (e.g. layout, subjects covered, depth of analysis):

_____
_____

What do you dislike about this workbook (e.g. layout, subjects covered, depth of analysis):

_____
_____

Are there any errors that we have missed (please state page number):

_____
_____

NEW EDITIONS OF THE CIM WORKBOOKS FOR 1997/98

The CIM Workbook Series is better than ever, order your copies now!

Using information and feedback gathered from lecturers and students the third editions of the acclaimed CIM Workbook Series have been updated and expanded where necessary. In addition, a revision section at the back of each workbook contains the most recent exam papers, specimen answers written by the senior examiners and a full glossary of key terms.

The CIM Workbook series provide the ideal companion material for CIM courses as well as revision guides for students nearing exam time.

Each workbook:
- is endorsed by The Chartered Institute of Marketing
- is approved by CIM Chief Examiner, Professor Trevor Watkins
- is written by the CIM Senior Examiners and experienced CIM Lecturers
- is written to help students pass their exams first time
- is in A4 paperback format
- is designed for interactive learning

Student quotes about Butterworth-Heinemann Workbooks:
'Readable, practical, useful for revision, relevant and up to date, on the whole well worth buying'
'Overall the layout of the book is very good – one of the best I have ever worked with'
'A user friendly publication'
'Best texts available at present and are well worth buying. I would definitely recommend them to anyone'

ALL WORKBOOKS WILL BE AVAILABLE IN JULY 1997

CERTIFICATE
All priced £15.99

Business Communications 1997–98
Shashi Misiura
0 7506 3576 2

Marketing Fundamentals 1997–98
Geoff Lancaster
Frank Withey
0 7506 3577 0

Sales and Marketing Environment 1997–98
Mike Oldroyd
0 7506 3574 6

Understanding Customers 1997–98
Rosemary Phipps
Craig Simmons
0 7506 3575 4

ADVANCED CERTIFICATE
All priced £16.99

Effective Management for Marketing 1997–98
Angela Hatton
Mike Worsam
0 7506 3579 7

Management Information for Marketing and Sales 1997–98
Tony Hines
0 7506 3578 9

Marketing Operations 1997–98
Mike Worsam
0 7506 3584 3

Promotional Practice 1997–98
Cathy Ace
0 7506 3580 0

DIPLOMA
All priced £17.99

International Marketing Strategy 1997–98
Paul Fifield
Keith Lewis
0 7506 3582 7

Marketing Communications 1997–98
Tony Yeshin
0 7506 3583 5

Strategic Marketing Management, (Planning and Control) 1997–98
Paul Fifield
Colin Gilligan
0 7506 3581 9

The Diploma Case Study Workbook
NEW!
Paul Fifield
0 7506 3573 8

To order, please contact: Heinemann Customer Services PO Box 381, Halley Court, Jordan Hill, Oxford, OX2 8RT
Tel: 01865 314333   Fax: 01865 314091

SALES AND MARKETING TITLES PUBLISHED BY BUTTERWORTH HEINEMANN

Many of these titles are recommended for further reading on CIM and other business courses.

STRATEGIC MARKETING
CIM Handbook of Strategic Marketing, The
October 1997 0 7506 2613 5 £35.00
Corporate Image Management
June 1997 9 810 080 859 £14.99
Creating Organizational Advantage
1995 0 7506 1937 6 £19.99
Creating Powerful Brands
February 1998 0 7506 2240 7 £19.95
Marketing Insights for the Asia Pacific
1996 9971 64 532 7 £16.99
Marketing Planner, The
1993 0 7506 1709 8 £14.99
Marketing Plans
1995 0 7506 2213 X £19.99
Marketing Plans Tutor Resource Pack
1995 0 7506 2304 7 £45.00
Marketing Strategy
1995 0 7506 0662 2 £19.99
Marketing Strategy
October 1997 0 7506 3284 4 £16.99
Market Focus
1993 0 7506 0887 0 £17.99
Market-Led Strategic Change
October 1997 0 7506 3285 2 £18.99
Market- Led Strategic Change Tutor Resource Pack
October 1997 0 7506 3900 9 £40.00
New Product Development
1996 0 7506 2427 2 £17.99
Retail Marketing Plans
1996 0 7506 2021 8 £17.99
Profitable Product Management
1995 0 7506 1888 4 £16.99
Strategic Marketing Management
June 1997 0 7506 2244 X £19.99
Strategic Marketing Management Tutor Resource Pack
June 1997 0 7506 2280 6 £40.00
Trade Marketing Strategies
1994 0 7506 2012 9 £18.99

GENERAL MARKETING
Business Law
March 1997 0 7506 2570 8 £19.99
CIM Marketing Dictionary, The
1996 0 7506 2346 2 £14.99
Economics
1990 0 7506 0081 0 £18.99
Economic Theory and Marketing Practice
1992 0 7506 0241 4 £16.99
Fundamentals and Practice of Marketing, The
1995 0 7506 0997 4 £12.99
GNVQ Advanced Marketing
Spring 1997 0 435 45257 6 £69.95
Marketing
1995 0 7506 2055 2 £16.99
Marketing (Made Simple Series)
1991 0 7506 0138 8 £9.99
Marketing Audit, The
1993 0 7506 1706 3 £14.99
Marketing Book, The
1994 0 7506 2022 6 £22.50
Marketing Case Studies
1995 0 7506 2011 0 £14.99
Marketing – Everybody's Business
1994 0435 45025 5 £11.99
Marketing Plan, The
1987 0 7506 0678 9 £12.99
Marketing Research for Managers
1996 0 7506 0488 3 £16.99
Marketing Research in Travel and Tourism
May 1997 0 7506 3082 5 £19.99
Marketing Toolkit
April 1997 0 7506 3550 9 £99.00
Marketing Toolkit Trainer Resource Pack
September 1997 0 7506 3551 7 £59.99
Pocket Guide to the Marketing Plan
1995 0 7506 2642 9 £6.99

INTERNATIONAL MARKETING
CIM Handbook of Export Marketing, The
1996 0 7506 2573 2 £60.00
International Encyclopaedia of Marketing, The
April 1997 0 7506 3501 0 £40.00
International Marketing
June 1997 0 7506 2241 5 £21.50
Relentless: The Japanese Way of Marketing
1996 0 7506 3208 9 £14.99

MARKETING COMMUNICATIONS
Advertising
1992 0 7506 0325 9 £9.99
Below-the-line Promotion
1993 0 7506 0548 0 £21.50
Creative Marketer, The
1993 0 7506 1708 X £14.99
Cybermarketing
1996 0 7506 2848 0 £16.99
Direct Marketing
June 1997 0 7506 2428 0 £14.99
Effective Advertiser, The
1993 0 7506 1772 1 £14.99
Fundamentals of Advertising, The
1995 0 7506 0250 3 £16.99
Excellence in Advertising
March 1997 0 7506 3129 5 £18.99
Integrated Marketing Communications
1995 0 7506 1938 4 £14.99
Marketing Communications
July 1997 0 7506 1923 6 £15.99
Practice of Advertising, The
1995 0 7506 2239 3 £18.99
Practice of Public Relations, The
1995 0 7506 2318 7 £18.99
Public Relations Techniques
1994 0 7506 1563 X £19.99
Royal Mail Guide to Direct Mail for Small Businesses, The
April 1996 0 7506 2747 6 £14.99
Writing for Marketing
June 1997 0 7506 3510 X £14.99

SERVICES MARKETING
Cases in Marketing Financial Services Teaching Notes
1994 0 7506 2319 5 £40.00
Management and Marketing of Services, The
July 1997 0 7506 3594 0 £17.99
Marketing Financial Services
1995 0 7506 2247 4 £19.99
Marketing Planning for Services
1996 0 7506 3022 1 £18.99
Services Marketing
March 1998 0 7506 2576 7 £19.99

MARKETING LOGISTICS
Managing Purchasing
1995 0 7506 1941 4 £18.99
Marketing Logistics
February 1997 0 7506 2209 1 £18.99
Strategy of Distribution Management, The
1986 0 7506 0367 4 £15.99

SALES
CIM Handbook of Selling and Sales Strategy, The
September 1997 0 7506 3116 3 £45.00
Direct Selling
March 1997 0 7506 2235 0 £14.99
Effective Sales Management
1993 0 7506 0855 2 £18.99
Pocket Guide to Selling Services and Products
1995 0 7506 2641 0 £6.99
Practical Sales and Management
June 1997 0 7506 33 61 1 £30.00
Sales and Sales Management
May 1997 0 7506 2849 9 £16.99
Selling Services and Products
1994 0 7506 1958 9 £12.99

CUSTOMER CARE
Customer Service Planner, The
1993 0 7506 1710 1 £14.99
From Tin Soldiers to Russian Dolls
1994 0 7506 1881 7 £19.99
Key Account Management
May 1997 0 7506 3278 X £24.99
Making Customer Strategy Work
October 1997 0 7506 3133 3 £18.99
Meeting Customer Needs
April 1997 0 7506 3391 3 £15.99
Relationship Marketing
1993 0 7506 0978 8 £18.99
Relationship Marketing for Competitive Advantage
1995 0 7506 2020 X £30.00
Relationship Marketing: Strategy and Implementation
September 1997 0 7506 3626 2 £30.00
Understanding Customers
March 1997 0 7506 2322 5 £17.99

SPECIALIST MARKETING
Business and the Natural Environment
June 1997 0 7506 2051 X £18.99
Creative Arts Marketing
1995 0 7506 2237 7 £19.99
Hospitality Marketing
1996 0 7506 2688 7 £16.99
Marketing
1992 0 7506 0165 5 £14.99
Marketing in the Not-for-Profit Sector
May 1997 0 7506 2234 2 £16.99
Marketing in Travel and Tourism
1994 0 7506 0973 7 £16.99

DIRECTORIES
The ABS Directories of Business Schools Postgraduate Courses
January 1997 0 7506 2947 9 £19.99
The ABS Directory of Business Schools Undergraduate Courses
January 1997 0 7506 2946 0 £19.99
Compendium of Higher Education
February 1997 0 7506 3294 4 £19.99
NVQ Handbook
1996 0 7506 2236 9 £25.00
Open Learning Directory
January 1997 0 7506 3338 7 £60.00

VISIT OUR WEBSITE!

For further information about these titles

http://www.bh.com